Summer Exhibition Illustrated 2015

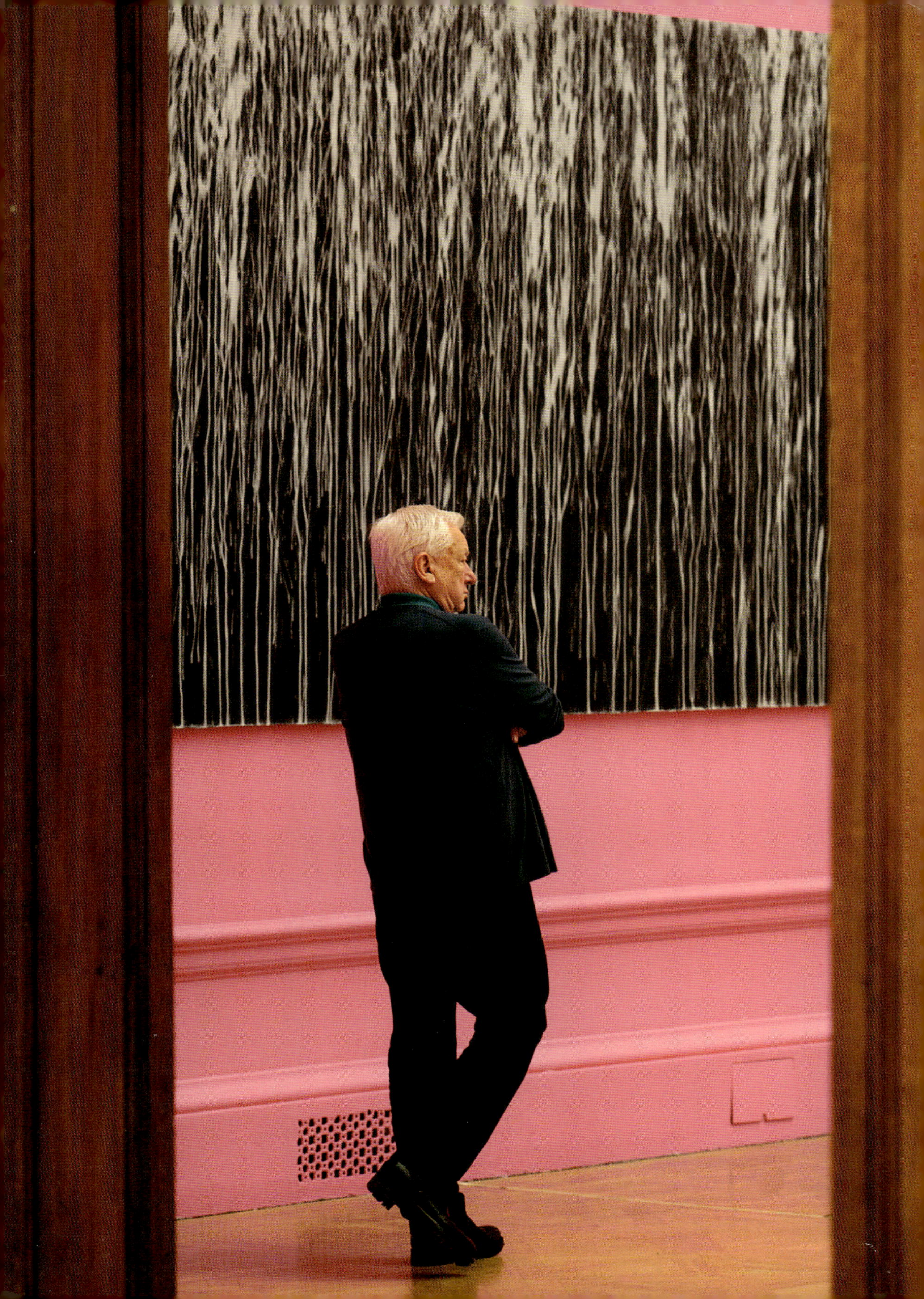

A Selection from the 247th Summer Exhibition
Edited by Michael Craig-Martin RA

Summer Exhibition Illustrated 2015

Royal Academy of Arts

Sponsored by

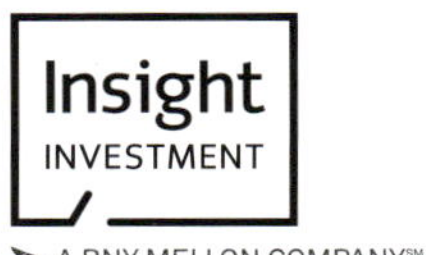

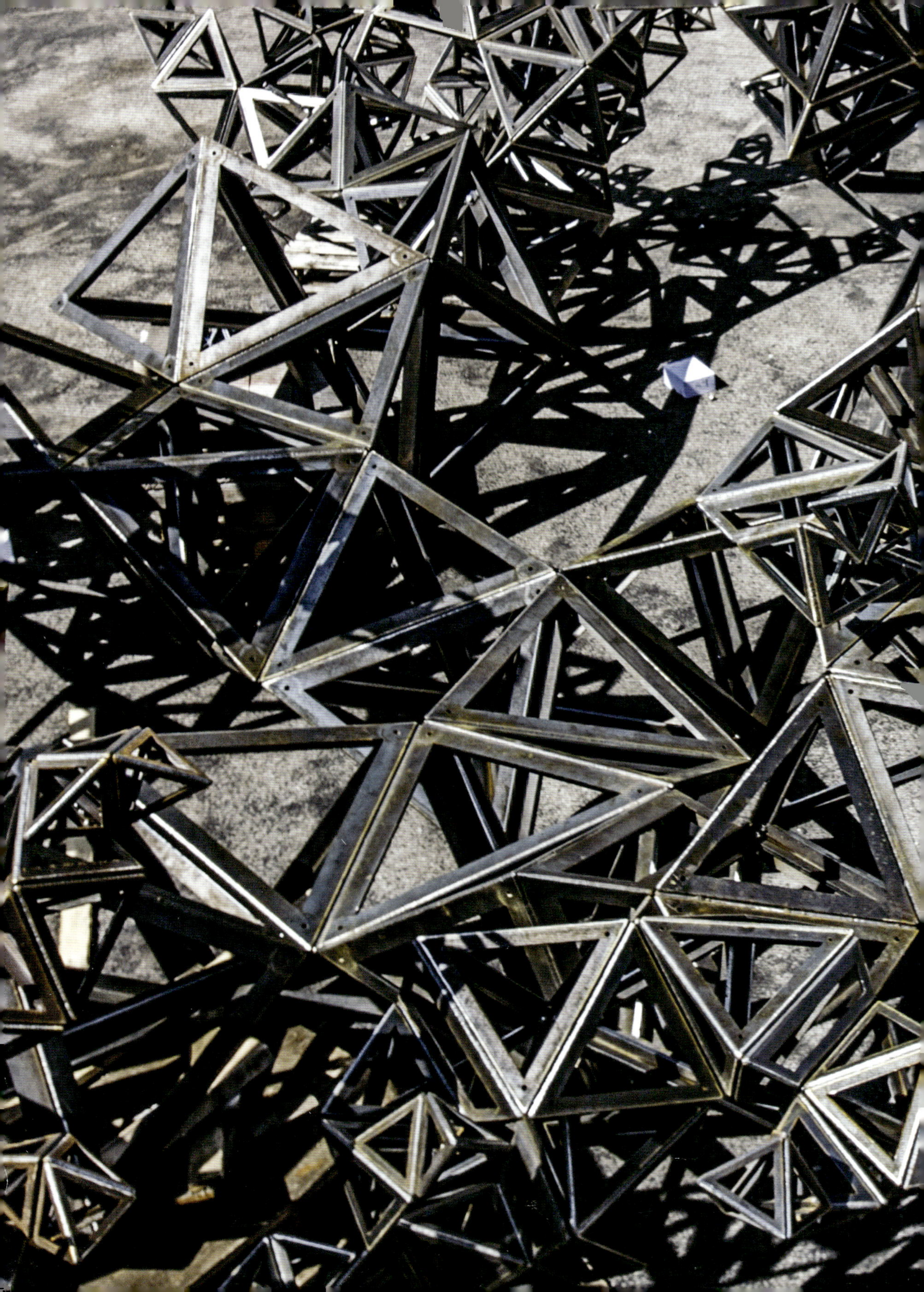

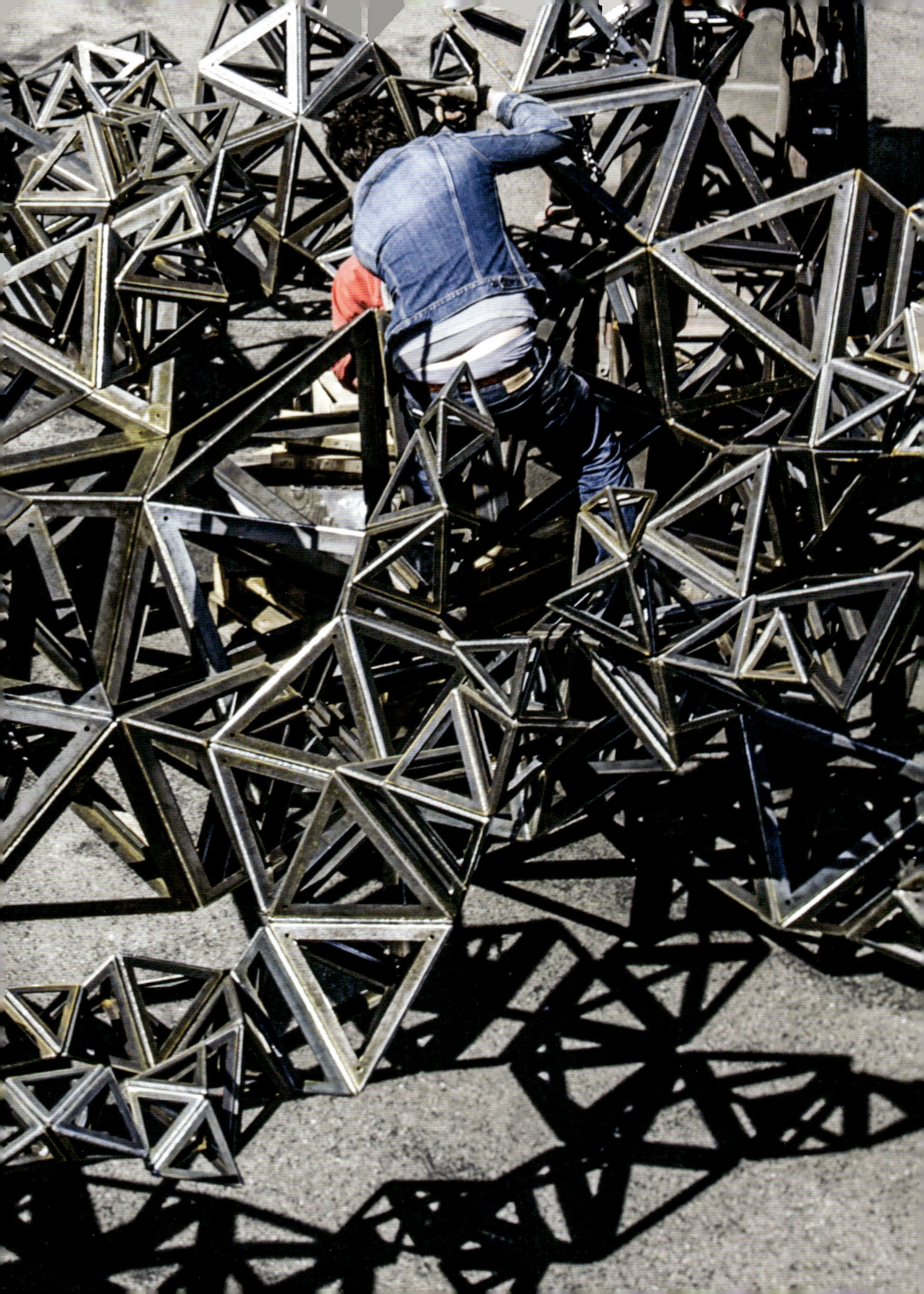

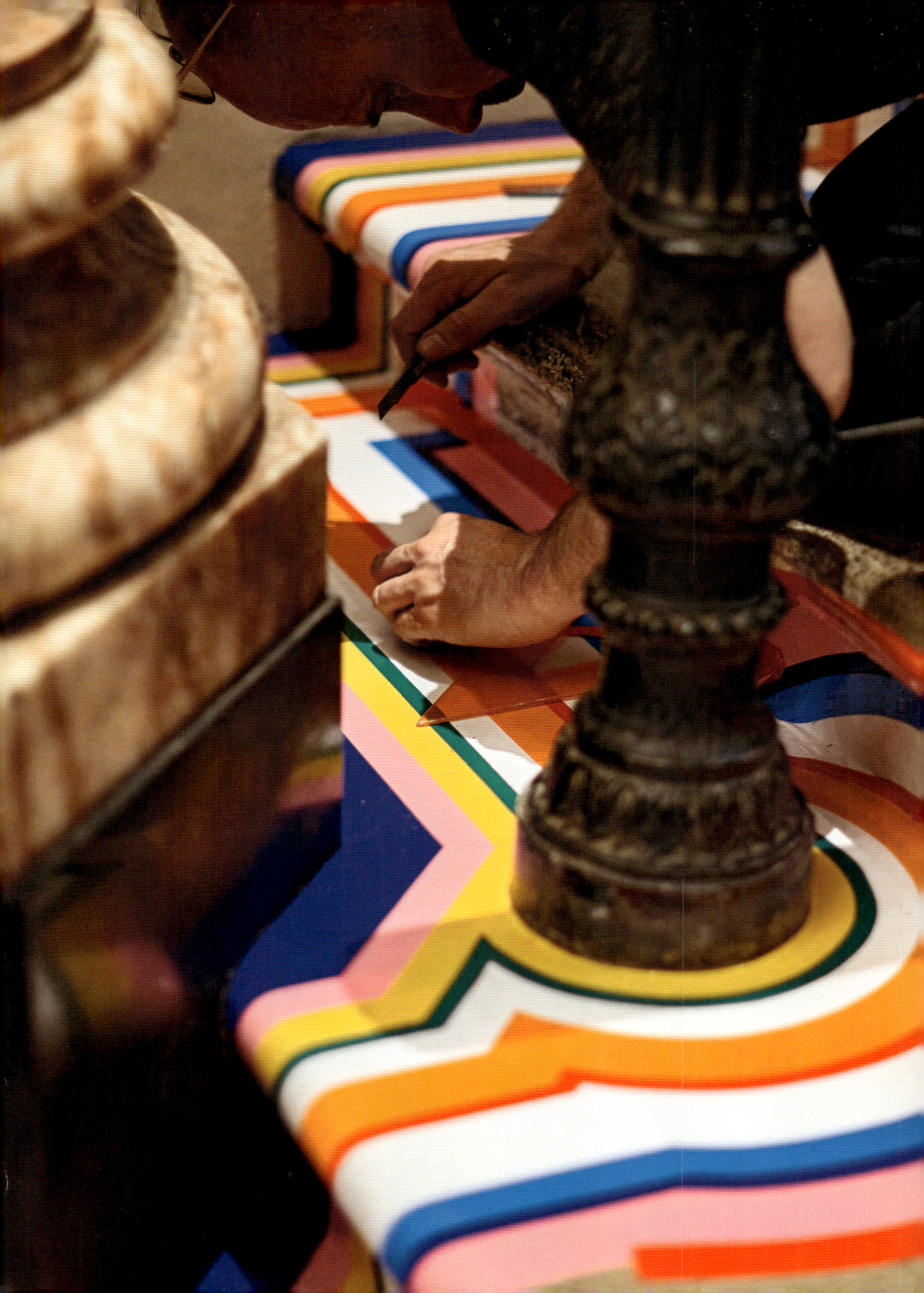

Contents

Sponsor's Foreword

The annual Summer Exhibition at the Royal Academy of Arts heralds the start of the British cultural summer season. From Conrad Shawcross's immersive courtyard installation, *The Dappled Light of the Sun*, to the vividness of the artworks within the Academy, the selection made by Exhibition Co-ordinator Michael Craig-Martin RA and his colleagues on the Hanging Committee breathes colour and light into the galleries' farthest reaches.

This is a landmark year for Insight's association with the Royal Academy Summer Exhibition. It is ten years since we began our partnership and it seems fitting that we should celebrate this milestone in the midst of such vibrancy and luminescence.

For 247 years, the Summer Exhibition has provided a platform for emerging and established artists alike to share their works with generation upon generation of visitors to the Royal Academy. It was this longevity, coupled with the Academy's seemingly limitless creativity, that captured our imagination exactly a decade ago.

Much has changed over the past decade, and much more has changed over the past 247 years. As we celebrate our enduring association with the world's oldest open-submission art exhibition, we hope you will share our enthusiasm for its illuminating contribution to the cultural life of the nation.

Abdallah Nauphal
Chief Executive Officer

Sponsored by

Insight
INVESTMENT
A BNY MELLON COMPANY℠

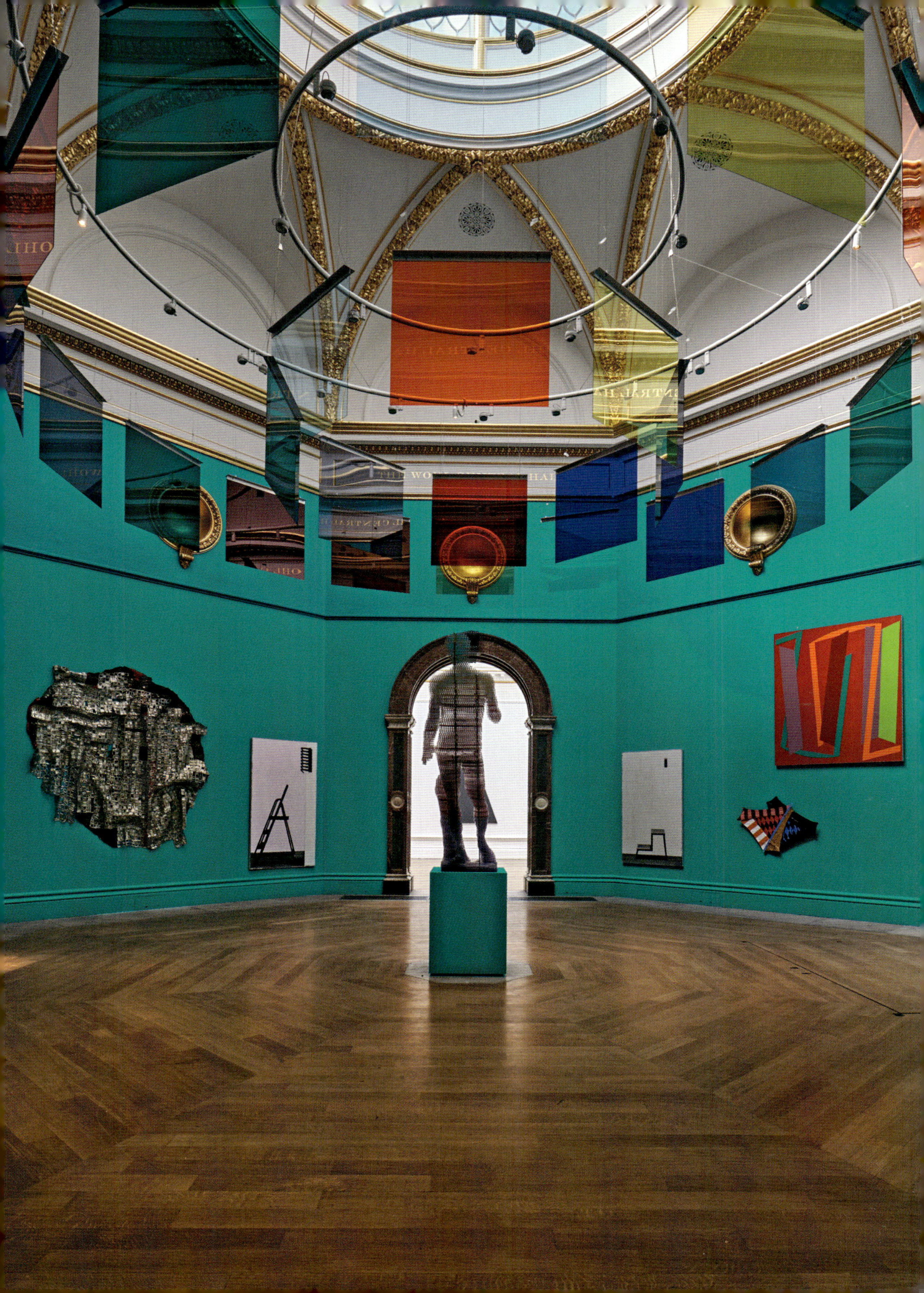

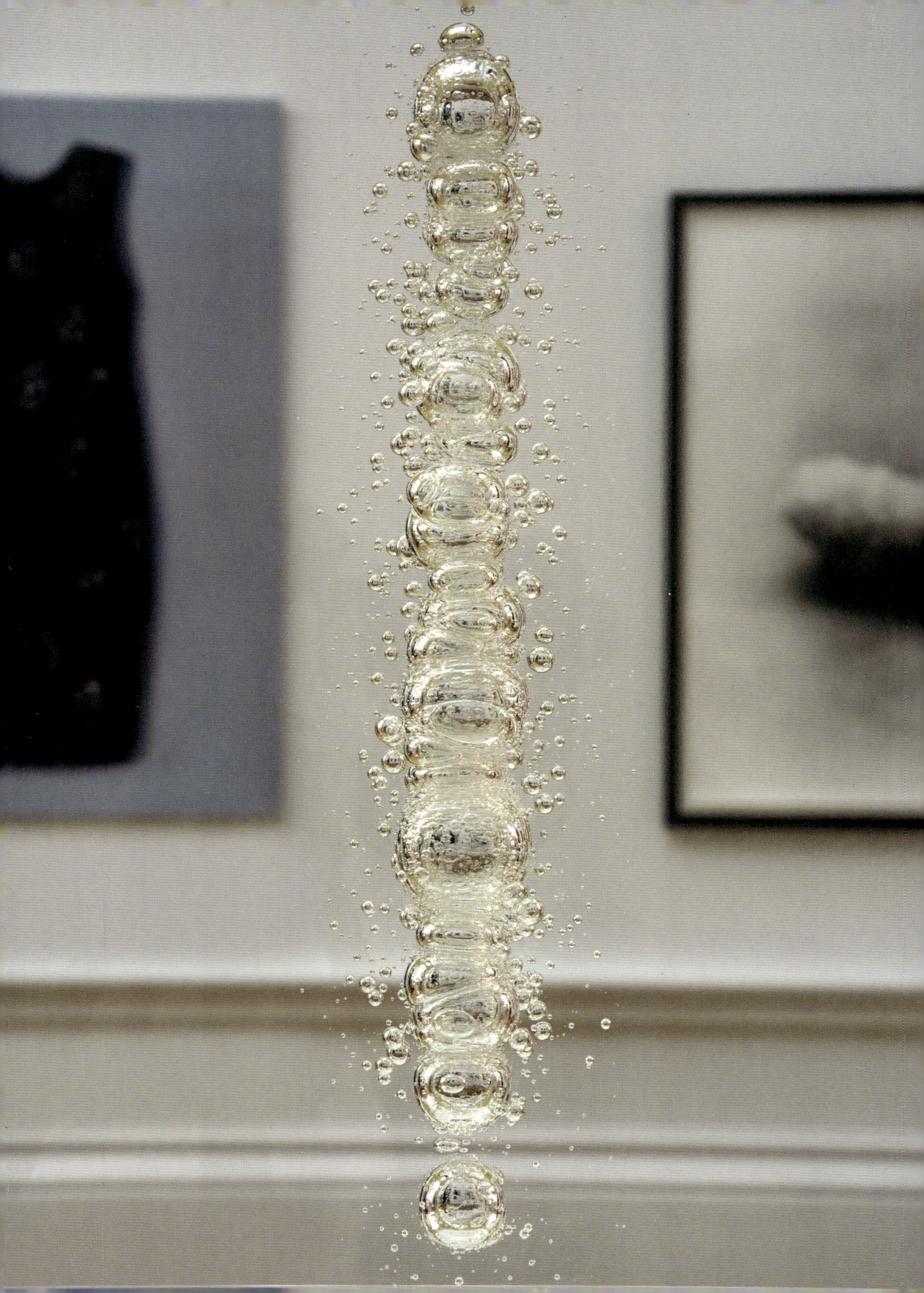

President's Foreword

This exhibition takes as its theme looking, and all the ways in which we encounter the world visually. The Summer Exhibition Committee has been led by Michael Craig-Martin RA in his role as Exhibition Co-ordinator and this year, perhaps more so than any other in the show's imposing 247-year history, the Co-ordinator has determined and shaped the exhibition's content, configuration and relationship with the Royal Academy's architectural spaces. The Summer Exhibition Committee as a whole paid especially close attention to the experience of visiting the exhibition, which itself extends well beyond the galleries of Burlington House.

Visitors to the Summer Exhibition trace a path that weaves through the Annenberg Courtyard, filled by an ambitious new installation by Conrad Shawcross RA, and then climbs the main staircase, traversing Jim Lambie's dazzlingly colourful intervention. Before entering the galleries by way of the Wohl Central Hall, they are greeted by the first of a number of walls painted in a solid block of bright colour. Indeed, each of the three main rooms is filled with a different and unexpected hue, chosen to produce an effect on the visitor, and dramatising the encounter with the exhibition space. These vividly coloured rooms are counterpointed by the careful placement and the diversity of the paintings, prints, sculptures and drawings to be found within them and the other gallery spaces. Michael and the committee have provided a masterclass in the art of curation. It is a comprehensive, confident and exciting exhibition that exploits the unique properties of this great event to the full.

On behalf of Council and my fellow Royal Academicians, I thank Michael Craig-Martin for the passion and vision he has brought to this year's Summer Exhibition. His task has been made simpler by the experience and support of his fellow committee members, the Academicians Norman Ackroyd, Olwyn Bowey, Gus Cummins, Jock McFadyen, David Remfry, Ian Ritchie, Mick Rooney, Alison Wilding and Bill Woodrow. We are also grateful to William Kentridge, recently elected an Honorary Academician, and Tom Phillips RA for their generosity and co-operation in arranging their dedicated galleries. Also deserving of our gratitude is Insight Investment, supporting the Summer Exhibition for a tenth consecutive year.

The Academy says farewell to Academicians who have passed away over the last twelve months. Memorial displays eloquently describe the talents of the painter William Bowyer, the sculptors Ivor Abrahams and Geoffrey Clark, and the architects Sir Philip Dowson PRA and Sir Richard MacCormac. It is with great sadness that we present their work in the Summer Exhibition for the last time.

Christopher Le Brun PRA
President, Royal Academy of Arts

Summer Exhibition 2015
A Masterclass in Looking

Richard Davey

In 1973 Michael Craig-Martin placed a glass of water on a glass shelf and gave it the title *An Oak Tree*. A year later, at his exhibition in the Rowan Gallery in Bruton Place in London, he located *An Oak Tree* at the centre of the longest wall. Positioned high above the eyeline, just out of reach, in what appeared to be an empty space, this provocative work was ignored by many visitors. Those who did see it and took the time to read the accompanying text provided by the artist found an explanation of the work set out in a traditional dialectical format: a short conversation between Craig-Martin the artist and Craig-Martin the enquiring sceptic. According to the former, this glass of water was now an oak tree because he had carried out an Aristotelian act of transubstantiation by changing the substance of the glass of water into a tree without changing its 'accidents', its 'colour, feel, weight, size…'. Like Marcel Duchamp's urinal, Craig-Martin's half-full glass seemed to push at the existential boundaries of art by using a 'readymade' object to focus attention on abstract concepts and theories. By placing an everyday object on a display shelf in an art gallery Craig-Martin was exploring questions that have occupied philosophers, art historians and critical theorists for much of the modern age: What is art? Who is an artist? How important is the artist's intention in defining a work of art?

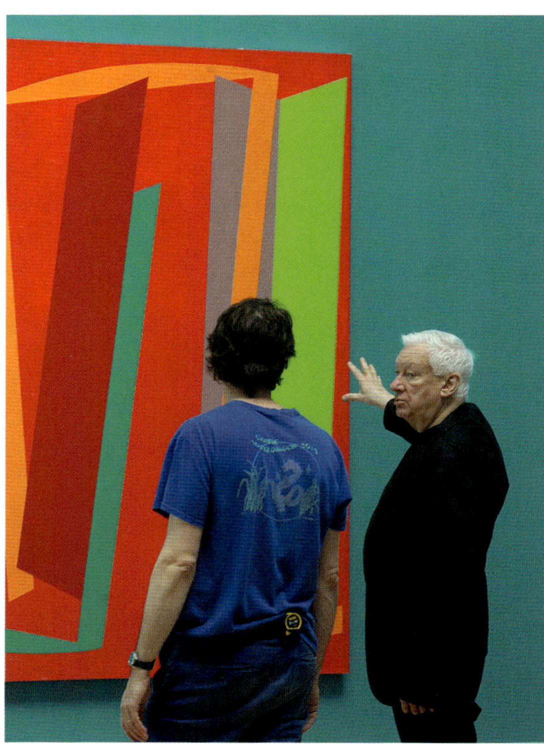

Michael Craig-Martin RA overseeing the installation of *Hommage à Henri* by Vanessa Jackson in the Wohl Central Hall

Such an emphasis on concept and philosophy rather than craft and painterly skill would have infuriated Sir Alfred Munnings, President of the Royal Academy from 1944 to 1949. In the now infamous presidential speech Munnings delivered to distinguished guests at the Royal Academy's Annual Dinner in 1949, among them Sir Winston Churchill, the Archbishop of Canterbury and Anthony Blunt, and to those listening to the live broadcast of his words on the BBC Home Service, Munnings launched an uncompromising attack on modern art and artists. He accused his fellow Academicians of 'shilly-shallying' and 'affected juggling', but reserved particular opprobrium for art critics and European artists, especially Matisse and Picasso. As if foreseeing Craig-Martin's own infamous work he went on to say: 'If you paint a tree – for God's sake try and make it look like a tree.'

For many modern artists, Munnings's very public assault on Modernism confirmed the Royal Academy and its annual Summer Exhibition as a symbol of reactionary conservatism in an art world that had been undergoing seismic shifts. Modernist ideas and radically experimental forms of art were becoming the norm rather than the exception. For more than half a century, the leading figures in modern art in Britain rejected membership of the Academy and never submitted their work for inclusion in the Summer Exhibition. In the last few decades, however, a corner has been turned. An increasing number of artists and architects representing the diversity of contemporary art practice have been elected and their impact on the works included in the annual show has been marked. Recent years have also seen the once male-dominated Academy transformed by the growing number of women who have been elected, with Eileen Cooper RA the first woman to be appointed Keeper of the Royal Academy, with responsibility for the Royal Academy Schools, in 2011. In December 2006 Craig-Martin was elected a Royal Academician, and now in 2015 he is co-ordinating the Summer Exhibition, which the Annual Dinner traditionally opens.

If *An Oak Tree* seemed to embody a particular focus on conceptual purity and enquiry in 'contemporary' artworks and exhibitions, the Summer Exhibition provides the opposite approach. Each year visitors find themselves assaulted by a visual cacophony, as paintings, prints, drawings, sculptures, photographs and architectural models fill the walls and floor spaces of the Academy's vast galleries without any obvious form of conceptual or stylistic unity. Diverse media, styles, forms and artistic backgrounds mingle in a chaotic, genre-defying democracy that can be both joyous and confusing.

The problem with *An Oak Tree*, Munnings would have said, is that it doesn't look like a tree. The title misdirects our engagement with the work. Instead of looking at it for what it is, a glass of water on a glass shelf, we instinctively respond to it in a Cartesian way, with our minds. We ask: How can this be an oak tree? What are the ideas shaping its production? How does this physical object illustrate these abstract, philosophical concepts? We search for meaning before we actually look. This is a reflection of the way in which images are increasingly used today: not as objects of visual experience and knowledge, but as icons standing for words and ideas, treated like hieroglyphs, as another form of written communication. But if we forget *An Oak Tree*'s title and begin by looking at it as a glass of water whose surface is a delicate interplay of light and shade, white and grey, transparency both solid and liquid, we find ourselves engaging with the work differently.

Seen as a diptych consisting equally of text and image, rather than as an image with an accompanying explanation, *An Oak Tree* becomes an exploration of the differences between the visual and the verbal, or between philosophical and practical approaches to our experience of being in the world. Craig-Martin believes that the realm of pure philosophy, as exemplified by his text, allows for conceptual perfectionism. When making or considering a work of art, however, we are always confronted by the limitations of the world. Objects have weight, colour, size and inhabit space, they can be touched, bumped into or broken. Brushes need to be washed at night if they are to be used the next morning, and etching plates need to be cleaned. This practical, or 'dishwashing', quality of art, which forces us to engage with the material world through sight and the other senses, is far more interesting to Craig-Martin than purist philosophical principles that take us out of physical reality and into the abstract realms of the mind.

Craig-Martin has been drawn to the visual elements of the world since his childhood. As a boy he was fascinated by architecture and design, and would rearrange the furniture in his bedroom so that it looked 'right'; he continues to be intrigued by what the visual can reveal that words cannot. This lifelong emphasis on looking and materiality, as both artist and teacher, fundamentally connects this champion of contemporary and modern art with Munnings and the Summer Exhibition. For unlike other exhibitions, which invariably begin by engaging the visitor's mind, focusing on particular curatorial ideas and approaches, the Summer Exhibition has no single theme or artistic focus. It is an exhilarating, exuberant celebration of the visual that begins with an act – in fact thirteen thousand acts – of looking. For when the Selection Committee, which comprises Royal Academicians, is confronted by thousands of anonymous, untitled potential exhibits its decision is almost always made by the fact that something momentarily catches the eye of one or more of its members. Then, while the exhibition is being hung, decisions about where to place individual works are made on a visual basis. In the galleries there are no names or titles, no conceptual vision driving the selection or reception of the show, just two-dimensional images, sculptures and architectural models to entice the visitor to look at and discover the world through their senses.

The six works that Craig-Martin has submitted for this year's show demonstrate his approach to visual knowledge. Familiar objects such as a wristwatch, a shirt, a coffee cup and an iPhone are made to seem unfamiliar through bold colours and simplified outlines. Although their highly graphic style evokes the Pop Art works of Andy Warhol and Patrick Caulfield RA, these are not just celebrations of consumer and mass culture. The deliberate lack of contextual elements – highlights, shadows and tonal gradation – encourages the viewer to re-examine these objects, seeing their shape and colour before their function and context.

Craig-Martin's paintings, prints and installations do not only put a primacy on visual knowledge, but they also structure how we look, emphasising and focusing in on the essentials. And this same concentrated, simplified and focused approach to the visual also underpins Craig-Martin's ideas for this year's Summer Exhibition.

Although some may feel overwhelmed and disoriented by the number and diversity of exhibits, Craig-Martin hopes that his imposition of clear structures on this visual chaos will enable visitors to see and appreciate individual works as well.

For Craig-Martin, the Summer Exhibition doesn't begin in the Beaux-Arts galleries of Burlington House, or even in the Annenberg Courtyard, but on the street outside. It starts among the buses, taxis, cars and bicycles heading towards Piccadilly Circus or Green Park, in the shops that line Piccadilly and the nearby arcades, and it emerges in the crowds of people hurrying to work or to meetings, stopping to take photographs, or casually strolling along and window shopping. As a buzzing image of the world in microcosm, Piccadilly provides both the route into and the very roots of the show, a vivid reminder of the materials and imaginative 'soil' from which art is made.

This year, visitors to the Summer Exhibition who pause outside Burlington House to look at the imposing façade of the Academy through the great entrance arch will find their view interrupted by a twisting cloud of oxidised metal. *The Dappled Light of the Sun*, a temporary sculptural installation by Conrad Shawcross RA, the youngest living Royal Academician, instantly transforms our experience of the courtyard and everything around it. Even if we try to ignore the work, its forty tonnes of weathering steel, fabricated into eight thousand tetrahedrons, demand our attention, for like all works of art *The Dappled Light of the Sun* structures our engagement with the space it inhabits. Not only do we see it in a context – the surrounding architecture, the Summer Exhibition, an urban location – but we come to it with our own contexts: our age, gender, background and our feelings, emotions and experiences on that day. For Craig-Martin and his fellow Academicians on this year's Hanging Committee – Norman Ackroyd, Olwyn Bowey, Gus Cummins, Jock McFadyen, David Remfry, Ian Ritchie, Mick Rooney, Alison Wilding and Bill Woodrow – this inescapable truth, that works of art and architecture are not isolated or rarefied objects but have their origins and existence within the physical world, and are therefore shaped by and shape the environment in which they find themselves, lies at the heart of their different but shared curatorial approaches.

In the context of the courtyard, *The Dappled Light of the Sun* seems both familiar and enigmatic, by turns inviting and threatening. Approaching its five geometric forms, set on a series of metal tripods that lift the entire structure 2.5 metres off the ground, we might be looking at a grove of trees that has grown up through the paving, their branches reaching up towards the sun, a harvest of tiny fruits or blossoms emerging at the end of each 'arm'. Some visitors will deliberately make their approach to the Academy through these angled trunks, wandering beneath the massive steel canopy among the areas of dappled shade that pattern the ground, their path dictated by the steel girders in their way and the people around them. They will look up, conscious of the enormous weight suspended just above their heads, and yet transfixed by the pattern of interlocking 'open' triangles that gives the structure its sense of airy weightlessness. Other visitors will walk around the work, ignoring it or looking at it from a distance through the corner of their eye, their experience less intimately engaged and yet still affected by its imposing presence, as their views of the surrounding buildings are filtered through its geometric forms.

Unlike Munnings, Shawcross is not interested in making his work look like something specific. *The Dappled Light of the Sun* might suggest a grove of trees, but it might also represent clouds, or tree roots exposed to the light. For those looking at it from the neighbouring offices of the Royal Society of Chemistry it might evoke a model of crystalline or atomic bonds. Shawcross has deliberately made the work's meaning a riddle so that it can unravel and develop like the work itself, being one thing at one moment, becoming another at a different moment, changing as endlessly as our viewpoints alter.

The work's essential building blocks are four differently sized tetrahedrons, with two connecting truncated tetrahedrons. As the most basic three-dimensional structure, the tetrahedron provided the ancient Greeks with the perfect symbol for the atom. For Shawcross, however, it offers not just simplicity but irrational complexity. Because a tetrahedron cannot be tessellated to create symmetrical, self-fulfilling patterns, Shawcross was forced to develop a series of rigorous construction rules that allowed him to join component tetrahedrons together into more complex sculptural forms. As a result *The Dappled Light of the Sun* is defined by asymmetry rather than symmetry, which lends it a sense of underlying organic chaos rather than rigorous mechanical order. Its tendril-like branches extend out from their central hubs, transformed into a series of lyrical optical curves despite the fact that their edges are straight; they can never reconnect with themselves, but are always reaching outwards and upwards, seemingly growing towards the light.

On first glance, *The Dappled Light of the Sun* seems to be about a sublime complexity, articulating a chaotic sense of structure that cannot be grasped rationally. But as you draw closer, the four triangles that make up each tetrahedron become more distinct, as do the soldered joins between each face, characterised by ripples that seem to flow down these seams like waves of molten

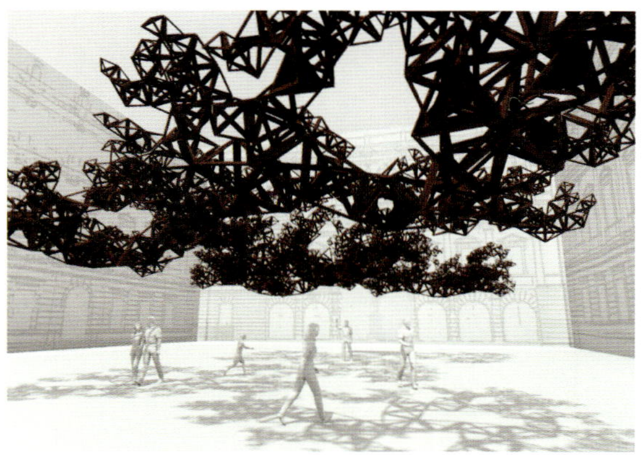

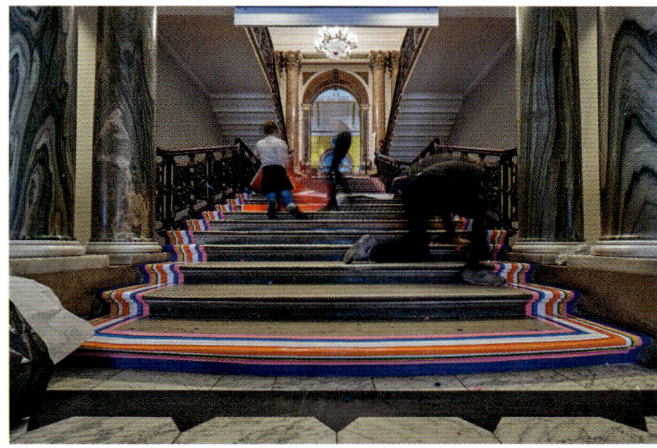

Top: Visualisation for *The Dappled Light of the Sun* by Conrad Shawcross RA
Above: Installation of Jim Lambie's kaleidoscopic staircase
Page 17: Installation of Gallery III in progress
Pages 18 and 19: The Wohl Central Hall, looking through to Gallery VI

metal or dribbles of paint, transforming hard-edged steel into something organic and fluid. Shawcross has devoted as much attention to these individual edges as he has to the mathematical and engineering rules that govern the construction of the whole, for this is a work united by the significance of each individual element, just as the Summer Exhibition celebrates the individual's position within the whole.

In 1904 Paul Cézanne wrote a now-famous letter to his fellow artist Emile Bernard, urging him to see nature in terms of 'the cylinder, the sphere, the cone'. Reflecting this basic lesson in how to paint and draw, Shawcross's monumental sculpture encourages us to see the simple geometric structures that lie beneath the complex organic forms of the natural world. But these triangles and tetrahedrons are not just about nature. Looking through them at the architecture of Burlington House we begin to see the underlying geometry of the façades, to notice those playful and abstract elements that transform the whole from a functional building into a work of art, to see the columns as tree trunks, the windows as deep pools of water, or as diamonds glinting in the sun. We are drawn to the individual triangles and rectangles whose repeating pattern transforms the surface into a playground for the eye.

But *The Dappled Light of the Sun* is not just about structure and design; it also gives us a different perspective on colour. As we stand beneath its steel canopy and gaze up through its branches we might see, depending on the weather, varying hues of blue and shades of grey caught like jewels in its complex latticework. By isolating and framing them, the artwork separates these colours from their original contexts so that we no longer see them as distant and intangible fragments of sky but as objects in their own right that appear both physically substantial and close by. Moving out from beneath the sculpture we might look up again, but now, gazing through the stone frame of the courtyard, it is as if we are looking up through a vast *Skyspace* by James Turrell HON RA. The distant sky becomes a ceiling holding us in, transformed into an abstract painting that we want to reach out and touch.

As we stand at the bottom of the steps leading into the main entrance of Burlington House, our experience of the world has been changed: what we thought we knew has been called into question by what we have seen. This sense of visual destabilisation continues as we walk up the grand staircase that leads to the Academy's main galleries. Each year the Summer Exhibition's co-ordinator is allowed to invite a number of artists who are not Royal Academicians to exhibit without undergoing the usual submission and selection process. This year Craig-Martin has selected a number of artists aged over

65 whose work received early critical recognition and praise, and yet is now less prominent than that of some of their contemporaries. Craig-Martin has also invited a few younger artists to create specific interventions that will anchor the exhibition within the building and thus highlight the significance of the relationship between works of art and their architectural settings.

The first of these commissions is by Jim Lambie, a Turner Prize nominee in 2005, who has covered the main staircase with his trademark strips of brightly coloured vinyl tape. As with the Shawcross sculpture, Lambie's work is defined by a rigorous but simple methodology: when it was laid down, the tape was made to follow the basic structure of the staircase precisely, reflecting and eventually magnifying any turns and indentations to make us highly aware of even the smallest architectural details and forms. The interplay of these different colours pulling and pushing at each other, advancing or receding before our eyes, leads to a mesmerising, psychedelic work that immediately alters our experience of the building.

Although the hard edges of the tape reflect the physical properties of the staircase, the colours dissolve its structural integrity. Instead of stairs we see zigzagged, edged rings of concentric colours flowing up, down and around the entrance. In the centre, a single line offers a moment of respite and focus in the midst of this giddy dance; an aperture that helps to pull our gaze through into another space. Applied in varying widths, the colours appear to ripple and breathe from side to side, pushing at the walls and balustrades like waves breaking on the shore. As we ascend this rainbow bridge, our feet may feel the solid ground of the building but our eyes are mesmerised by the shifting, insubstantial world of colour that lies immediately ahead.

There is a tendency for colour to be seen in a subsidiary, subservient role, as a descriptor for other things – blue sky, red hair, black heart – but rarely as something distinctive in its own right. Scientists and philosophers tell us that we all see colours differently, and that they are not really properties of an object but a product of subjective neural processes in our minds. Lambie's staircase fundamentally disrupts and calls into question our engagement with the world. As these vivid colours cascade around us, the familiar becomes strange and the solid becomes fluid. More than decoration, this is a passport to a new world.

At the top of the stairs, the entrance wall leading into the exhibition has been painted an intense buttercup yellow. Unlike the staircase flowing beneath our feet, this sunburst explodes upon the eye with a physical intensity that is almost blinding. As one of the primary colours, the first to be processed by the eye and the most visible colour in the spectrum, yellow has both the same essential simplicity as Shawcross's tetrahedrons but is equally difficult to use. With pigments derived from such toxic metals as cadmium, lead and chrome, yellow requires consideration and care not only in its handling but also in its application: if applied too liberally its demanding presence dazzles and diminishes surrounding colours, leaving a composition unbalanced. Craig-Martin's use of yellow in such a prominent position is therefore a clear statement of intent for the visual focus of the exhibition. This is not colour pushed into the background to sit quietly, but colour that forces us to look and to take notice. It is a colour deliberately chosen to have an impact upon the retina, not only cleansing the visual palate but making us look with the whole body, tasting the world with the tongue of our eye.

Craig-Martin has used bold wall colours in his installations and exhibitions since he was invited to make a site-specific work for the British School at Rome in 1993. Usually he paints every wall in a space, but in the Summer Exhibition he has restricted himself to just three of the galleries: the octagonal Wohl Central Hall, which has been transformed by a vivid turquoise, and the large rooms to either side. The Lecture Room, to the east, is painted a light blue that brings it a sky-like spaciousness and gives a sense of coherence to the disparate sculptures, drawings and prints exhibited there, while Gallery III to the west has been brought to life with an electric magenta that animates without overwhelming the paintings hung on its walls.

One of the first things visitors see as they enter the galleries and stand in the Wohl Central Hall is *Applied Projection Rig*, a monumental sculpture by the 2002 Turner Prize nominee Liam Gillick. Consisting of a double corona of 24 panels of coloured Plexiglass suspended from the gallery ceiling, the work fills the air with a blizzard of colour. Looking up at the dome through a rainbow of transparent coloured shards we see endless reflections and colour combinations that filter our view of the room's classical architecture and Craig-Martin's turquoise walls. The walls no longer appear solid, the colour is no longer fixed. What we might consider permanent appears to be in flux, transformed by washes of coloured light that, like a rainbow, are always just ahead of us.

In 1666 Isaac Newton, then a young Cambridge scientist, opened the shutters in his study just enough to allow a thin beam of light to travel through a prism he had placed in its path. Reflected on the opposite wall he saw a spectrum of seven colours, which, when returned to white light through a second prism, provided him with visible proof that colour is the product of light. In his work Gillick has effectively filled the Wohl Central Hall with an enormous 'prism' that also reveals the passage of

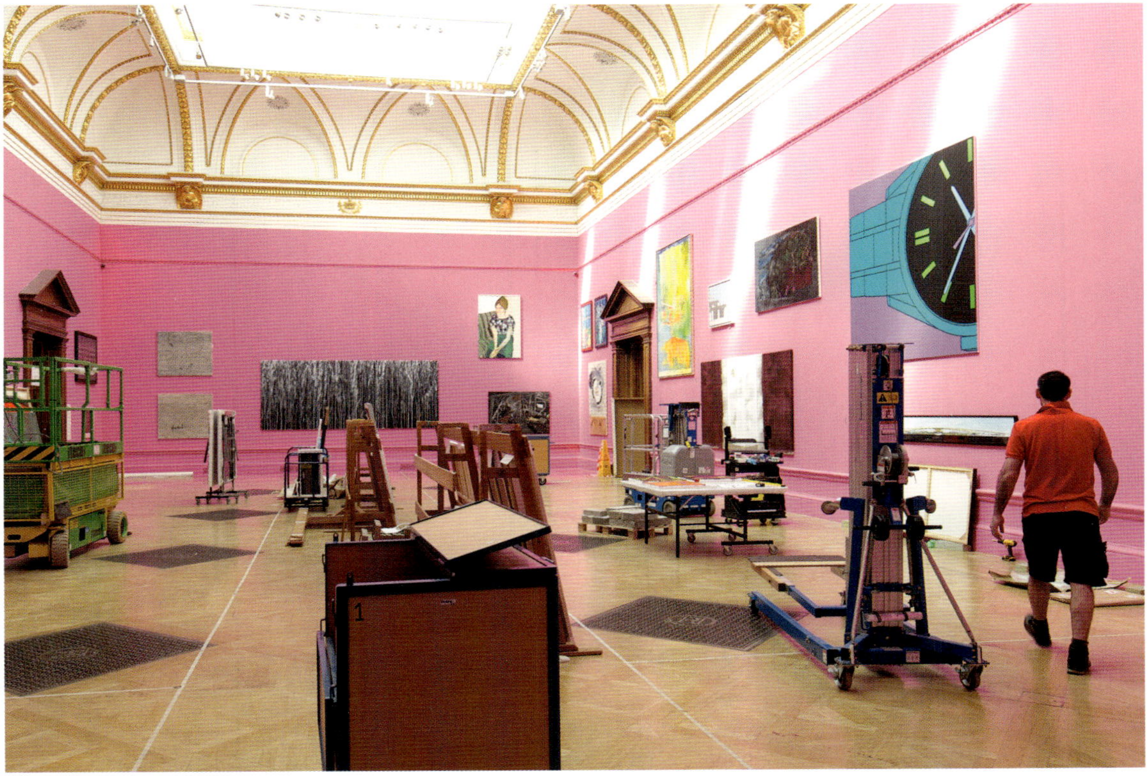

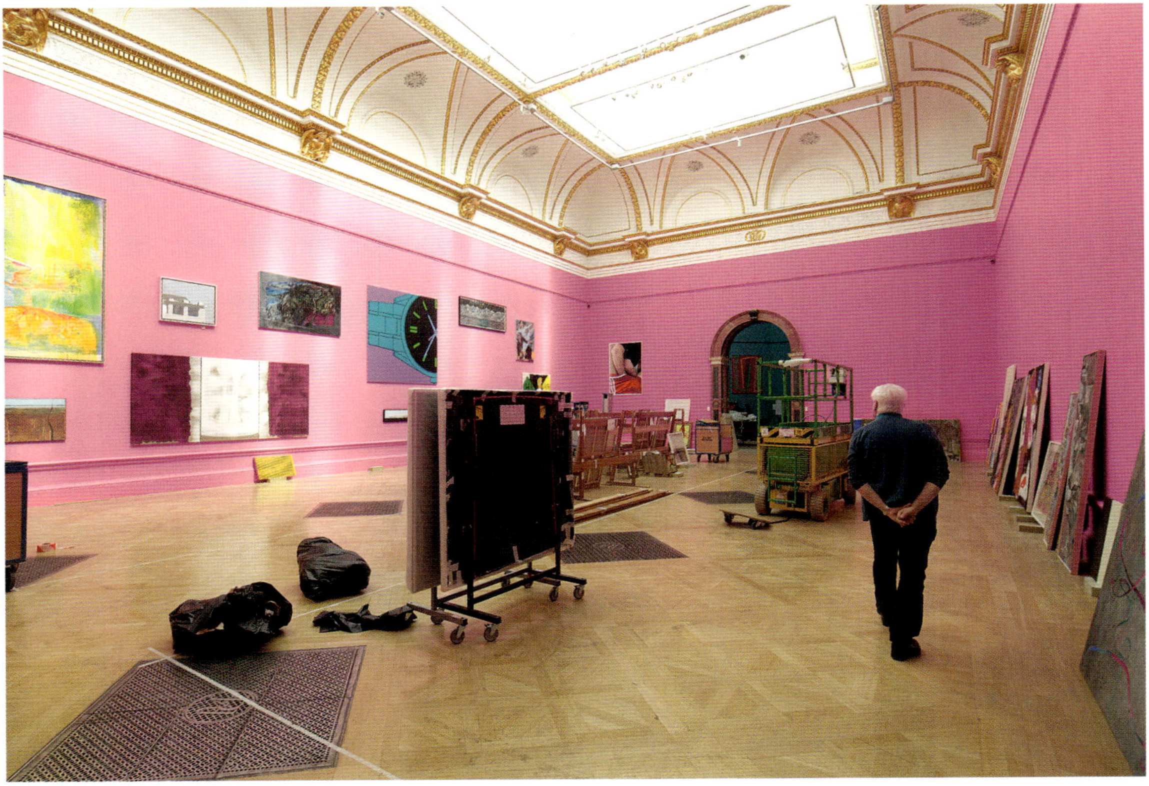

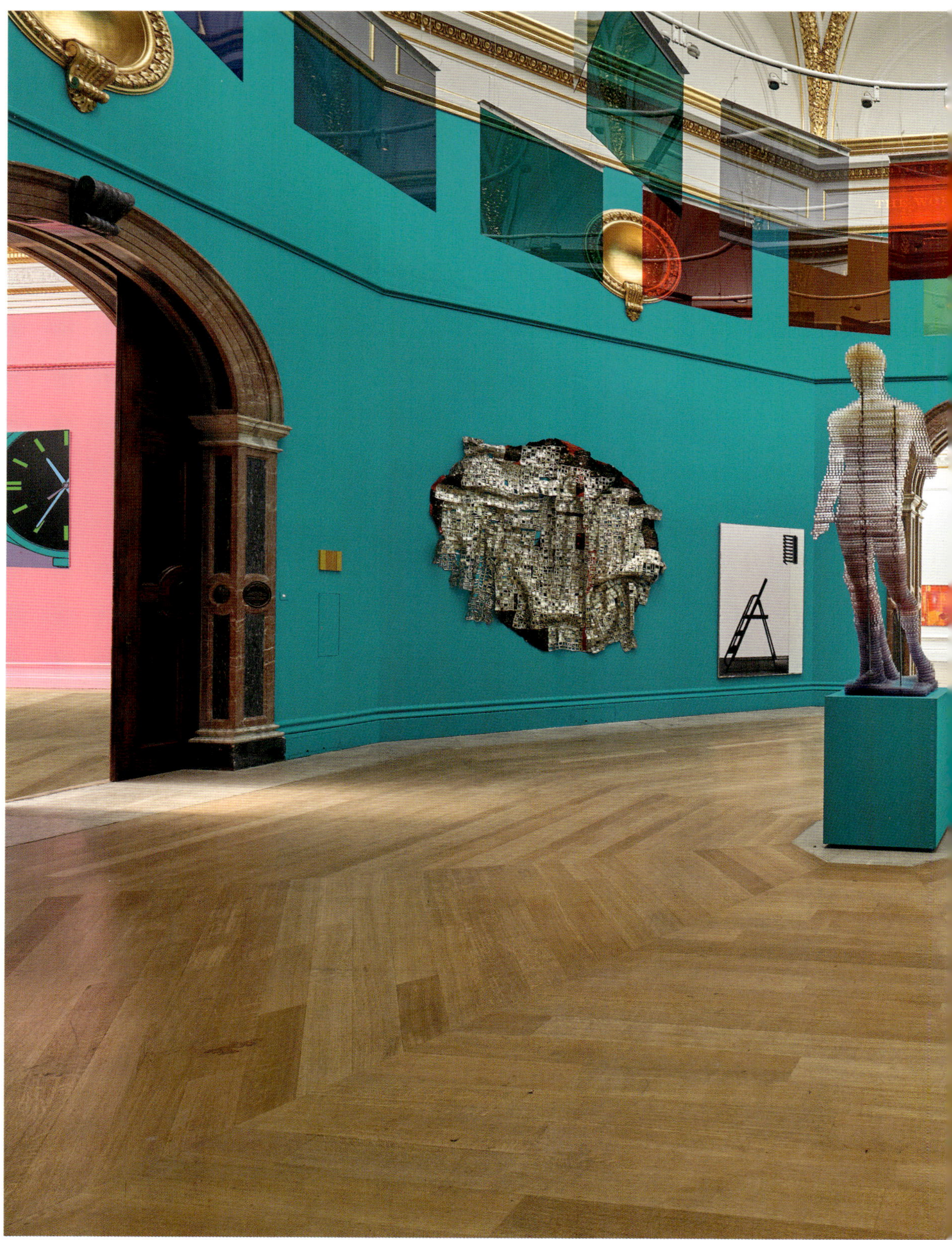

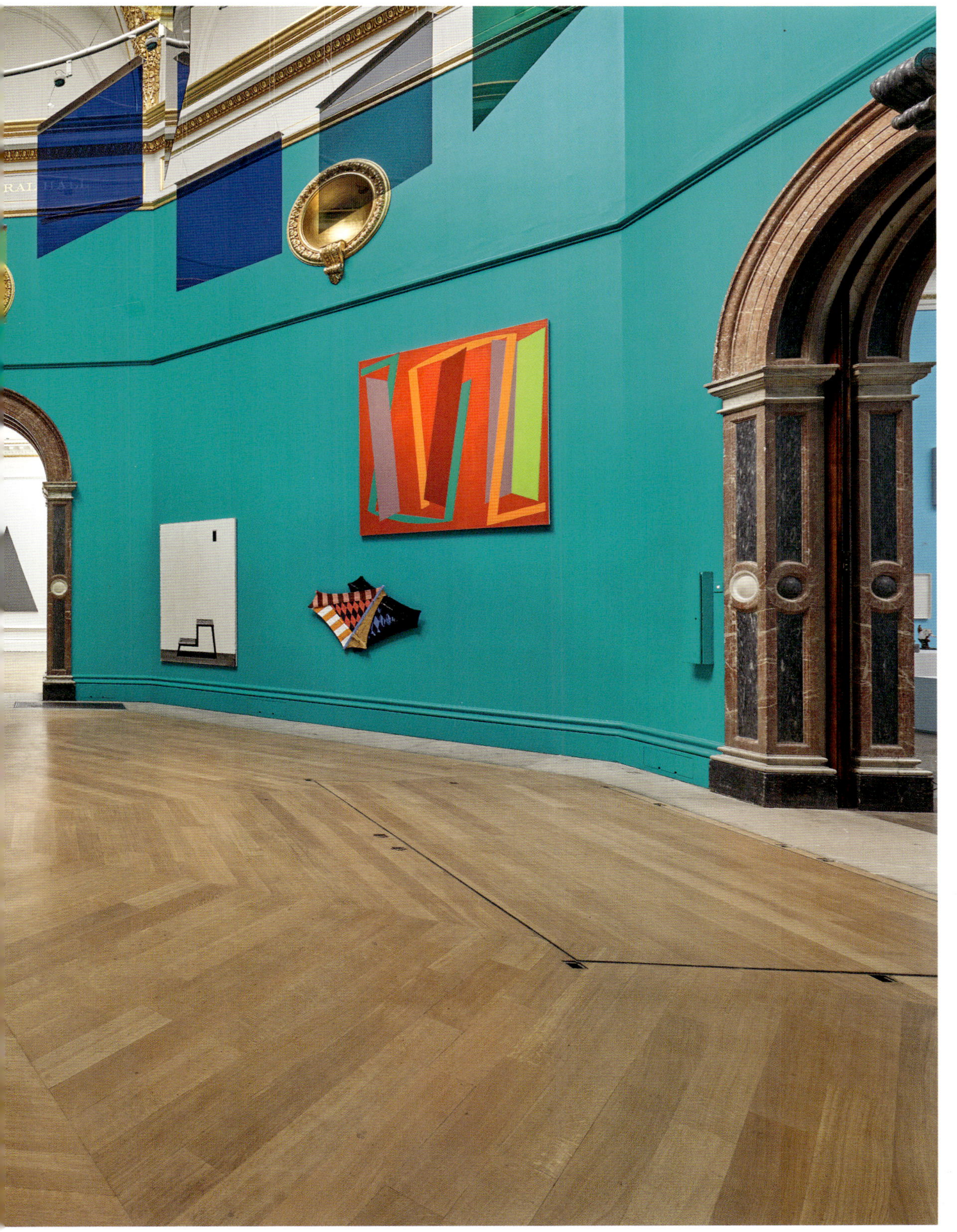

light through space; a dazzling, multi-coloured bridge that both connects us to the world outside and alerts us to the teeming mass of atoms and photons around us. For although the air that surrounds us appears to be a void, as the German artist Anselm Kiefer HON RA notes, every cubic centimetre is actually filled with billions of atoms constantly oscillating between form and formlessness.

Matthew Darbyshire's sculpture *Doryphoros*, positioned directly beneath *Applied Projection Rig*, also exploits and exposes the dynamic world of shifting light and fluid boundaries. Based on the celebrated Greek sculpture by Polykleitos of the *Doryphoros* (Spear-bearer), Darbyshire's figure, which is made out of layers of clear multi-wall polycarbonate, sprayed on their underside with car-body lacquers that flow through the graduating tones of Photoshop's colour scale, seems to dissolve before our eyes. As the edges of this idealised human body melt into nothingness, and the colours fade into transparency, we are left grasping for an elusive form that is both there and not there.

Fractured into numerous horizontal layers, held together by two tall metal rods, and with no discernible outline to define and contain its once-beautiful form, Darbyshire's *Doryphoros* seems to undermine the classical ideal of beauty embodied by the original sculpture. Using mass-produced materials and colours referenced from contemporary digital processes, the work celebrates the ordinary and the individual in much the same way that in 1863 the French poet and critic Charles Baudelaire urged his painter of modern life to discover beauty in the ever-changing fashions of his or her own culture and context rather than in the impossible ideals of the past. As we stand looking at the shimmering, evanescent body of *Doryphoros*, and gaze mesmerised at a form that appears always to be changing and new, we no longer see any difference between the ideal and the real, the practical and the perfect. Instead we see them held together and combined in a semi-transparent form in which we might glimpse the lingering presence of universal and eternal beauty in an assembly of materials that are very much of the here and now.

If Gillick's *Applied Projection Rig* offers a bridge between the visible and invisible worlds, and Darbyshire's *Doryphoros* forms a visual connection between everyday and universal beauty, Alan Charlton's *Grey Triangle* (p. 149), seen through the arch surrounding the Wohl Central Hall's north door, provides another type of visual bridge. Charlton is one of the group of invited artists aged over 65 whom Craig-Martin wants particularly to celebrate. After studying at Sheffield and Camberwell in the late 1960s, and then at the Royal Academy Schools from 1969 to 1972, Charlton has spent the subsequent 43 years making grey paintings. Like all his works, this simple grey triangle activates the space around it, transforming how we see the exhibits hanging nearby and the white wall on which it is displayed. We are drawn to its simplicity and honesty. There is nothing here to distract our gaze, no narrative or pattern, just a single colour contained by the most basic of shapes, pulling us in and forcing us to engage with the highly refined product of Charlton's years of concentrated looking and visual discovery. As with Craig-Martin's paintings, the spareness of Charlton's canvas teaches us how to look, encouraging us to see with heightened physical awareness, reminding us that colour is a point of connection with our bodies.

We often overlook grey, associating it with the shadow that always follows a solid body, seeing it as a nondescript hue that enlivens other colours while itself remaining in the background. We dismiss it as being produced by mixing those 'non' colours, black and white. But if white is created by the mixing of the three primary colours of light, and black is the product of the three primary colours of pigment and matter, then grey can be seen as the product of all the primary colours and therefore the meeting point between light and matter, the visible and invisible, form and formlessness. Consequently, we encounter more than a colour when we look into the dim shadows of the world, or examine the surface of Charlton's *Grey Triangle*: we find a boundary between the universal and the particular.

Norman Ackroyd RA, who has selected this year's print galleries, uses grey to portray the currents of wind and the waves of light that move through the earth's atmosphere. His dramatic landscapes are never merely concerned with physical geography, they portray the invisible forces that occupy the space around them. His etchings celebrate the way that distant rainstorms paint the horizon with broad streaks of grey, mist softens and obscures a mountain's contours, and shafts of sunlight throw a patchwork of light and shadow across the earth. The towering cliffs of the Yorkshire headland in Ackroyd's large etching *Morning Sunlight Bempton* (p. 158) have dissolved beneath broad strokes of white and grey that cascade down their surface like waterfalls of light. Like Lambie's strips of brightly coloured tape, these stripes cause our gaze to ripple and flow across the print's surface as if transported by the invisible wind currents that buffet these gannet-filled skies.

Ackroyd's etchings often resemble monochrome watercolours, their fluid washes of grey conveying a sense of immediacy that perfectly captures the ephemeral atmospheric moments that are his subject. But whereas watercolours are fixed and unchanging once the paint dries on the paper, prints have a playfulness more akin to music. The original plate may stay the same, but

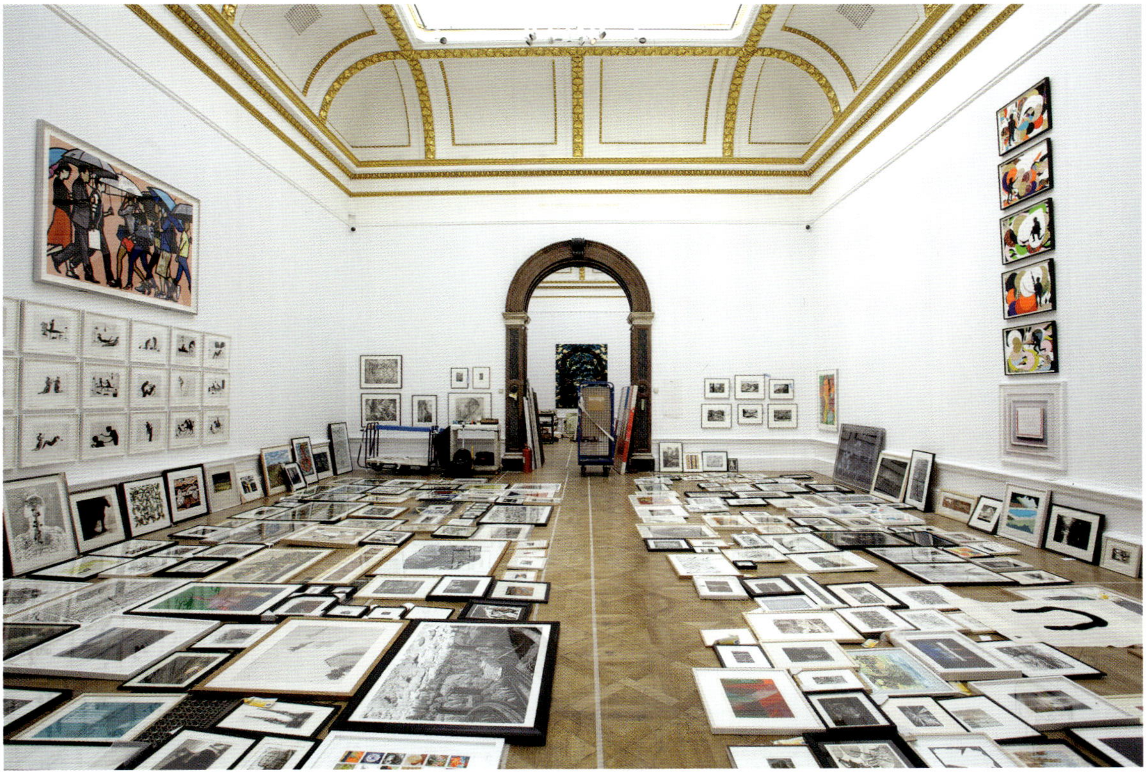

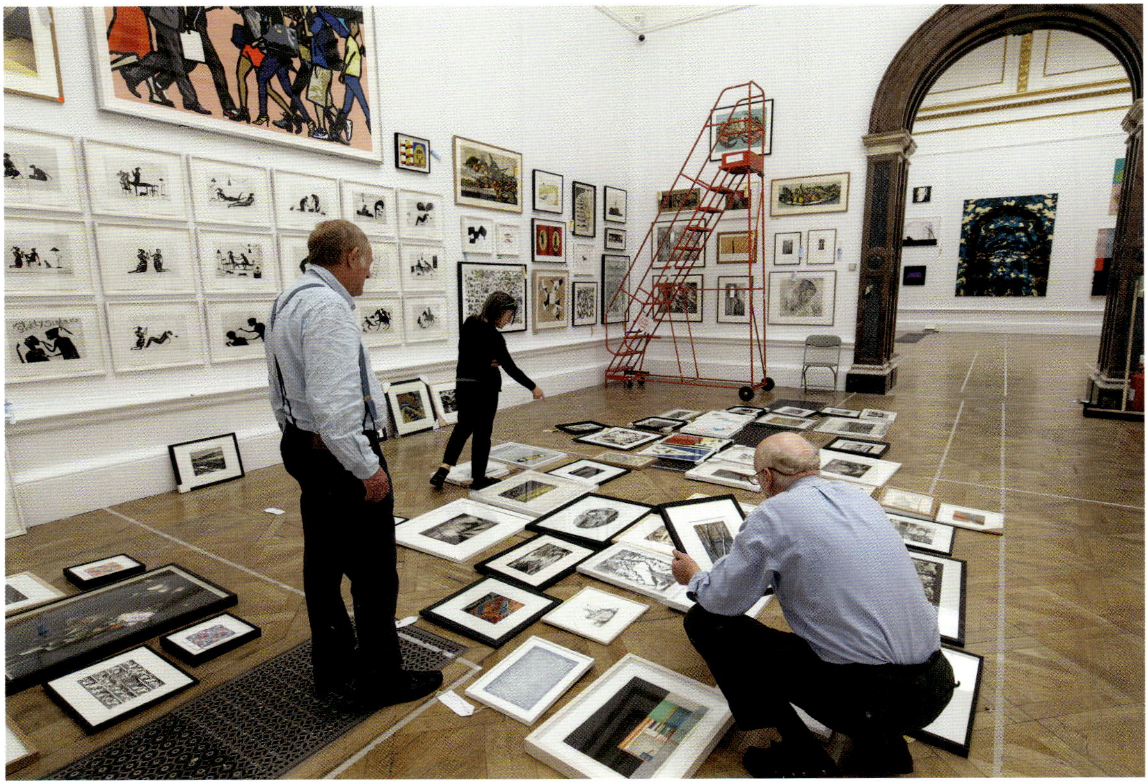

each time it is inked and printed something slightly different emerges as the ink densities change and the pressure applied by the press is varied. Printmaking is an inherently dynamic medium, providing artists with opportunities for play and variation and allowing them enormous freedom to experiment with a range of different possibilities and permutations.

For Ackroyd, prints are the visual equivalent of poems rather than novels, or lieder rather than operas. Prints, he believes, have a subtle intimacy and a sense of understatement that demand close attention. Regardless of their size, they draw the viewer in with visually compelling areas of mark-making and small detail. Even looking at the largest prints we invariably stand close to the surface so that our gaze can become lost in the clusters of intricate hatchings that allow three-dimensional forms to emerge. There is something viscerally exciting about the complex counterpoint that is created when different marks are combined, and there is something mesmerising about the unintentional puddles of intense black ink that congregate between tiny networks of lines to form a raised skin on the surface of the paper. Paying attention to these small details requires us to look at a print with a concentration and care that are often not required when looking at a painting, sculpture or photograph. Instead of looking at it as a whole we are instinctively drawn into its individual parts, those visual crevices where shadows develop and forms are only hinted at.

Ackroyd's prints can also be found in the architecture room, which has been hung by the architect Ian Ritchie RA. Among the architectural models, drawings and photographs are Ackroyd's *Galapagos* prints, commissioned in 2009 for the new Sainsbury Laboratory at the University of Cambridge. For Ritchie, these works epitomise the relationship between landscape and architecture that has been the focus of his hang. The dark, brooding forms of these islands may emerge like skyscrapers from the translucent waves of sea mist surrounding them, but Ritchie's interest, like Ackroyd's, is not so much in the physical structure of things but in the layers of dynamic natural forces around them that shape and control our experience of the world.

Ritchie's own prints explore how in this world nothing is static and everything exists in a state of constant motion: the air, the sun, our bodies, light and sound. In Ritchie's etching *Light Leaving the Earth* the long streaks of white that dart like fireflies in the night or meteor showers in the black void of space suggest not only the passage of light and energy to and from the earth but also wind blowing through a field of long grass. They represent the sunlight streaming into the Academy, passing through Gillick's corona, or the phototropic

Page 21: Installation of Gallery V in progress with (from left) Norman Ackroyd RA, Alison Wilding RA and Bill Woodrow RA

Top and middle: The Lecture Room at different stages of the installation
Below: Alison Wilding RA with *Erebus (Man on Fire Version II)* by Tim Shaw RA

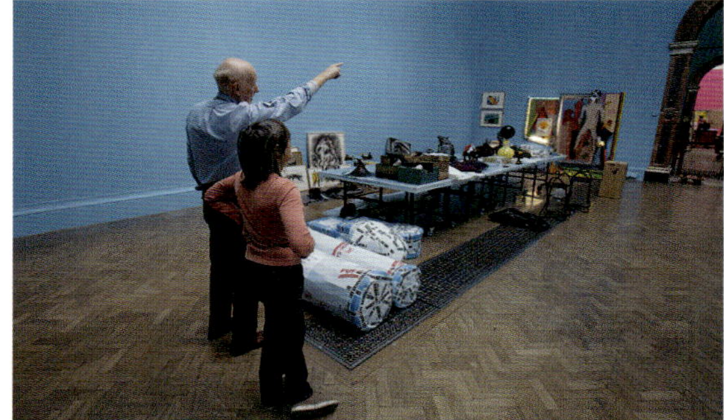

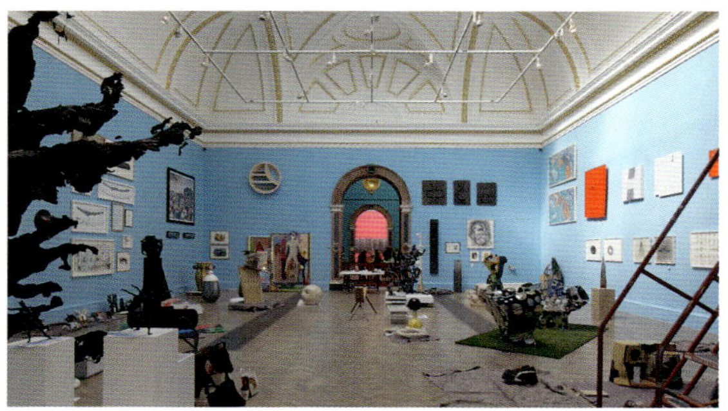

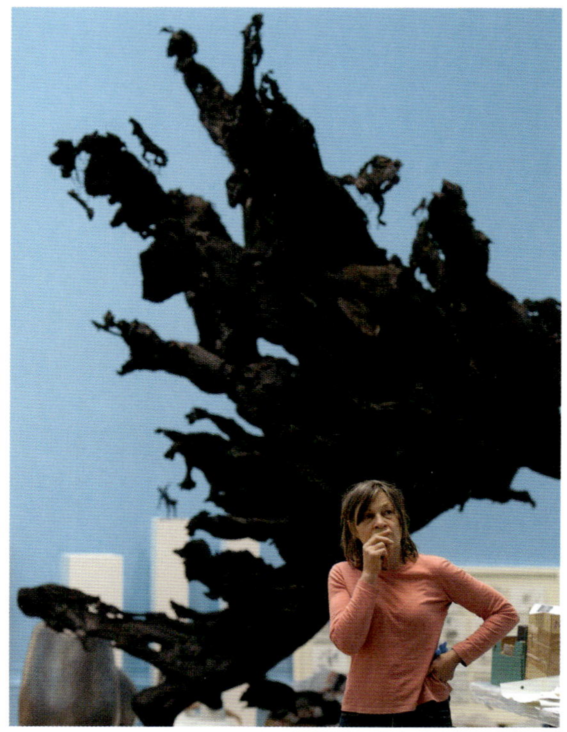

forces that turn the branches of trees towards the light of the sun, or pull the water up through the tangled roots of Ackroyd's *Isabela Mangroves*.

In his carborundum print *Disequilibrium* (p. 104), Ritchie nods to our own precarious position and impact on the world. Balancing an orange square on an orange triangle on an orange circle, and floating them in a bright magenta space above a series of interlaced curves that suggest the earth's surface, Ritchie offers a vision of the 'invented landscape' that we inhabit, a combination of the man-made and natural in which disparate, individual forms must co-exist in a delicate and fragile harmony.

But Ritchie sees the 'invented landscape' of architecture as playing a more active role in shaping and moulding our daily experience. He believes that architecture is not just a space for living, but an experience for the eyes and the skin, something to be both seen and felt. He likens our experience of architecture to the way in which a child unconsciously measures his passage through space and time by trailing his fingers along some metal railings. As we walk past stone, glass, brick and steel our eyes and bodies tingle and vibrate with the differing sensations these materials produce. Just as mist, wind, sunlight and shadow provide the visual and sensory context through which we encounter reality, buildings also surround us with a constantly changing environment of colour, texture, shape and volume that causes the world to oscillate, fragment, coalesce and vibrate around us.

Our sensory reaction to architecture is not only provoked by our corner-of-the-eye response to materials and physical construction. Buildings are brought to life by the ever-changing passage of light across their surfaces, with shadows holding our gaze and highlights dazzling our eyes. As they creak and echo to the sound of the wind our eardrums vibrate, while draughts cause our skin to tingle at their unexpected touch. Like Gillick's Plexiglass corona, these highlights, shadows, echoes and draughts are signposts to the constantly changing world that surrounds us, providing a physical point of connection with the teeming atomic world that Ritchie envisions in *Light Leaving the Earth*.

A world veiled in light and atoms is also the subject of the two paintings submitted by Bill Woodrow RA, who, with Alison Wilding RA, has hung the sculpture room. The origin of the larger of Woodrow's paintings (*Untitled*) lay in three separate sheets of paper, each dominated by a large amorphous yellow shape painted from pollen collected by bees and then mixed with a binding agent. These painted sheets became Woodrow's 'stone', the base material in which he saw a world forming, in this case a wide plain fringed by a range of snow-capped mountains that is an idea of landscape rather than a specific place. But as with Lambie's staircase, Woodrow has created a pictorial space that is both visually and spatially ambiguous. He has shrouded the physical geography in layers of colour whose camouflage of swirling patterns turns two dimensions into three and three into two, dissolving the difference between the mountains and the plains, the solid earth and the flowing rivers, exposing the atomic realm where such distinctions do not exist.

A similar mountainous scene is also the subject of *Plain Ranger* (p. 192), Woodrow's sculpture submission, although inevitably three dimensions demand and exploit a different response from the viewer. Seen from a distance, *Plain Ranger* appears two-dimensional, its different planes coalescing into an apparently flat surface. But this initially simple visual narrative becomes more complex the closer we get, as the work's three-dimensional cubist construction starts to reveal itself. Woodrow's differently angled planes begin to open out, exposing nooks and crannies whose siren call invites our gaze to play among the intriguing shadows that fill these occluded spaces. But the invitation is not just visual: we long to touch the work as if we were standing in such a landscape; to feel its rocky screes beneath our feet, the snow melting against our skin, the cold water rushing between our toes. We want to probe its crevices with our fingers, feel the sharp edges of its corners, and caress the different surfaces of the wood and cardboard like a child feeling her way around the world. But we cannot, and this unspoken cultural prohibition makes the desire all the more tantalising; so we must imagine it in our mind's eye, feeling the sensations of these different materials as a ghostly echo on our skin.

The sense of feeling through seeing is even more acute in Wilding's sculptures *Killjoy* and *Baby Shimmy*. The abstract simplicity of *Killjoy* (p. 183) forces us to look at its shapes, materials and textures without any intervening associations. Accordingly, when our eyes caress the small iron sphere balanced on a larger iron half sphere, we perceive their weight and smoothness, we become lost in the warm colour of their oxidised surfaces while imagining their cold touch against our skin. In our mind's eye we can even pinch and hold those intangible points of connection where these forms balance on each other and on the ground. Upon seeing the bleached feather that pierces the sphere, we focus on the contrast between its soft, weightless delicacy and the heaviness of the metal rather than thinking of the bird from which it came. For as we look now we first encounter substance and form rather than specific objects; we see weight, colour and texture rather than defined meanings. This sense of feeling through looking is not restricted to sculpture, however. We unravel the tangled compositions of *The Brothers Tzoveleki* (p. 66) and *Re-Assemble,* two paintings submitted by Gus Cummins RA, using our eyes to feel our way around these industrial junkyards of the imagination. Our gaze shudders across corrugated surfaces and skips across perforated covers, it hula-hoops around thin metal circles, pushing aside heavy metal girders. Blurring the boundary between the abstract and the figurative, Cummins invites us to see the essential visual beauty of even the most functional of man-made objects.

Sculptures only come to life when we walk around them. Until we move away from the fixed viewpoint from which we look at a painting, their outlines will always be fixed and unchanging. Circumnavigating a sculpture allows its different aspects to reveal themselves, so that our experience of it is constantly changing, yet even when we do this we can never see the whole sculpture at once: whichever angle we choose we are chasing shadows, our efforts to find an all-encompassing viewpoint doomed to failure. But this is what gives sculptures their energy: they demand not just a visual but a physical engagement; we can't just look, we have to move around, through and under them, watching as they constantly change before us, with shadows, highlights and differing perspectives transforming hard-edged profiles into a series of different propositions that can never be fixed or tied down. Whether wood or metal, plaster or fabric, hard or soft, large or small, the sculptures enfolded by Craig-Martin's sky-blue walls invite us to contemplate a world whose edges fizz and vibrate as they melt into the surrounding air. They inspire us to walk towards the horizon, going from simplicity to detail, reminding us that what we see of reality is never complete but always partial, shaped by the specific context of the place we are in.

An awareness of the uncertain, partial nature of the world underpins the work of the South African artist William Kentridge HON RA. Kentridge is showing nine drawings and prints in the Small Weston Room, which is traditionally hung floor to ceiling with small paintings. This year, however, we find ourselves standing in a clearing in a wood, surrounded by large linocuts and ink drawings of South African trees. Craig-Martin intends this to be a space of reflection, like Shawcross's monumental steel grove, somewhere to pause for thought and breathe in a different air. These drawings are also a place of reflection for Kentridge, who uses the process of making art as a way of making sense of the world.

Kentridge thinks through his body, accessing knowledge through his senses and then expressing these sensations through the different gestures and marks he uses within his drawings. His works are thus the physical expression of his ideas. In some of his prints and drawings here we find a single mark, a bold, expressive gesture that perfectly conveys his immediate, unconsidered physical response to what he has seen. This is not the sort of intelligence contained in rational thought, but the intelligence and world-knowledge found, as Kentridge puts it, 'between one's shoulders and one's fingertips'. Other drawings, in contrast, are more detailed, their knowledge gained from an intimate and close attention to nature, which celebrates the significance of individual leaves on a tree. In *The Periphery – All Text Tree*, however, Kentridge has constructed the tree's trunk and branches from a collage of random texts. When we gaze upon the world, our minds are not empty, but filled with quotations and memories, thoughts, ideas and snatches of music that shape the way we see things. These are not the product of a conscious narrative, but fragments of our past story that bring colour to our present experience.

Kentridge has drawn these trees onto pages torn from an encyclopaedia and the *Shorter Oxford English Dictionary*, his ink obscuring and rewriting the facts contained within the printed pages. This is a deliberate act by the artist, who sees uncertainty as a fundamental 'category of knowledge' and who wants to challenge ideas that are fixed and unmoving. For the same reason, after tearing pages out of books to create a base collage on which to work, he reassembles them in a deliberately random order to reflect the partial nature of all knowledge. Visual knowledge, Kentridge believes, can take sense and deconstruct it, and take nonsense and see the sense in it. His drawings connect disparate pages through a spider's web of black lines that link together words and ideas into new and unexpected narratives.

We find a similar use of the visual to rearrange words and reconstruct narratives in the Summer Exhibition's last room, which houses the two completed versions of *A Humument* by Tom Phillips RA (p. 200). Phillips began this almost lifelong project on 5 November 1966, while he and R. B. Kitaj were browsing for books in Peckham Rye. Phillips said to Kitaj that he would use the first book he found for threepence to construct a new artwork. The book he came across was a copy of W. H. Mallock's 1892 novel *A Human Document*, the title of which Phillips contracted to *A Humument*.

Over the intervening years Phillips has constructed two completely unique reworkings of Mallock's text, as well as an opera and an app, seeing *A Humument* as a work that cuts across a number of artistic genres. Here, eyes are inevitably drawn to the passages of text that now pattern each page, the black printed words standing out against the paper around them like beacons of promise hinting at the new worlds that lie waiting to be born in our minds. As we read these short poetic texts we are drawn into the disjointed lives of characters such as Bill

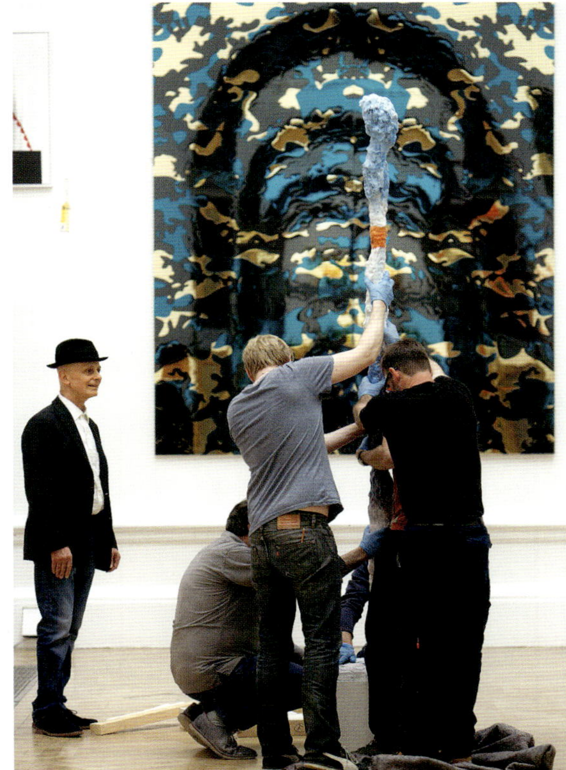

David Remfry RA overseeing the installation of *So Long Ago and Far Away* by Rebecca Warren RA in Gallery IV, in front of *Mimic (Black)* by Paul Hosking

Toge and Irma, which have been constructed by Phillips from a complex set of rules that he has developed over the years to help him in the discovery of the hidden text.

Looking at these pages we are again in the realm of *An Oak Tree*, confronted by a dialogue between visual and verbal knowledge. Although our initial response is to read these pages as we would any book, Phillips sees each page as both a text and a landscape, searching for its poetic narrative while responding to it visually, looking for colours, light, shade and texture. Once he has identified the words he wants to use, he begins to use the visual prompts he has found to deconstruct the original linear narrative, using a patchwork of collage, intricate patterns and minute figurative paintings to create ribbons of colour and pattern across the whole, obscuring and hiding large areas of text to reveal the new meaning he has found. What we encounter in the three rows of *A Humument* that line the gallery is what we find whenever we look out across the world and see the blurring of foreground and horizon: that the constraints imposed by linear time and space are set free by the visual.

The galleries given over to architecture, printmaking and sculpture, as well to the works by Kentridge and Phillips, offer particularly concentrated reflections on the nature of visual knowledge, but throughout the Summer Exhibition Craig-Martin and the other members of the Hanging Committee have selected and hung a number of key works that contribute further insights into the act of looking and visual thinking. Some have been placed in strategic positions at the end of sight lines to draw the eye through the whole length of the building; some are framed by a series of arched doorways, giving them a sense of mystery and intrigue when seen from a distance; some are hidden among the general mix of works. These points of reference not only enable us to see with new eyes, but they also help to provide the visual connections that unite the different spaces and disparate exhibits of the show.

When we look into the vast gold, teal and black mirrored surface of Paul Hosking's *Mimic (Black)* (p. 120), we see images of ourselves disappearing into the far distance in a version of reality transformed by playful symmetrical patterns, where the distinction between near and far, self and other has been collapsed. As we are drawn into this compelling surface, these patterns fragment our vision, so that at one moment we see both ourselves and the rooms around us clearly, and at the next, everything is obscured and tinted, and what we think is familiar has been called into question, distorted and camouflaged into an Andy Warhol-like version of itself. Through Hosking's mirrors, as through all art, the world is transformed and we see ourselves differently.

Antony Stokes's black-and-white photograph *Cover, Pen-y-Bont*, hanging in the Wohl Central Hall, asks us to step back and think about the difference between knowledge and sight. Before us we know we see a car tightly wrapped in a sheet of fabric, a wing mirror giving away the identity of the hidden object. But what we actually see is a billowing grey shape like a cloud, its bottom edge puckered and rippled like a deflating balloon. What fascinates Craig-Martin is when the division between the known and the seen is blurred, and we can perceive both the car and the cloud, just as he once saw both a glass of water and an oak tree.

To the left of the main entrance, leading our eye through to the largest gallery, hangs *Can't or Won't?* (p. 31), a large yellow and red abstract painting by the current President of the Royal Academy, Christopher Le Brun PRA. Le Brun makes no attempt to paint anything recognisable. Hemmed in and contained by the turquoise walls of the Wohl Central Hall, his broad strokes of yellow and red pull our eye into their simple narrative. They tell the story of the painting, recording each thought and each decision, each movement of the arm and stroke of the brush as it deposits a layer of paint on the canvas. The resulting work expresses the drama of pushing 'coloured mud' around a surface, the game of push and pull played between these two primary colours that pulls us into silent, uncertain depths. Look to the far end of the largest gallery and we see the same story told in the large print *Mississippi River Blues* by Richard Long RA. Both these monumental, abstract works reveal in the vibrant physicality of their mark-making the transition from mind to hand, abstract thought to physical act, which is mirrored in our act of looking, as our physical response to these dynamic surfaces leads to a thought, an emotion, an idea.

In Gallery I, hung by Olwyn Bowey RA and Gus Cummins RA, is *Julie and Rob* (p. 87), a monumental tapestry portrait by Grayson Perry RA. This vast work with its anonymous couple demands our immediate attention. But then out of the corners of our eyes and at the edges of our perception, we notice tiny movements of colours, and we look away and begin to discover the smaller works that surround it. For however large and compelling an object is, our gaze is always democratic; it is always moving: shifting from large to small, from people to objects, always inquisitive and open, just as the Summer Exhibition strives to be.

Many of the small works in this gallery reflect the attentive, loving gaze that informs and shapes Bowey's own paintings. Among the dynamic forms of abstract and contemporary art that have increasingly come to fill and excite the walls of the Summer Exhibition, the tradition of figurative painting championed

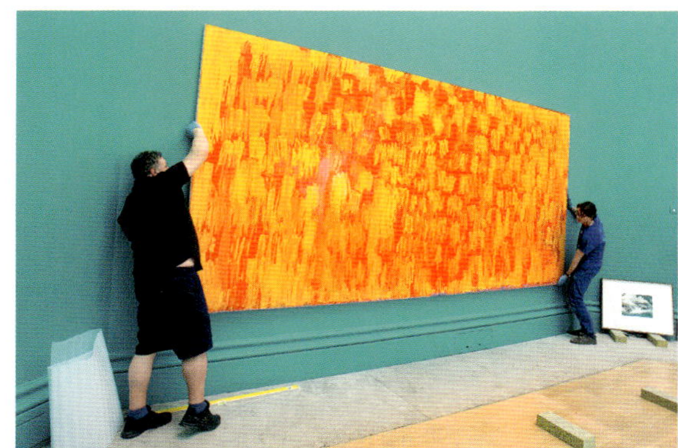

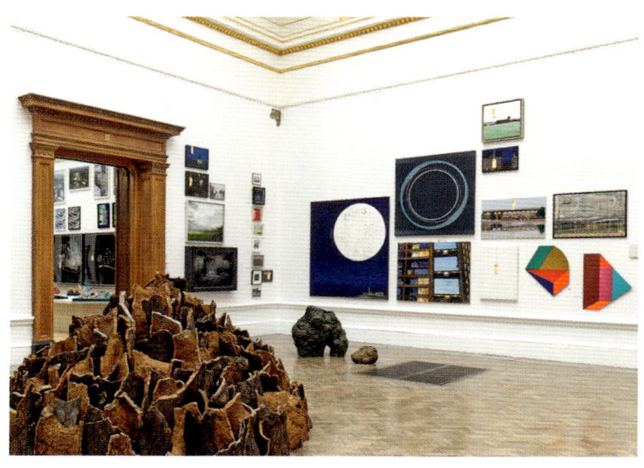

Top: Installation of *Can't or Won't?* by Christopher Le Brun PRA in the Wohl Central Hall
Above: Gallery II with *Cork Dome* by David Nash RA in the foreground

by Munnings and continued by Bowey and other Academicians might seem out of place, a retrograde step along the path of Modernism. But Bowey's works are not about fashion or concerned with artistic trends, they are about the same timeless, universal act of seeing that informs all art, the translation of a look into a mark, and in Bowey's case a million looks, each lovingly attentive to those often unnoticed things that surround us, a fallen tree, a hedge, plants in a greenhouse, allowing us to see the shape and colour of each individual element within the whole. As Christopher Le Brun has noted, Bowey 'looks on behalf of those too busy to look'. For those who are caught up in the speed and constant change of modern life, her canvases reveal the beauty and everyday wonder of the overlooked and uncelebrated corners of the world.

The attentive look also allows us to reach out into the unknown and approach the things we fear. In his dramatic drawing of a prowling wolf, David Remfry RA, who has hung Gallery IV, contemplates the gap between man and nature. This is an archetypal image of the hungry wolf, captured in a furtive moment slinking away from us, its mouth open and salivating, but Remfry invites our eyes to look at what we fear and to confront the danger of the other. As our gaze becomes tangled in its matted fur and traces the curves of its back, tail and belly, we are no longer other, the gap has been bridged.

Seeing the other is also the focus of the paintings submitted by Mick Rooney RA, who has hung Gallery VIII. His fantastical narratives apply the same loving attention to the world as Bowey's, depicting unnoticed elements in fascinated detail; the multi-coloured labels on an old battered suitcase, the grain in a wooden table, individual tresses of curling hair. But just as the eight-year-old William Blake saw a tree filled with angels, Rooney sees rooms filled with flying fish, and the night sky filled with multiple moons. For while a painting can express an emotion, embody a physical movement or capture what we see in front of us, it can also reveal what we see inside ourselves. It can give form to our hopes, express our dreams, and reveal the possibility of magic and wonder in the world, for sight and vision are not ruled by the boundaries of reason and logic but by the limits of our imagination.

Wandering through each of the Academy's galleries we are bombarded with colours, lines, shapes and textures that provoke memories of other works. When we walk past Rose Hilton's painting *Red Studio* (p. 141) we might see a family likeness between the hesitant borders and coloured hatching of her isolated figure and the uncertain boundaries of Matthew Darbyshire's *Doryphoros*; or when looking at Tim Head's interlocking and intersecting semi-opaque circles (p. 142) we might recognise the shifting patterns we saw earlier in Liam Gillick's double corona. These echoes and reflections create visual connections that send our gaze running across, around and through the different galleries of the Academy to knit together individual works into a cohesive whole.

This is particularly apparent in Gallery II, hung by Jock McFadyen RA, where our eyes ricochet endlessly between the connections of geometry, colour and texture that underlie this joyous and idiomatic room. McFadyen's painting of a large white moon suspended magically over Calton Hill speaks to the two circles next to it, while his almost ethereal pale blue and pink landscape *Uist* reflects the emptiness of his *Dungeness Beach* opposite. A small group of celebrity portraits may look out of place, but are in fact the perfect inhabitants for McFadyen's reinterpretation of the British landscape, where the unremarkable rubs shoulders with the picturesque and the historic sits alongside the contemporary. His room constructs a landscape inhabited by ordinary people and celebrities, everyday and remarkable scenes, the urban and rural; built from colours, light, textures and patterns that reflect all the fun of a day at the seaside, or a picnic in the park. Encircled by the diverse works of McFadyen's extraordinary landscape we don't worry about the different genres and categories of art: abstract and figurative, still-life and portraiture, painting, photography and sculpture, amateur and professional. Instead we stand and look, joining the invisible dots that can lead to new ideas and unknown pleasures.

So we leave the cool interior of Burlington House and stand beneath *The Dappled Light of the Sun* again. As we look up through these steel branches, we might now imagine the Summer Exhibition as a tree, with Lambie's staircase a rainbow trunk leading up to the galleries that form the branches, and each work a leaf in the dense vegetation of the canopy. Then, as we stand again on Piccadilly, we become aware of the invented landscape around us, our senses tingling in anticipation as we prepare to walk out into a world where shadows beckon and colours tease and the air around us is made to pulsate and vibrate by the buildings on either side. We might find ourselves longing to taste with the tongue of our eye, or to trail our fingers along the railings that stand outside. We know that before us there now lies an uncertain world of infinite, unfolding possibilities, a world waiting to be discovered and experienced through our vision and other senses. For this is the unique role of the Royal Academy of Arts and its Summer Exhibition: to offer its visitors a masterclass in looking and the distinctiveness of visual knowledge that inspires us to rediscover the world around us.

Wohl Central Hall

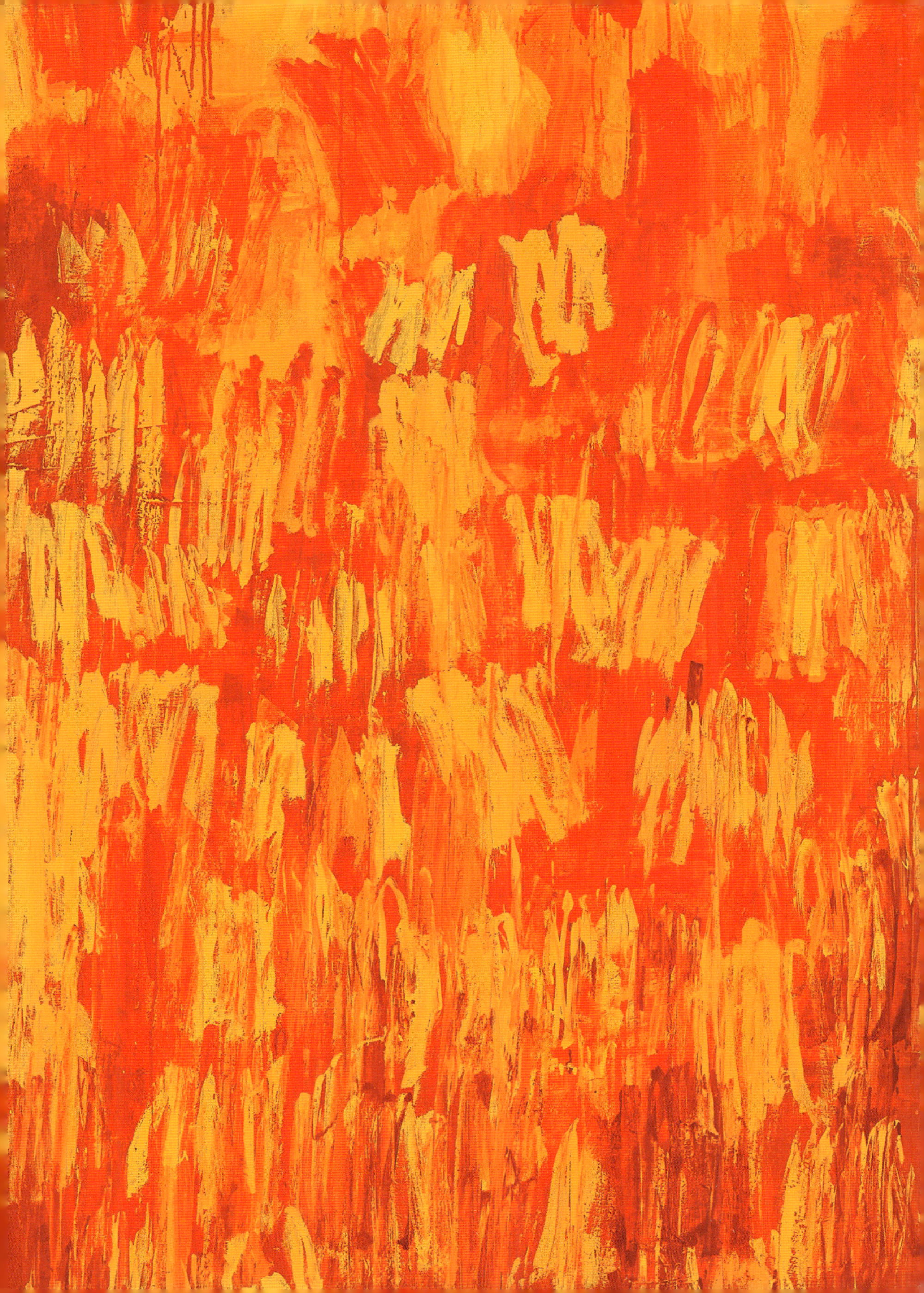

Jim Dine HON RA
Night
Mixed media
130 × 101 cm

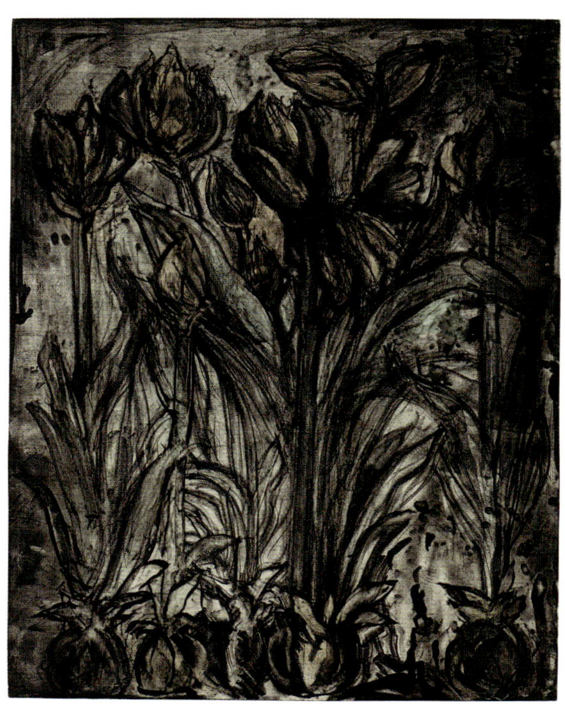

Dr Leonard McComb RA
Jasmine Flowers Provence, Turkish Bowl V&A
Oil
67 × 57 cm

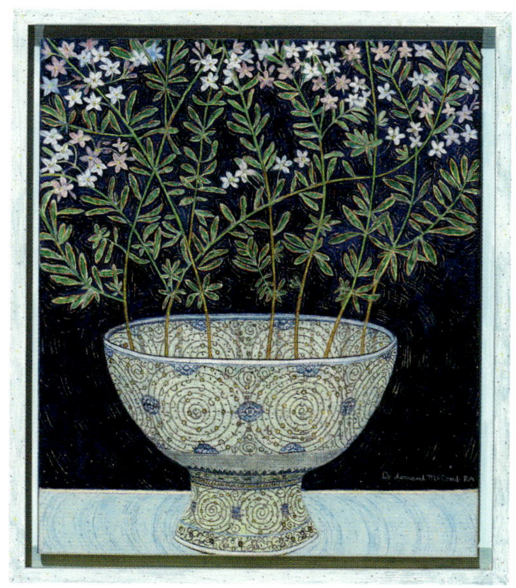

Christopher Le Brun PRA
Can't or Won't?
Oil
220 × 440 cm

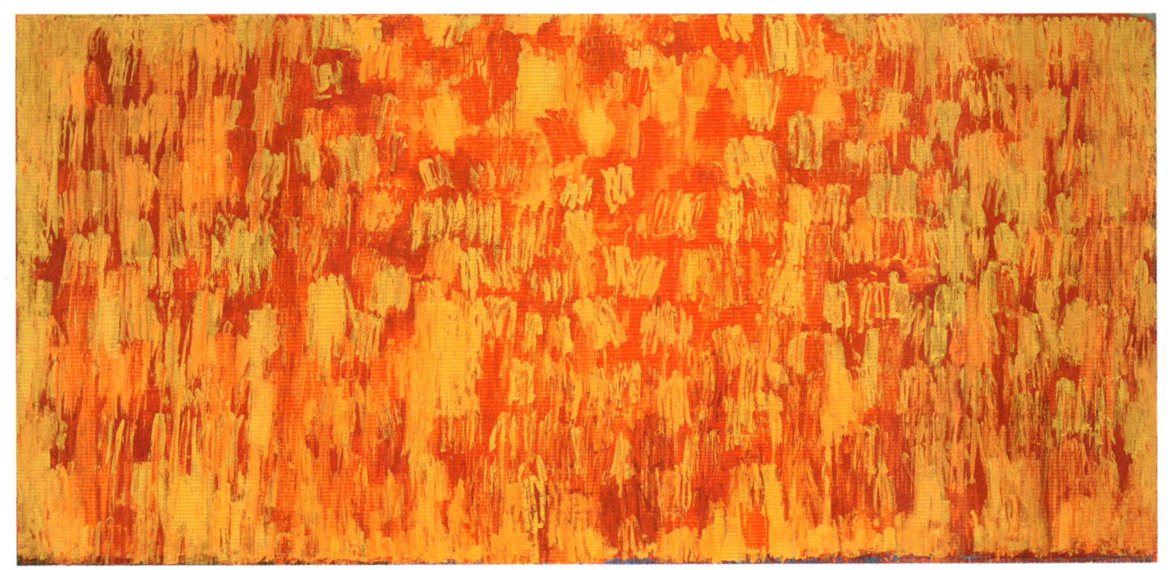

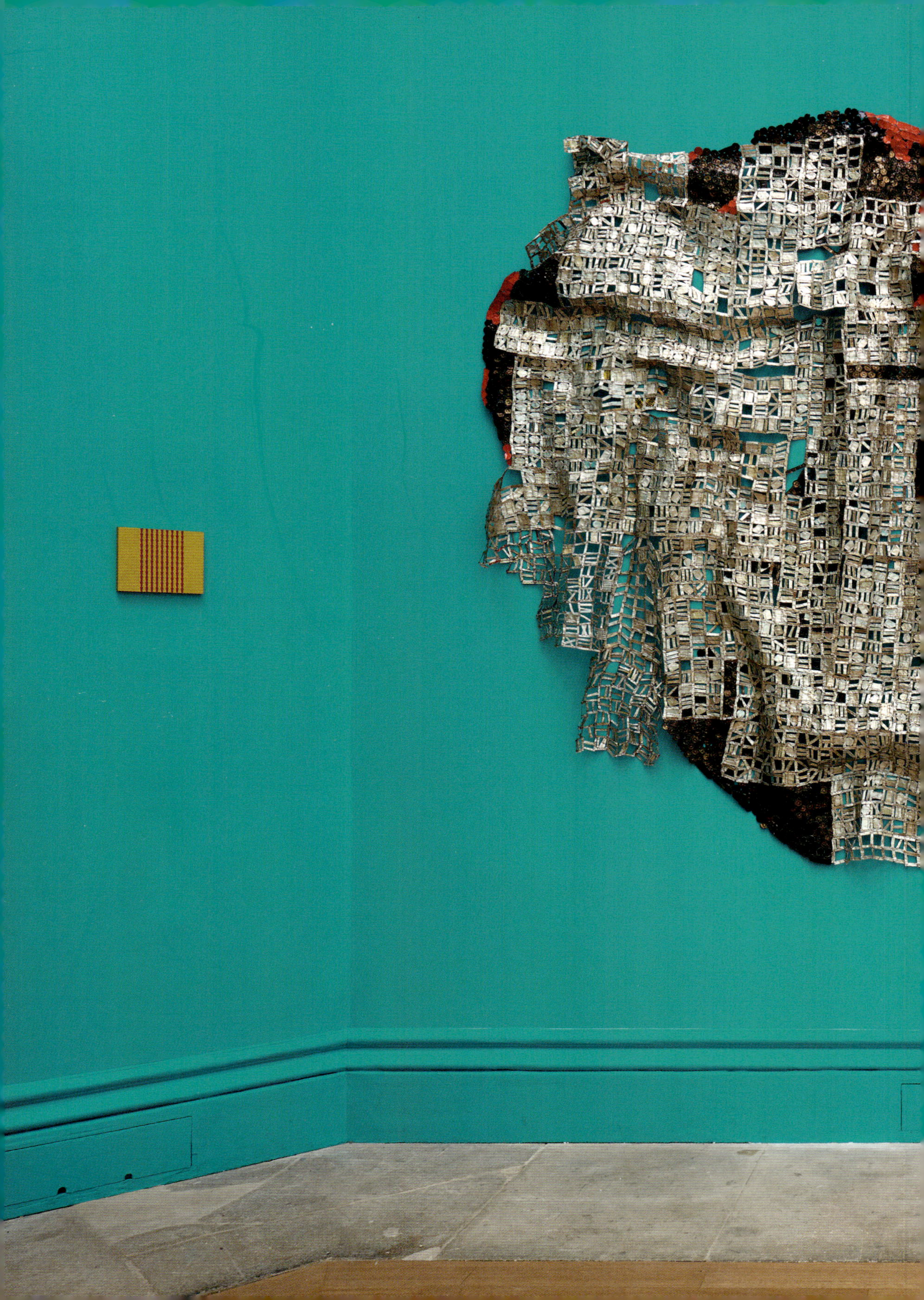

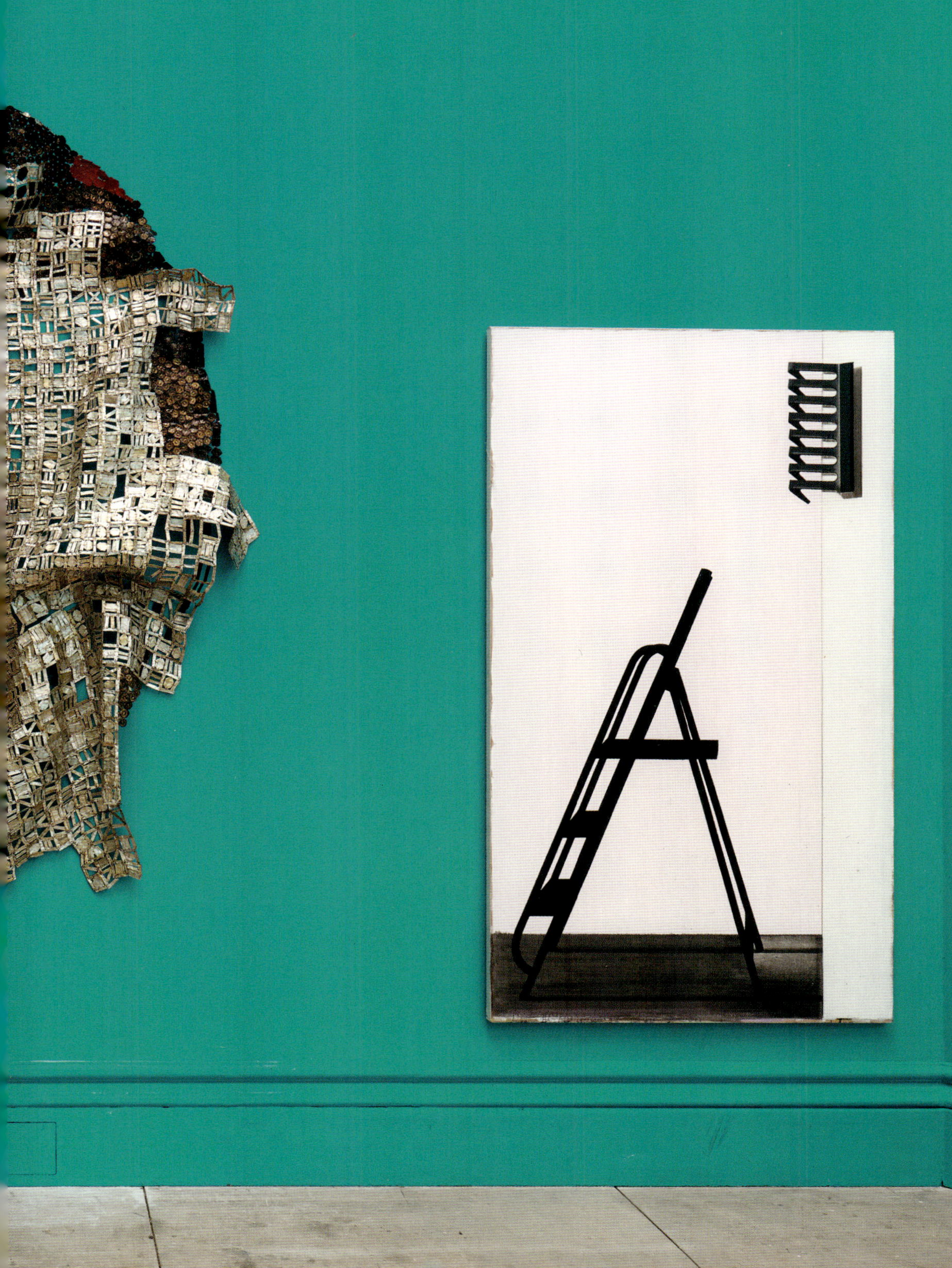

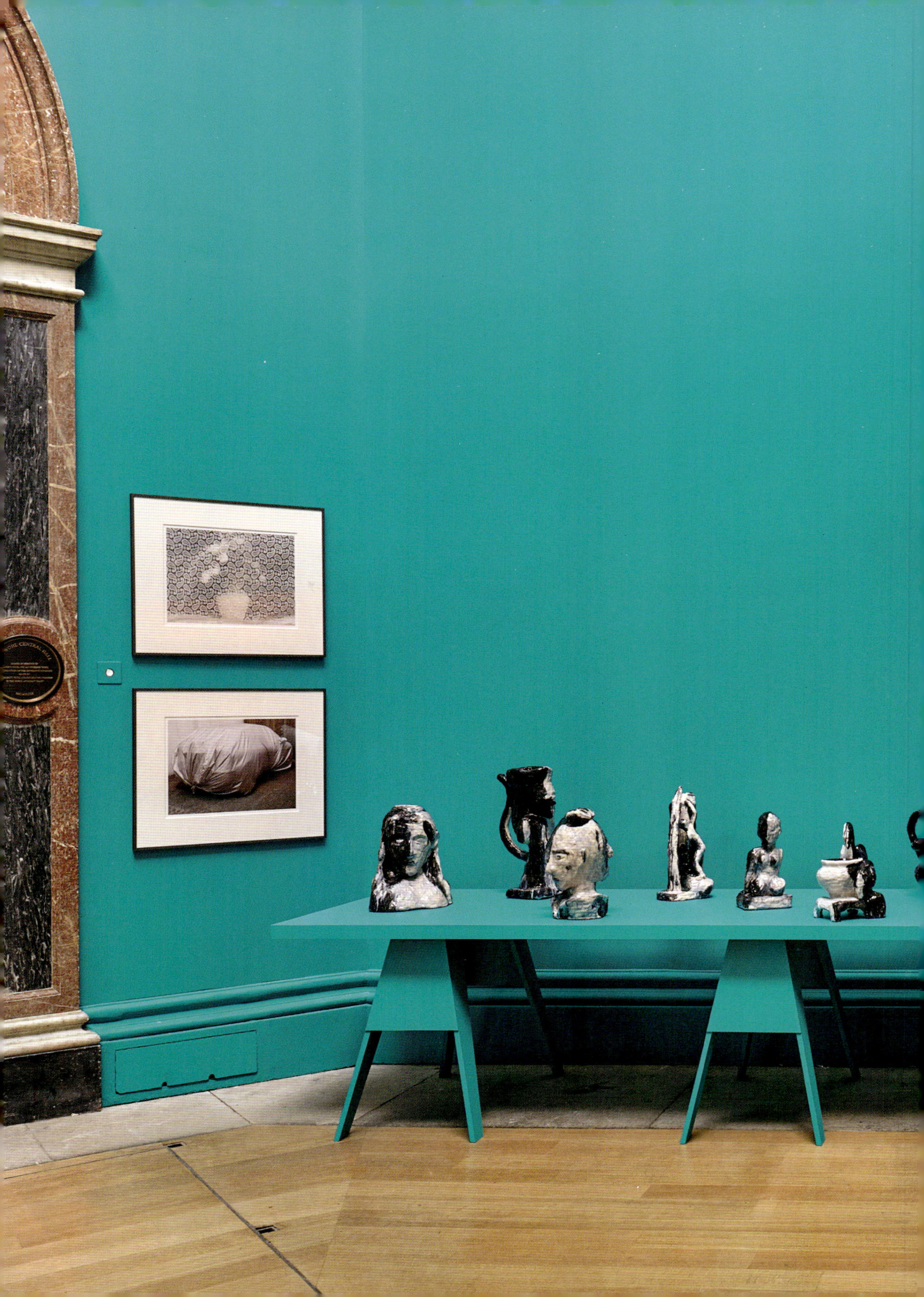

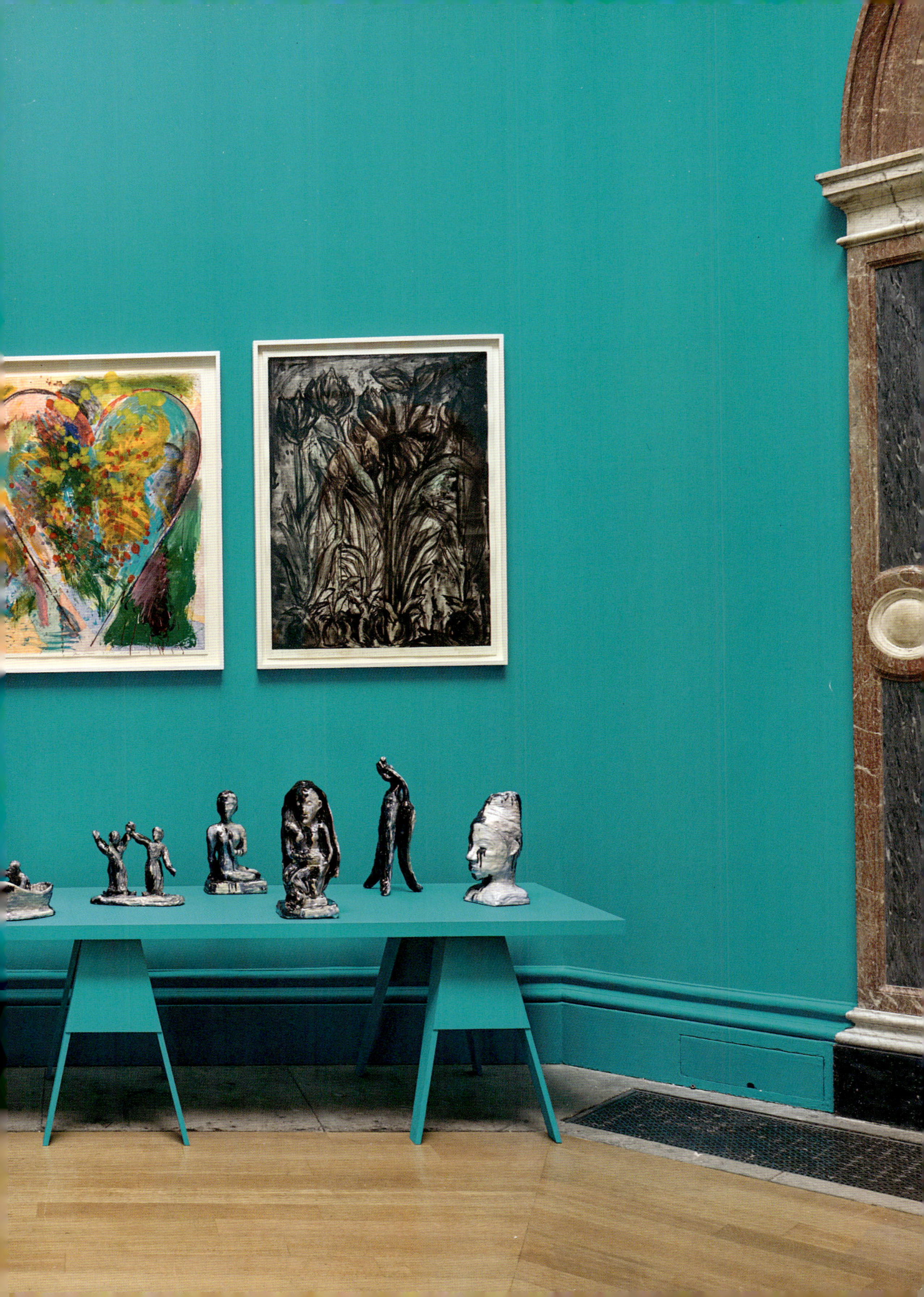

Anthony Stokes
Paisley (Welsh Pears), Tynewydd
Inkjet print
64 × 76 cm

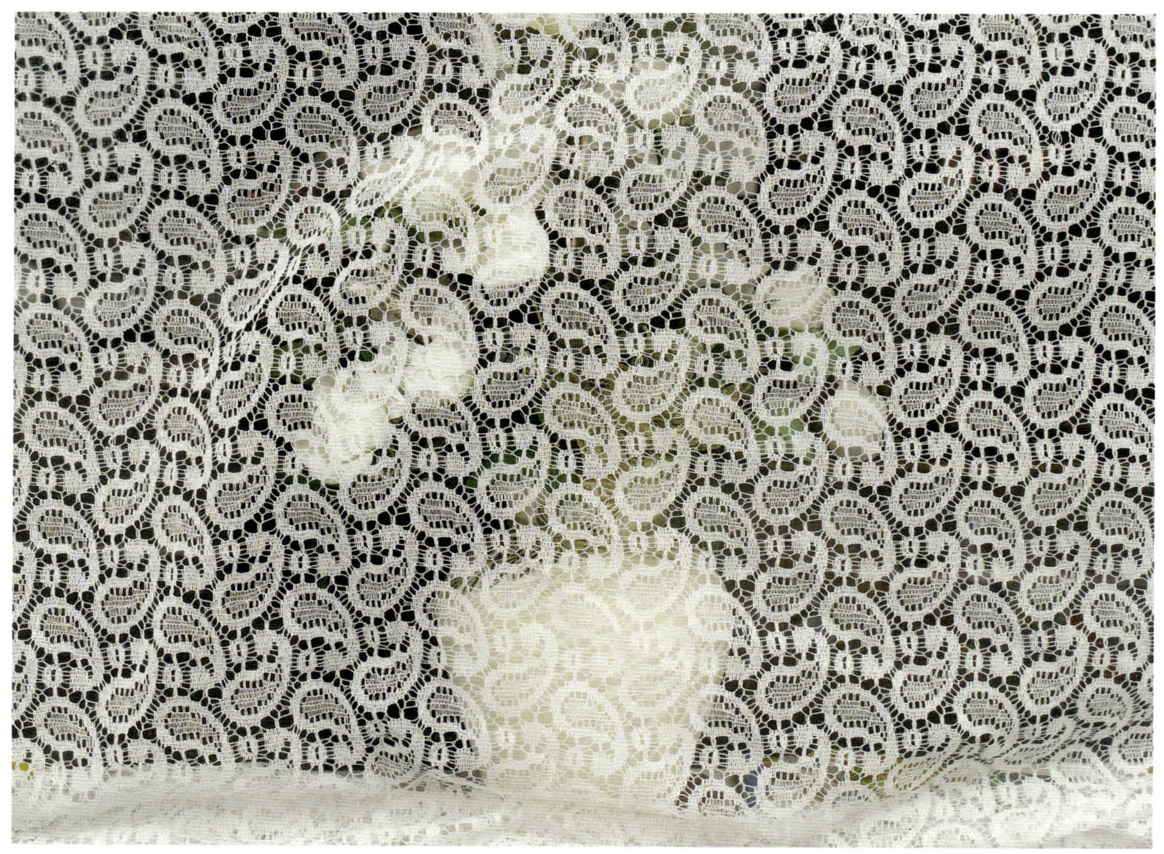

Michael Simpson
Squint (17), Second Version
Oil
230 × 130 cm

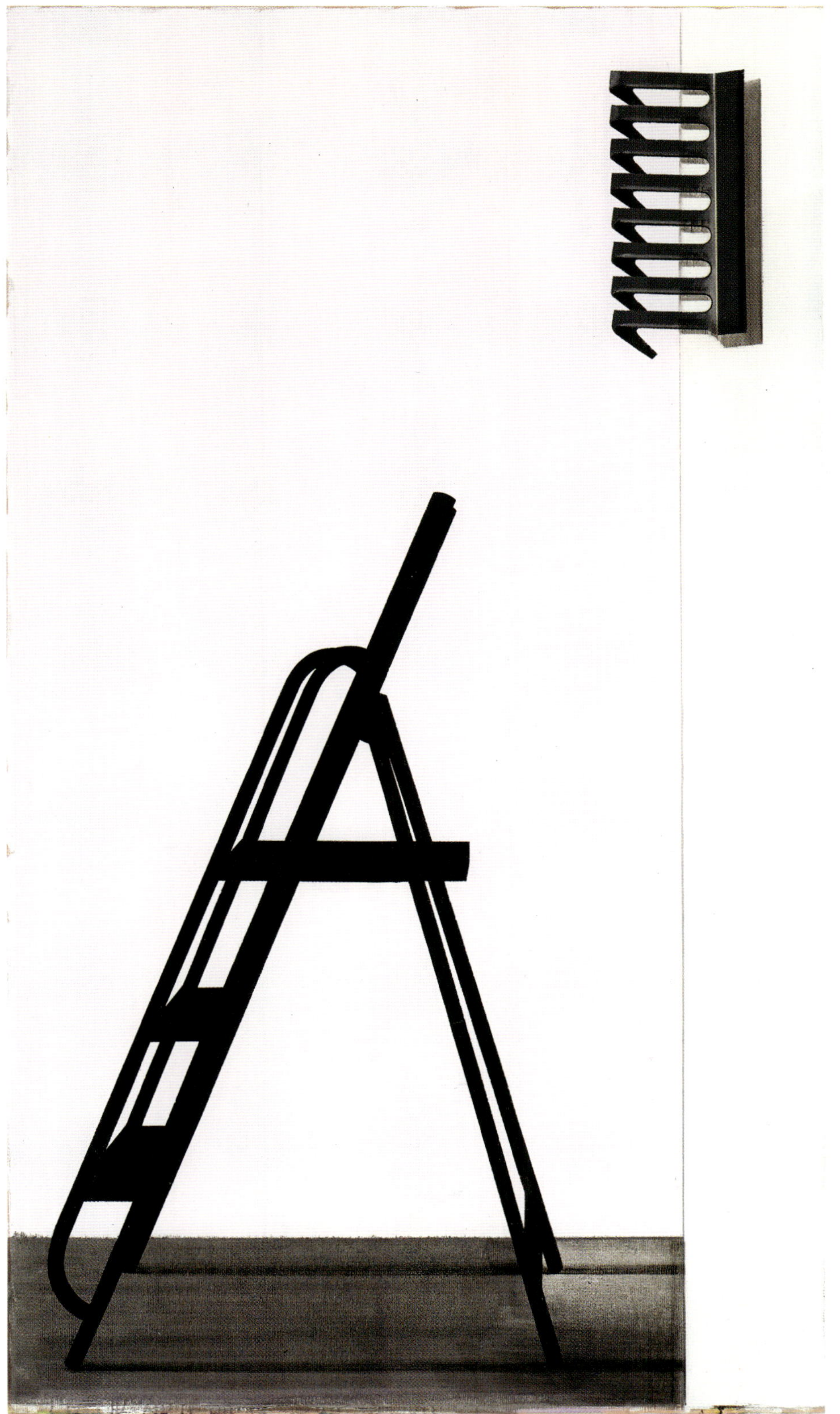

Vanessa Jackson
Hommage à Henri
Oil
214 × 183 cm

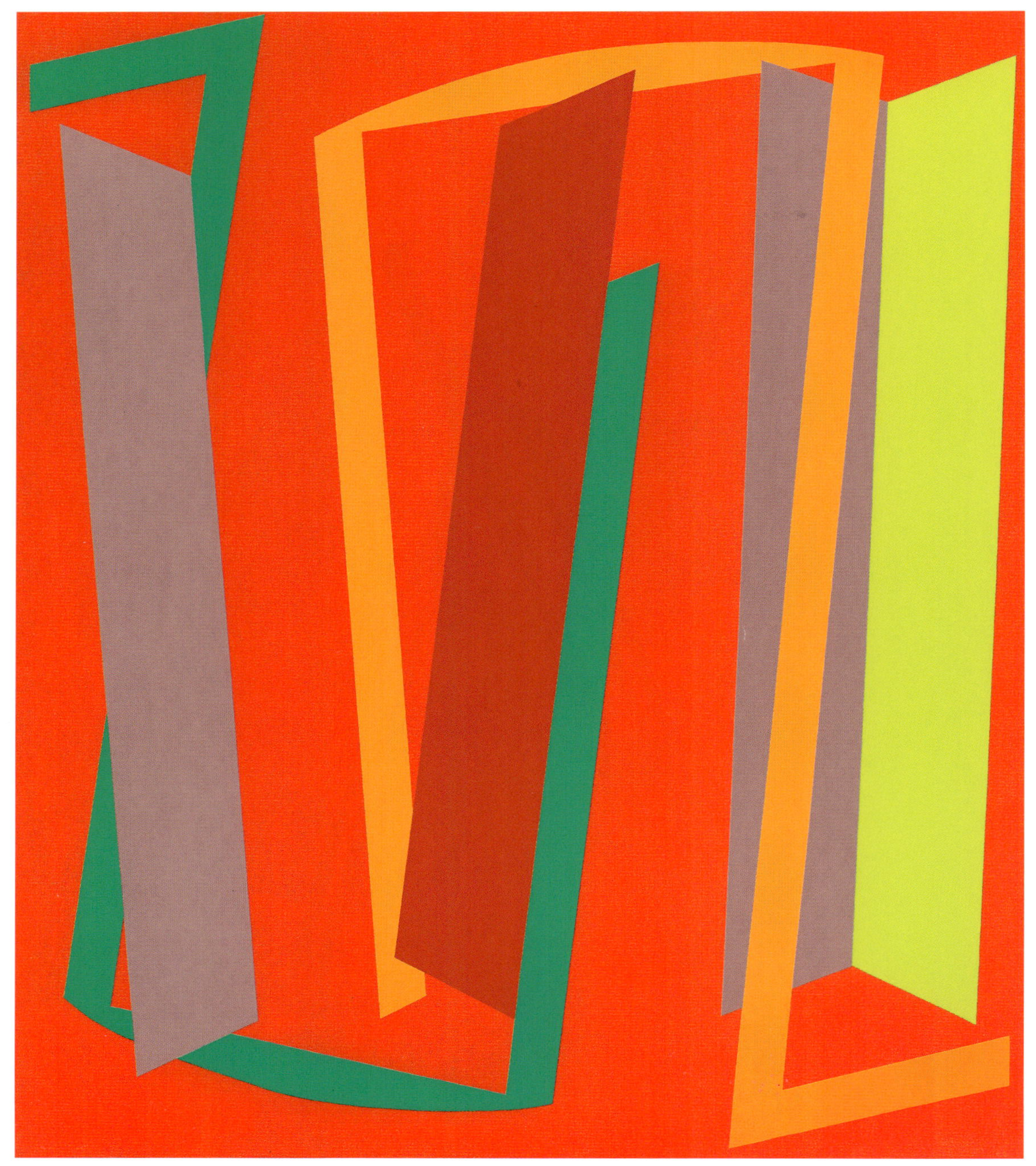

Stephen Buckley
Racer
Oil and enamel
95 × 126 cm

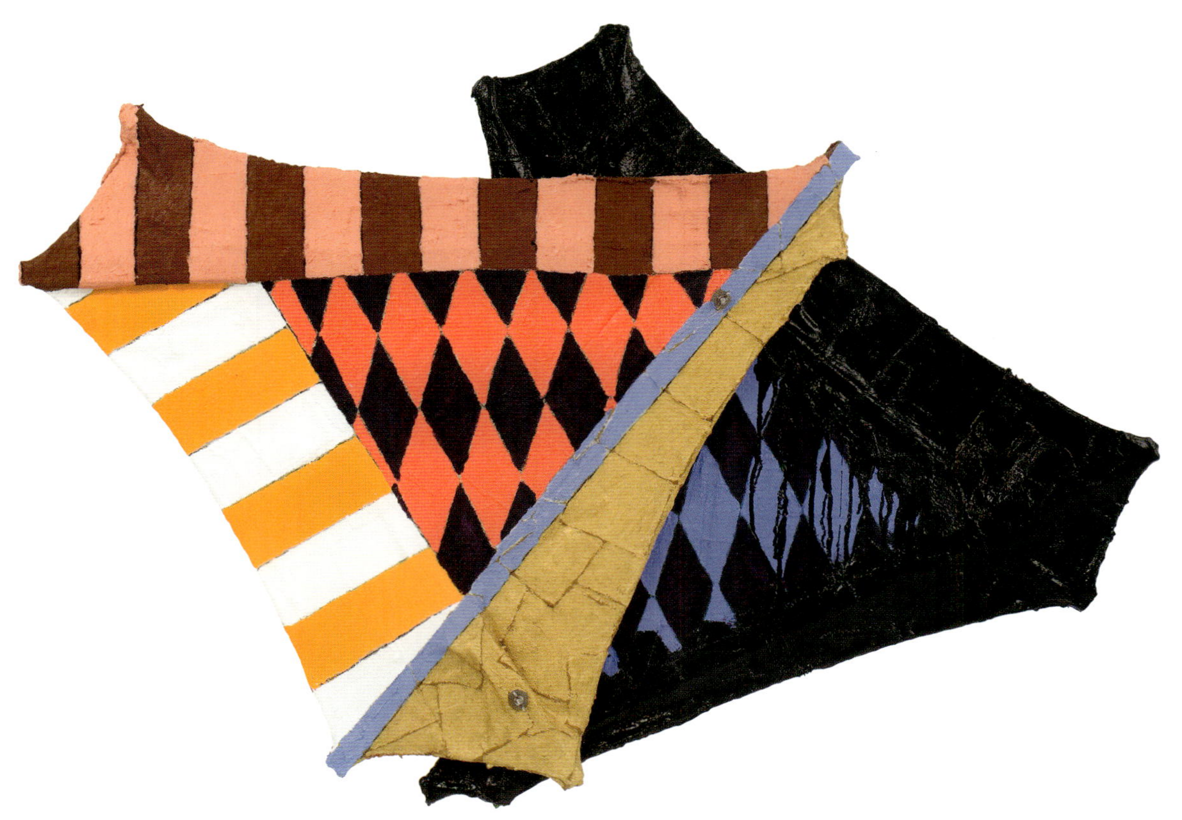

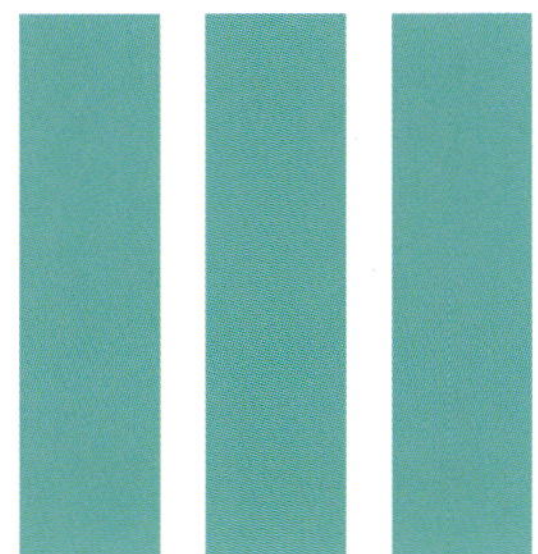

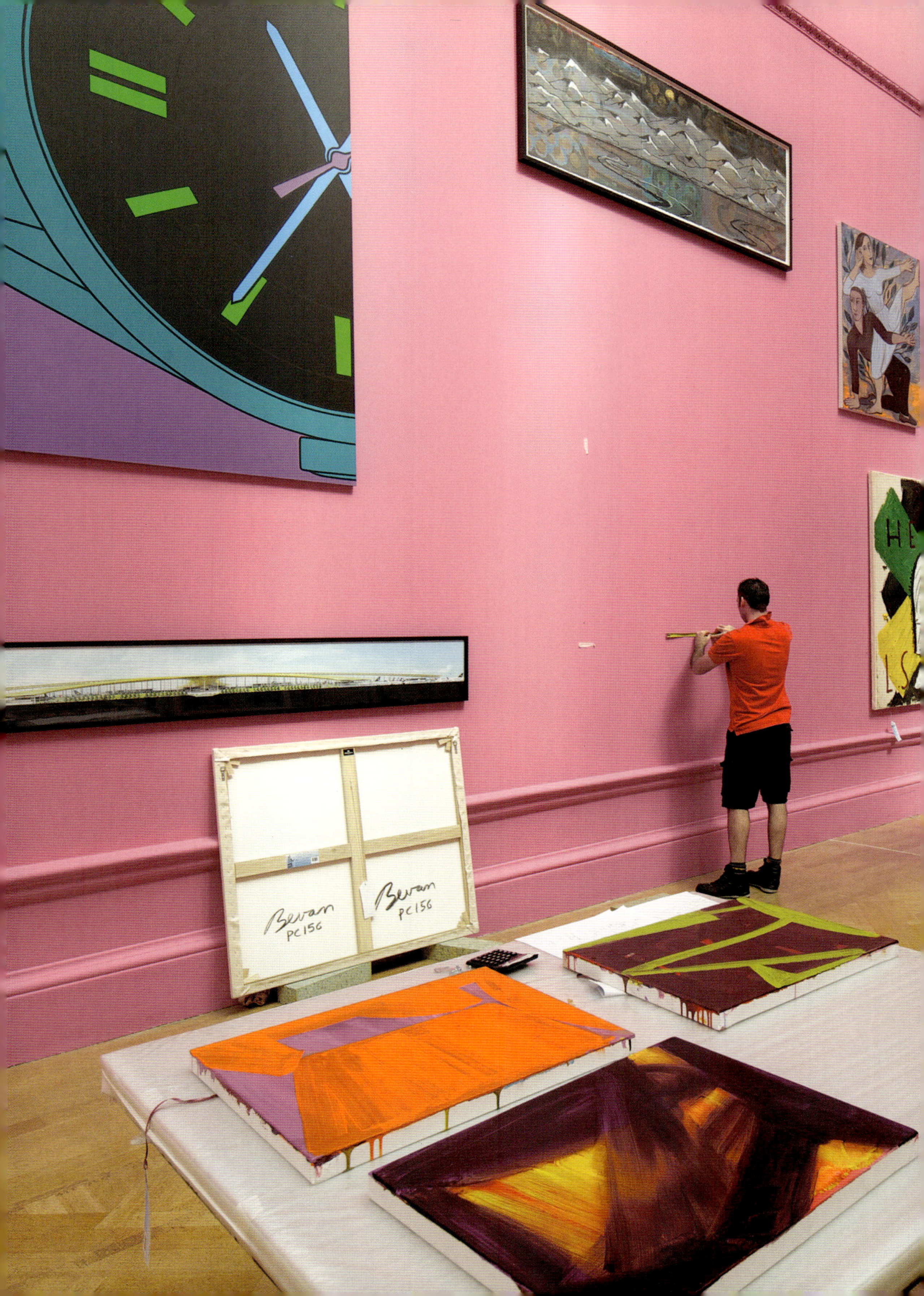
Bevan
PC156
Bevan
PC156

Prof Humphrey Ocean RA
Drift
Oil
81 × 100 cm

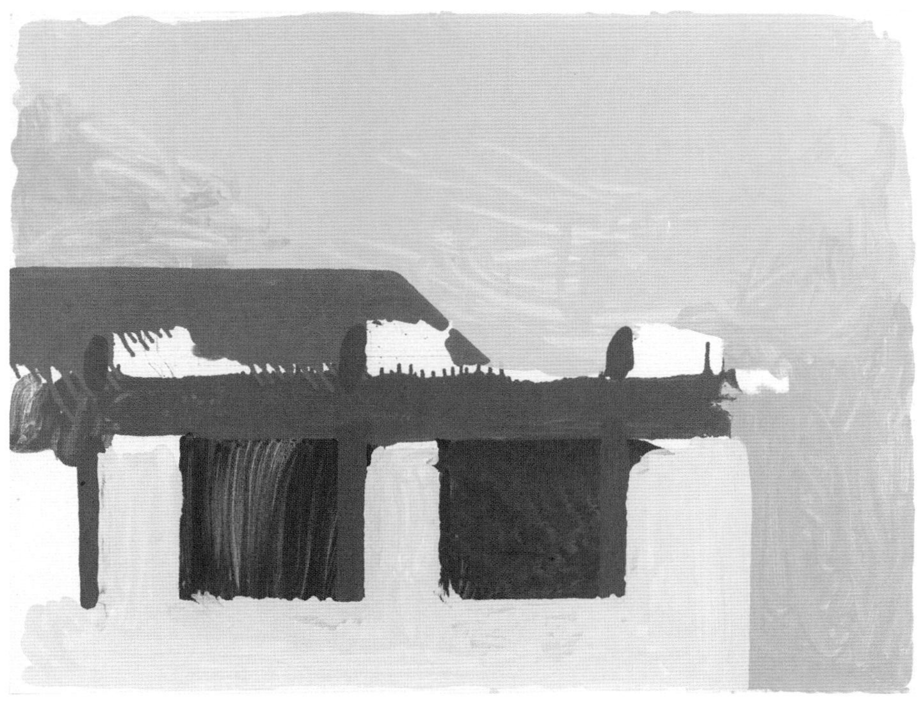

Michael Craig-Martin CBE RA
Untitled (Watch)
Acrylic on aluminium
250 × 250 cm

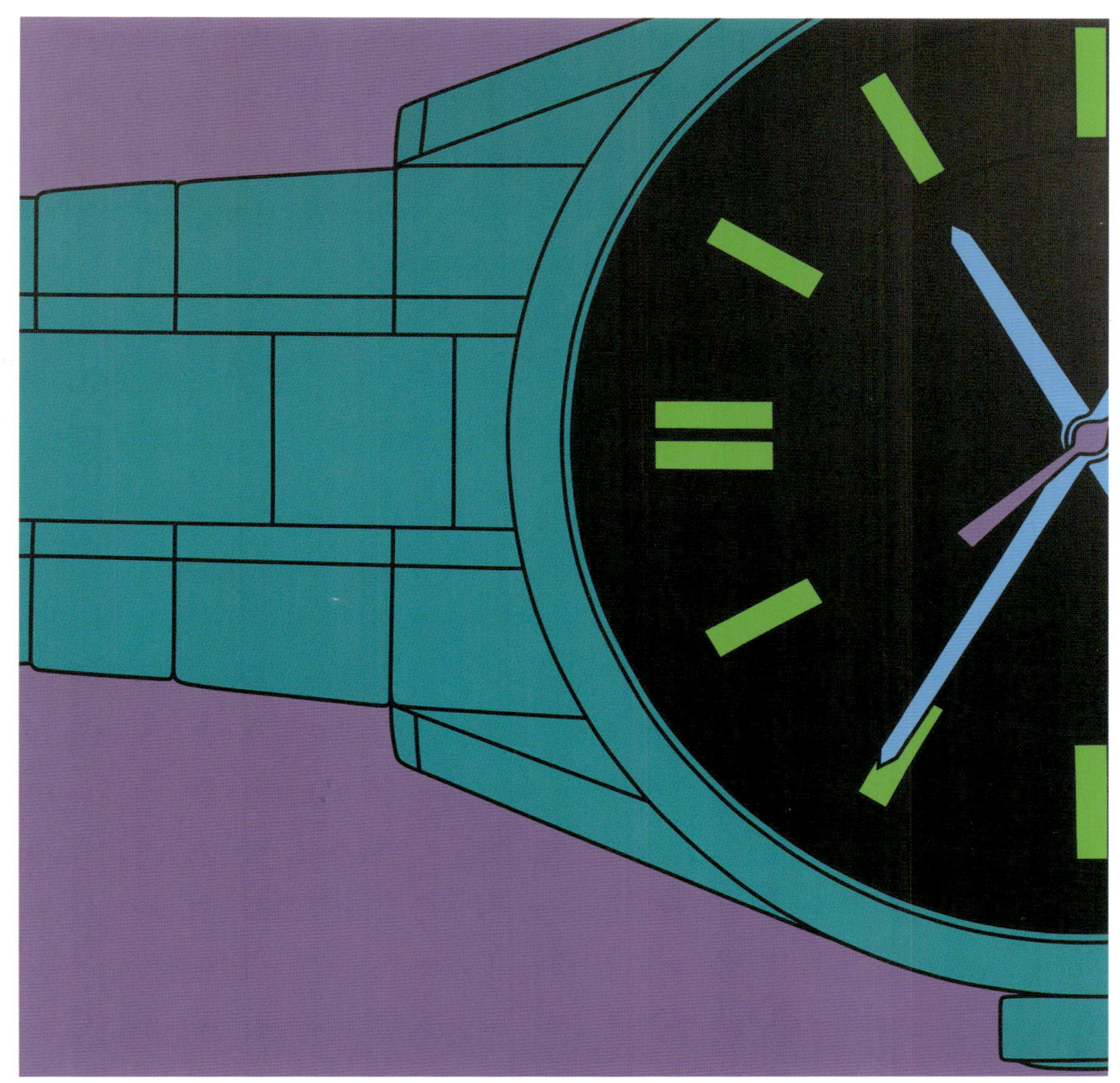

Rose Wylie RA
Herr Rehlinger in White Armour
Oil
186 × 169 cm

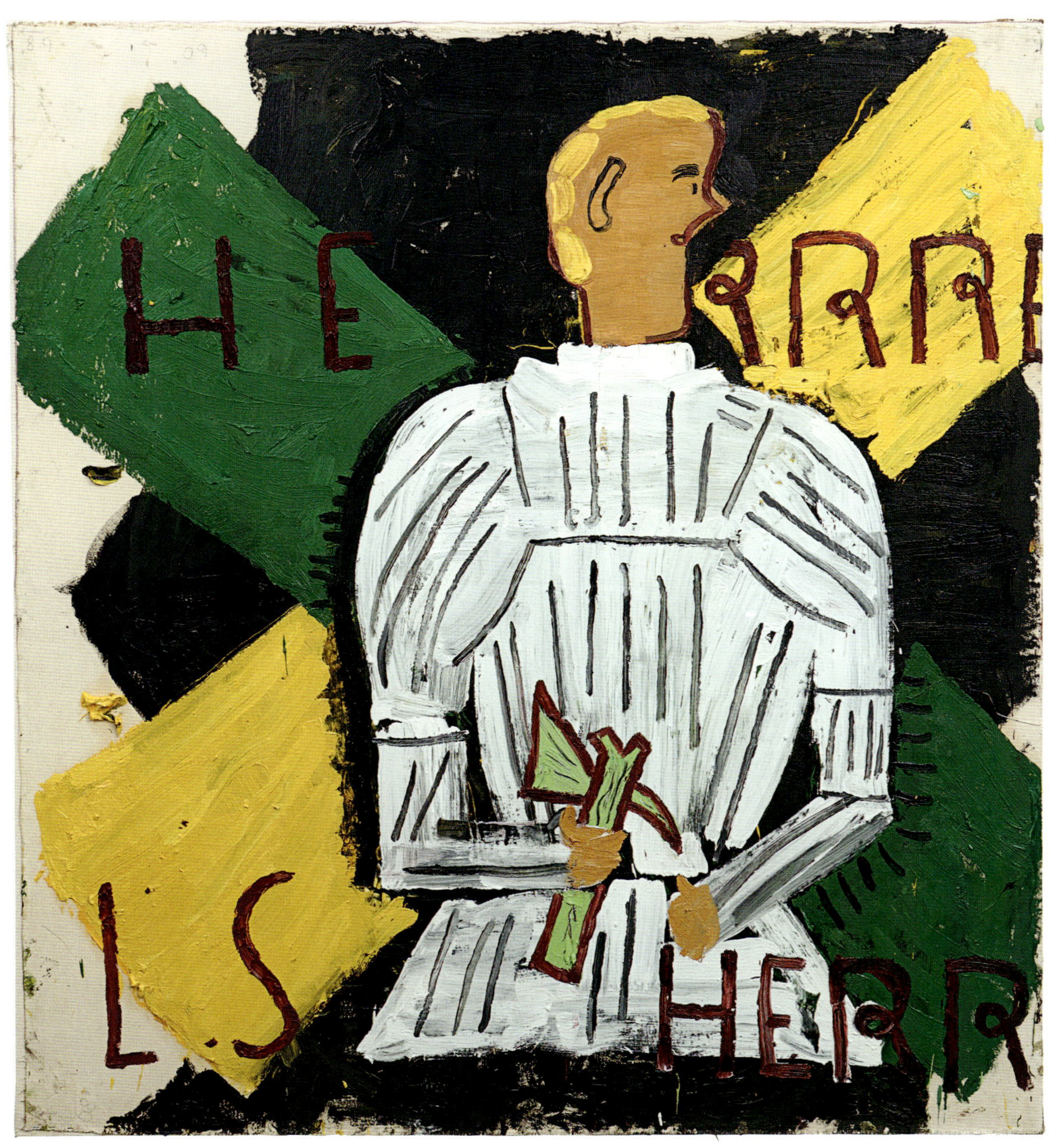

Chantal Joffe RA
Megan in Spotted Silk Blouse
Oil
183 × 122 cm

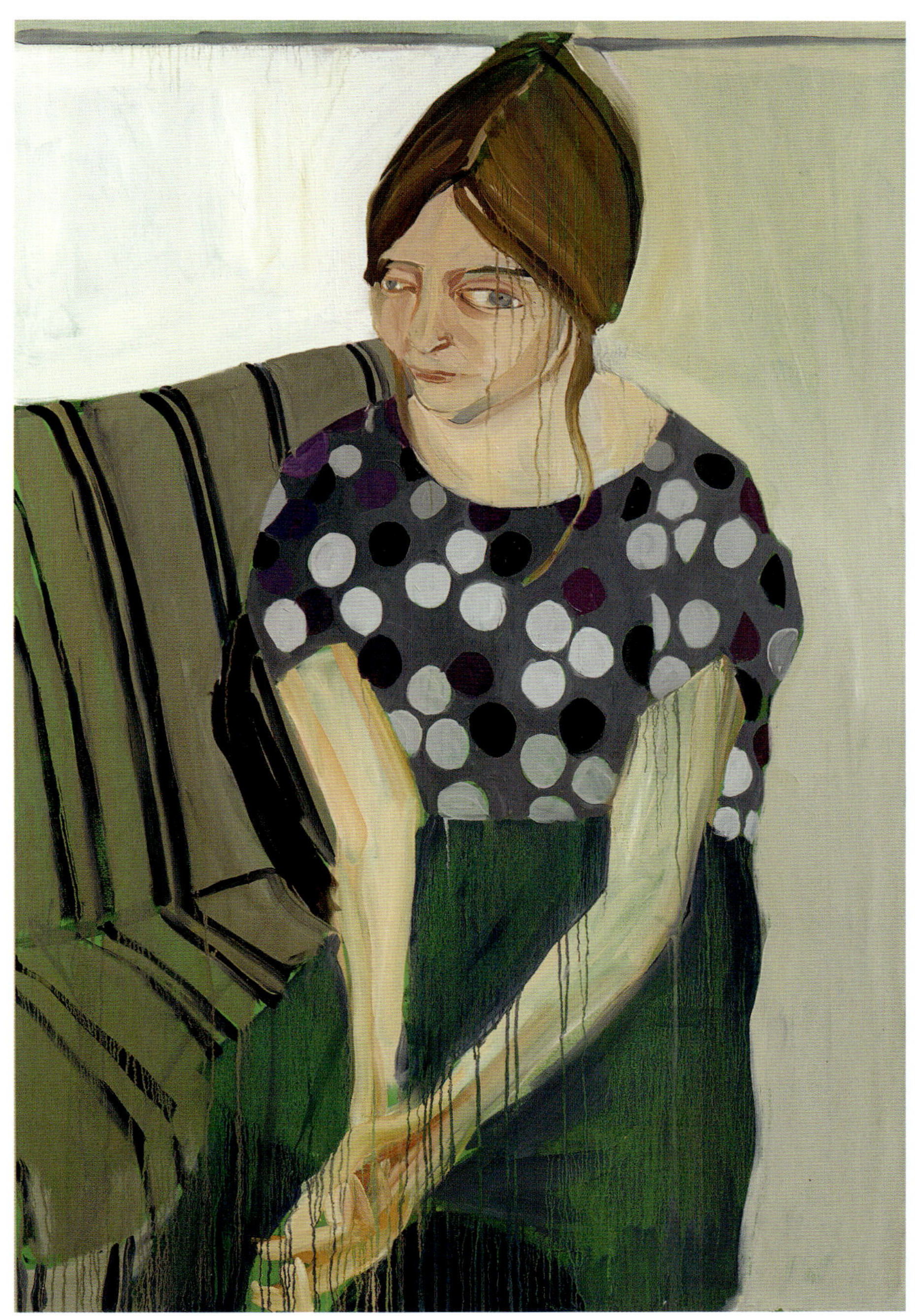

Tom Phillips CBE RA
Music
Oil
125 × 184 cm

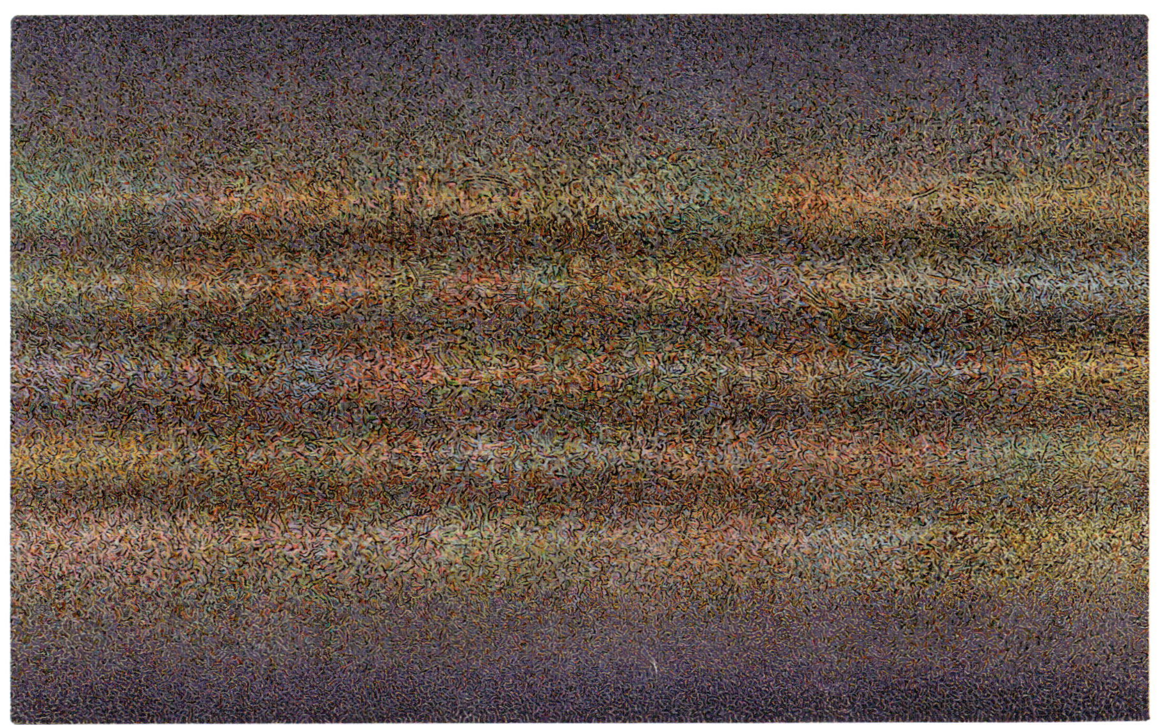

Jasper Johns HON RA
Untitled
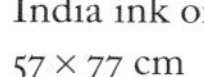
India ink on paper
57 × 77 cm

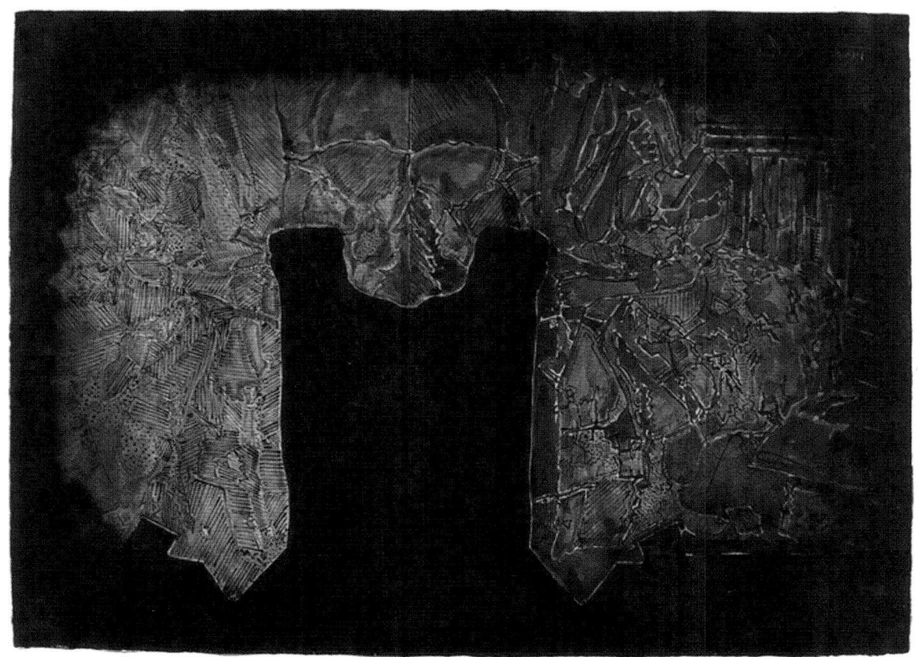

Tess Jaray RA
Light 2 (Diptych)
Work on panel
72 × 120 cm

Frank Bowling OBE RA
Pickerslift
Acrylic
277 × 188 cm

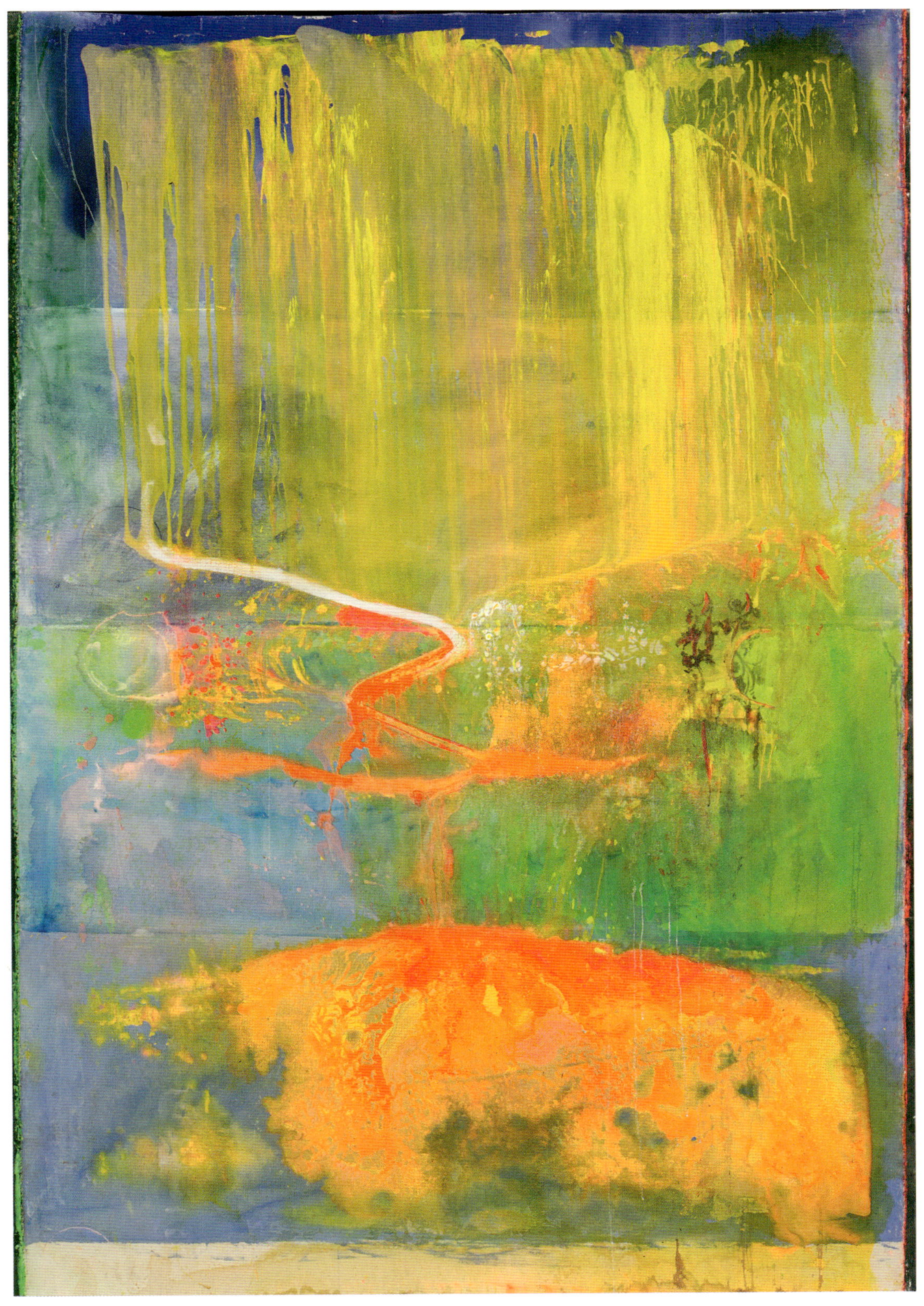

Terry Setch RA
Dolly Mixtures
Mixed media
122 × 244 cm

Timothy Hyman RA
Descent into Covent Garden
Oil
53 × 180 cm

Prof Stephen Farthing RA
Drone on the Range
Acrylic
200 × 159 cm

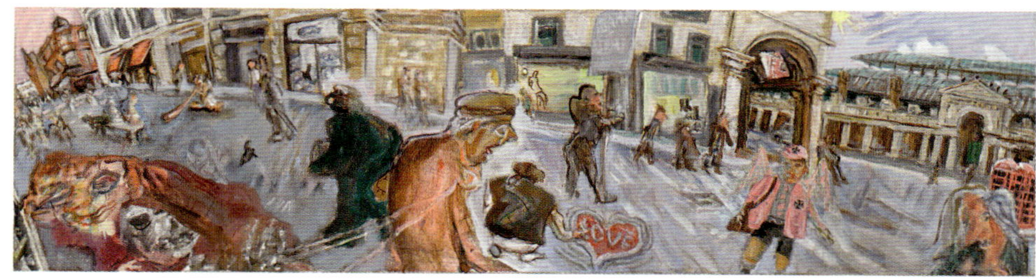

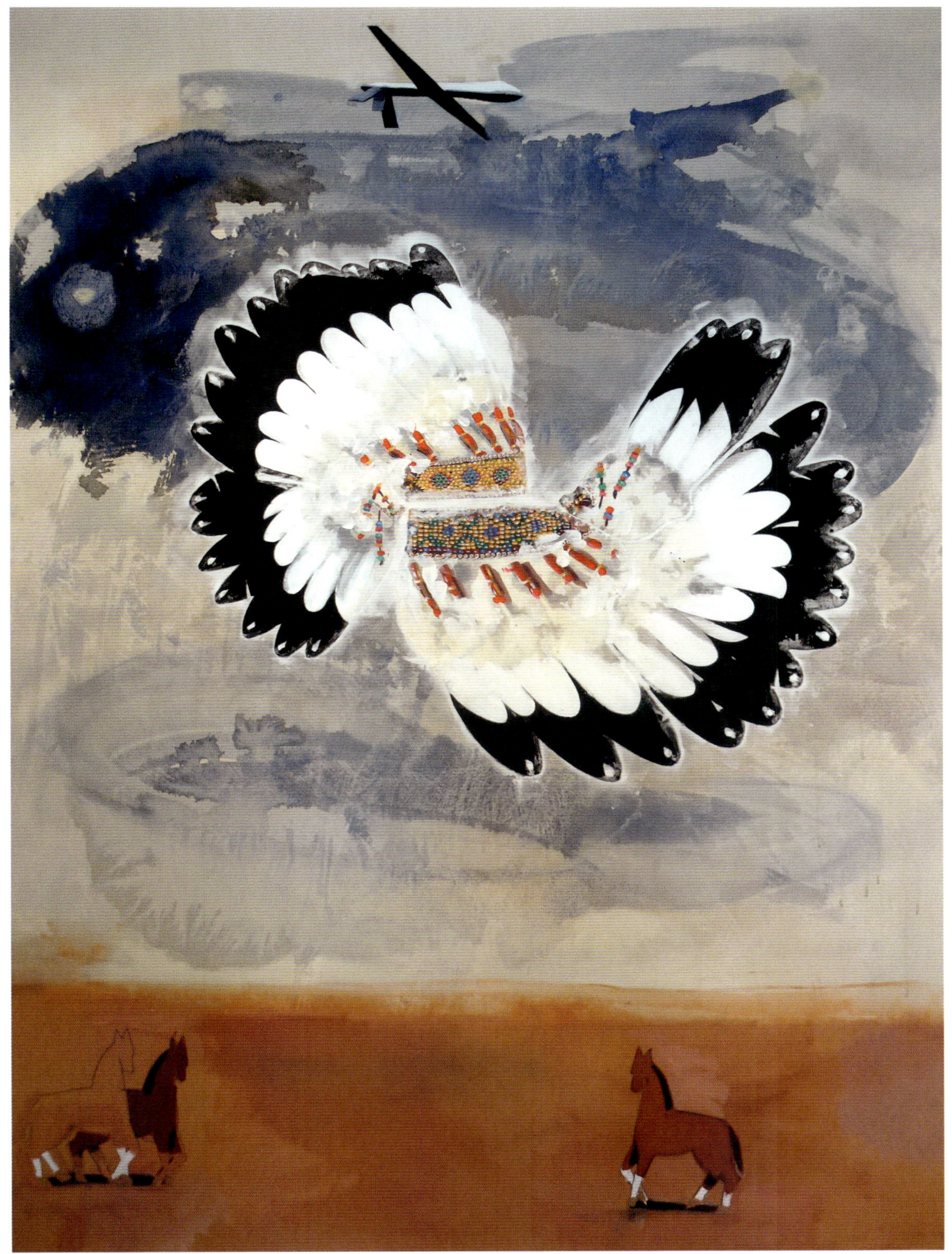

Dr Barbara Rae CBE RA
Inlet
Acrylic and mixed media
183 × 183 cm

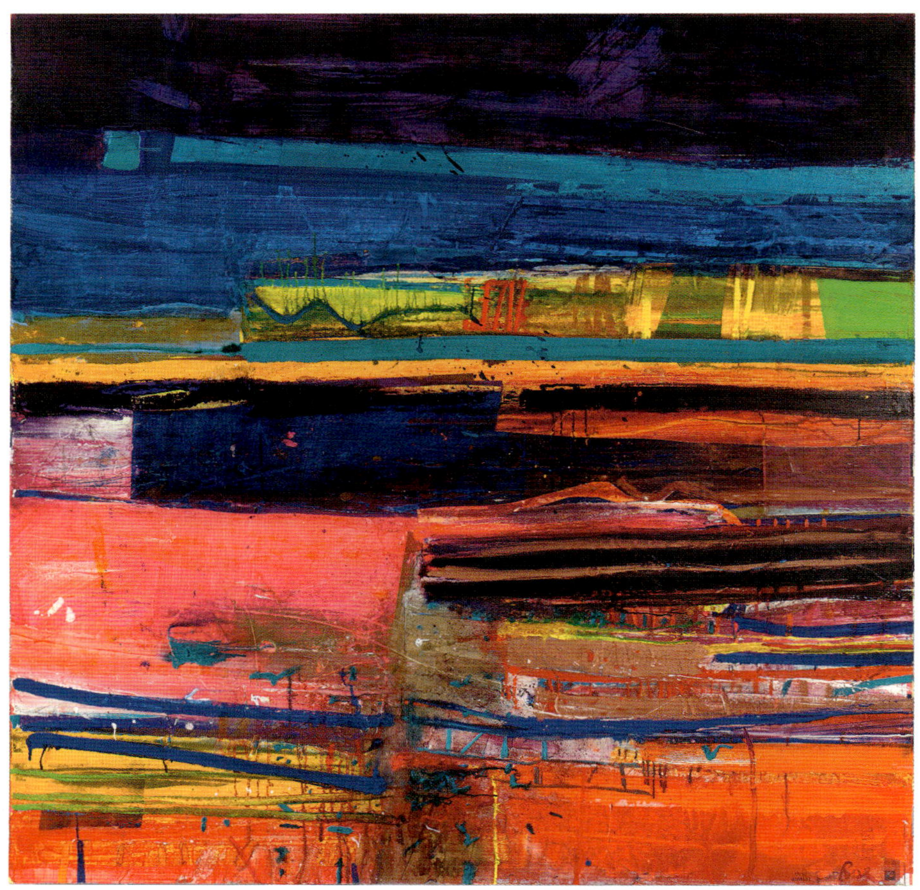

Mali Morris RA
Stradella
Acrylic
168 × 193 cm

Gillian Ayres CBE RA
Tremenheere
Sugar-lift aquatint and carborundum print
98 × 114 cm

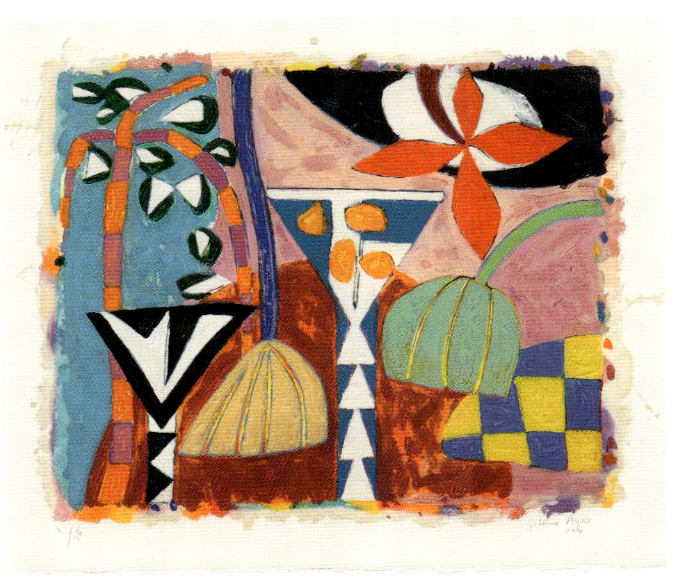

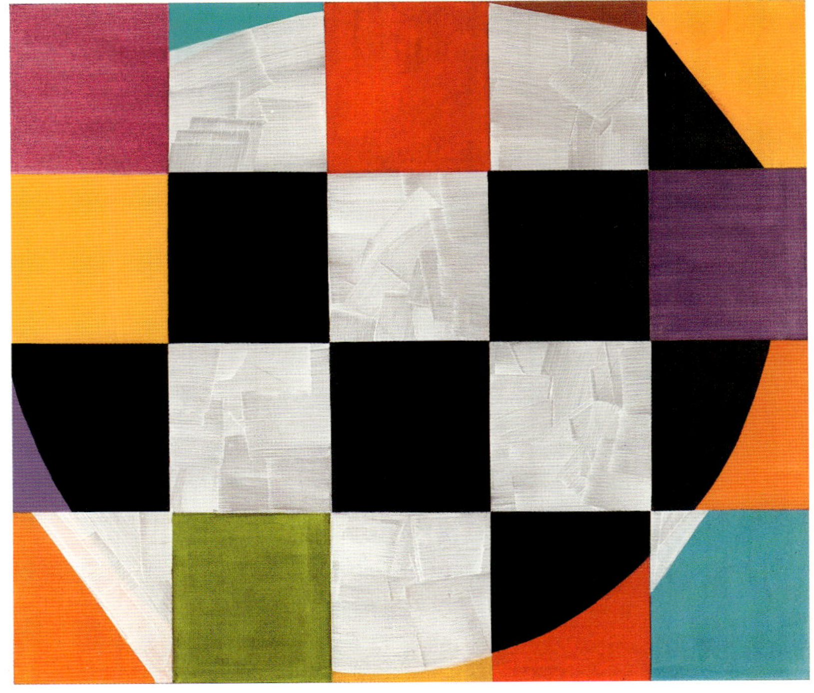

Wolfgang Tillmans RA
Arm and Legs
Inkjet print on paper
138 × 209 cm

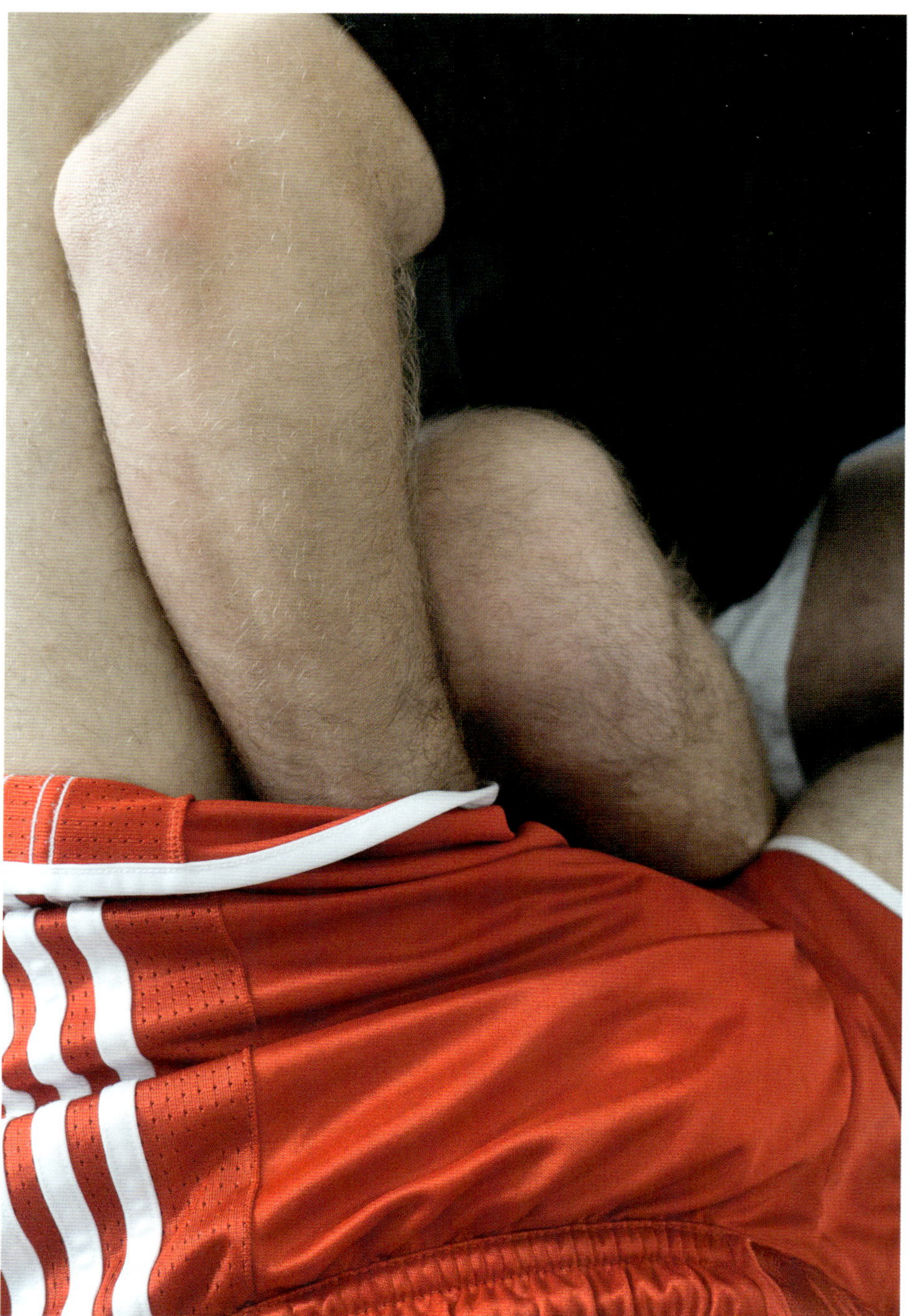

Ed Ruscha HON RA
Flying Gator #1
Acrylic
81 × 96 cm

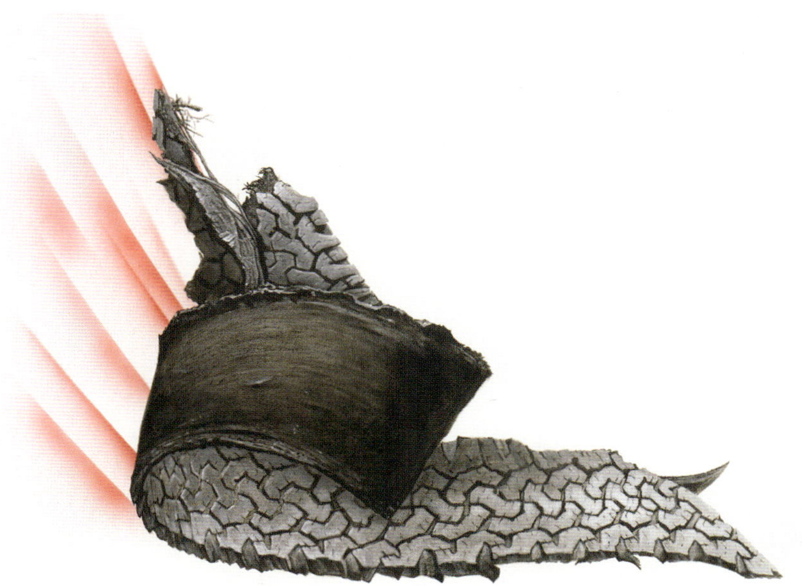

Eileen Cooper RA
Dancing and Solitude
Oil
137 × 106 cm

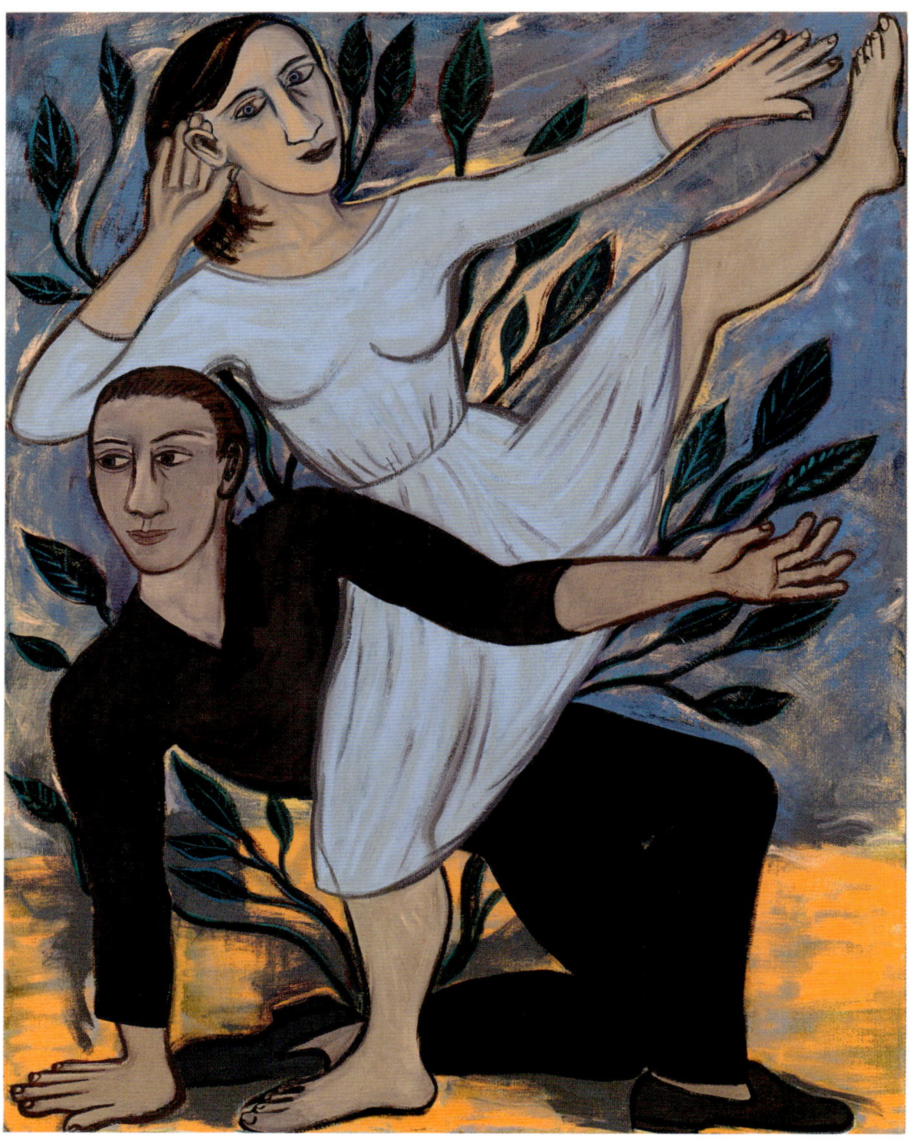

David Remfry MBE RA
Untitled
Oil
162 × 112 cm

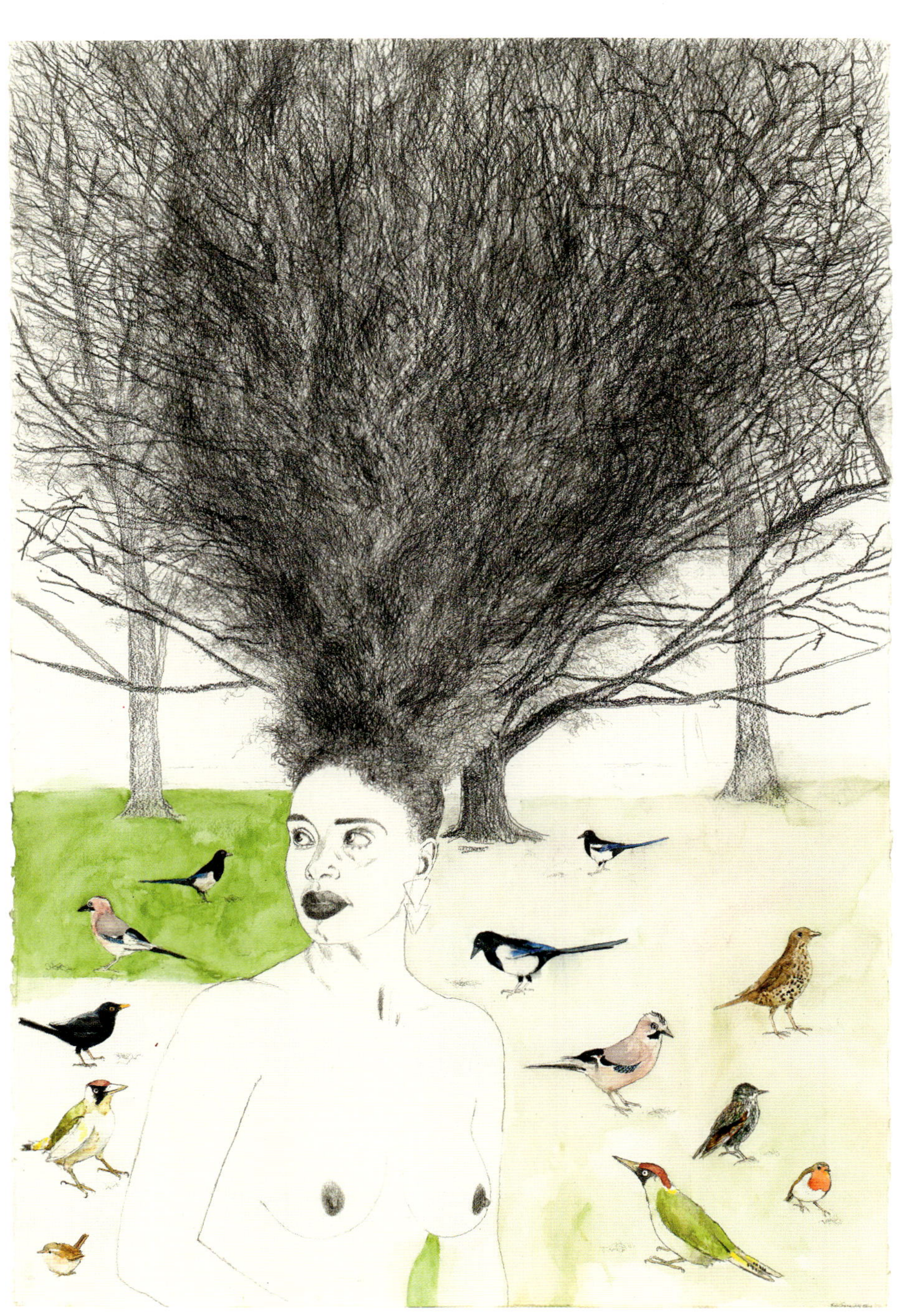

Tony Bevan RA
Tree No. 7
Acrylic and charcoal
165 × 240 cm

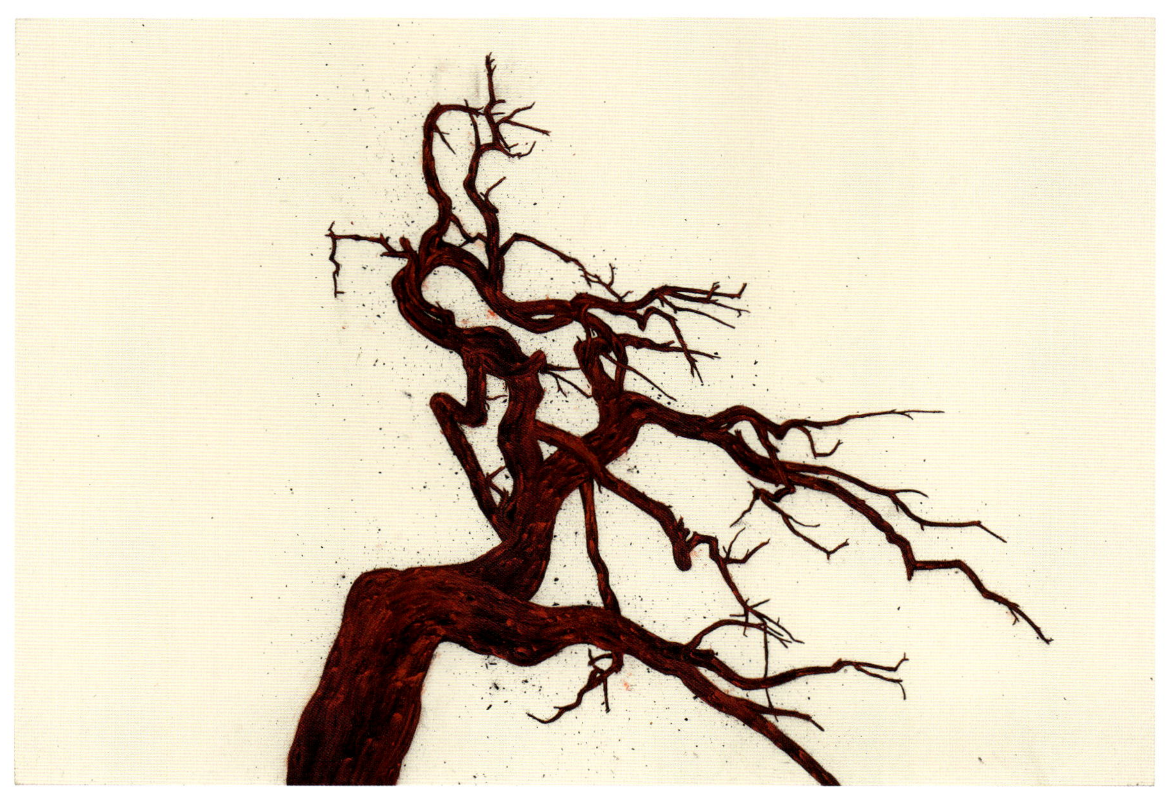

Jock McFadyen RA
Jura
Oil on board
68 × 91 cm

Olwyn Bowey RA
Fallen Tree in Blossom
Oil
194 × 112 cm

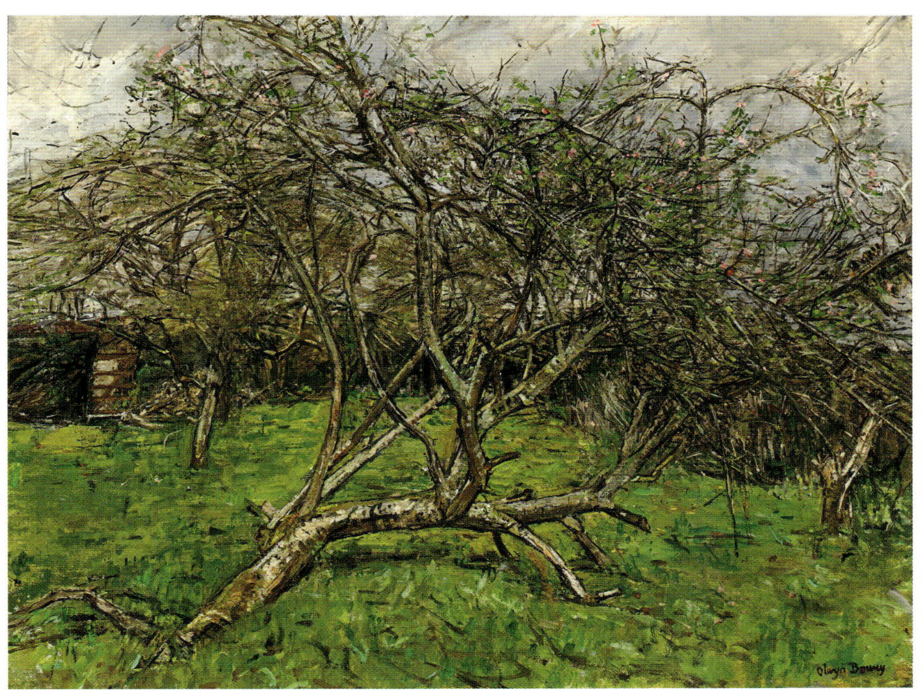

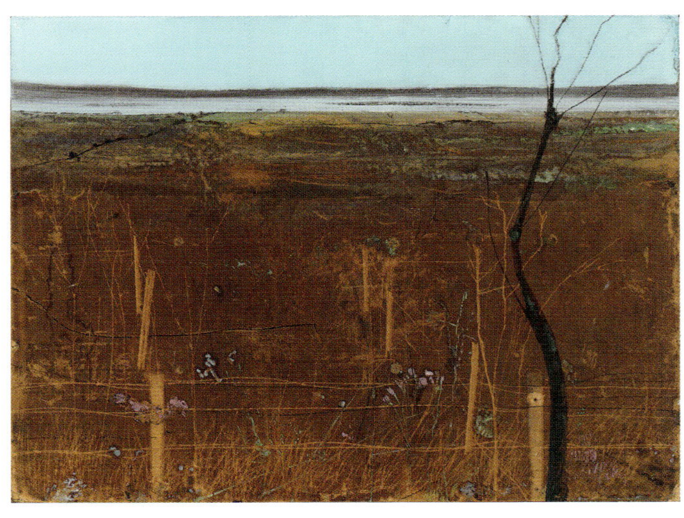

Stephen Chambers RA
Stealing Things: Bag Snatcher
Oil
44 × 54 cm

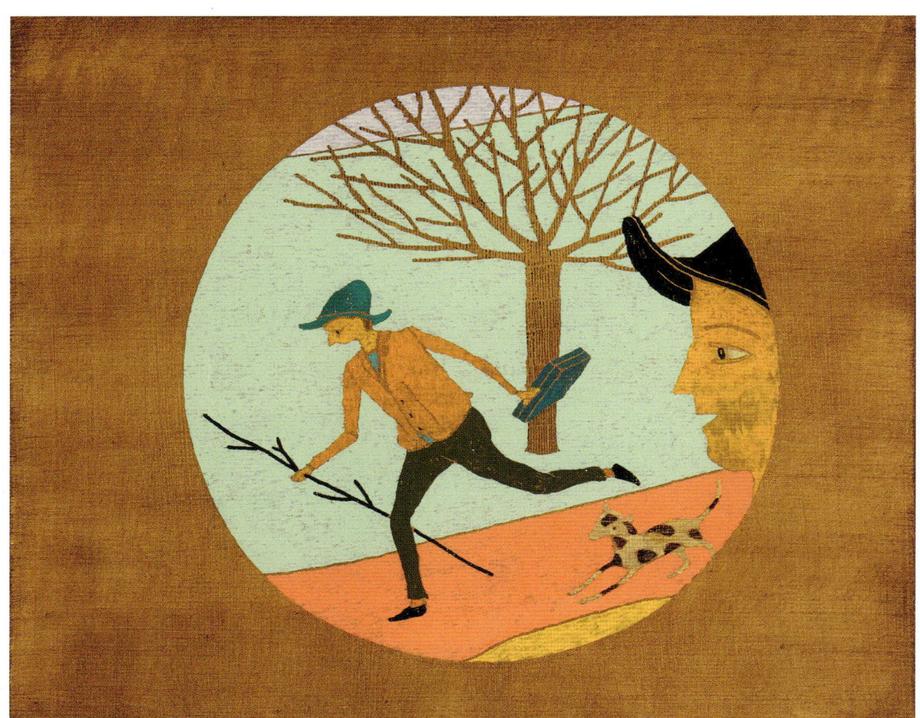

Derek Boshier
Reigning Apps and Blogs
Acrylic
183 × 122 cm

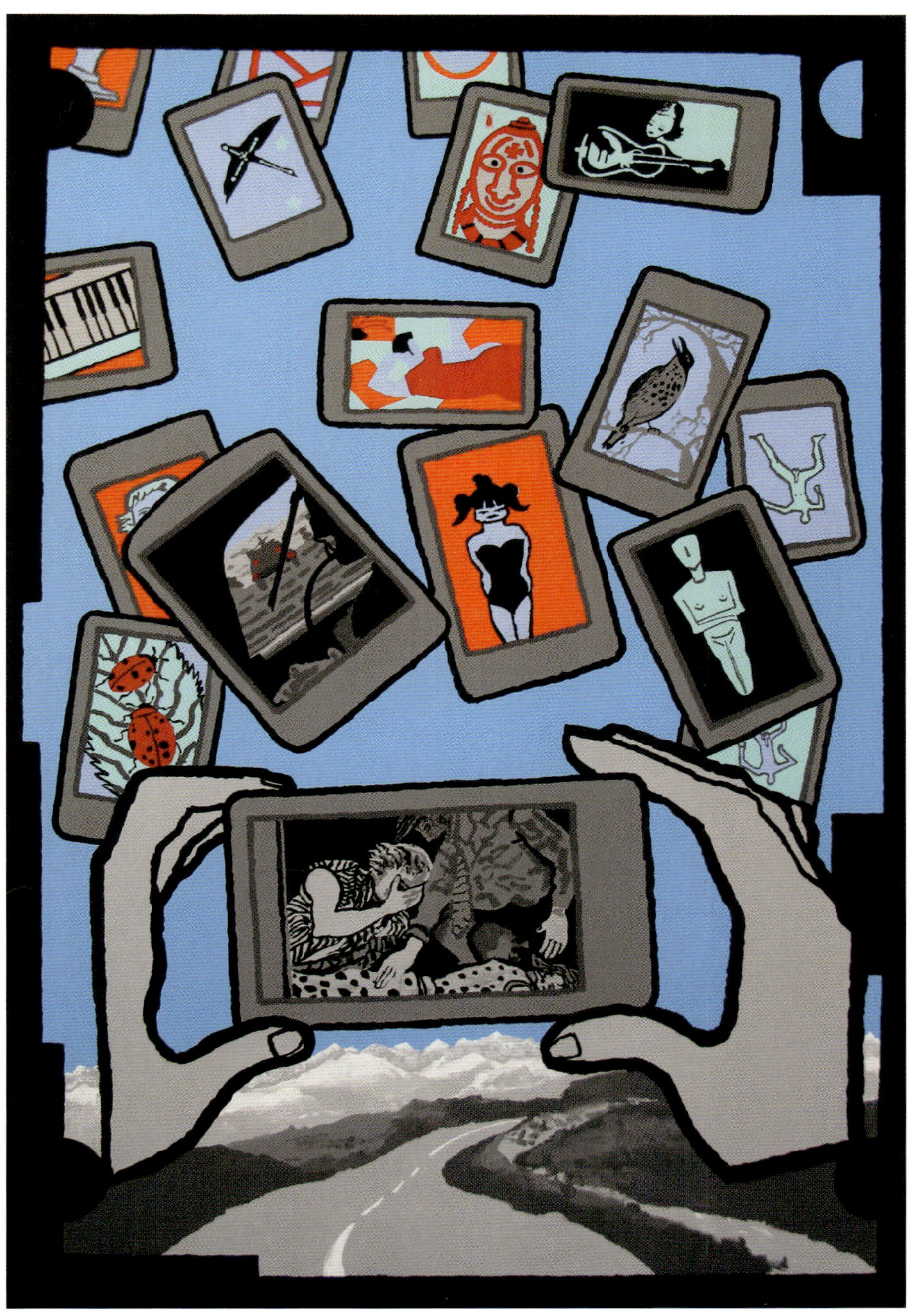

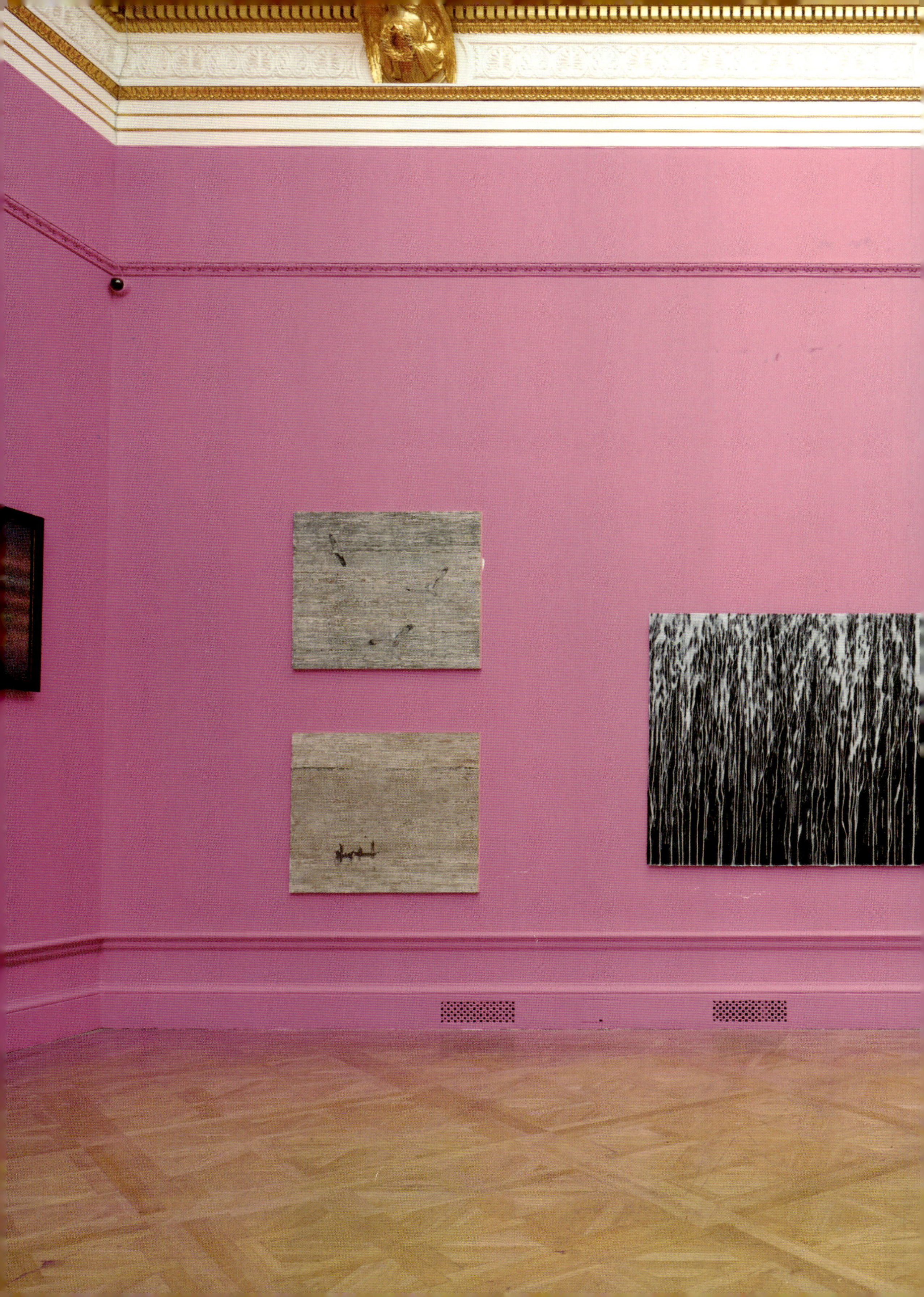

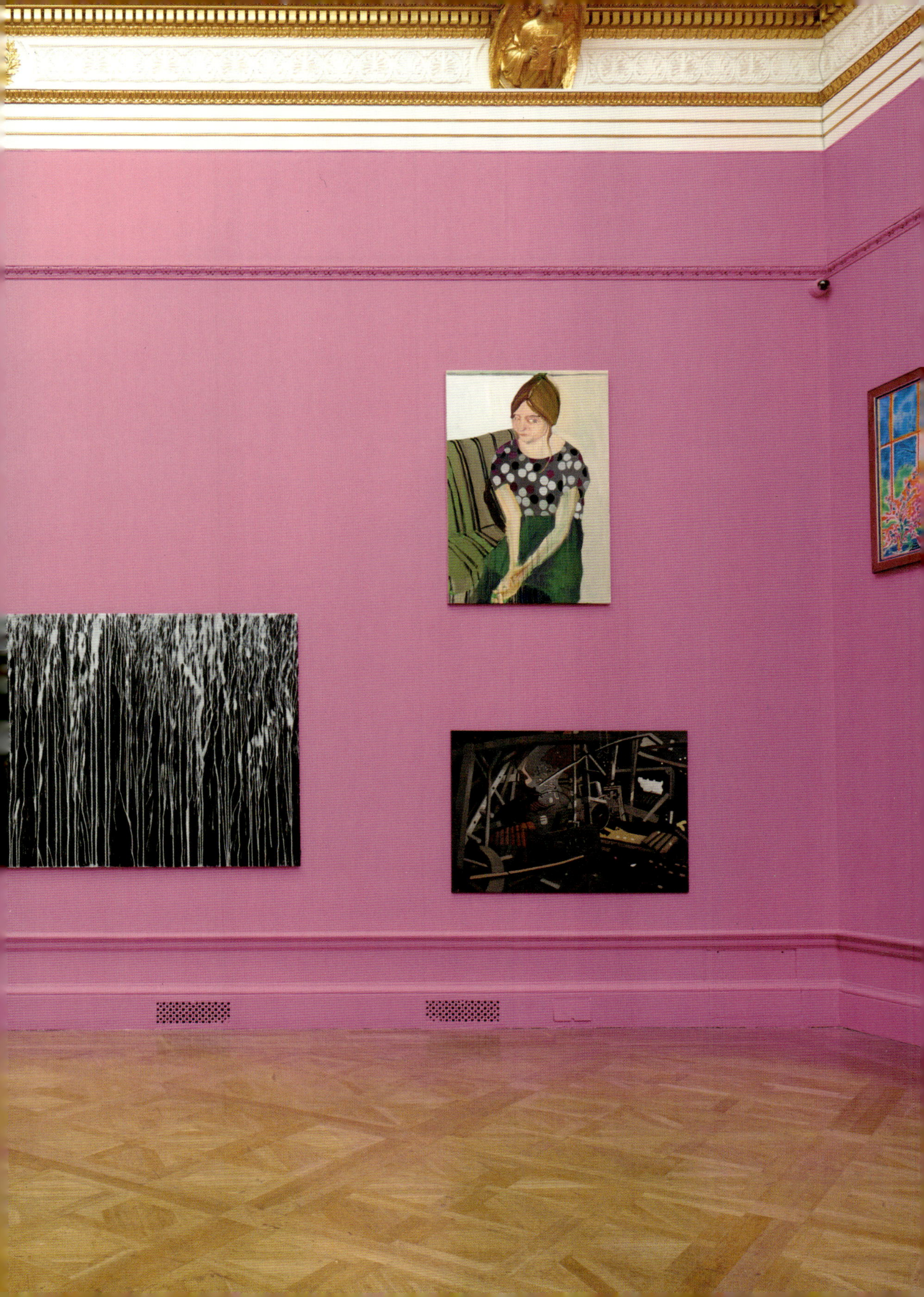

Anthony Whishaw RA
Come Dance With Me (2012–2015)
Acrylic and collage
173 × 305 cm

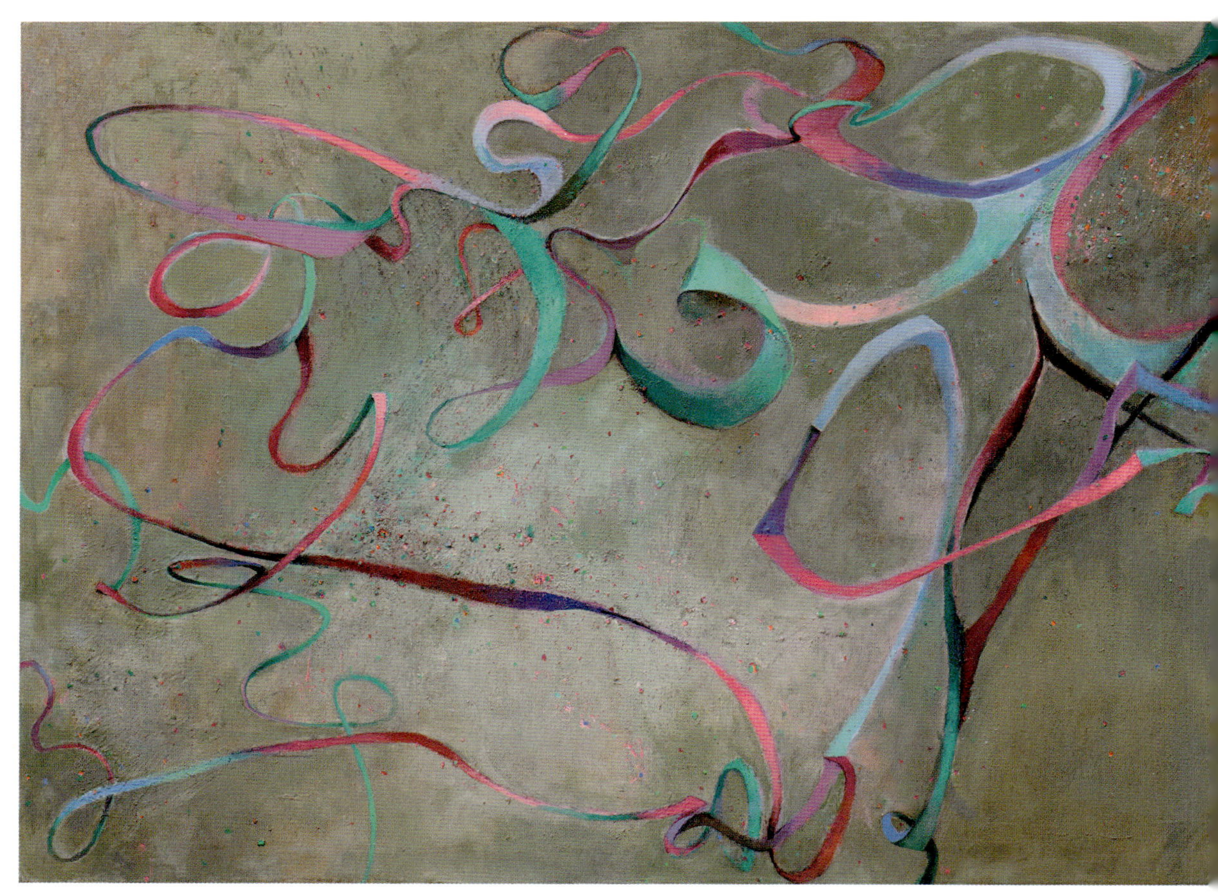

Philip Sutton RA
Heather's Finished Painting
Oil
138 × 108 cm

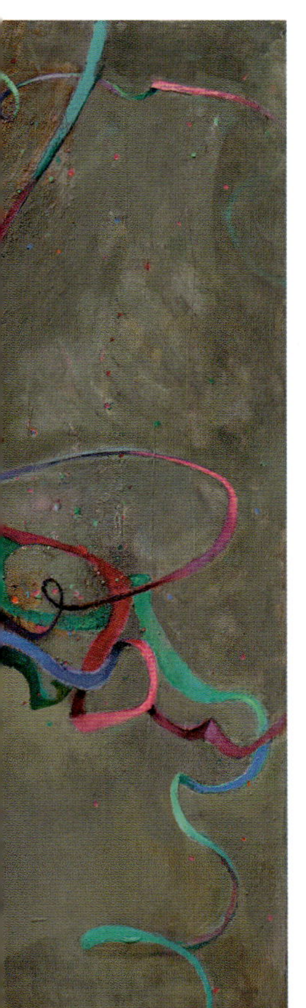

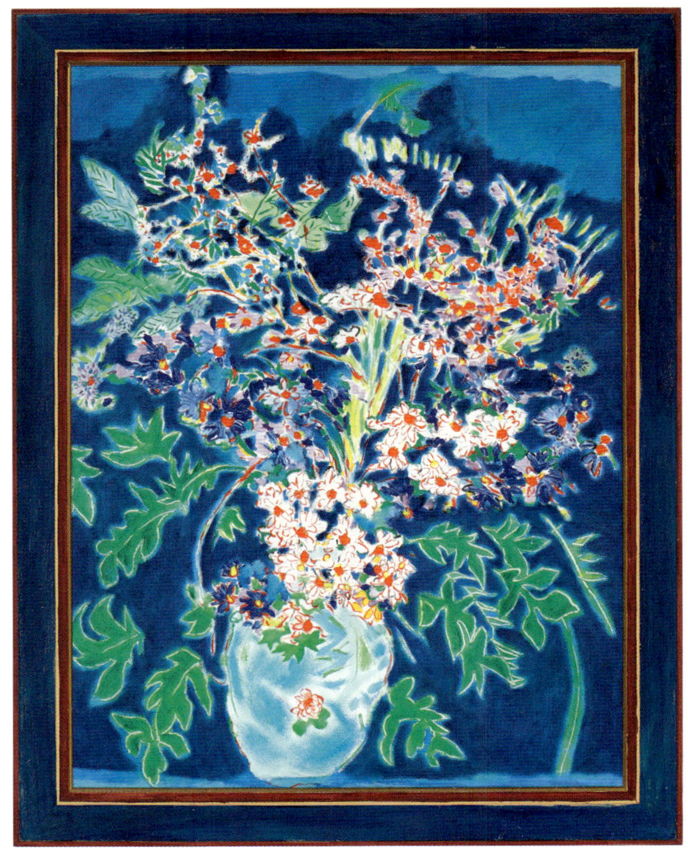

Gus Cummins RA
The Brothers Tzoveleki
Oil and wax
124 × 178 cm

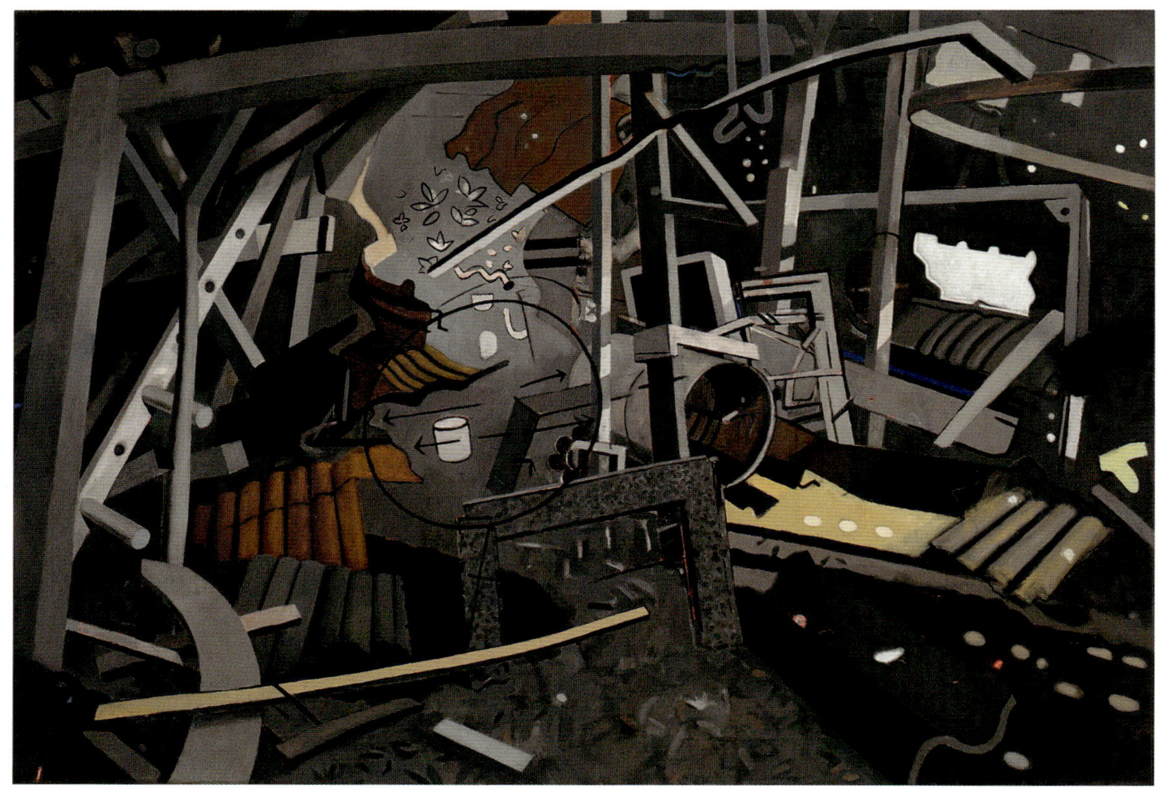

Mick Moon RA
Noon Fishing
Acrylic
122 × 140 cm

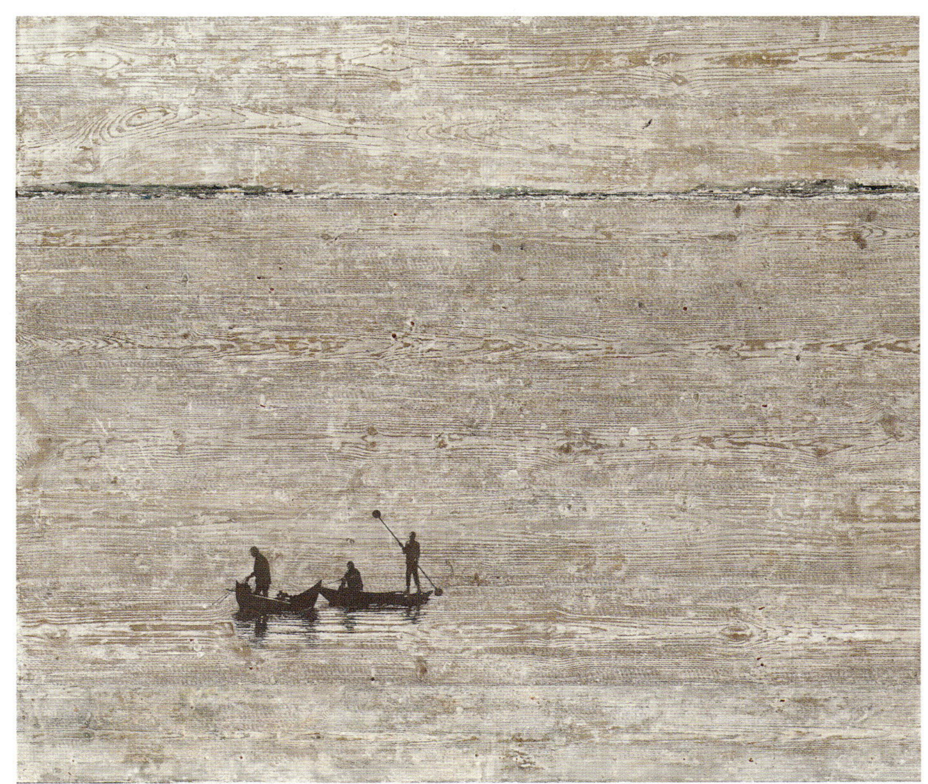

Basil Beattie RA
Far From Somewhere
Oil and wax
213 × 198 cm

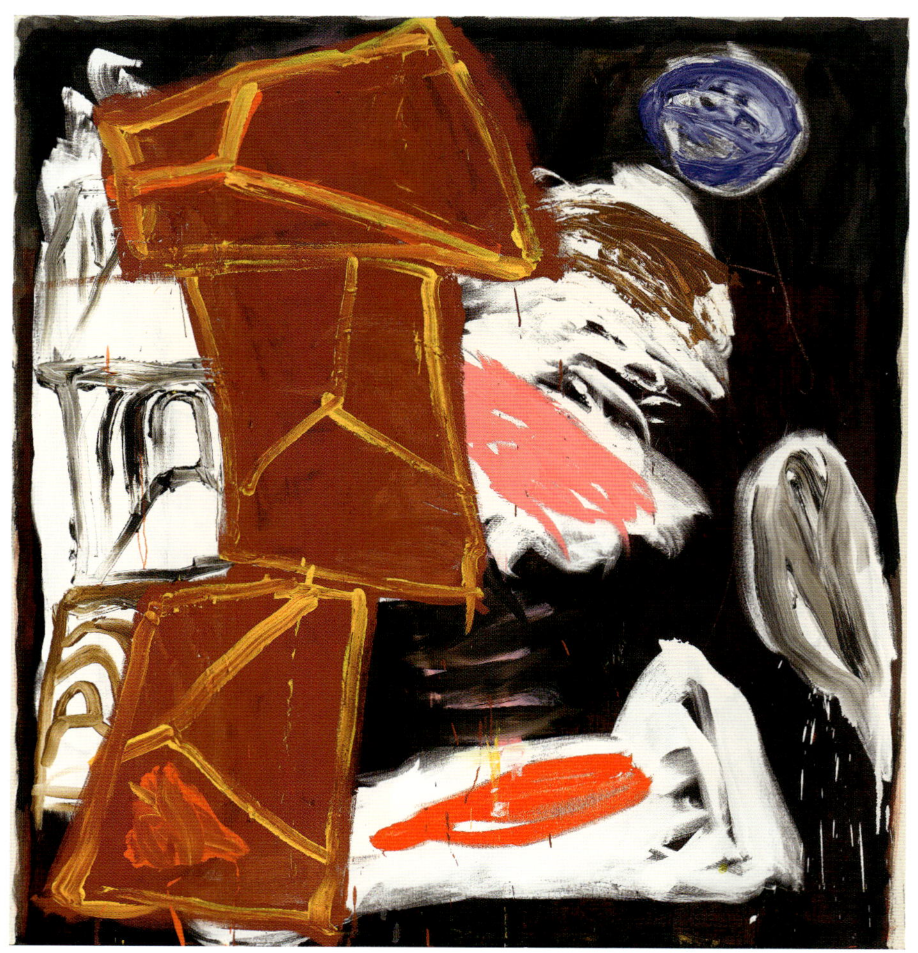

Hughie O'Donoghue RA
Animal Farm
Oil
207 × 241 cm

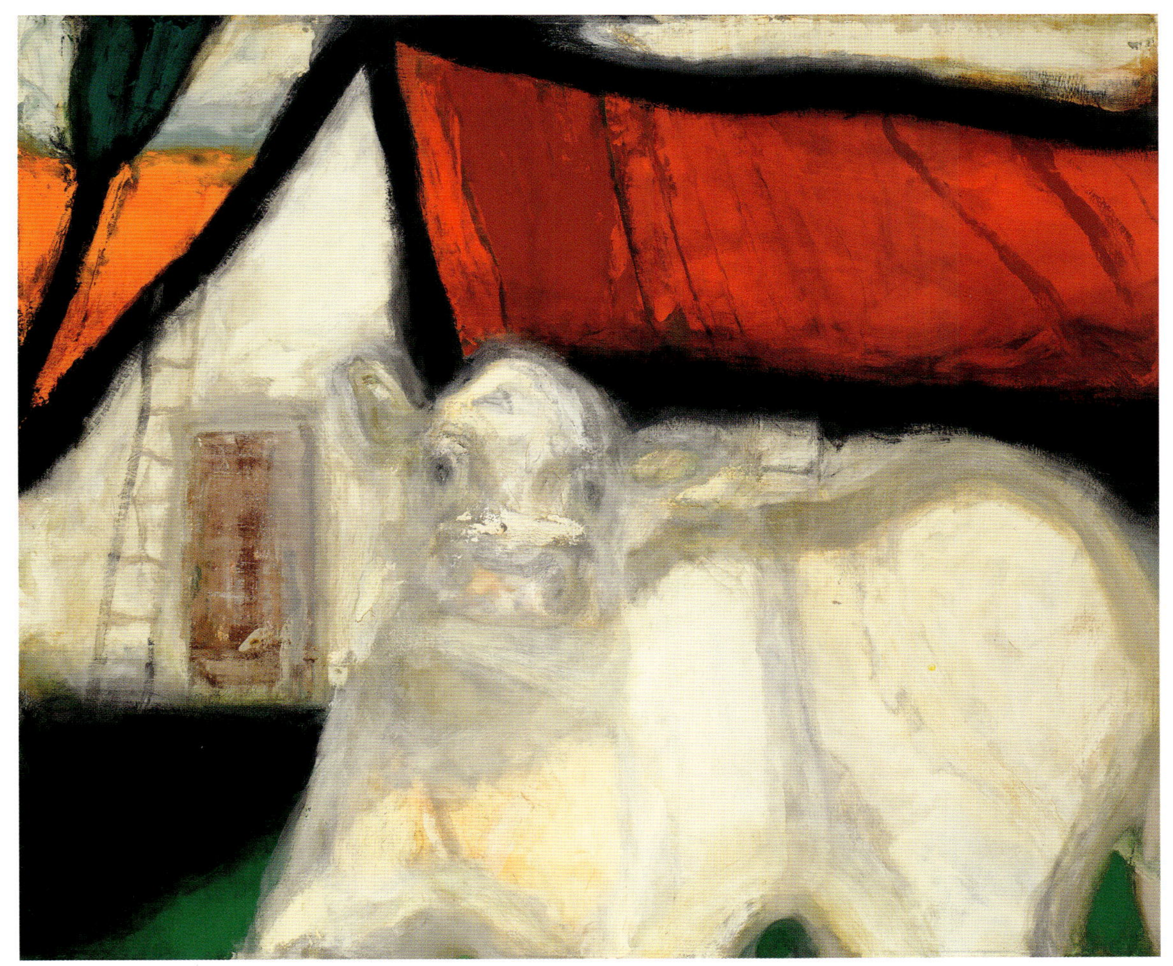

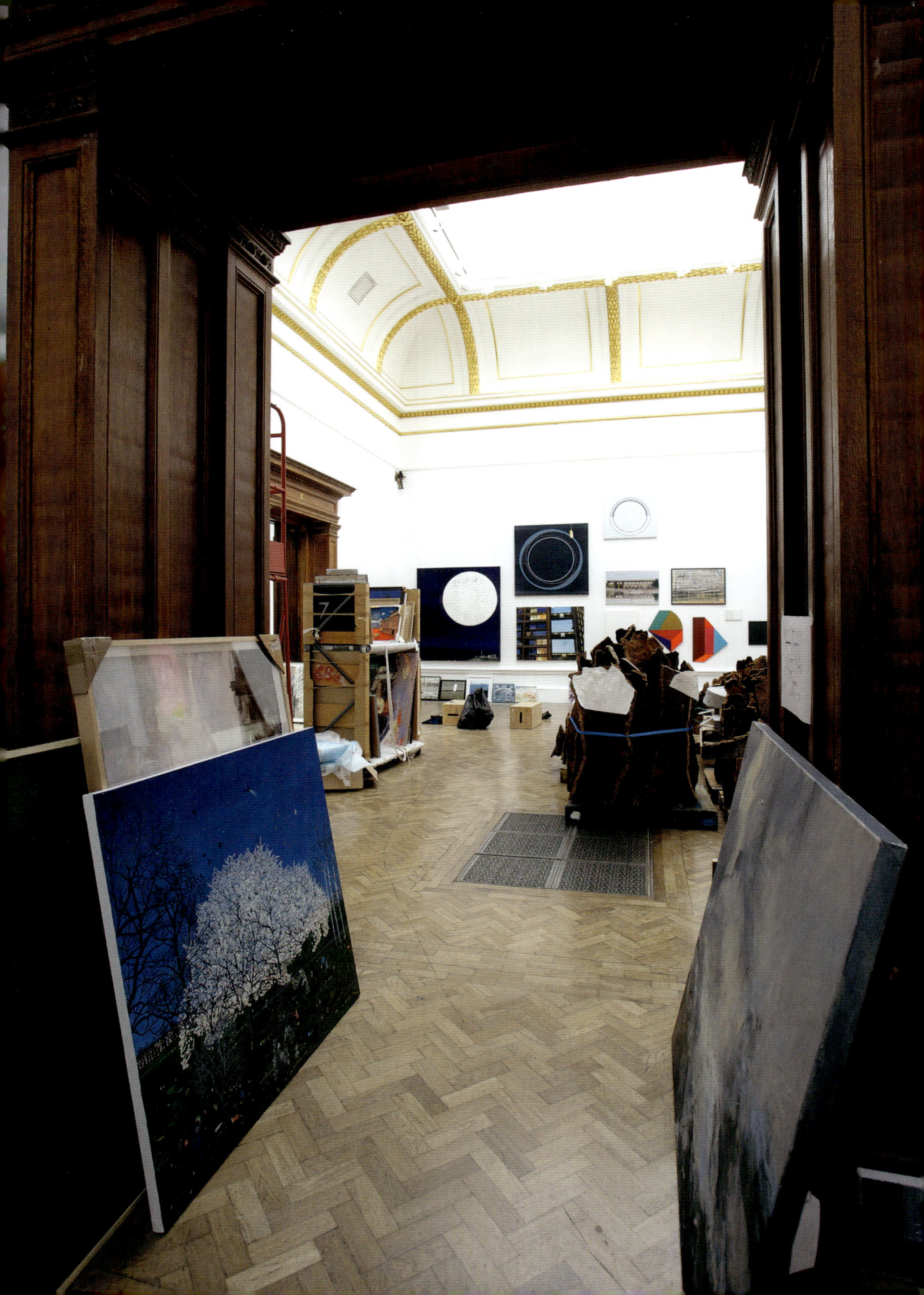

Carol Robertson
Circadian Stream 2
Oil
153 × 153 cm

Nigel O'Neill
5 Colour Painting 4 and *5*
Acrylic on birch plywood panels
86 × 68 cm and 92 × 68 cm

David Nash OBE RA
Cork Dome
Cork
H 120 cm

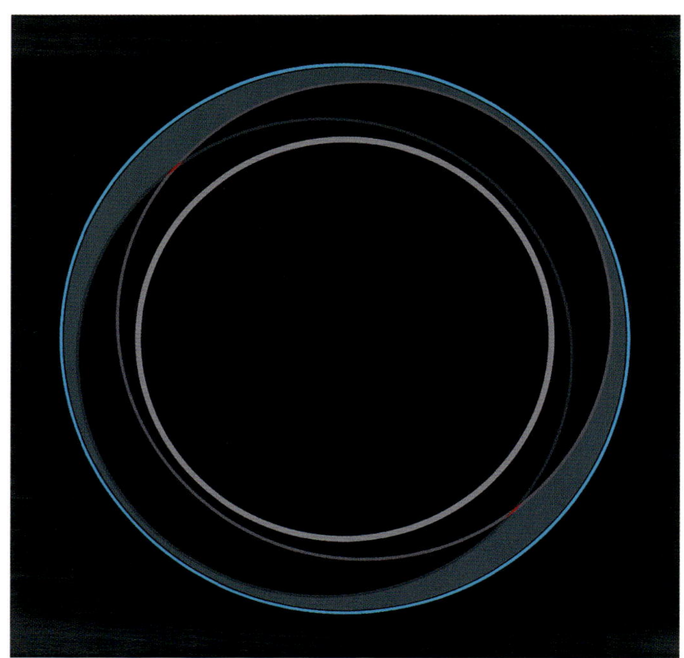

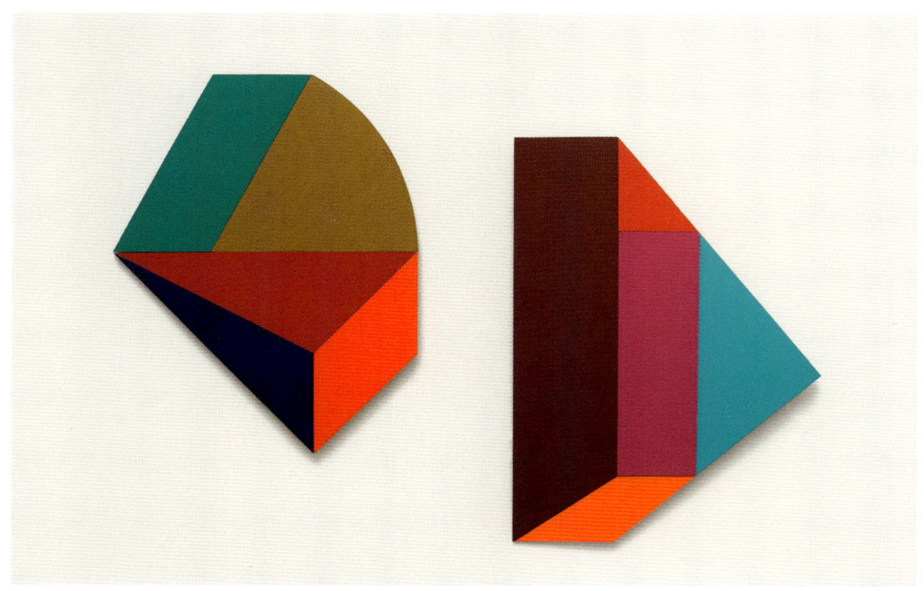

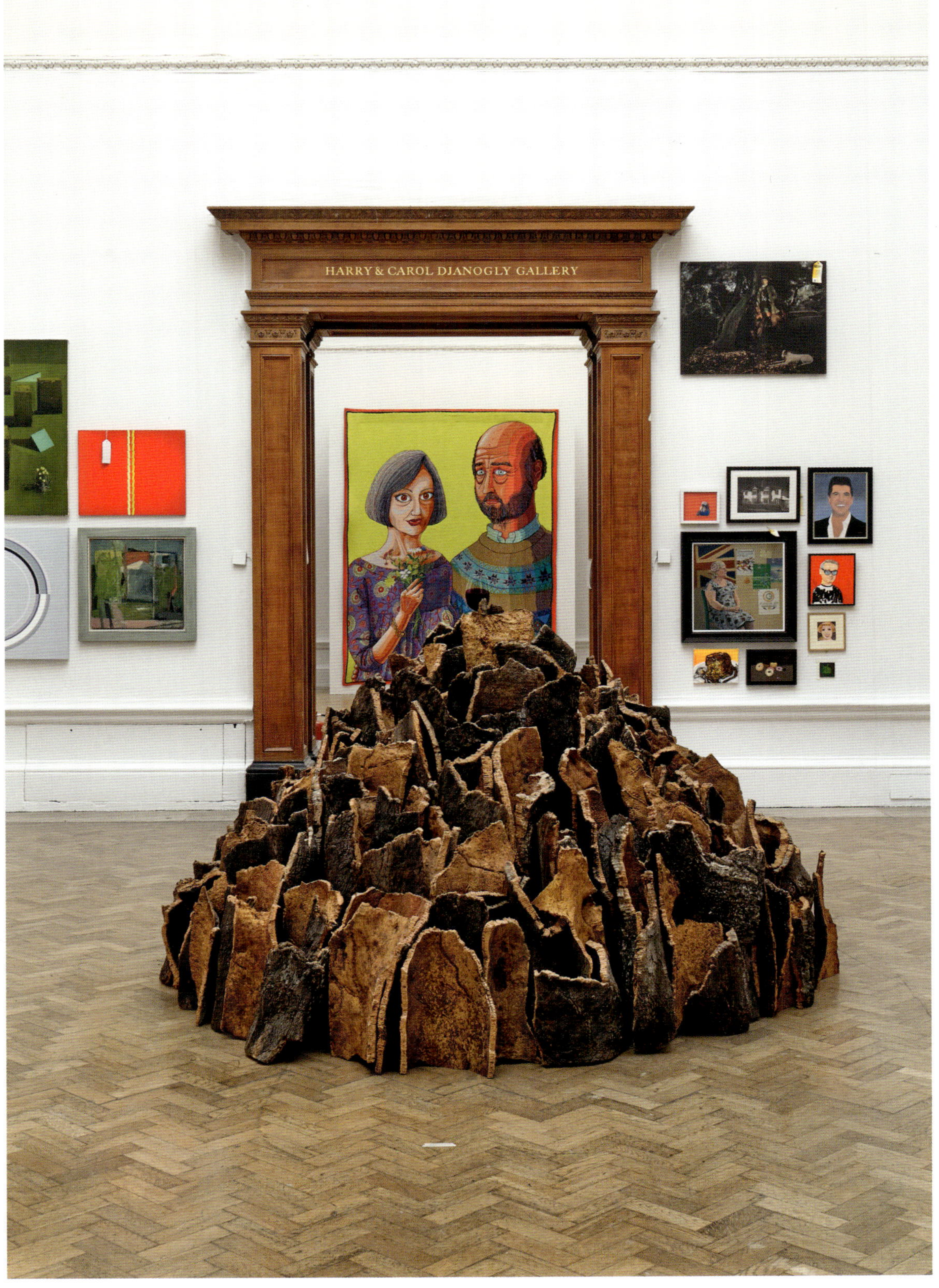
HARRY & CAROL DJANOGLY GALLERY

Benjamin Sullivan
Backs
Oil on panel
26 × 37 cm

David Aston
Untitled
C-type print
73 × 95 cm

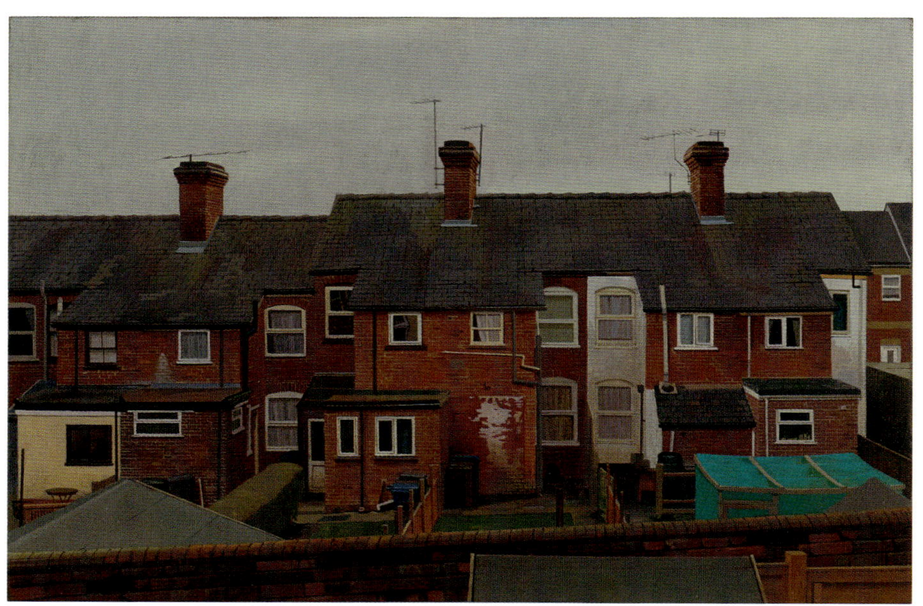

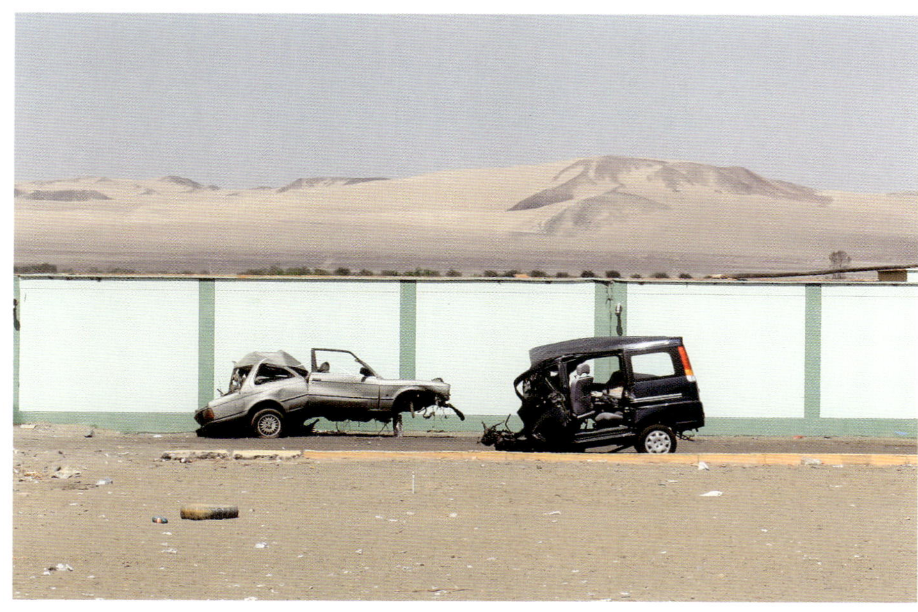

Elise Ansel
Feast of the Gods II, After Bellini and Titian
Oil
122 × 152 cm

Rachel Heller
Sit Down Prose
Pastel and charcoal
45 × 33 cm

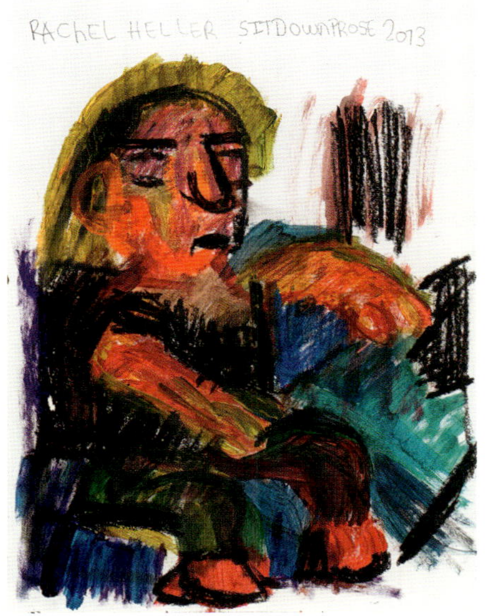

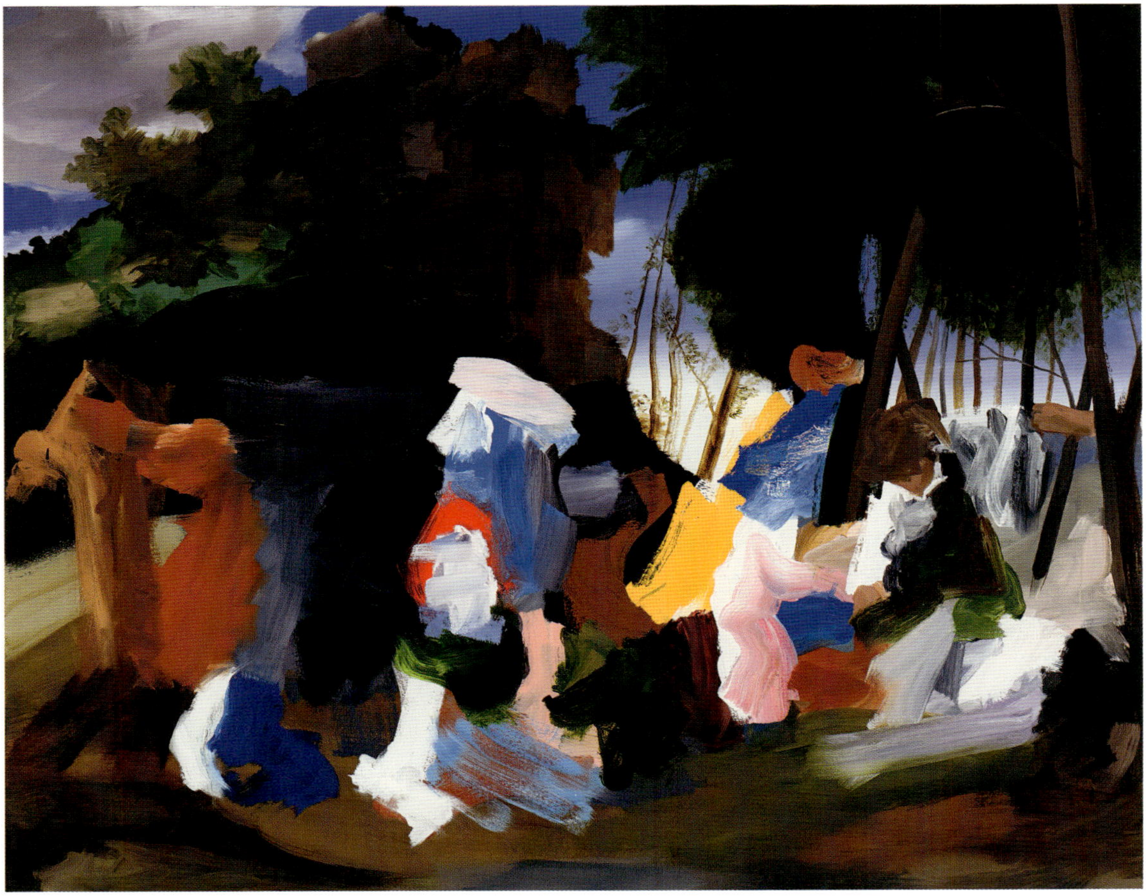

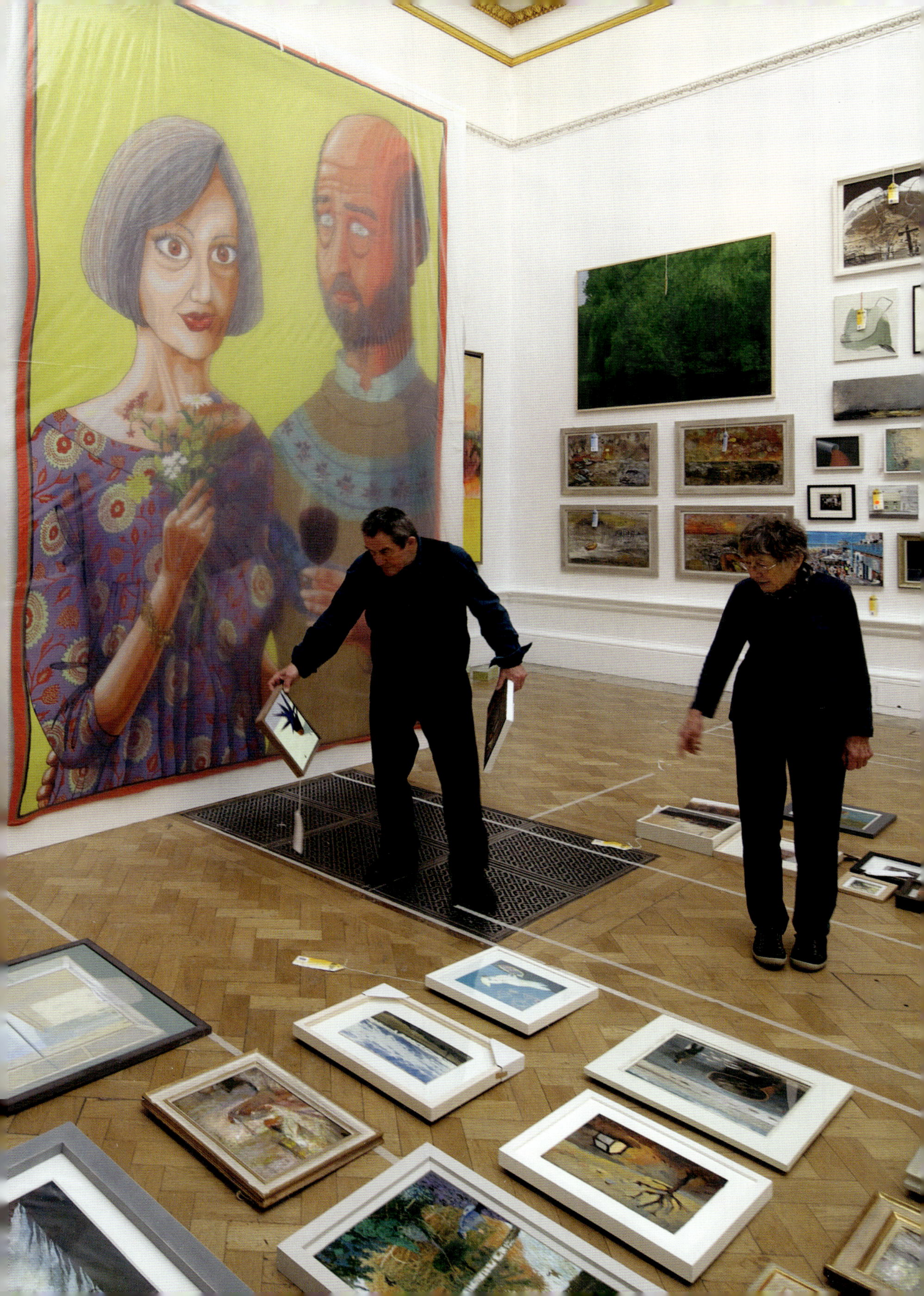

David Humphreys
Monday Landscape
Mixed media
43 × 74 cm

Melissa Scott-Miller
Railings and Magnolia Tree
Oil
62 × 61 cm

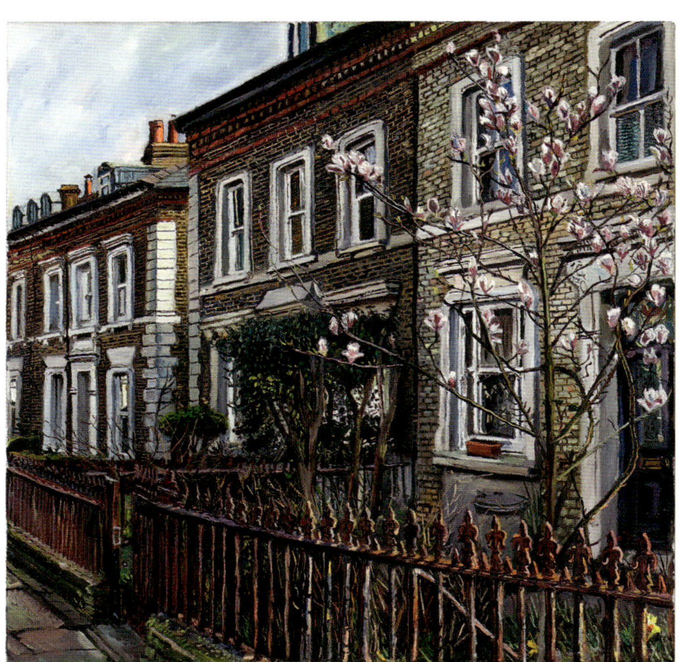

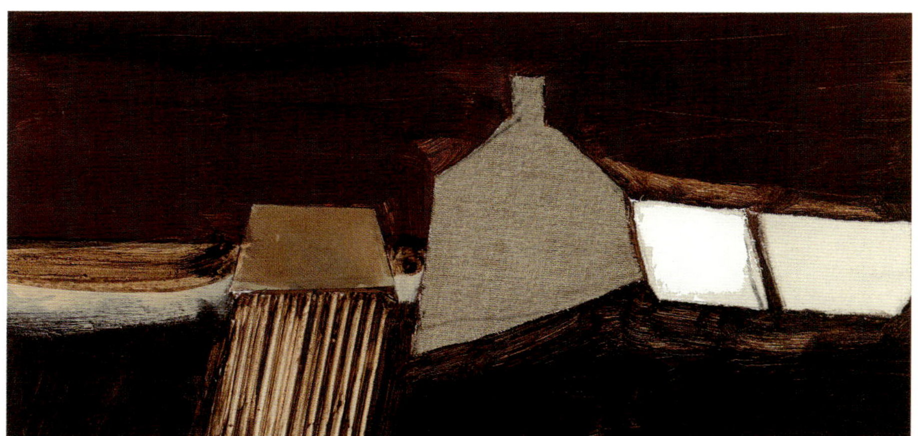

Eileen Hogan
Melting Snow, Kensington Gardens
Oil
129 × 129 cm

Harvey Kimberley
House
Oil
25 × 30 cm

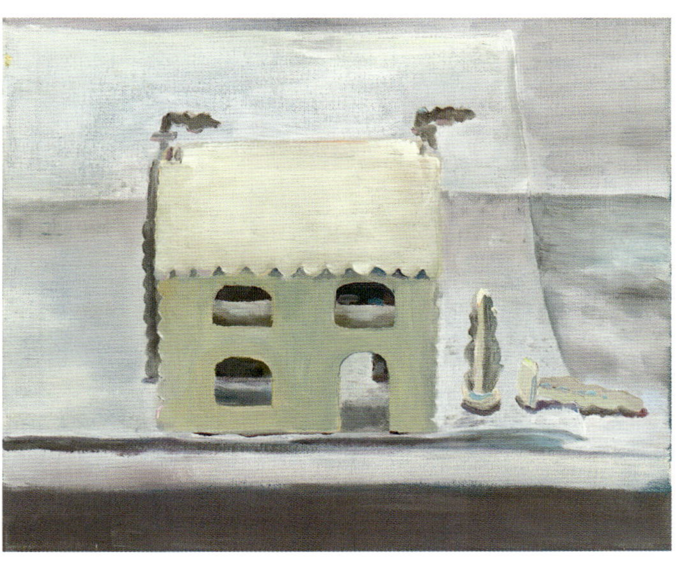

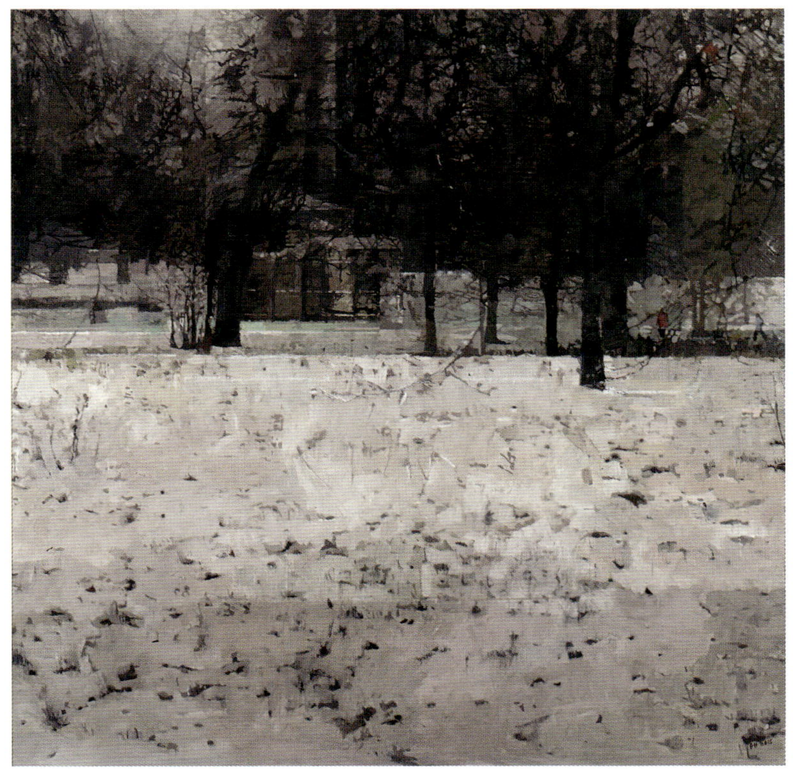

Dame Elizabeth Blackadder DBE RA
Seafood Medley
Screenprint
76 × 87 cm

Diana Armfield RA
Study of Sunflowers
Chalk
51 × 43 cm

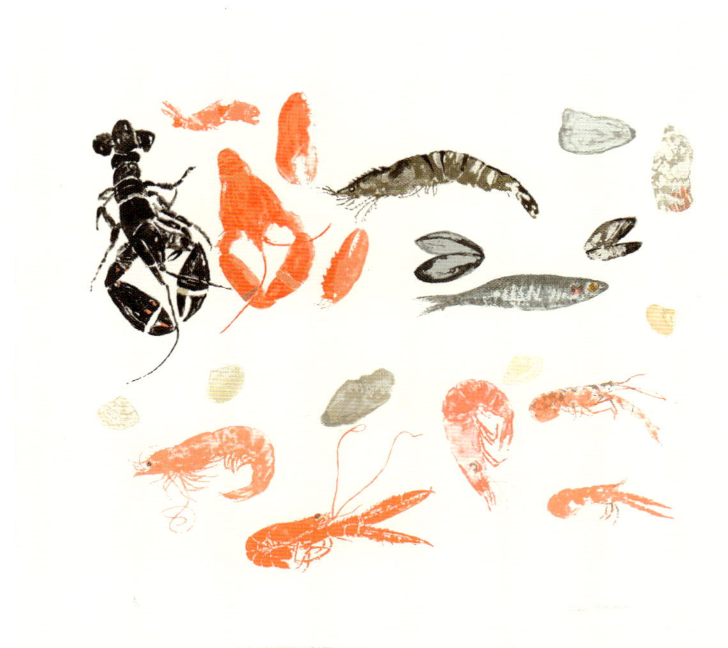

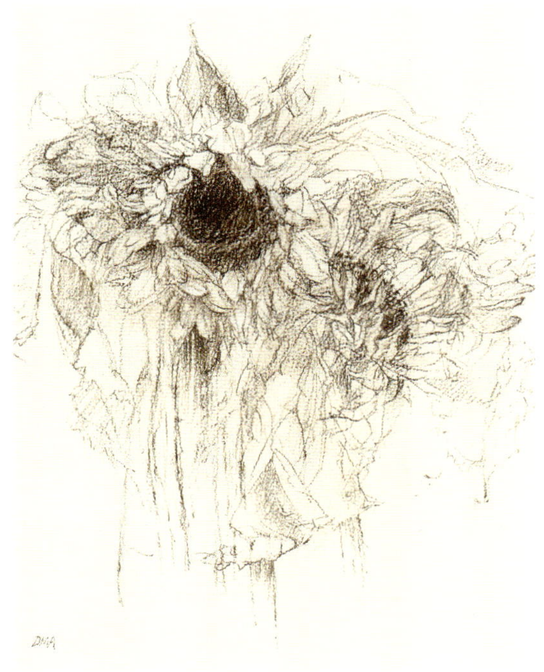

Arthur Neal
Corner of the Studio
Oil
90 × 82 cm

Bernard Dunstan RA
Trying on Stockings
Oil
21 × 29 cm

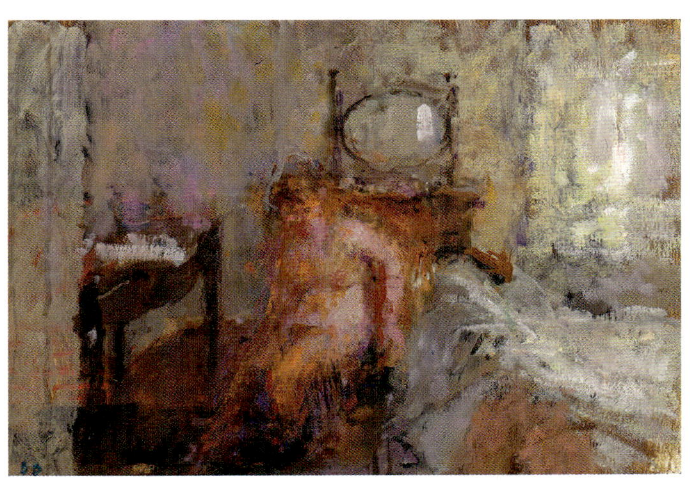

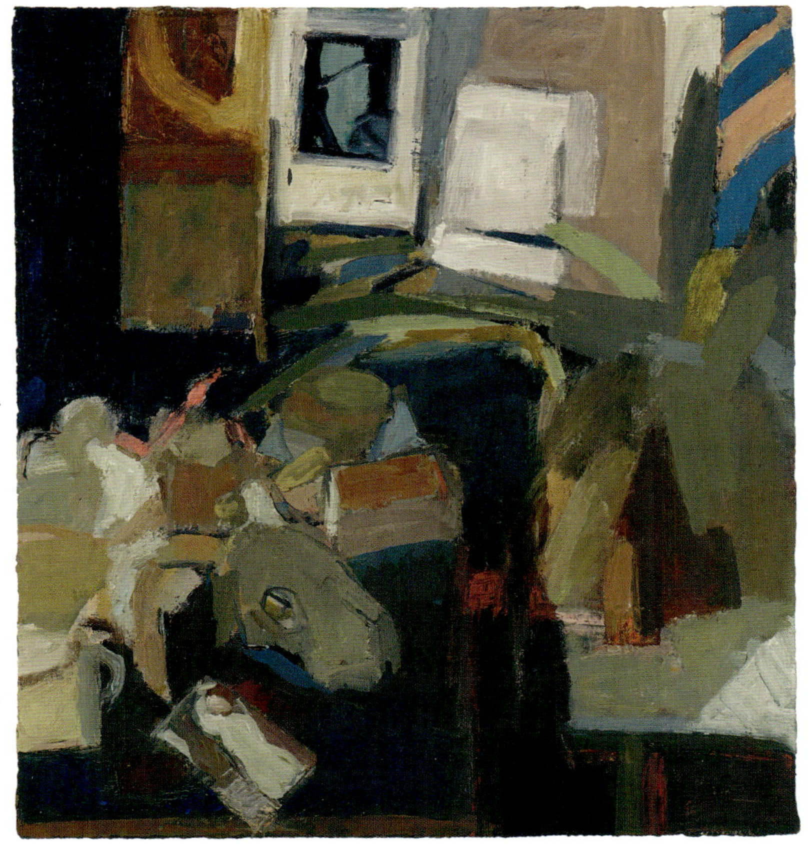

Karl James Ullger
Bayview Clock Tower
Mixed media
50 × 48 cm

John Miles
Dorothy
Mixed media
41 × 51 cm

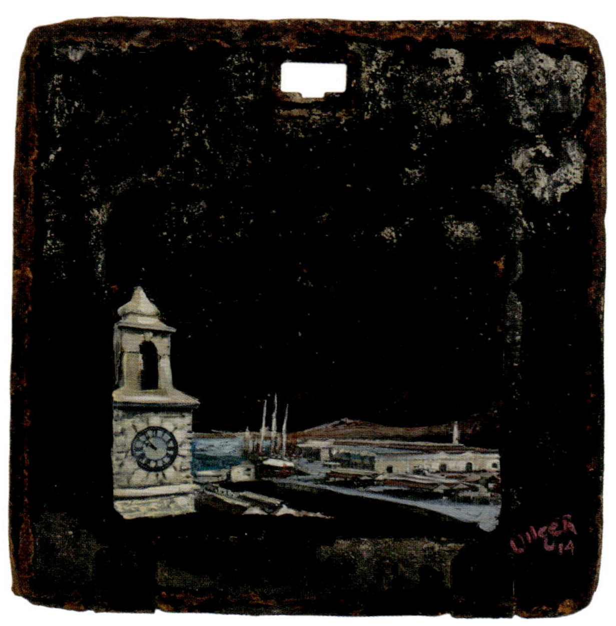

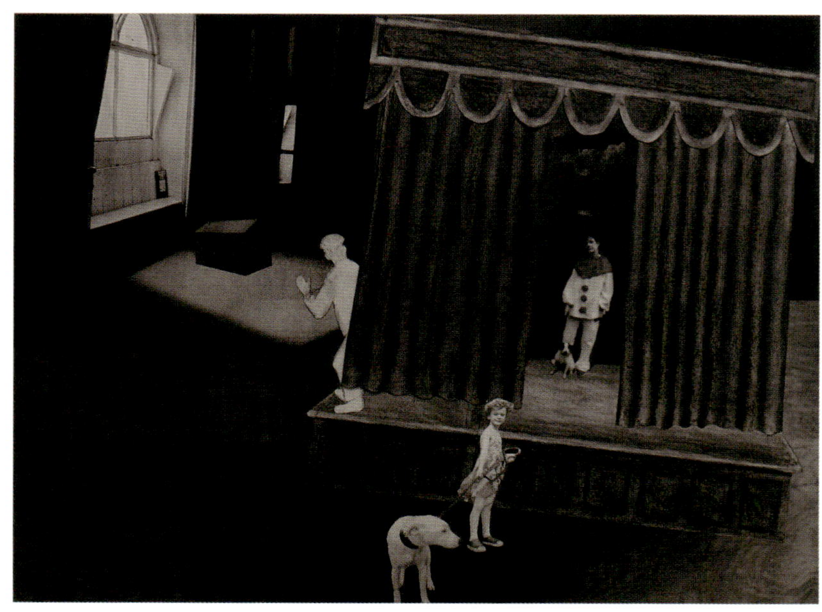

Rebecca Salter RA
Untitled
Ink and woodblock on Japanese paper
49 × 94 cm

Dr David Tindle RA
Window with Screen No. 2
Acrylic on board
80 × 66 cm

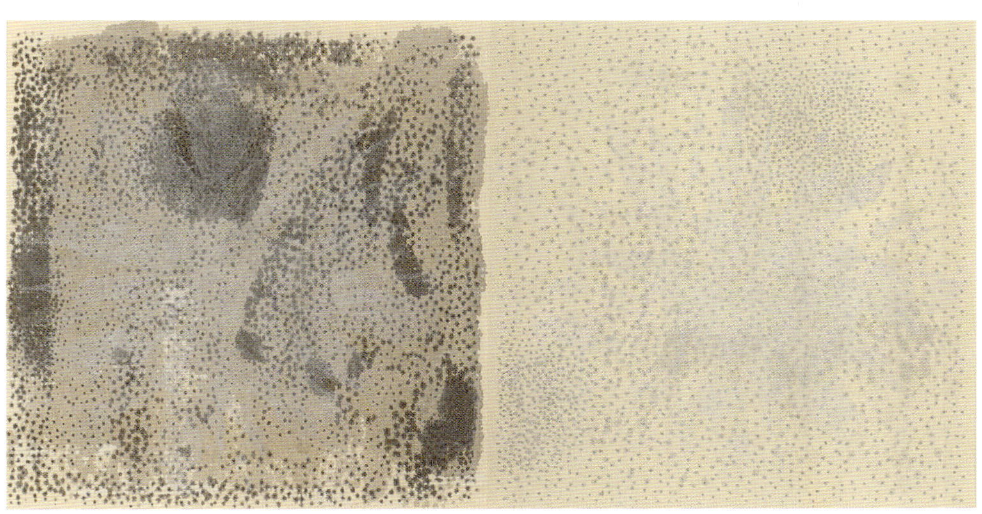

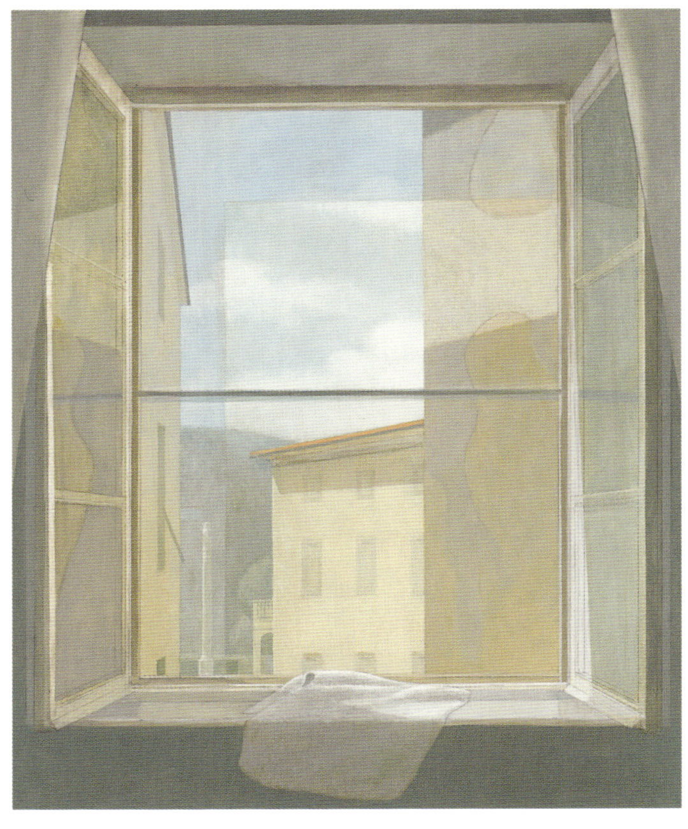

Susan Wilson
Summer Garden Notting Hill
Oil on linen
76 × 127 cm

Francis Tinsley
Distant Lake
Oil
26 × 30 cm

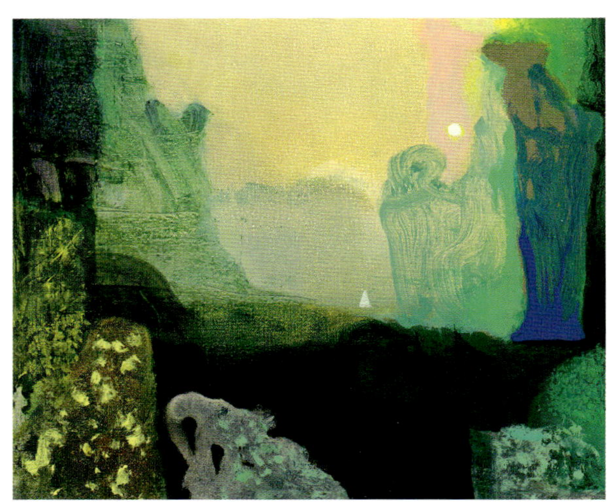

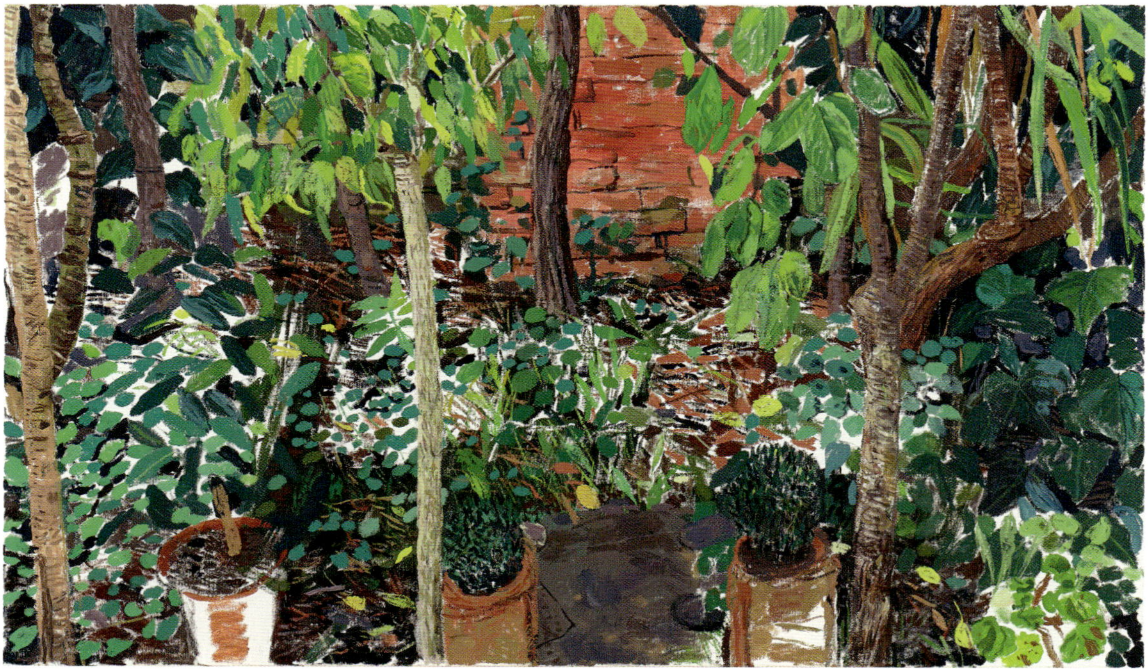

June Berry
Elderly Couple Walking
Oil
40 × 48 cm

Francis Bowyer
Quiet Moment at Le Grand Colbert, Paris
Watercolour
74 × 92 cm

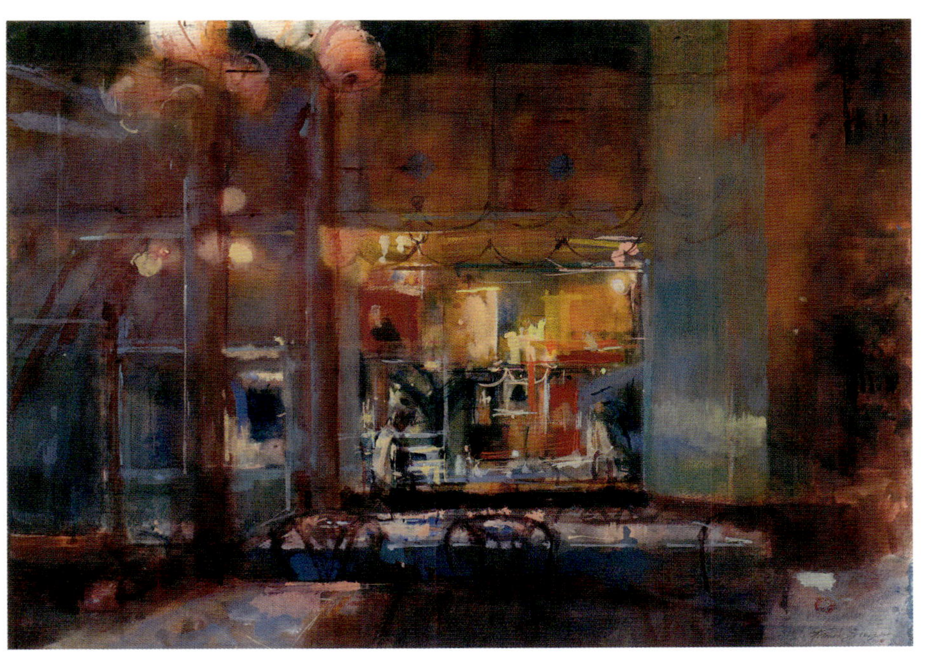

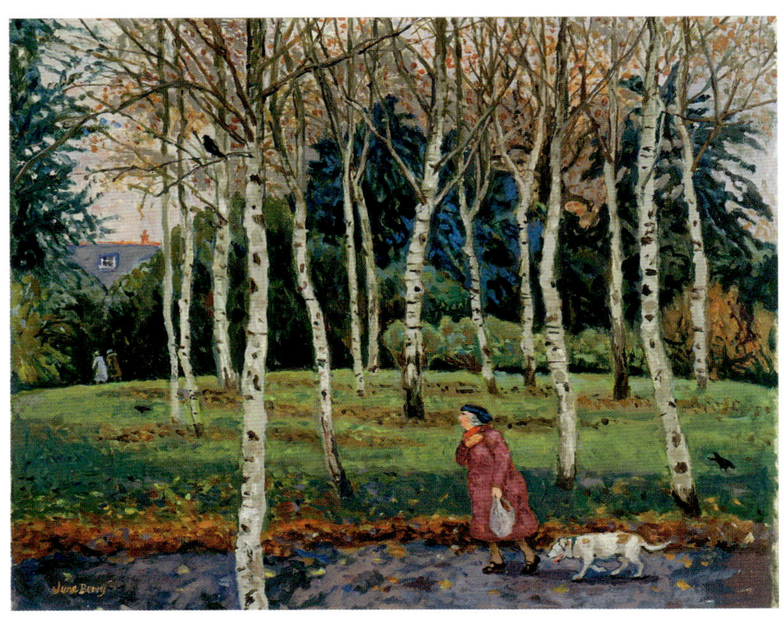

Clyde Hopkins
A Short Life and Its Trouble
Oil on linen
33 × 28 cm

Grayson Perry CBE RA
Julie and Rob
Tapestry
400 × 300 cm

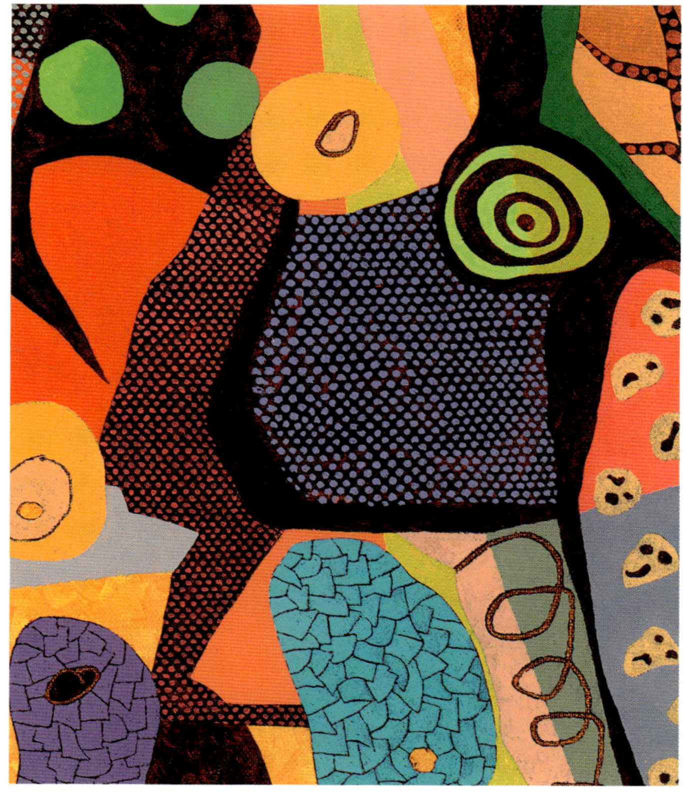

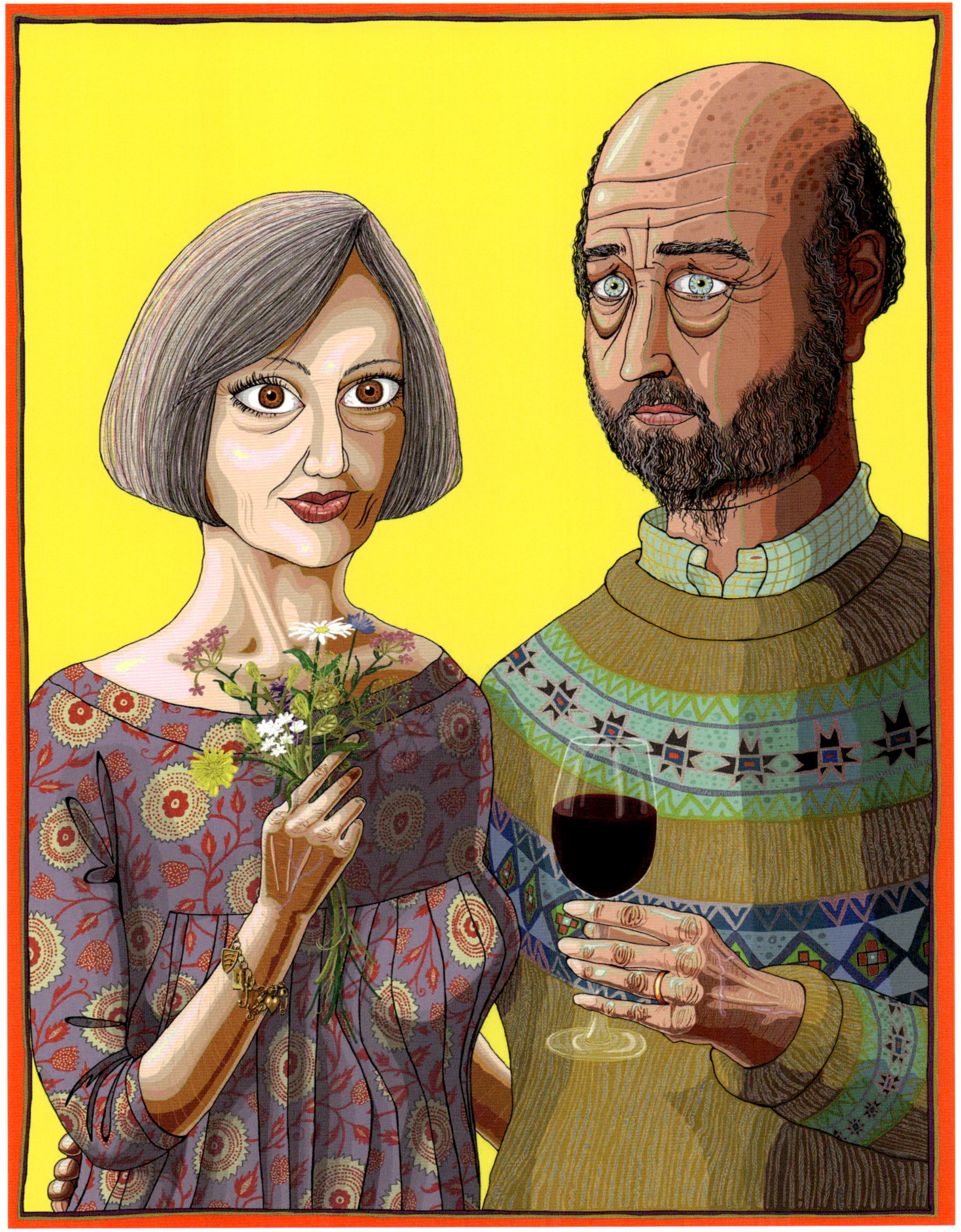

Luciana Meazza
Happy
Acrylic
80 × 120 cm

Louisa Mahony
Untitled
Oil
36 × 26 cm

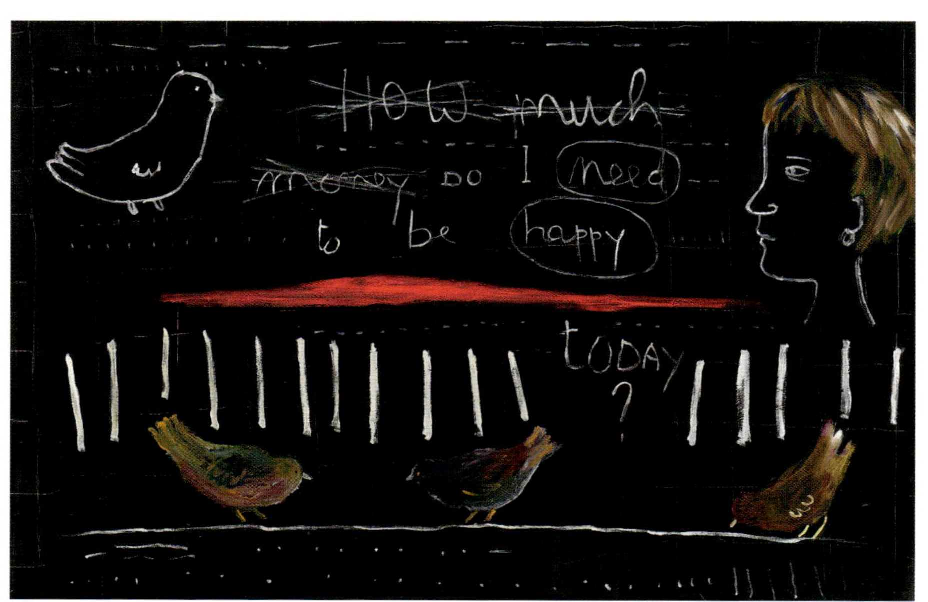

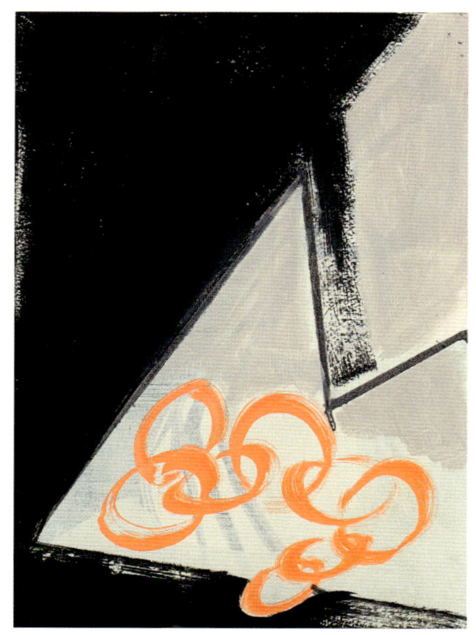

Sheila Girling
Measure Up
Handmade paper and acrylic
98 × 76 cm

Stuart Newman
Periscope Dazzle
Acrylic
33 × 33 cm

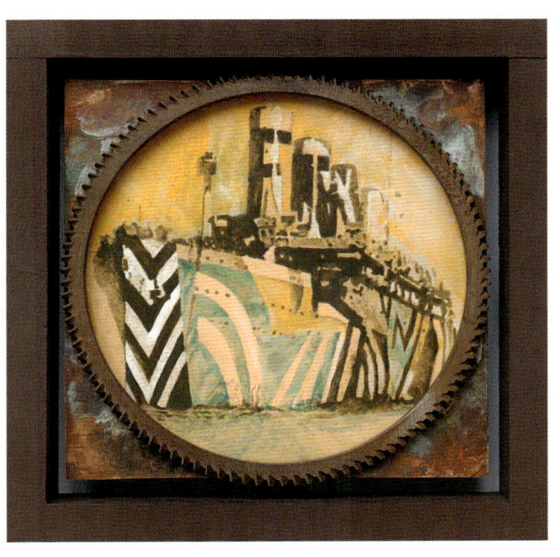

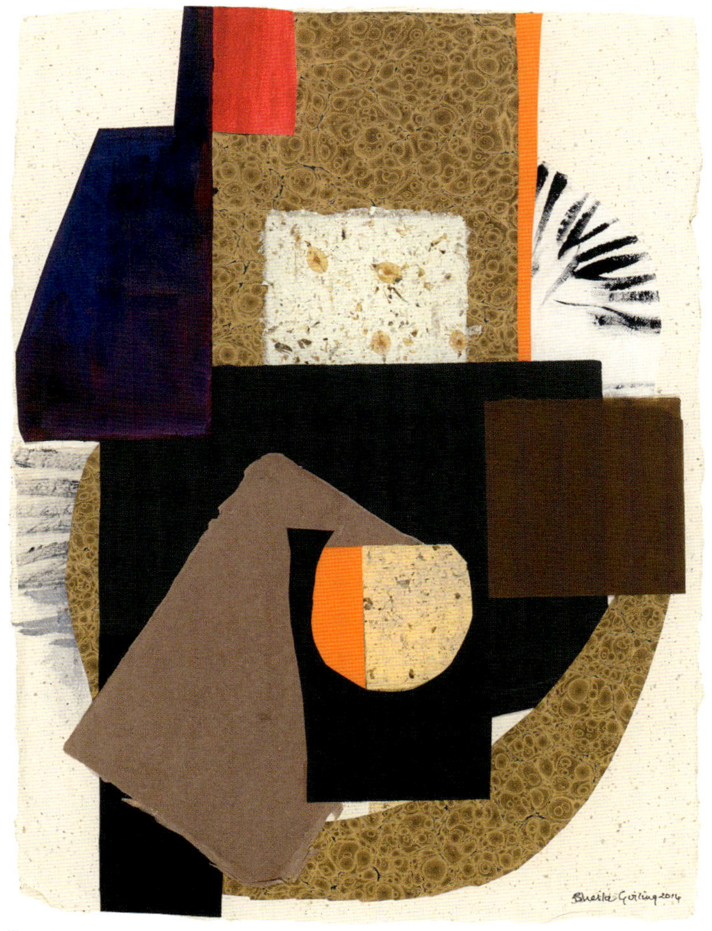

Large Weston Room

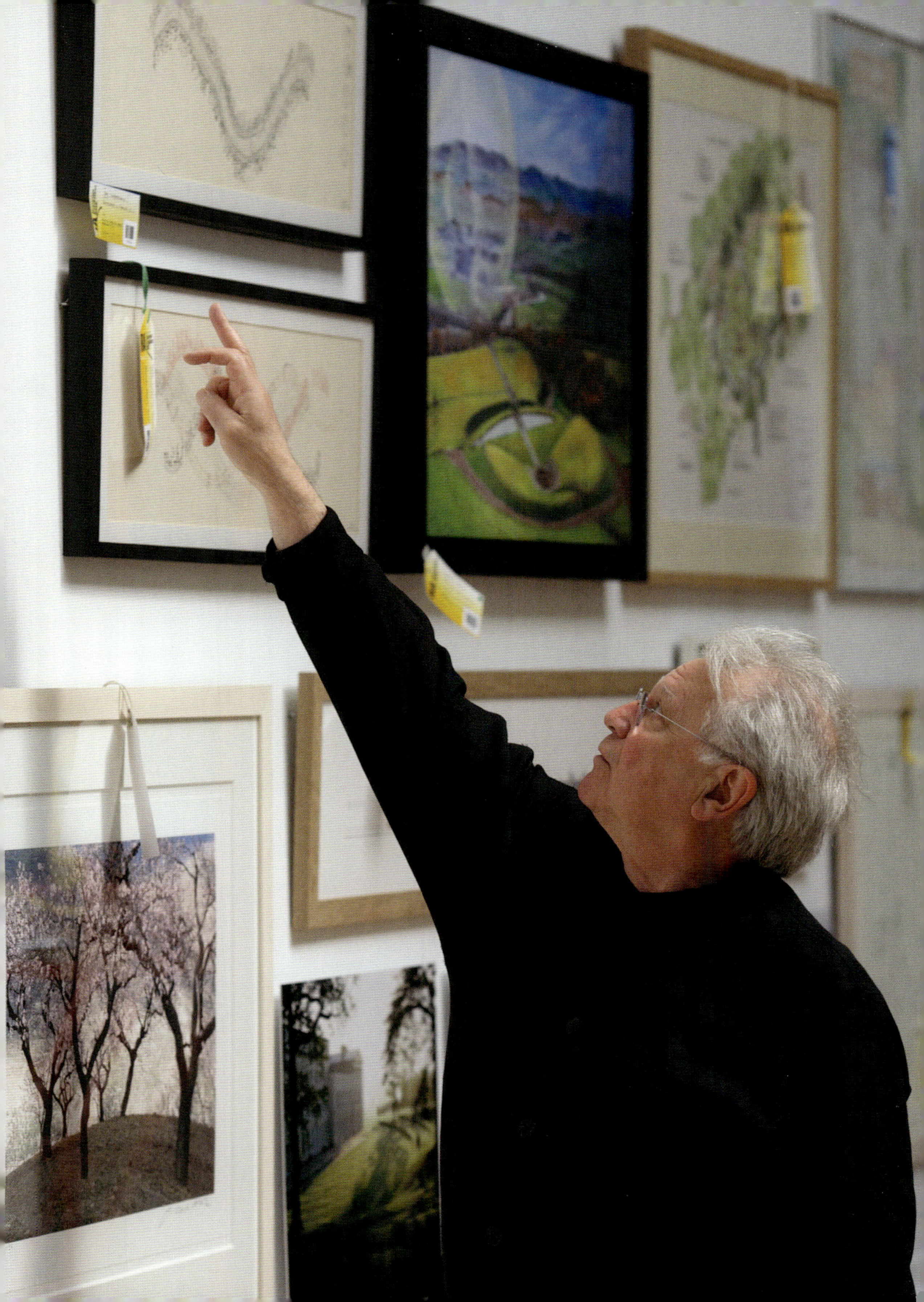

Lord Rogers of Riverside CH RA
Aerial View, Beijing Airport Competition
Computer-generated image
120 × 240 cm

Andy Earl
29 Planes
Photograph
60 × 190 cm

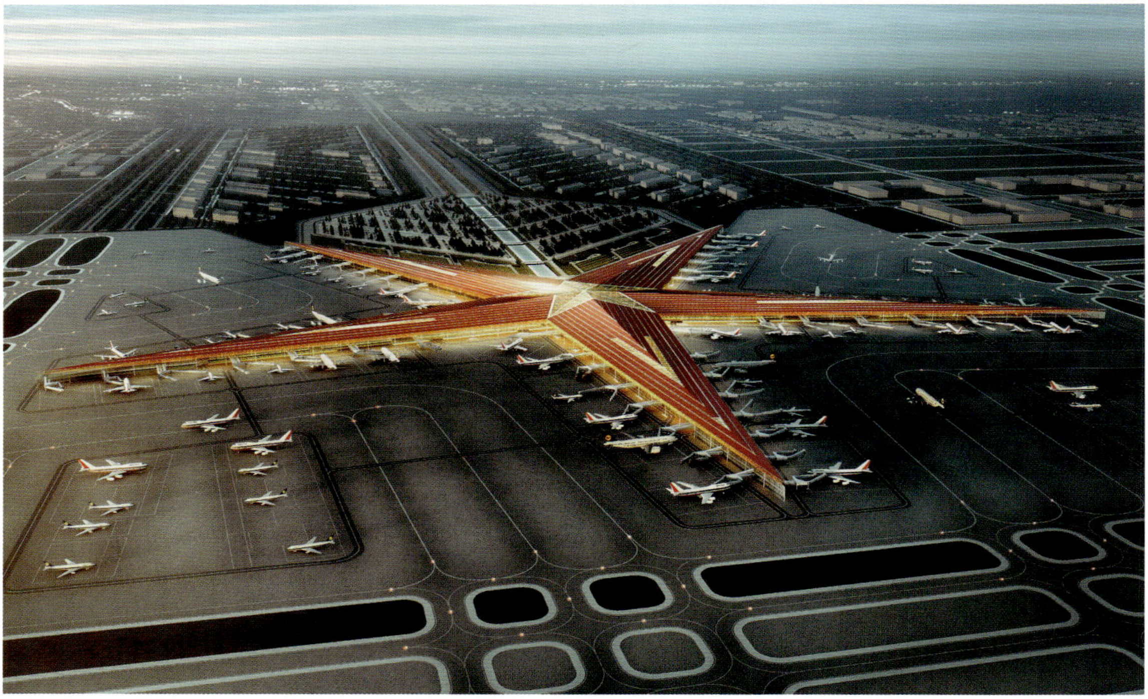

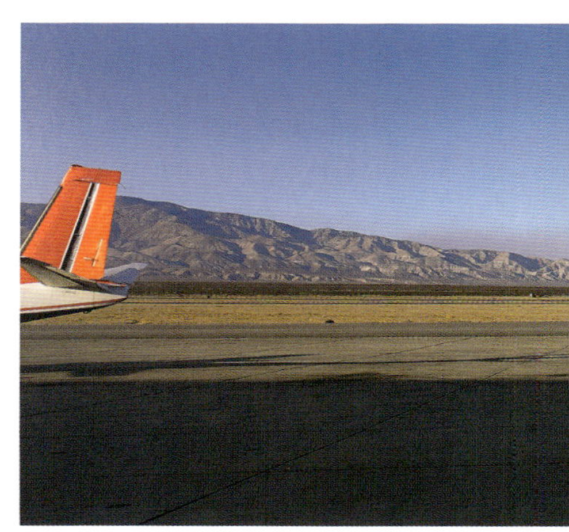

Lord Foster of Thames Bank OM RA
Mexico Airport Structure
Photoprint
170 × 160 cm

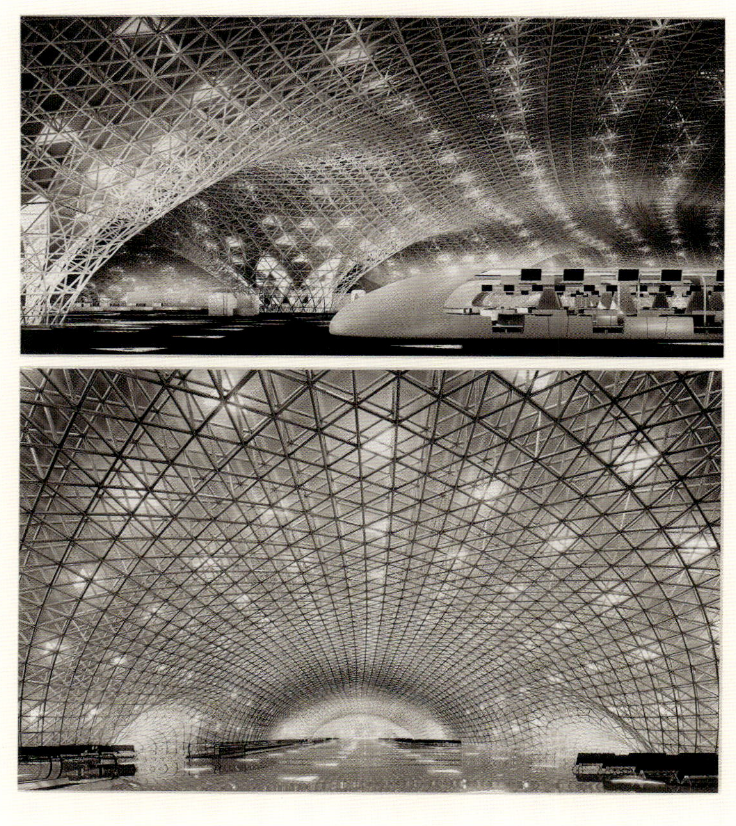

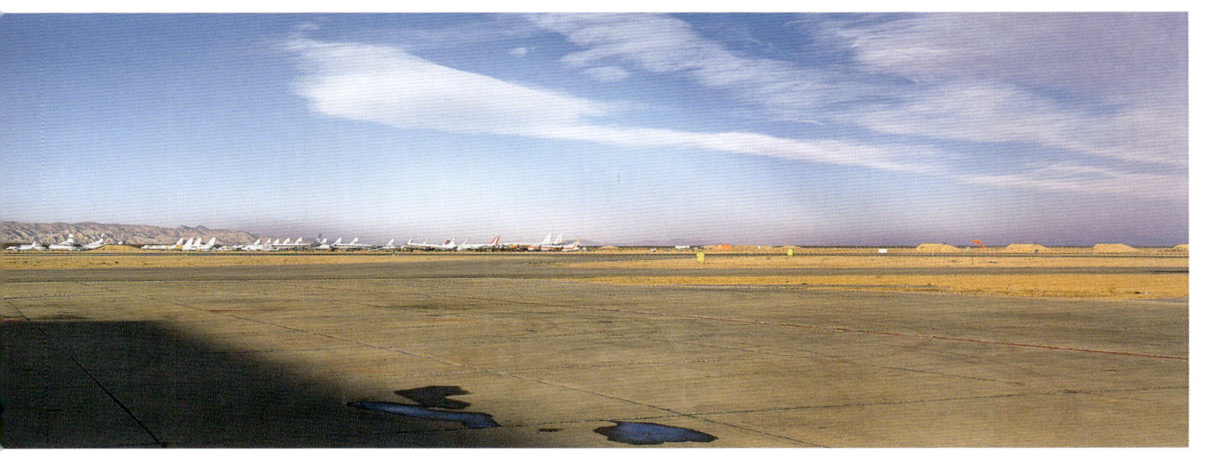

Sir Nicholas Grimshaw CBE PPRA
Wimbledon Master Plan, London, UK
Hardwood and etched metal
5 × 30 × 30 cm

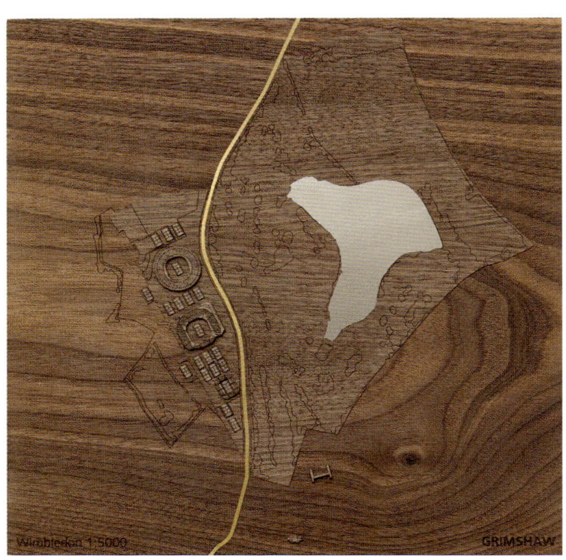

Louisa Hutton RA
Now Is Here
Fine art print
84 × 59 cm

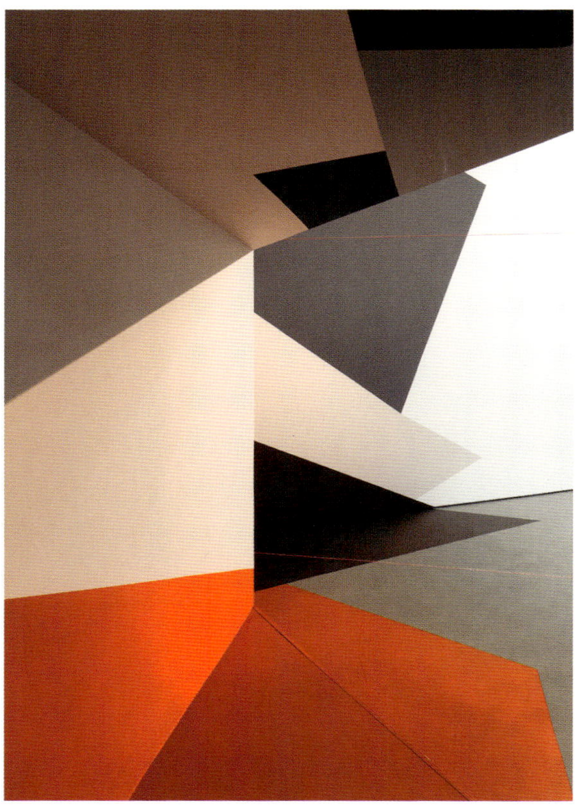

The late Sir Philip Dowson PRA
Old Church Banyuls
Watercolour
13 × 17 cm

Prof Trevor Dannatt RA
Art and Illusion, Hydra
Watercolour
41 × 31 cm

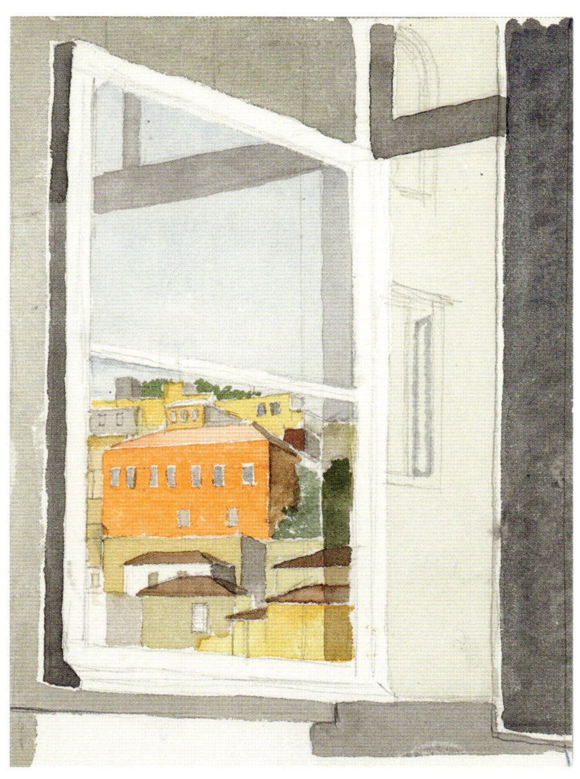

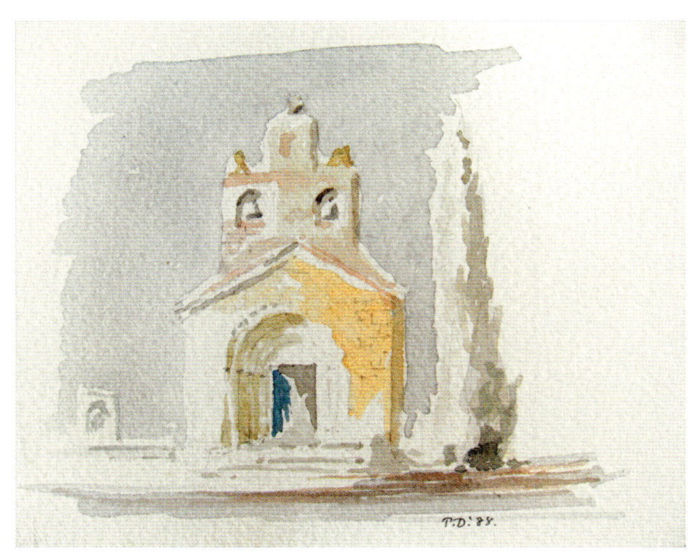

Kim Wilkie
Led by the Land
Photograph
82 × 123 cm

Chris Wilkinson OBE RA
Modular Blueprint
Acrylic
93 × 93 cm

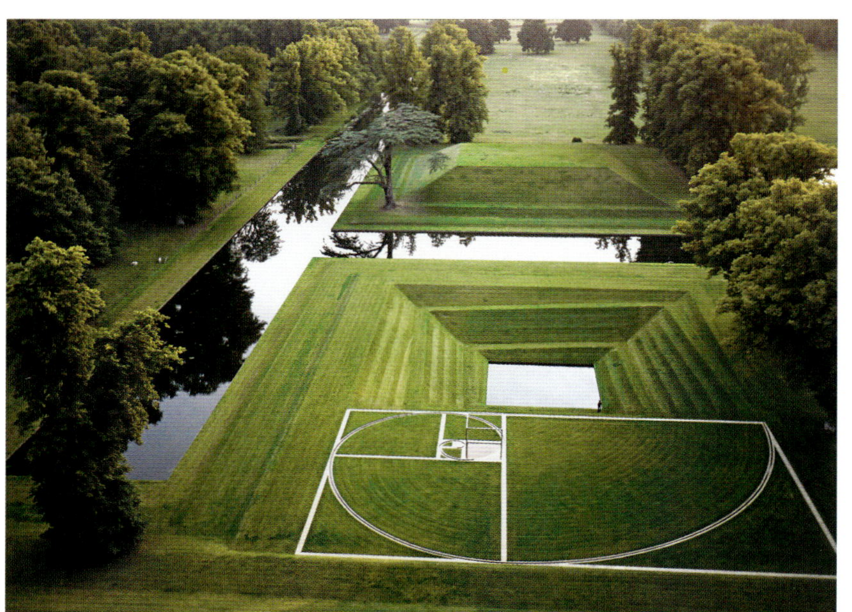

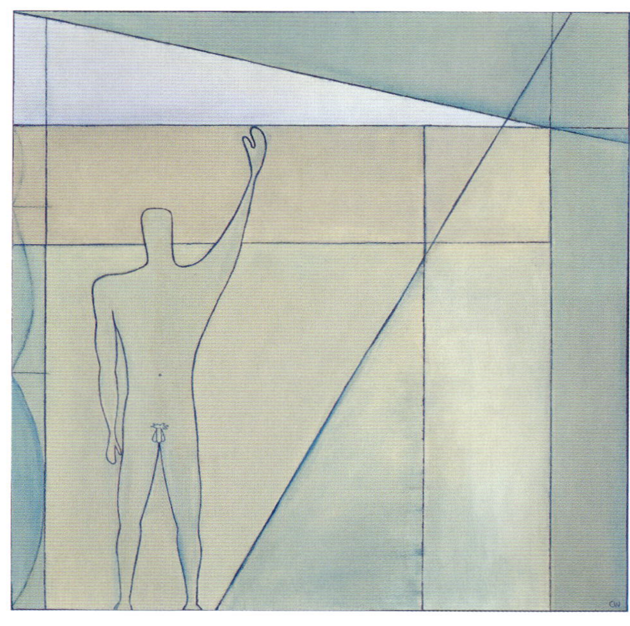

Prof Piers Gough CBE RA
Creek Wharf 1
Aluminium and print
20 × 30 cm

Sir David Chipperfield CBE RA
Views of Museo Jumex
C-type print
105 × 60 cm

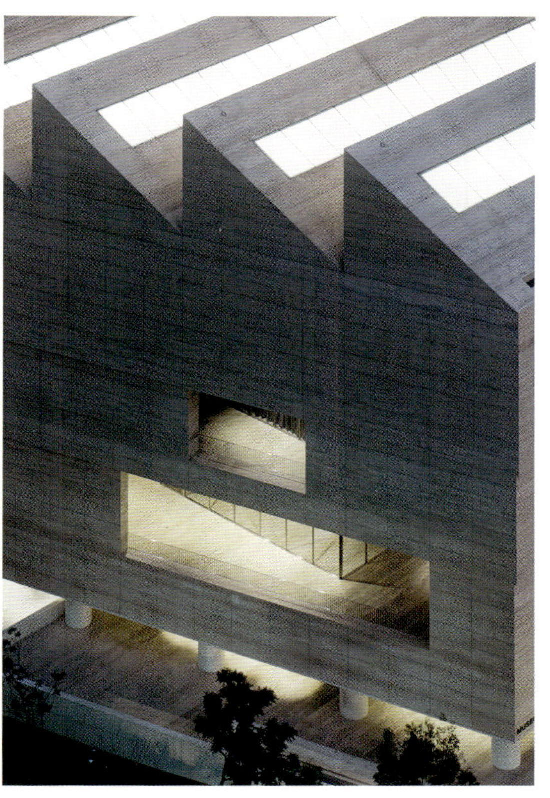

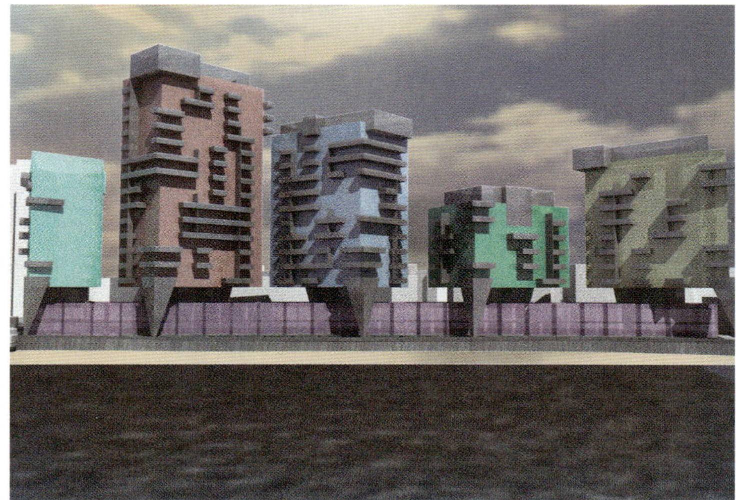

Eric Parry RA
8 St James's Square: Three States
Giclée print mounted on aluminium composite backing
75 × 170 cm

Spencer de Grey CBE RA
RMK HQ Yekaterinburg
3D print, acrylic and metal
51 × 101 cm

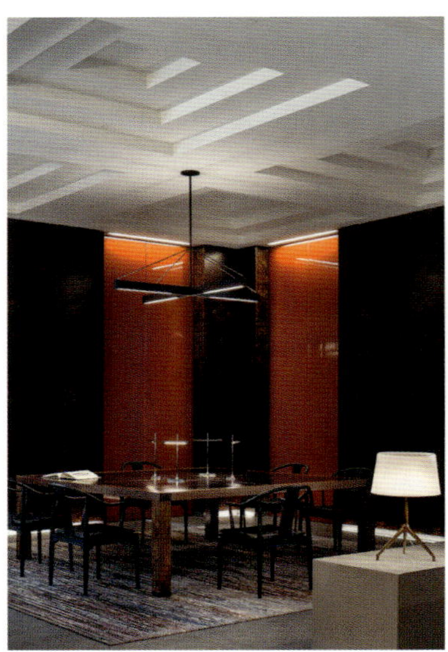
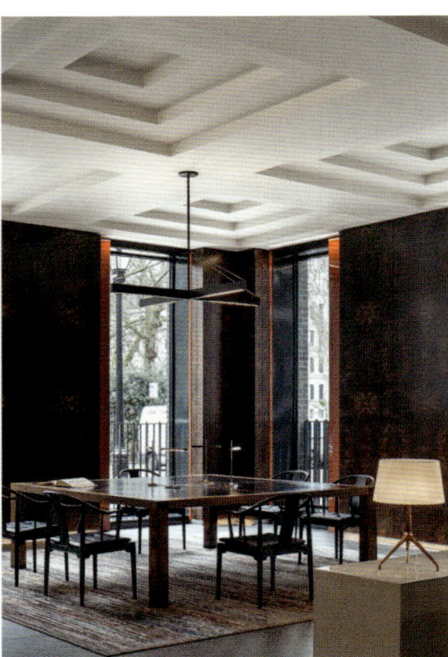
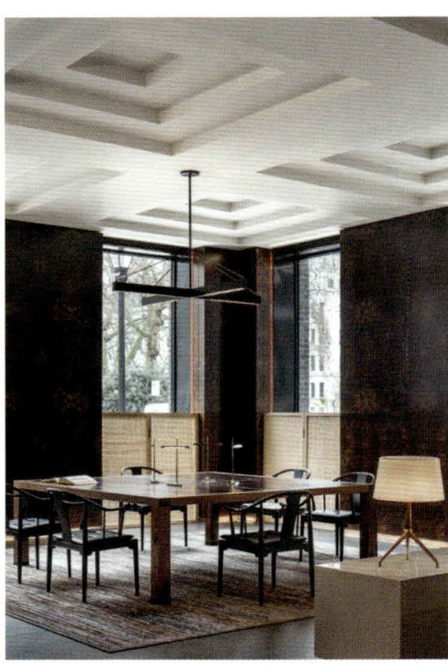

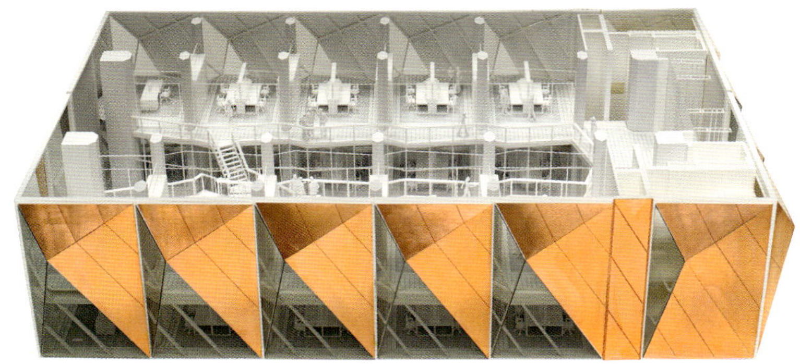

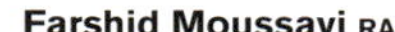

The late Sir Richard MacCormac CBE RA
St John's College, Oxford, Garden Quadrangle
Photograph on aluminium
42 × 30 cm

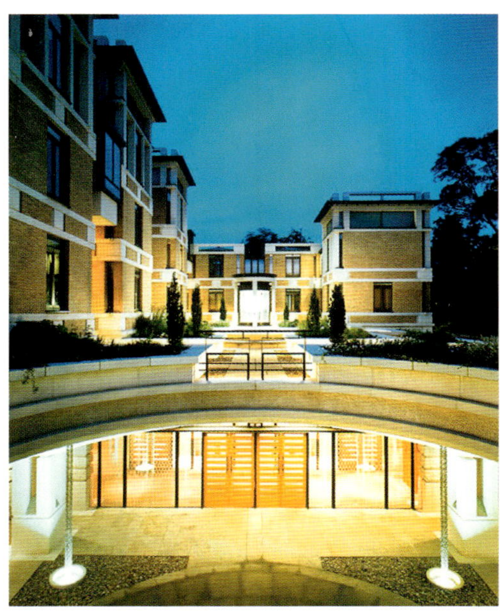

Farshid Moussavi RA
Montpellier Housing 2
Paper
70 × 58 cm

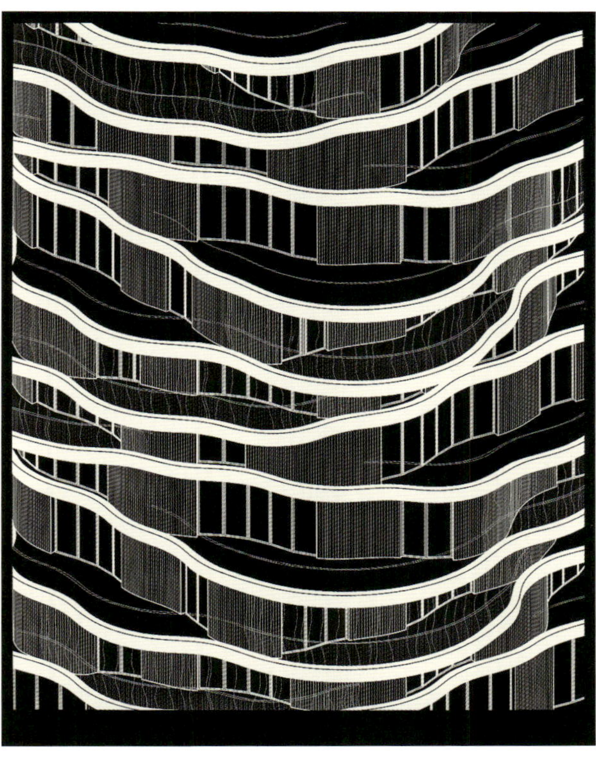

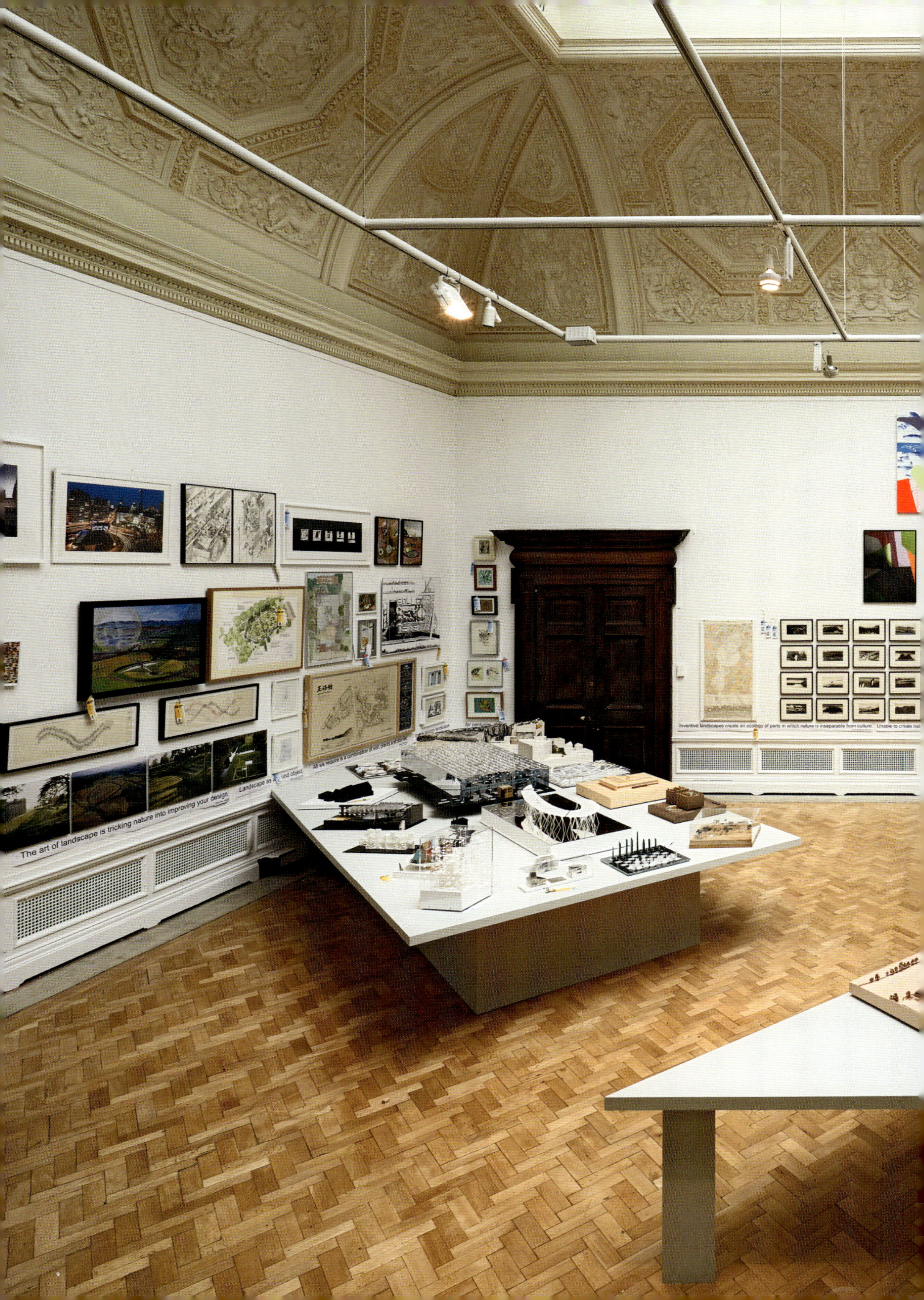
The art of landscape is tricking nature into improving your design.
Inventive landscapes create an ecology of parts in which nature is inseparable from culture.

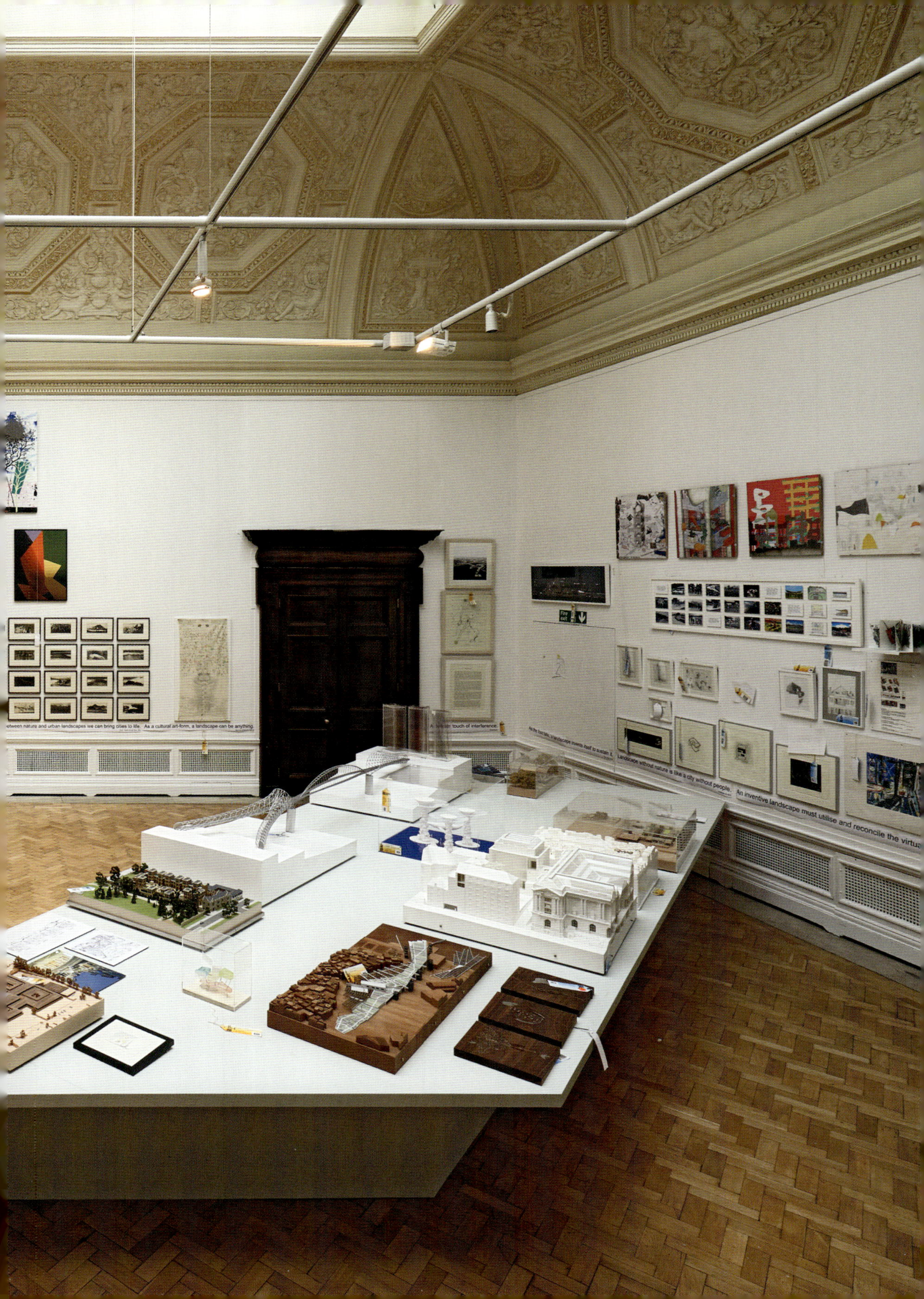
between nature and urban landscapes we can bring cities to life. As a cultural art-form, a landscape can be anything.
Landscape without nature is like a city without people
An inventive landscape must utilise and reconcile the virtua

Senator Renzo Piano HON RA
Wooden Shape
Wood
H 10 cm

Sir Michael Hopkins CBE RA
Harvard University – The Richard A. and Susan F. Smith Campus Center
Wood
H 20 cm

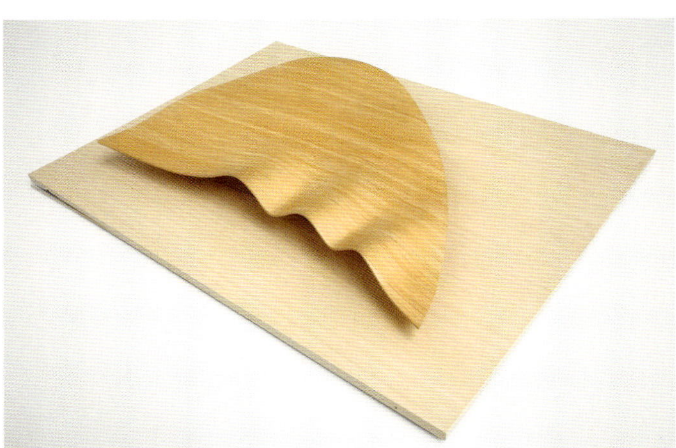

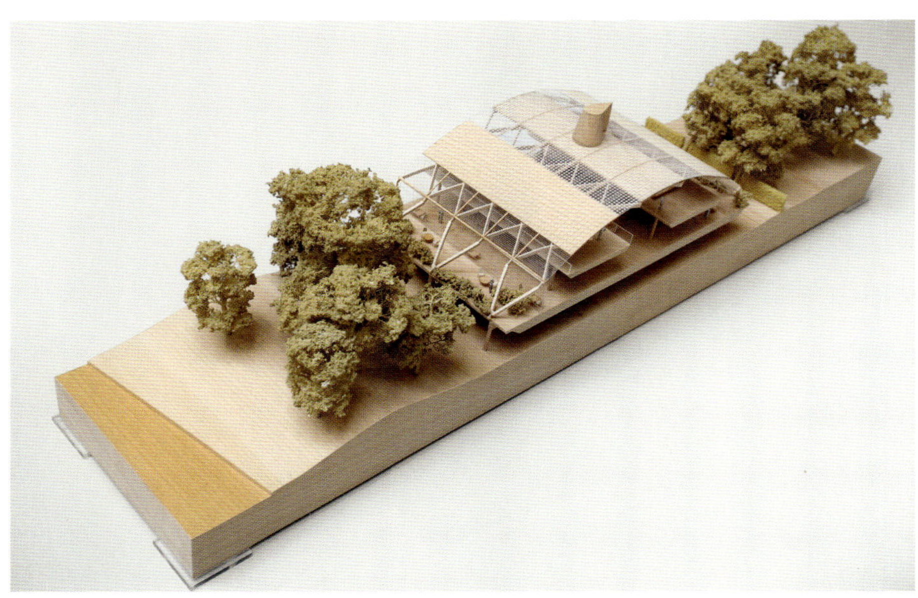

Stanton Williams
The Sainsbury Laboratory, Cambridge
Timber model
H 14 cm

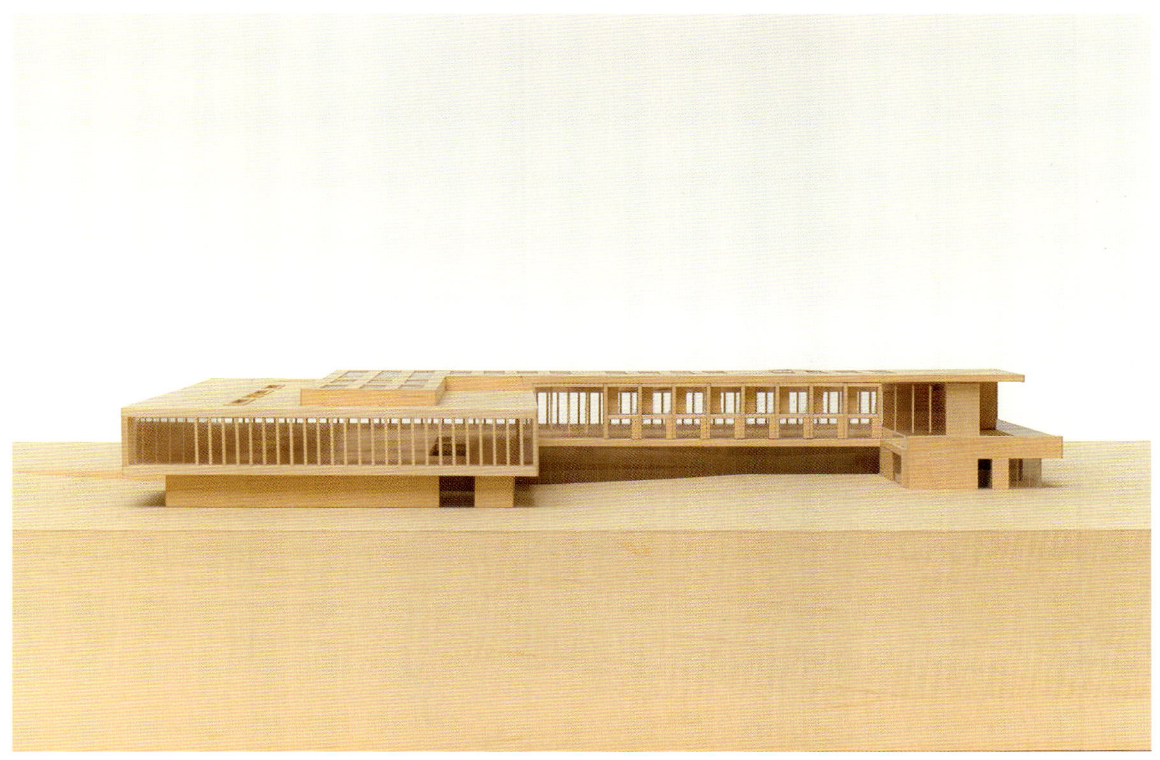

Michael Manser CBE RA
Enderby Place: Façade Model
Mixed media
52 × 51 × 46 cm

Prof Ian Ritchie CBE RA
Disequilibrium
Carborundum
42 × 29 cm

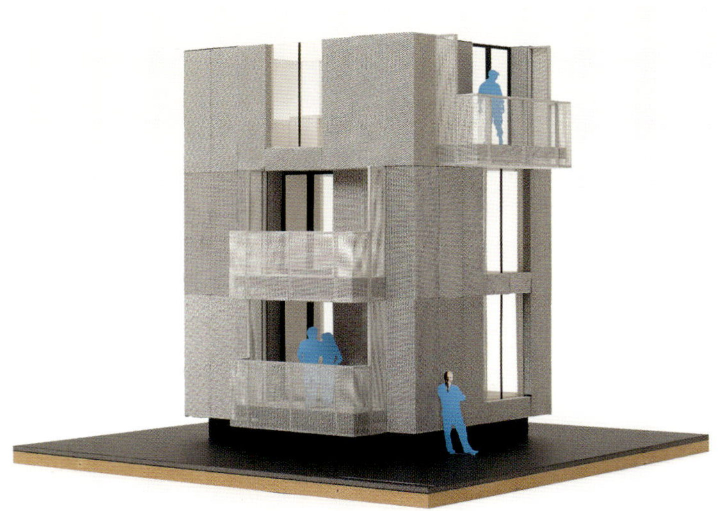

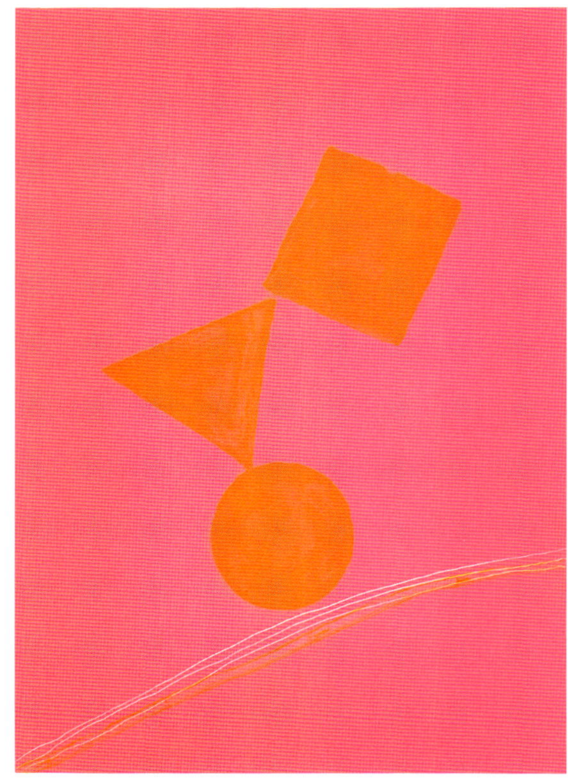

Paul Koralek CBE RA
Thoughts on Paper
Ink
31 × 40 cm

Leonard Manasseh OBE RA
Bustly Black
Ink on paper
43 × 33 cm

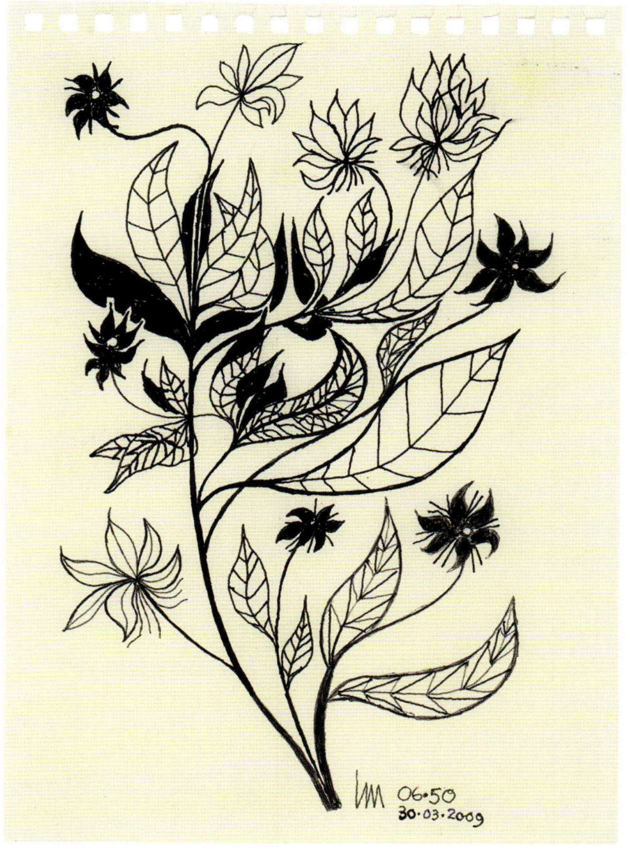

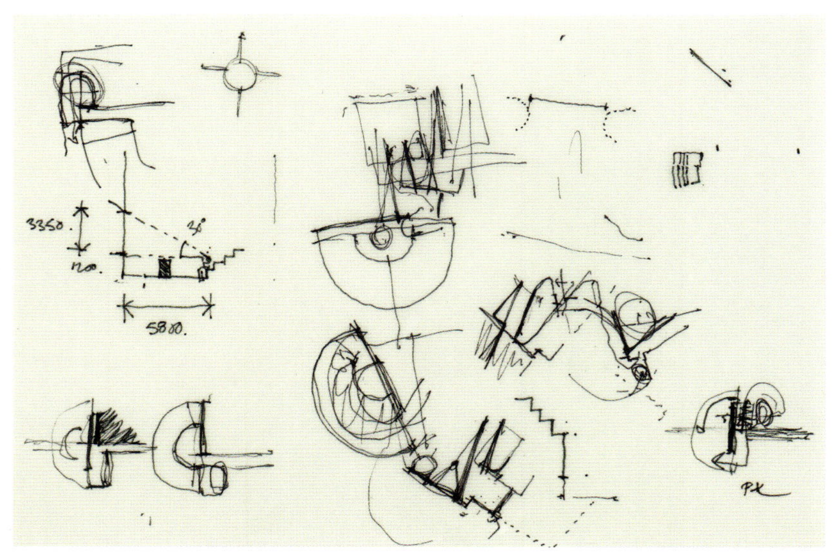

Eva Jiricna CBE RA
Villa Sekyra, Prague (detail)
Duratrans
135 × 80 cm

Dame Zaha Hadid DBE RA
Beijing New Airport – Roof Perspective
Acrylic on black paper
86 × 120 cm

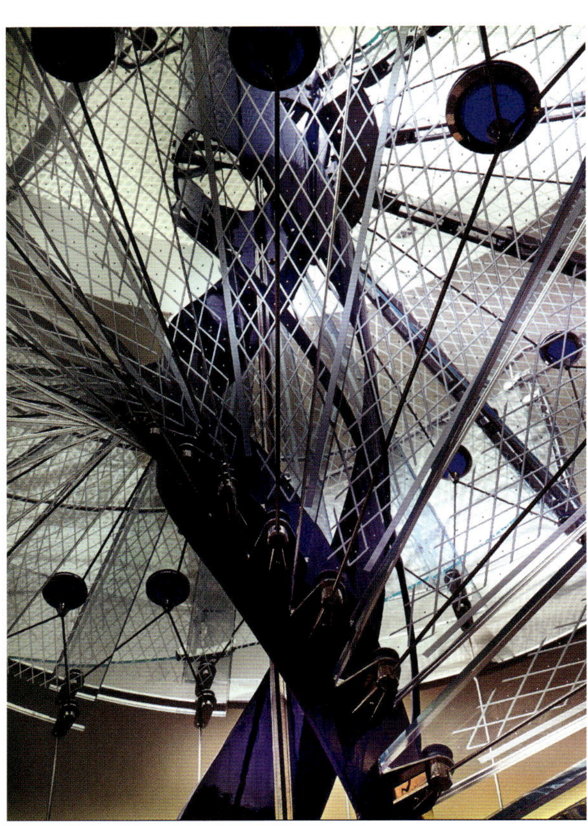

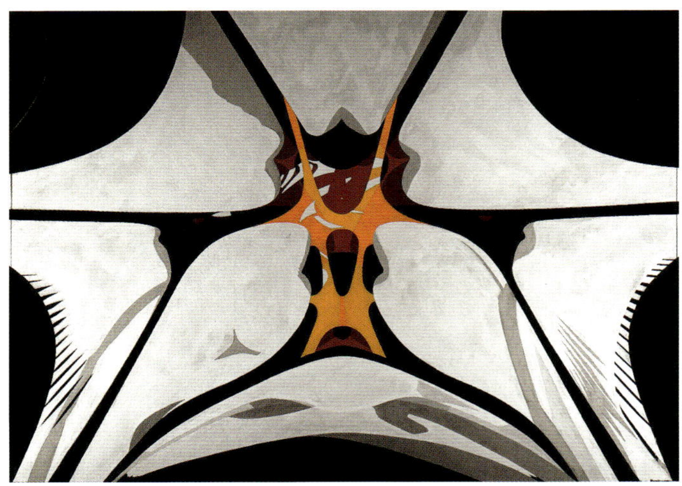

Thomas Heatherwick CBE RA
Maggie's Yorkshire
Hemiwood, acrylic, SLS print, cherry-wood veneer, metal and landscape material
28 × 57 × 82.5 cm

Prof Tadao Ando HON RA
Tall Green Project (Diptych)
Japanese paper, pencil, Indian ink, water-based pen and photograph
40 × 50 cm

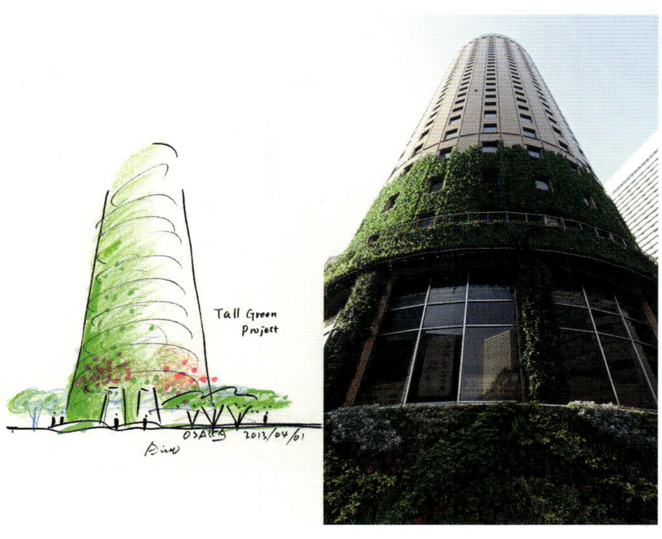

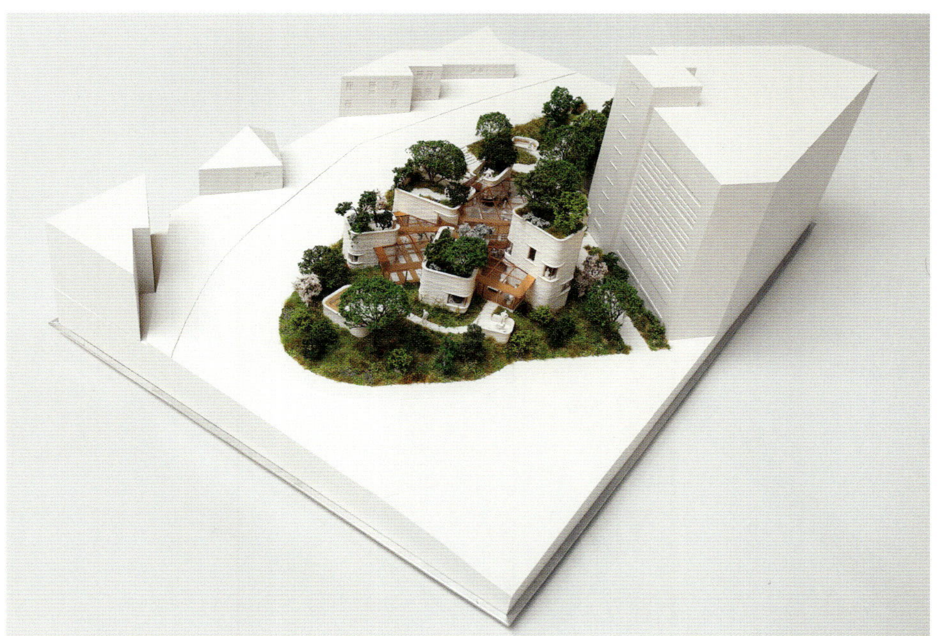

Prof William Alsop OBE RA
Total Eclipse of the Landscape
Acrylic
120 × 150 cm

Prof Sir Peter Cook RA
Vertical University: The Possibilities
Print from collage
63 × 63 cm

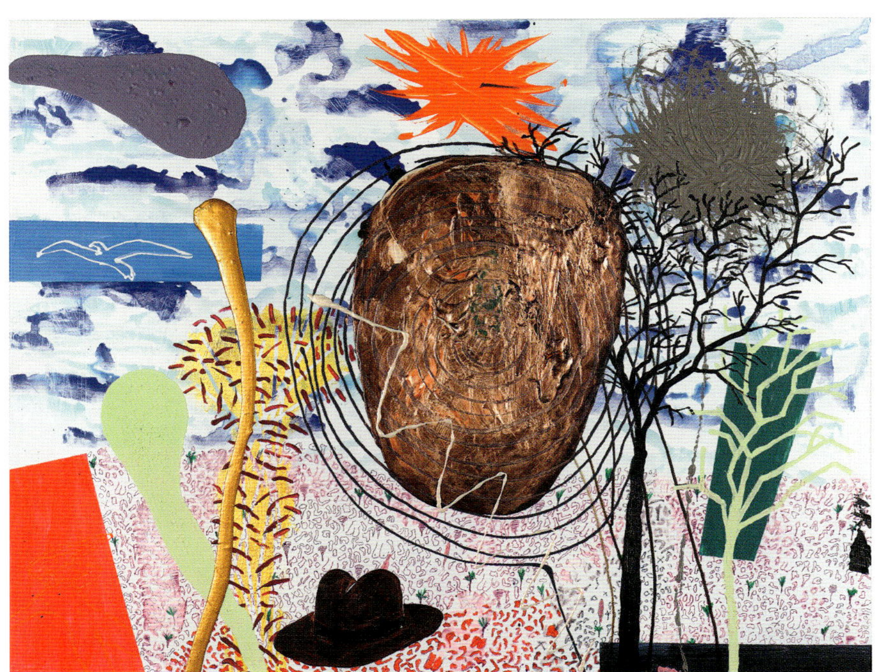

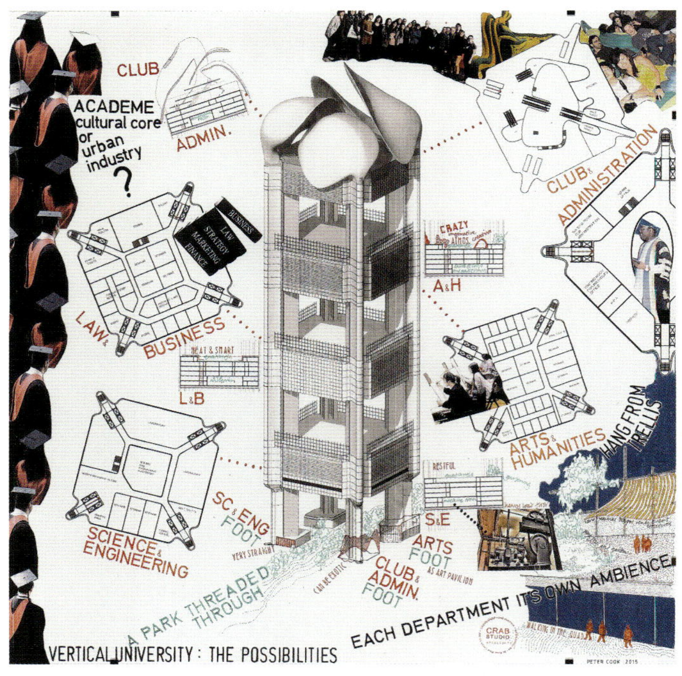

Prof Gordon Benson OBE RA
Illuminated Metropolis (detail)
Hand-finished digital-pigment print with screenprint
120 × 160 cm

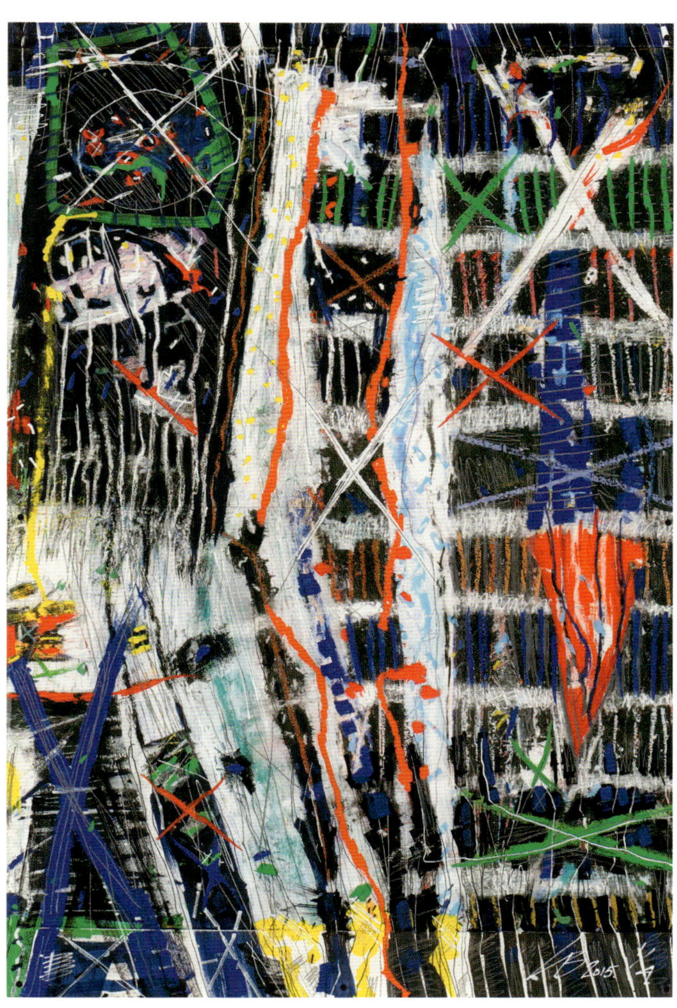

Small Weston Room

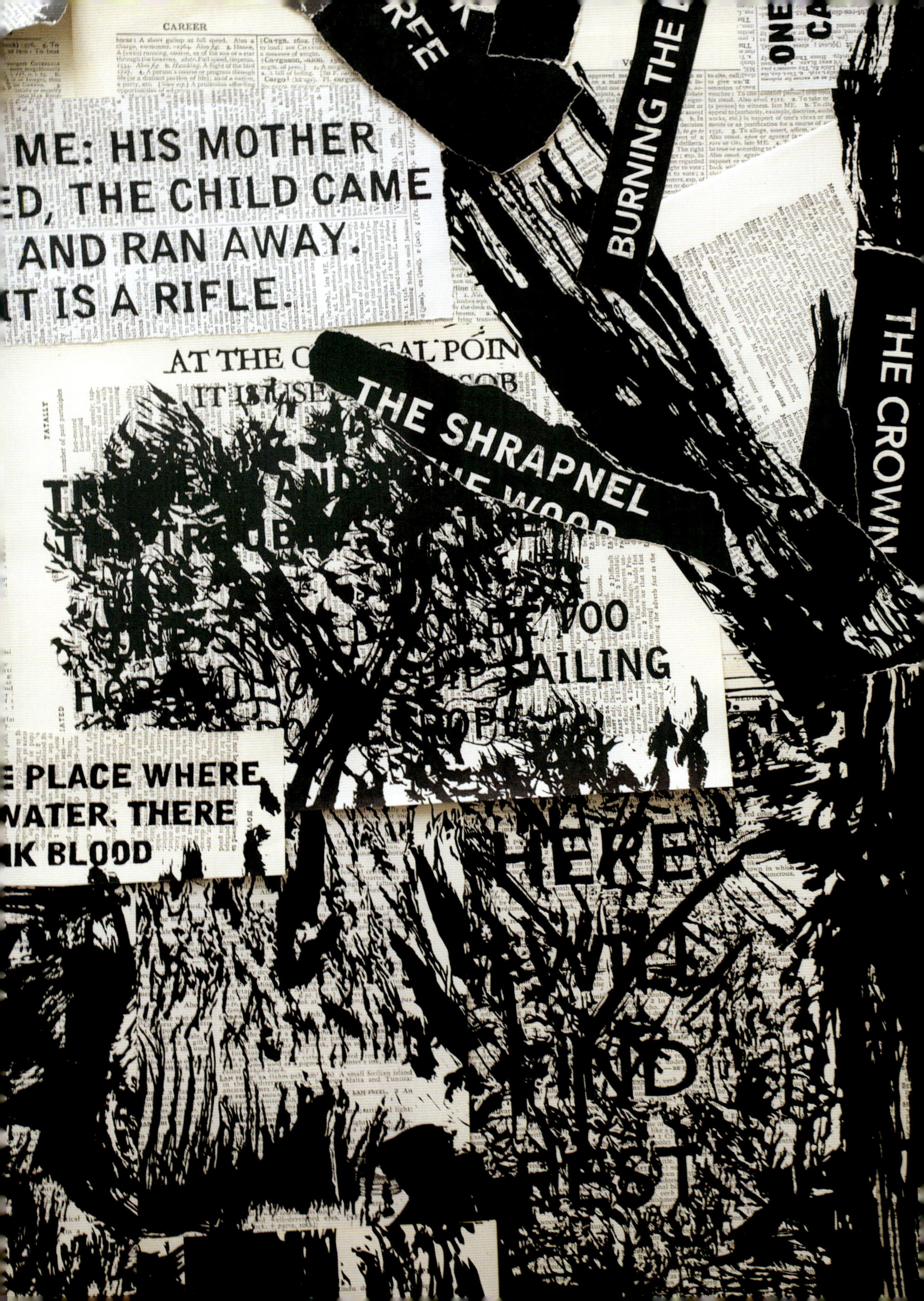
CAREER
ME: HIS MOTHER
D, THE CHILD CAME
AND RAN AWAY.
T IS A RIFLE.
BURNING THE
THE SHRAPNEL
THE CROWN
PLACE WHERE
WATER. THERE
K BLOOD
HERE

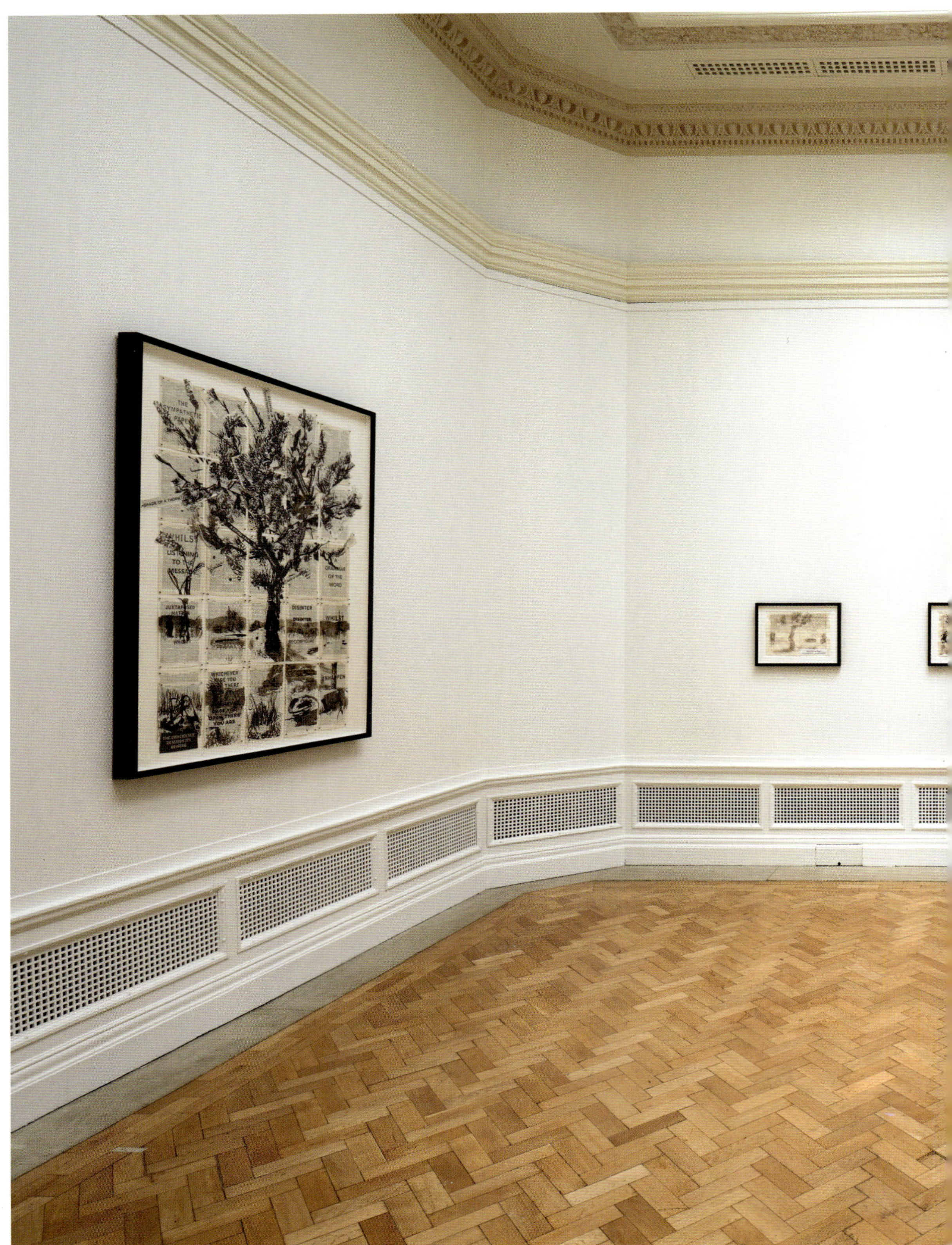
THE
SYMPATHETIC
OF THE
WORD
DISINTER
DISINTER
WHILST
WHICHEVER
THERE
YOU ARE

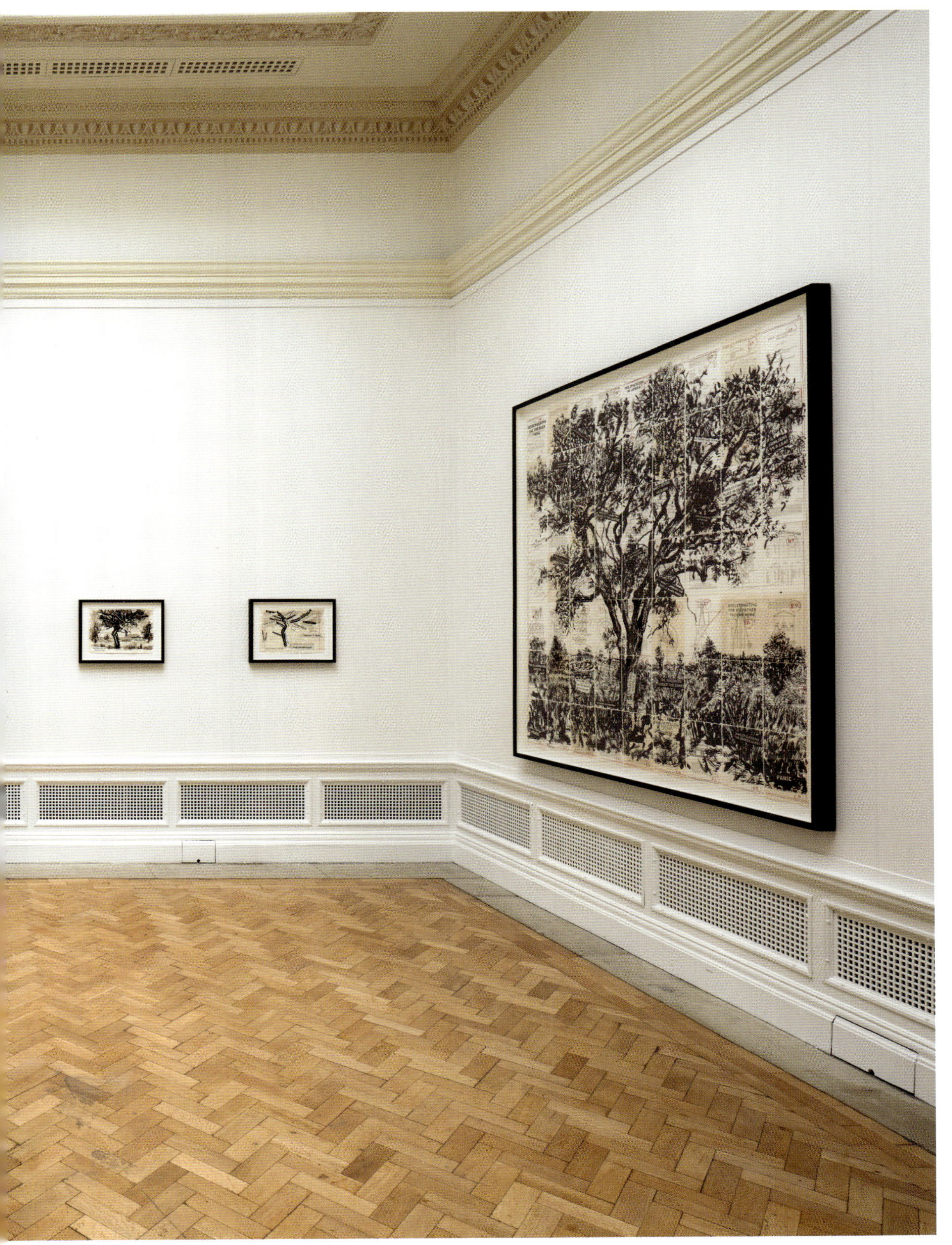

William Kentridge HON RA
Untitled
Indian ink and red pencil on handmade paper
44 × 57 cm

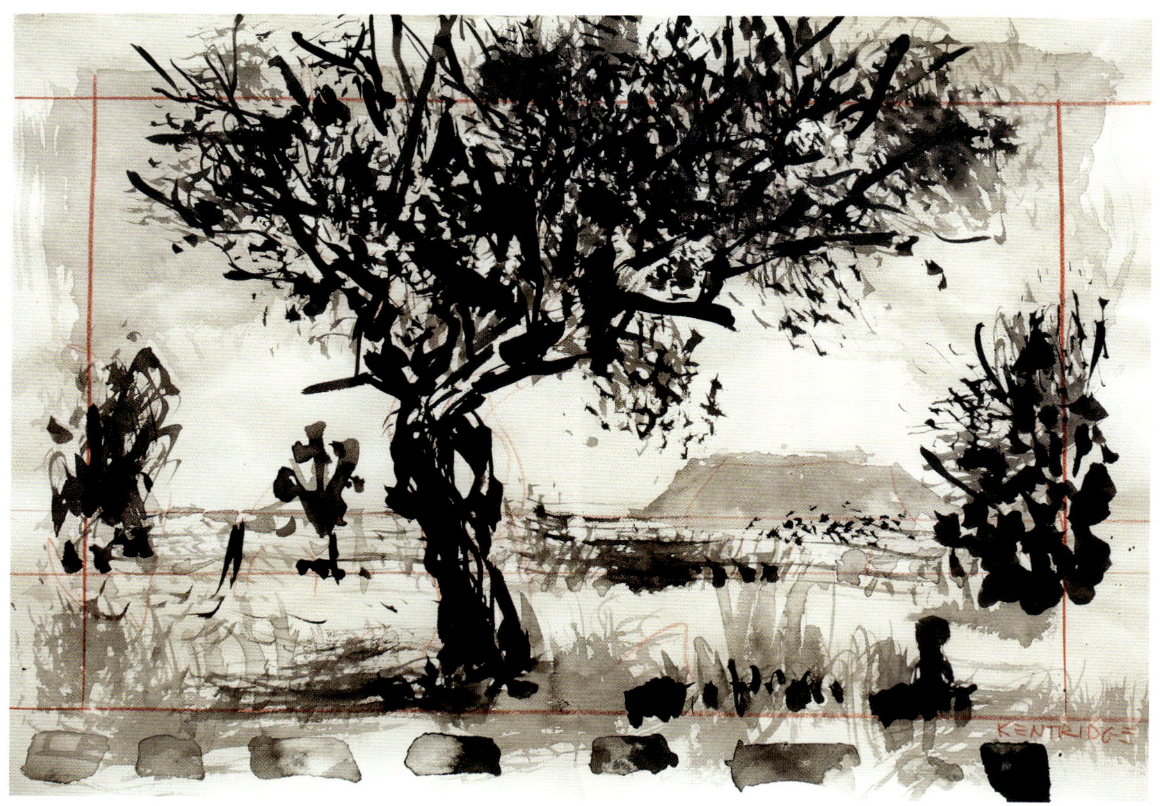

William Kentridge HON RA
Untitled (Remembering the Treason Trial)
Indian ink and red pencil on handmade paper
44 × 57 cm

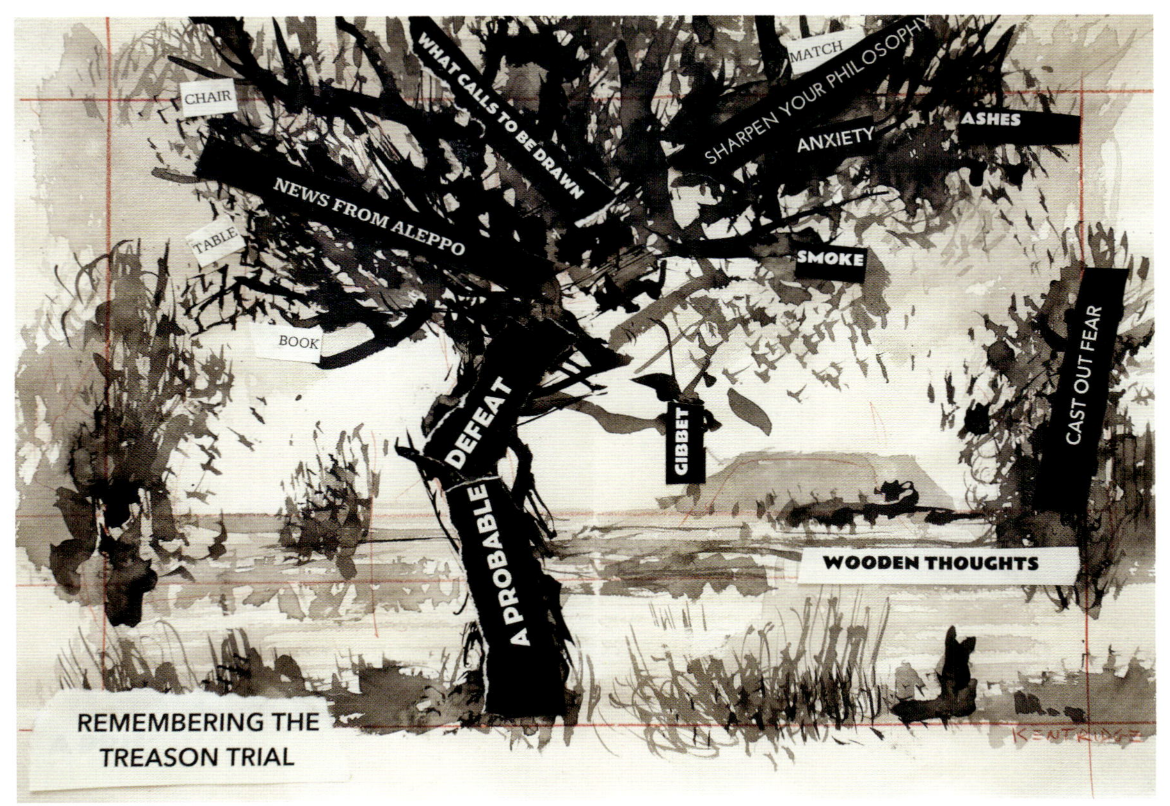

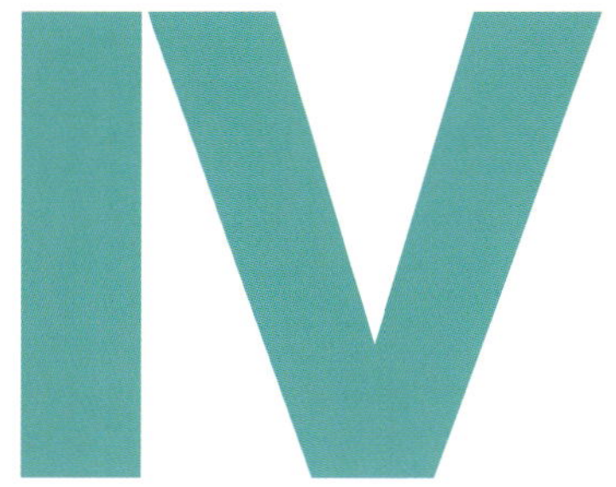

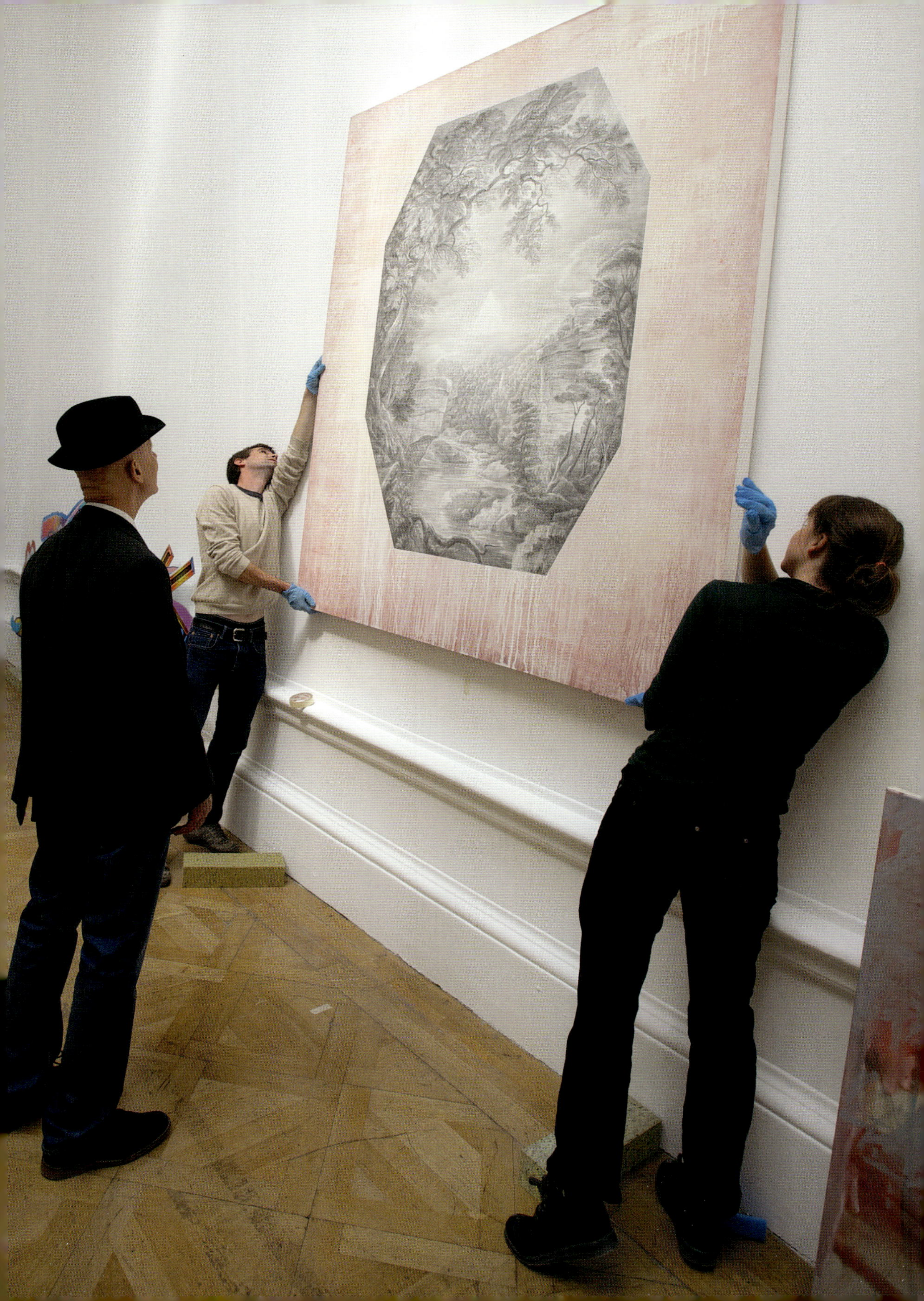

Andrew Cranston
Exercise in the Still Night
Oil
50 × 105 cm

Rita Barros
Shoe
Archival inkjet print
50 × 68 cm

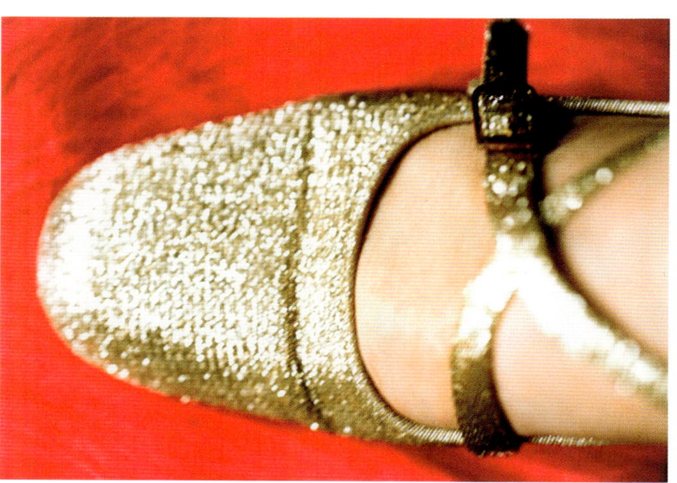

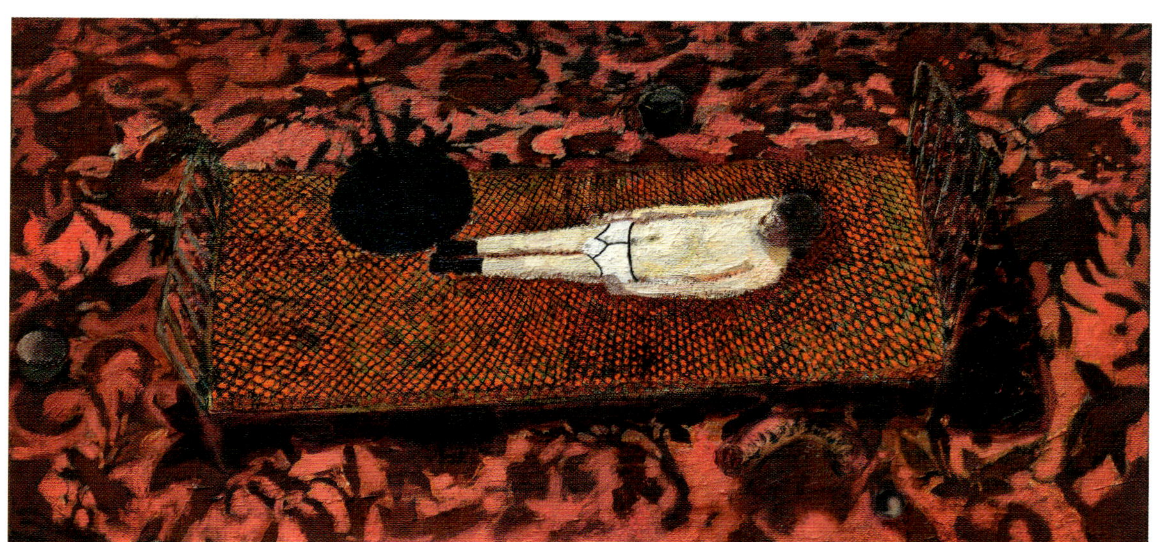

Güler Ates
Amer Fort and Orange Yellow
Archival digital print
64 × 42 cm

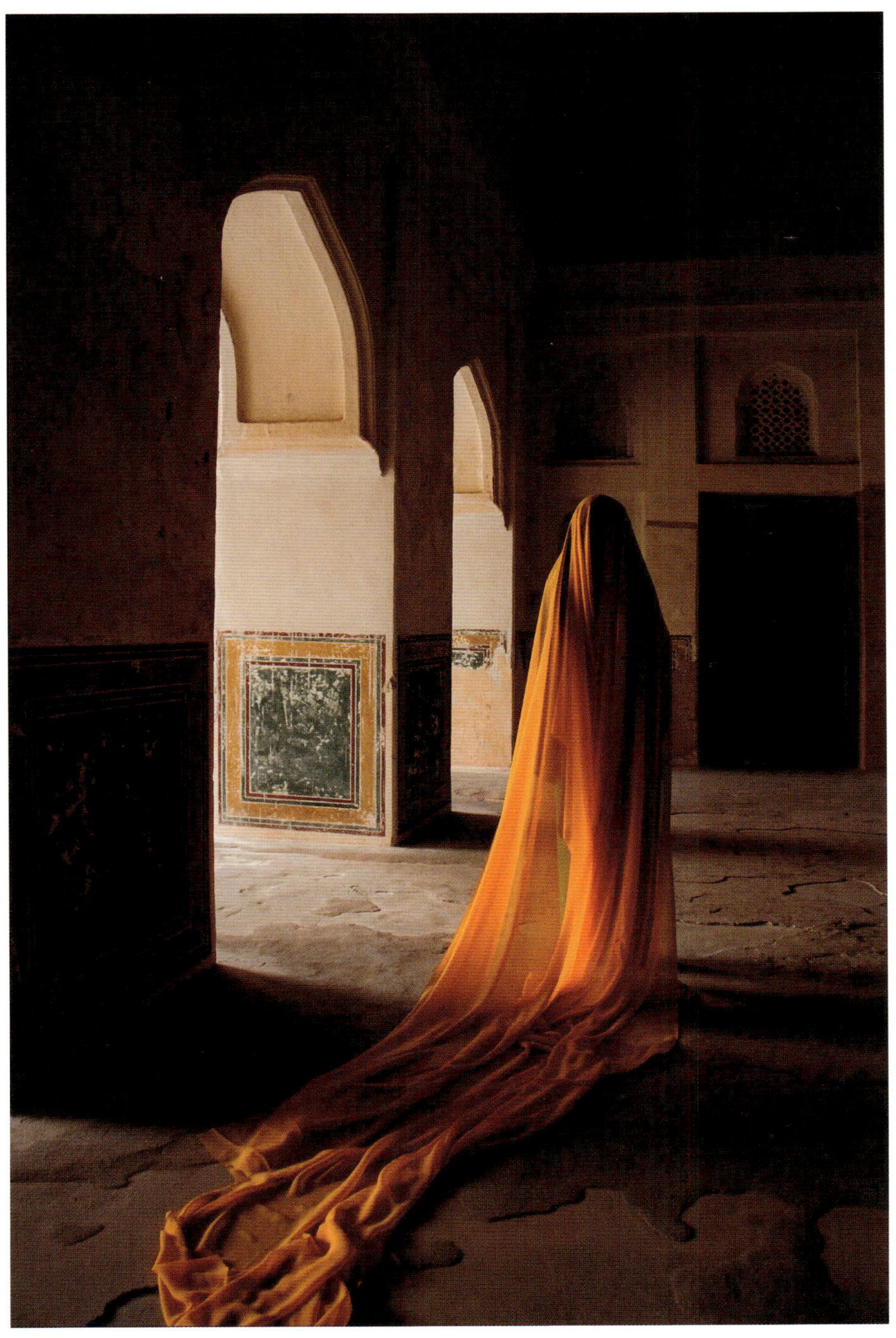

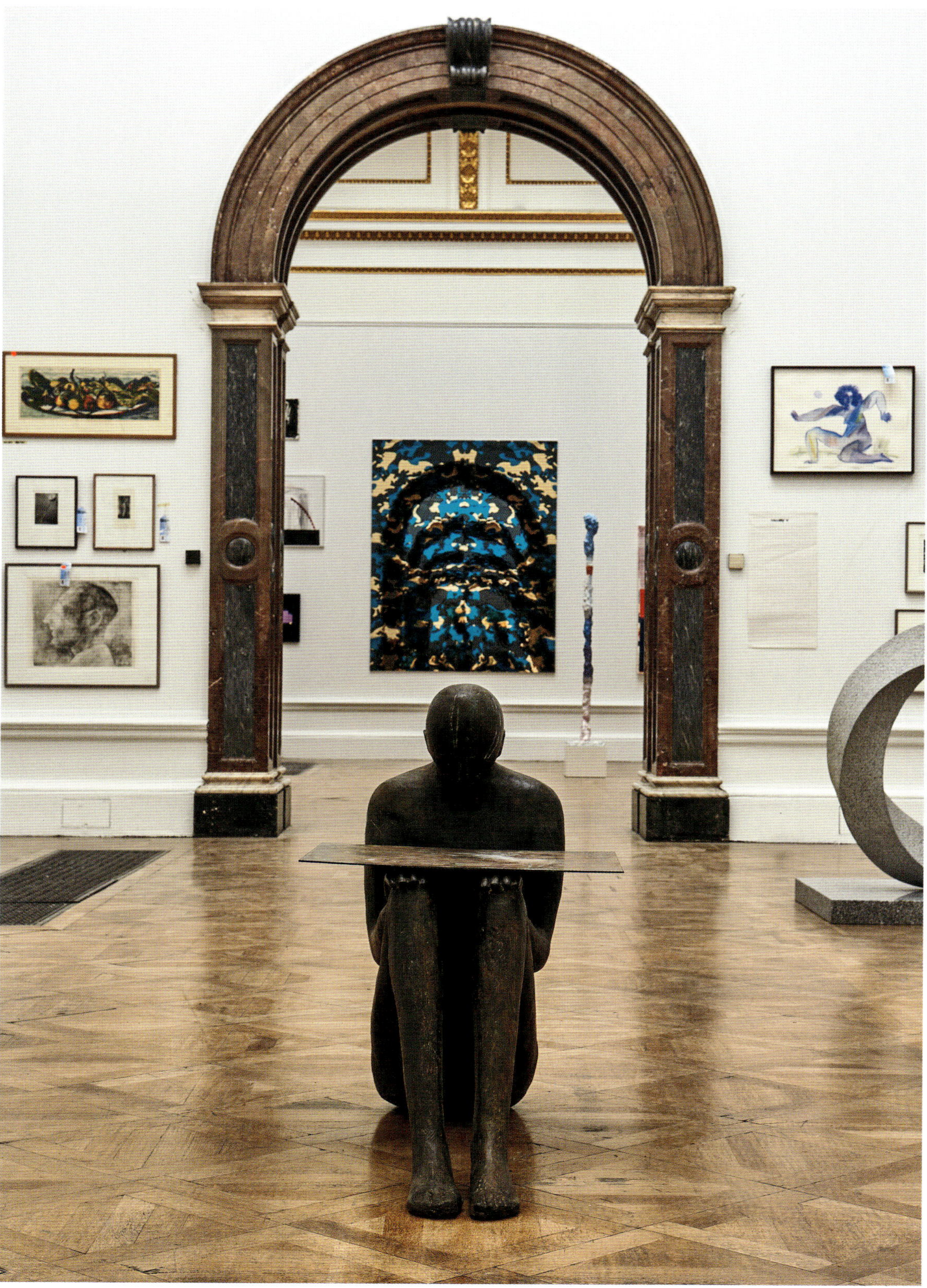

Rebecca Warren RA
Long Ago and So Far Away
Bronze
H 273 cm

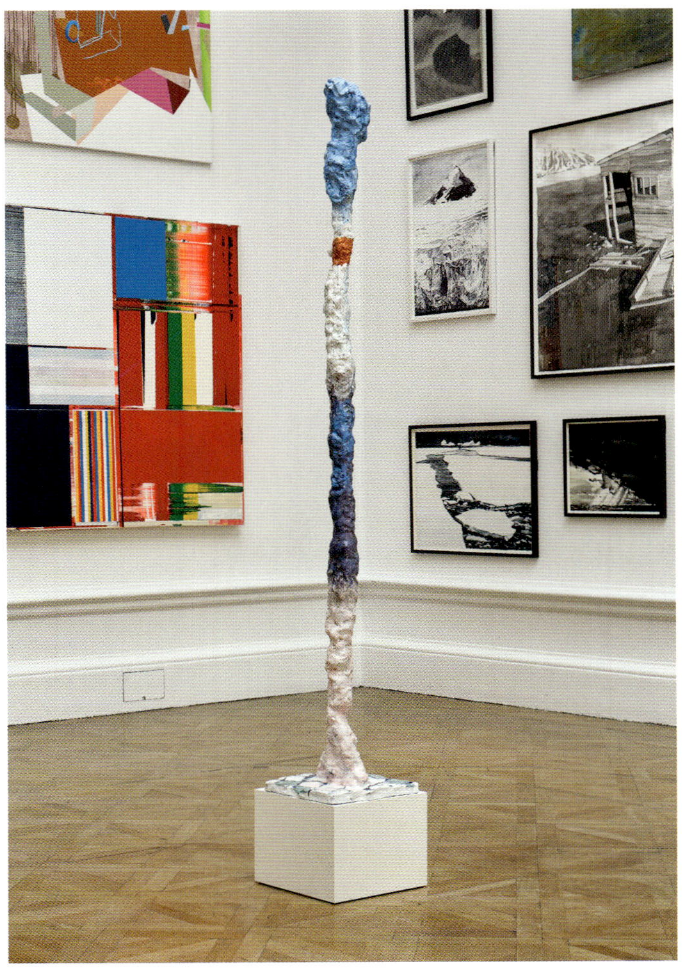

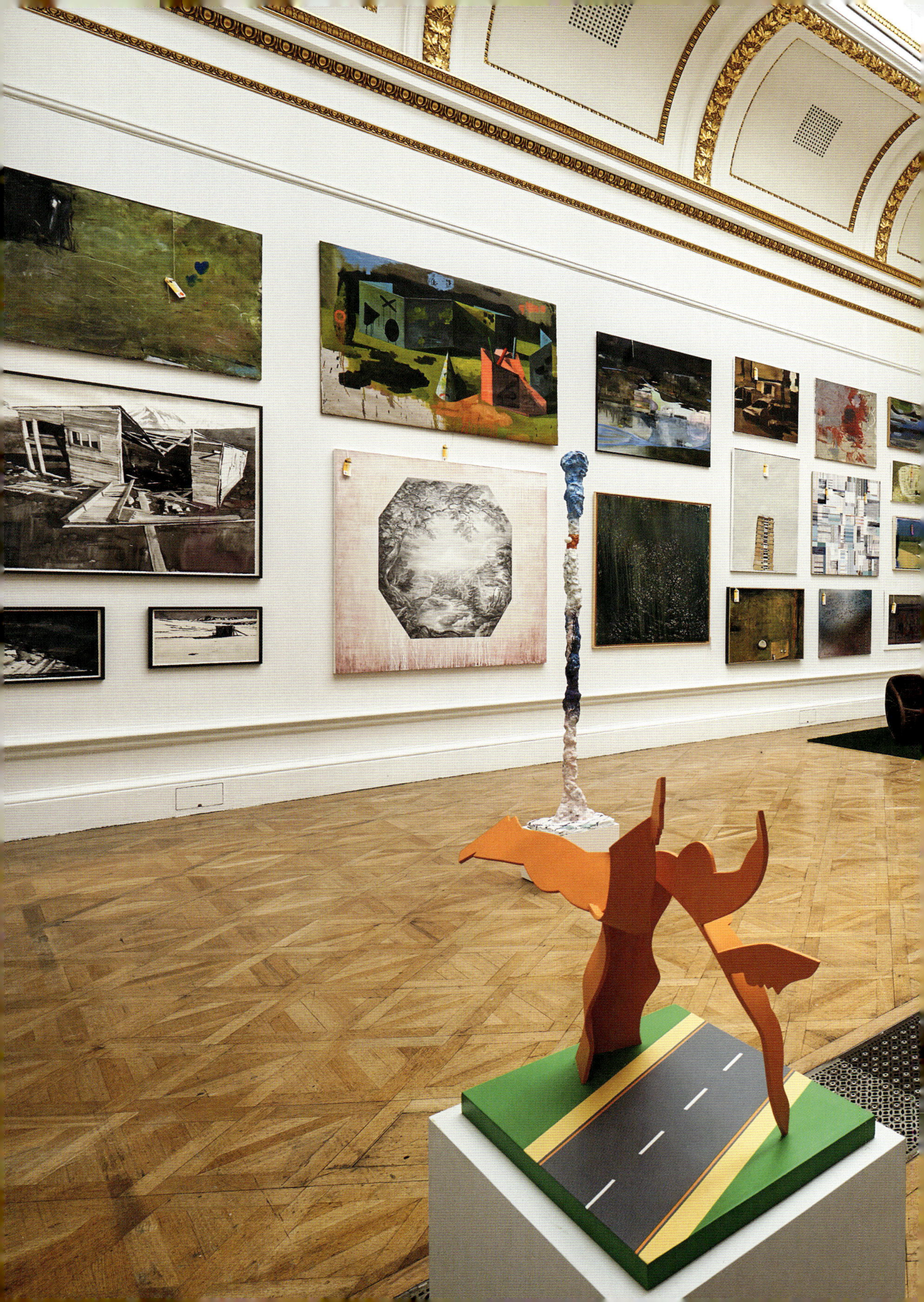

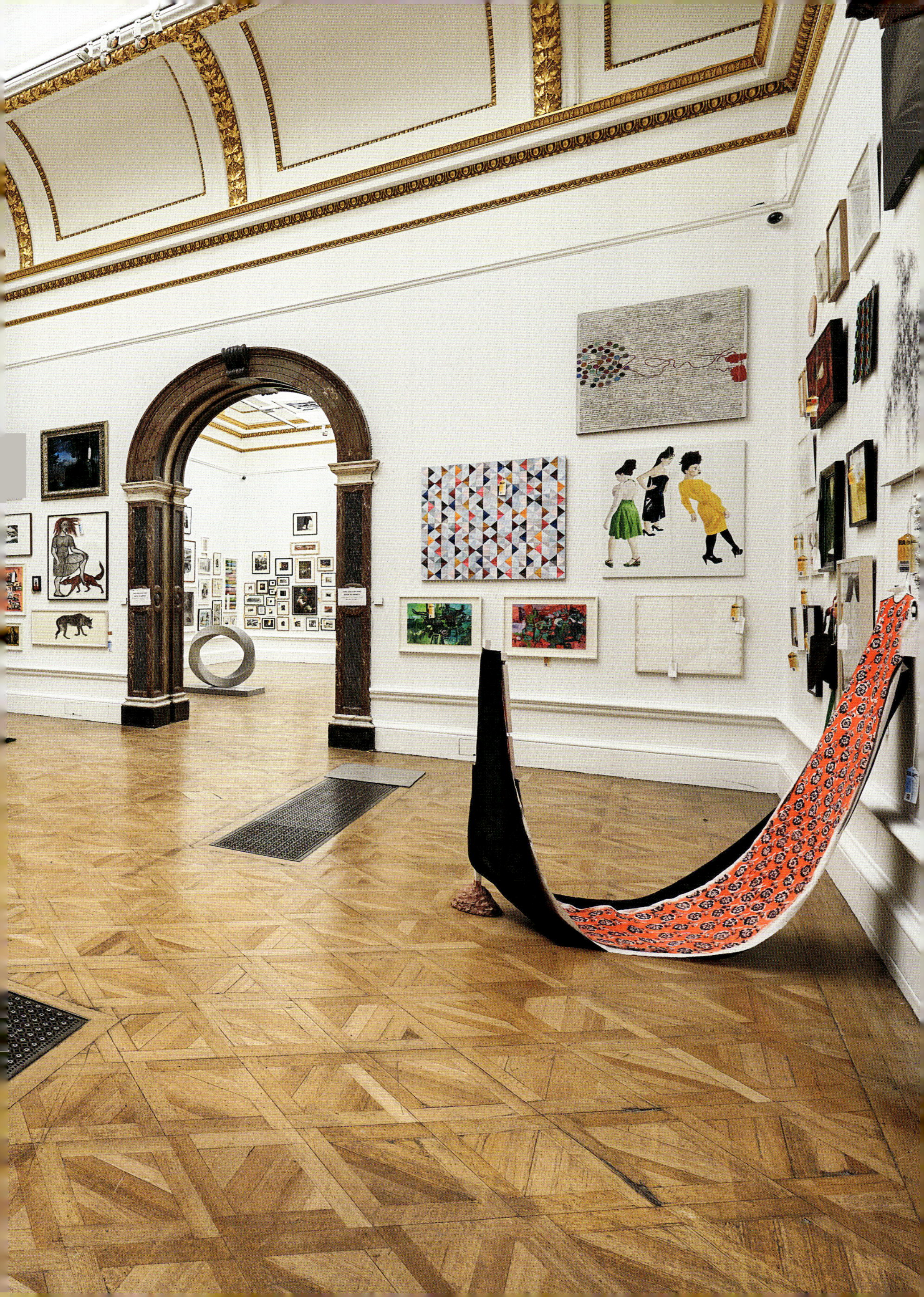

Vanessa Teperson
When Seasons Change
Oil and mixed media
122 × 152 cm

Emma Stibbon RA
Collapsed Shed, Svalbard
Ink and charcoal on paper
142 × 183 cm

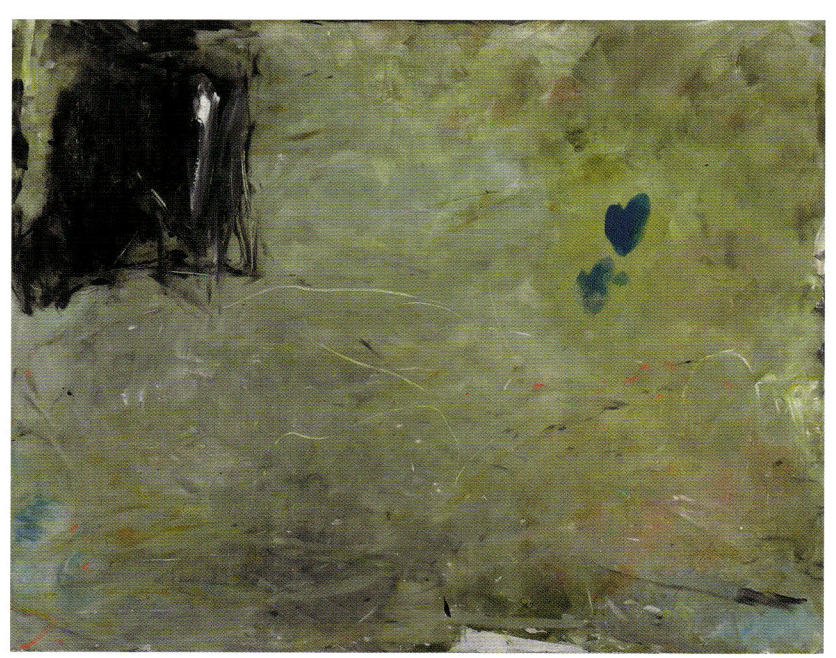

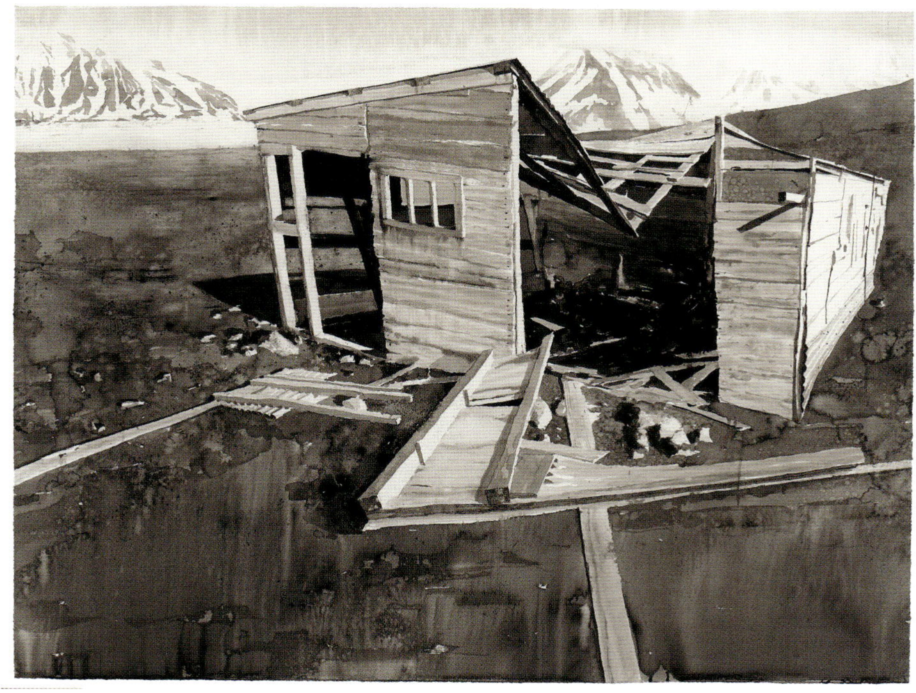

Ermioni Avramidou
Rainfall
Acrylic and ink on paper
168 × 141 cm

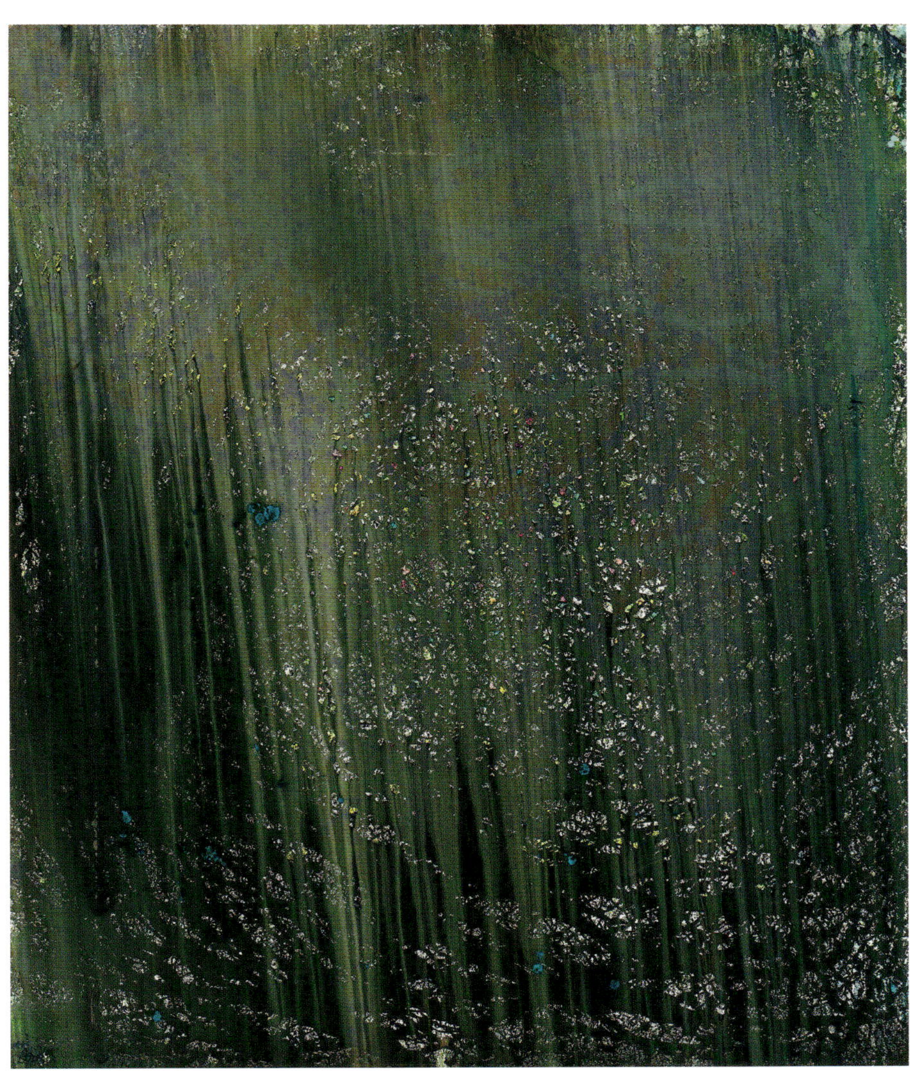

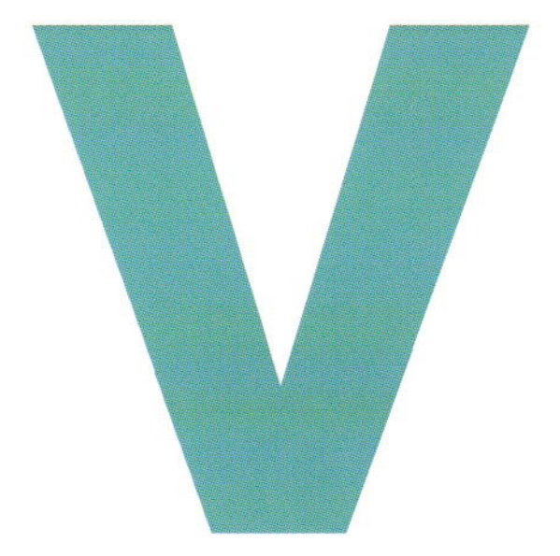

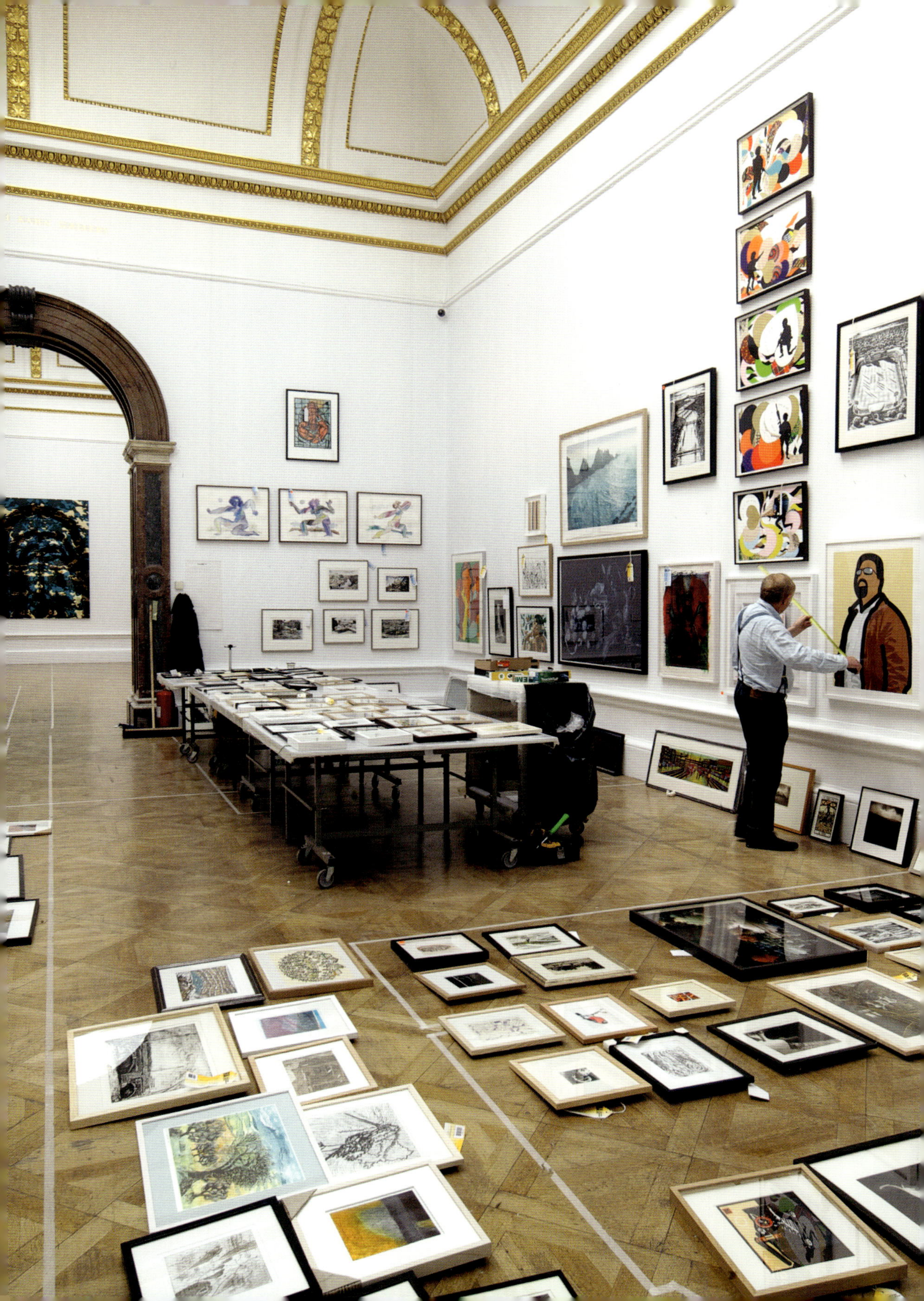

John Duffin
Thames Bridges East
Etching
80 × 46 cm

Prof Sir Quentin Blake CBE RDI
Big Healthy Girl II
Watercolour pastel
56 × 76 cm

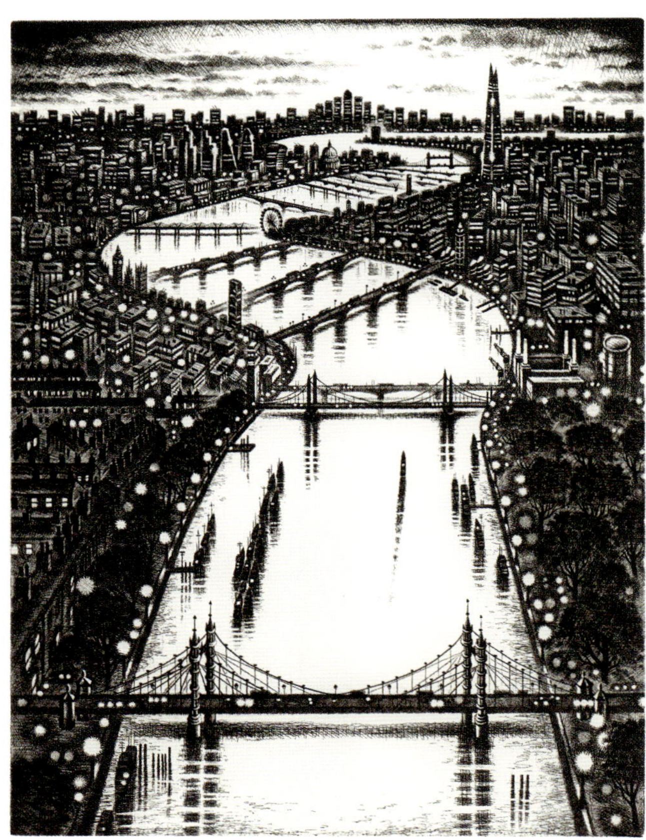

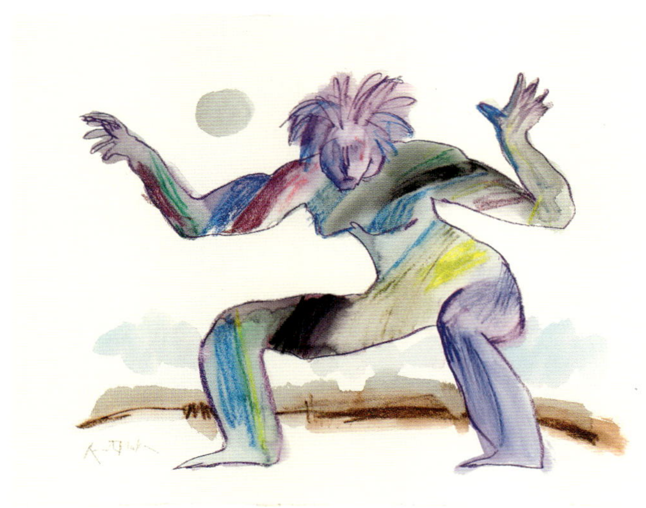

Julian Opie
Walking in the Rain, Seoul
Screenprint
150 × 220 cm

Yinka Shonibare MBE RA
Love in a Time of War 2
Digital print with gold leaf on Somerset Velvet 330 gsm paper
49 × 66 cm

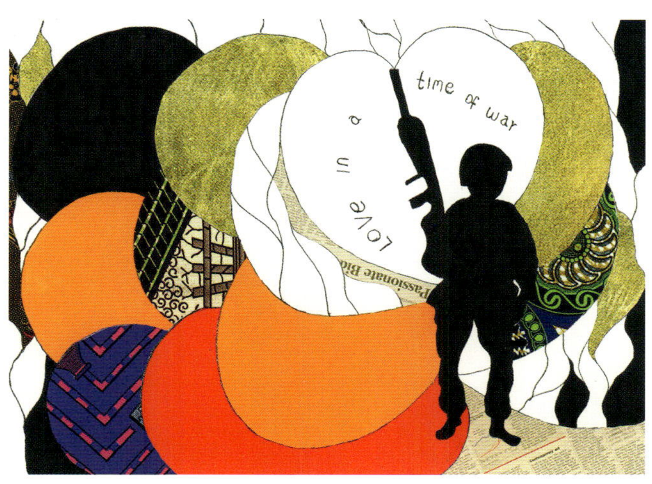

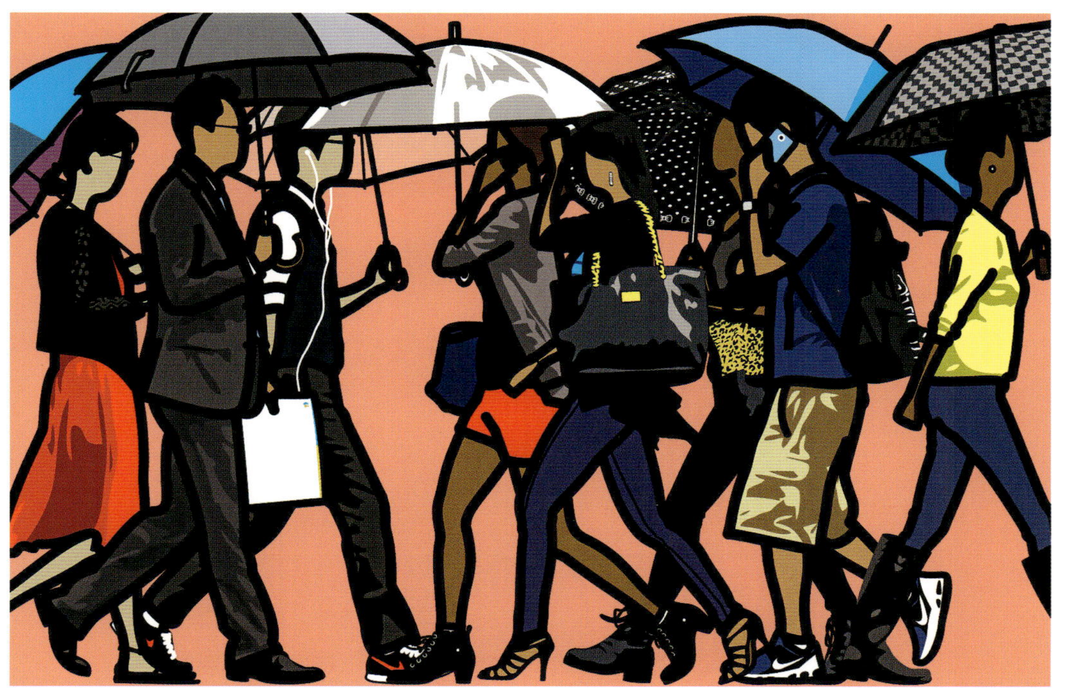

Sally McKay
Rapidly Scrawled Life
Etching and sugarlift
14 × 18 cm

Cornelia Parker OBE RA
Stolen Thunder III
Print
78 × 78 cm

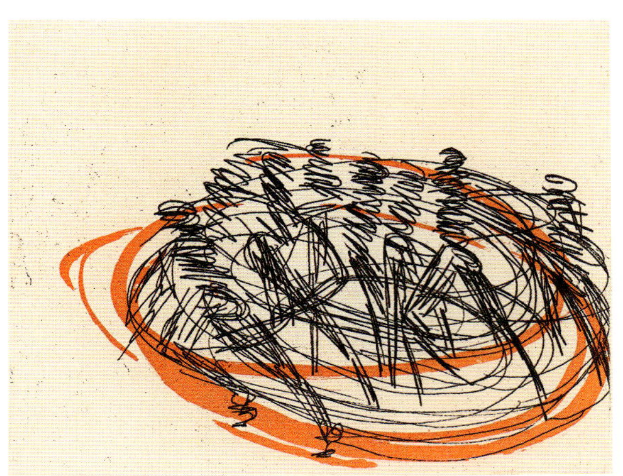

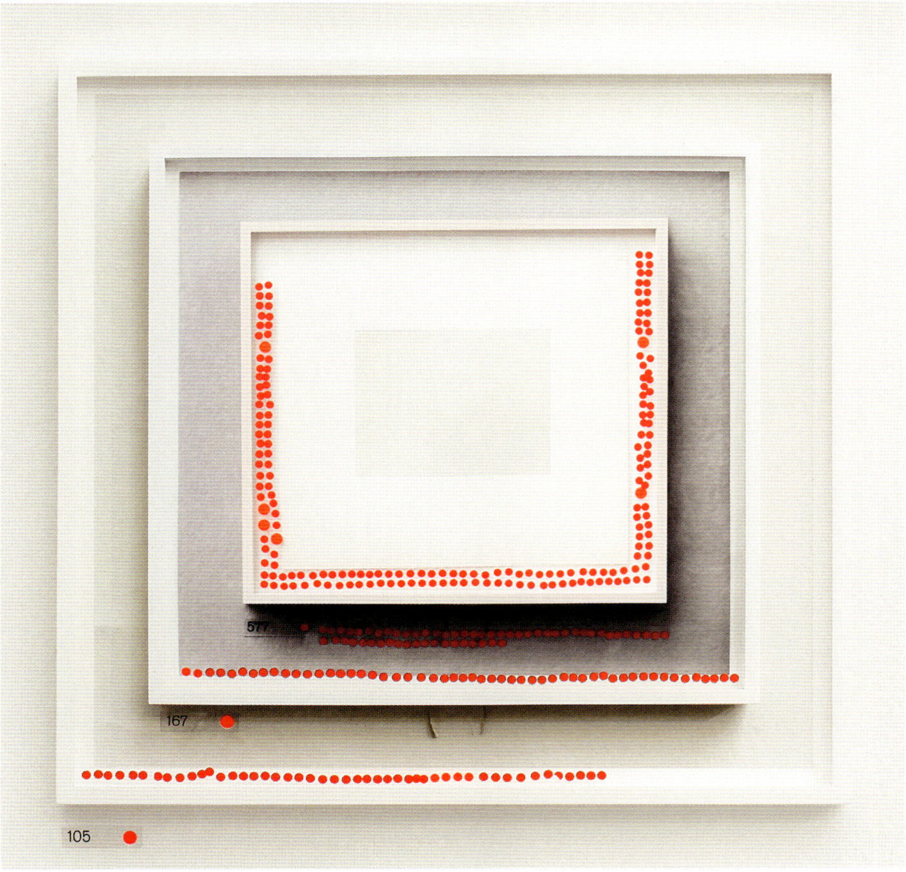

Prof Ian McKeever RA
Eagduru Study (IN2014-134)
Mixed media
24 × 36 cm

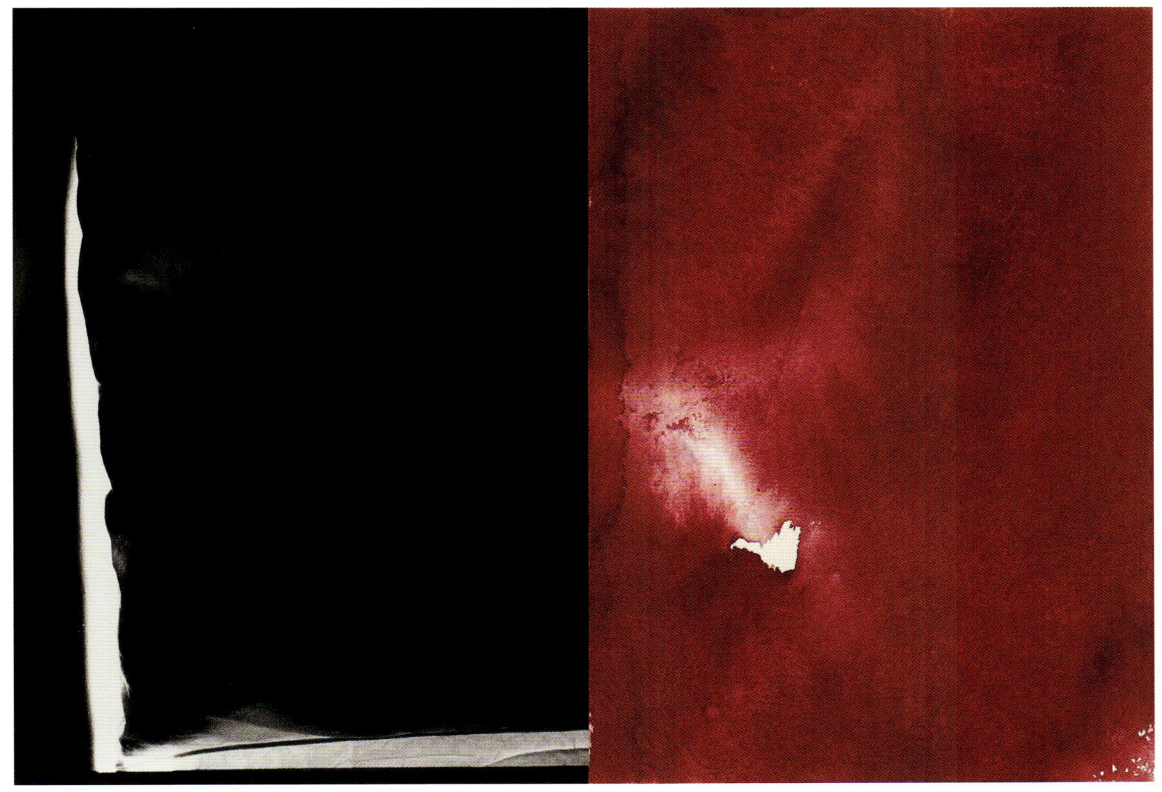

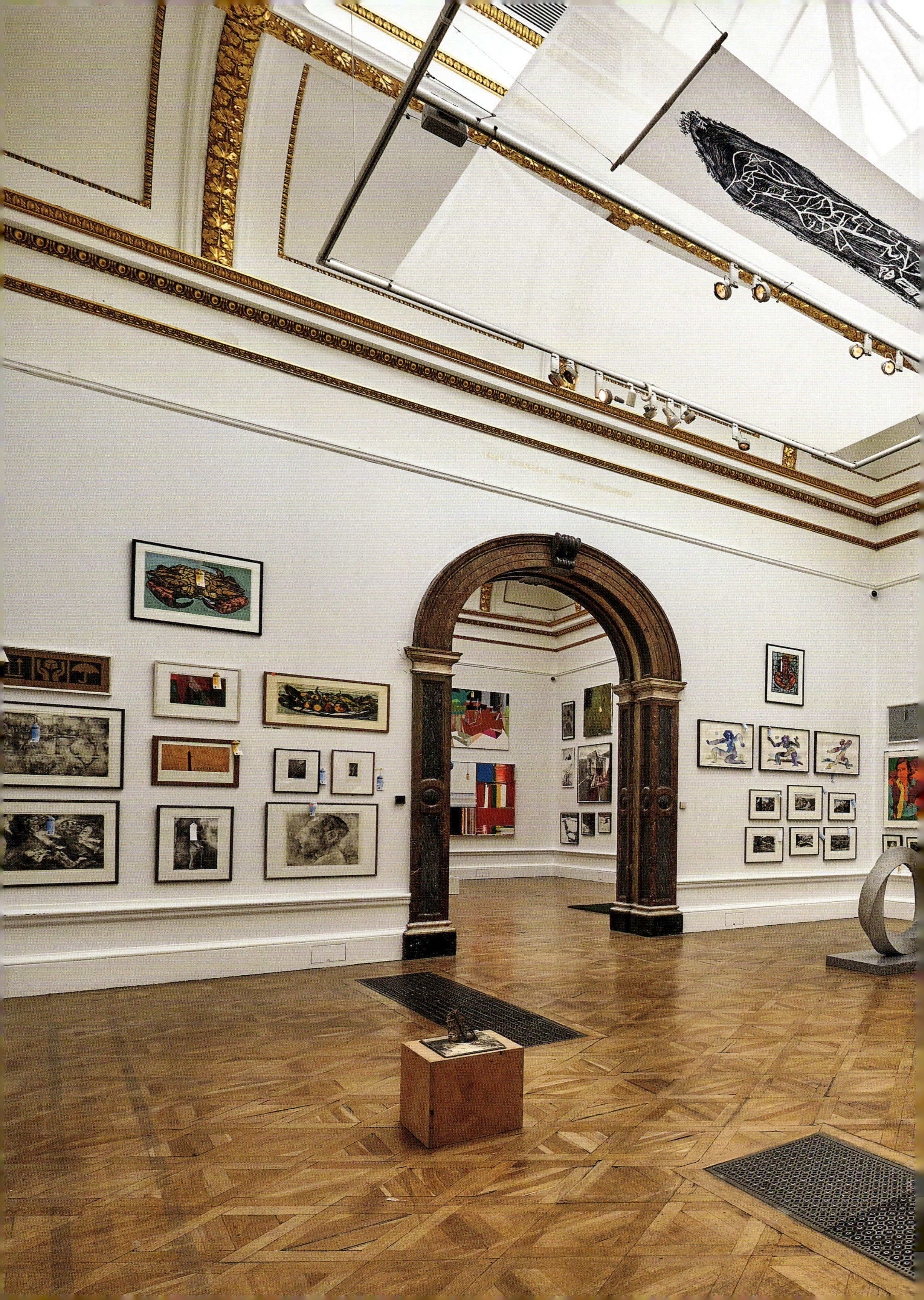

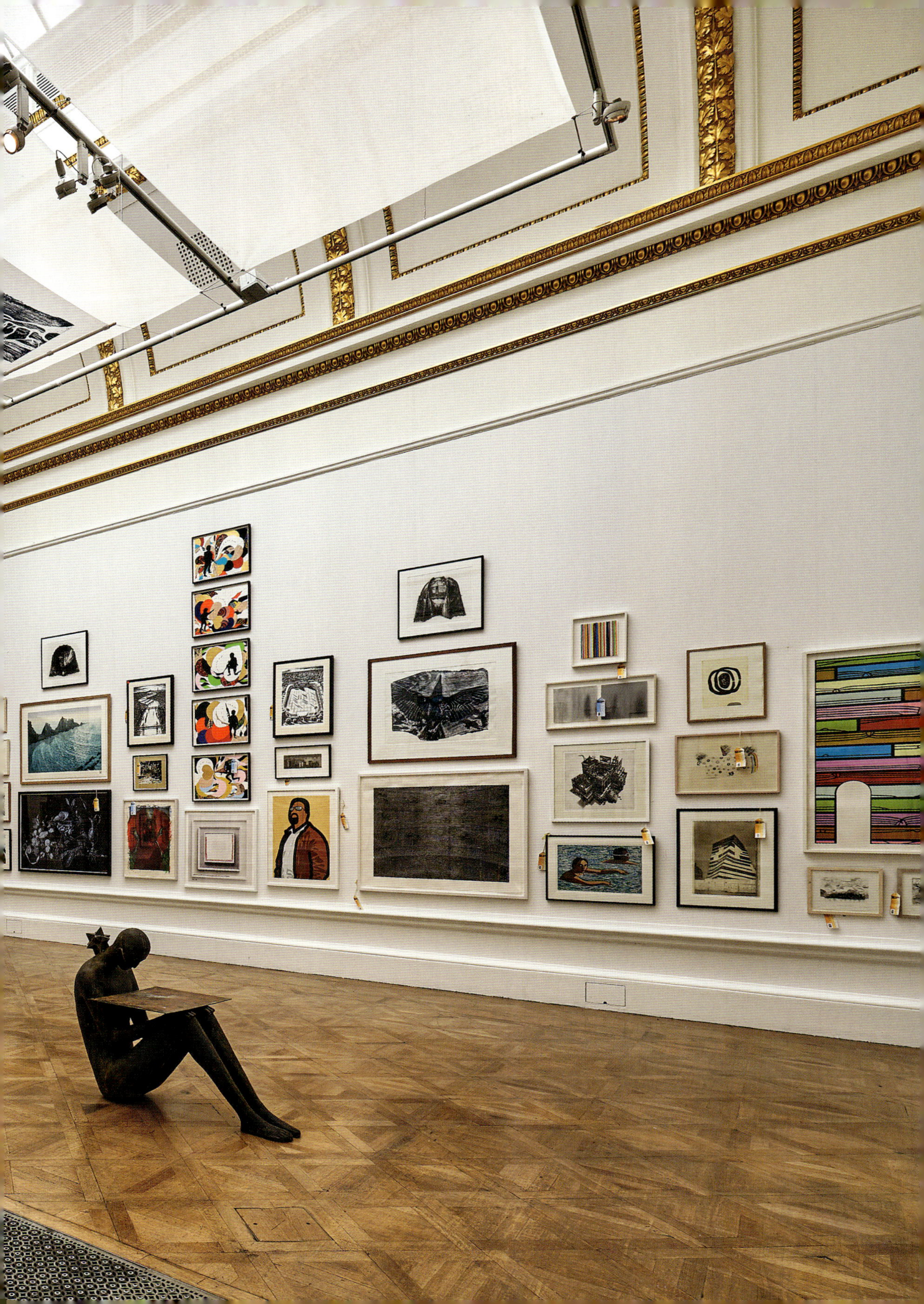

Hilary Daltry
Eden Valley Apples
Woodcut
31 × 80 cm

Peter Freeth RA
Dreamer
Aquatint
55 × 62 cm

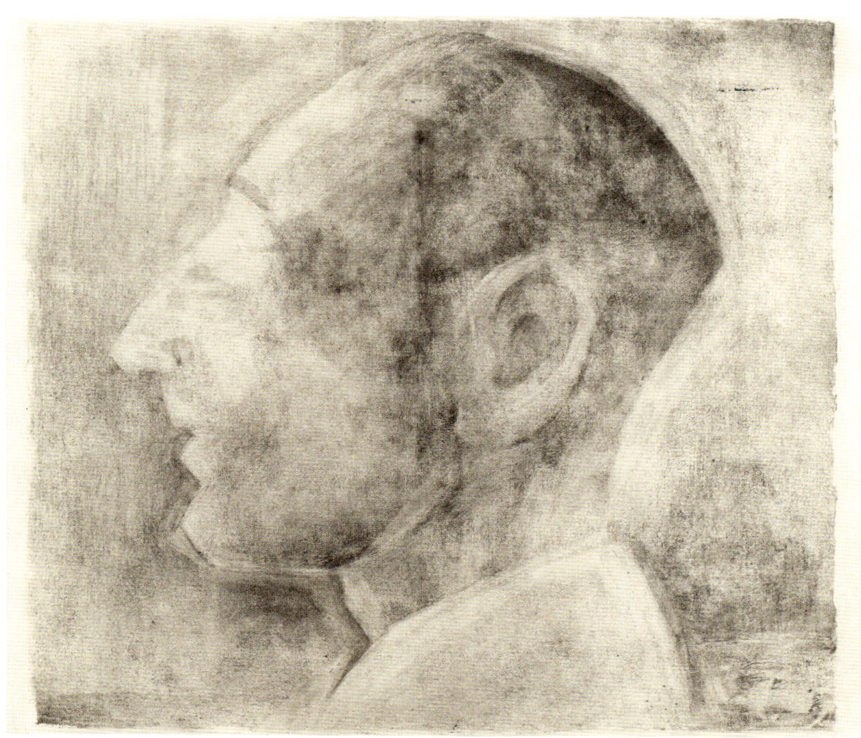

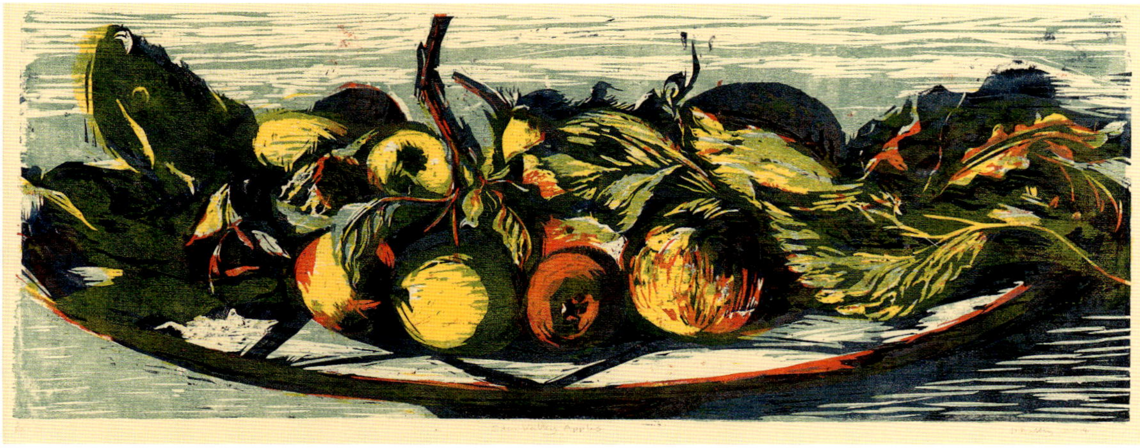

Anne Desmet RA
Grasshopper
Wood engraving
24 × 34 cm

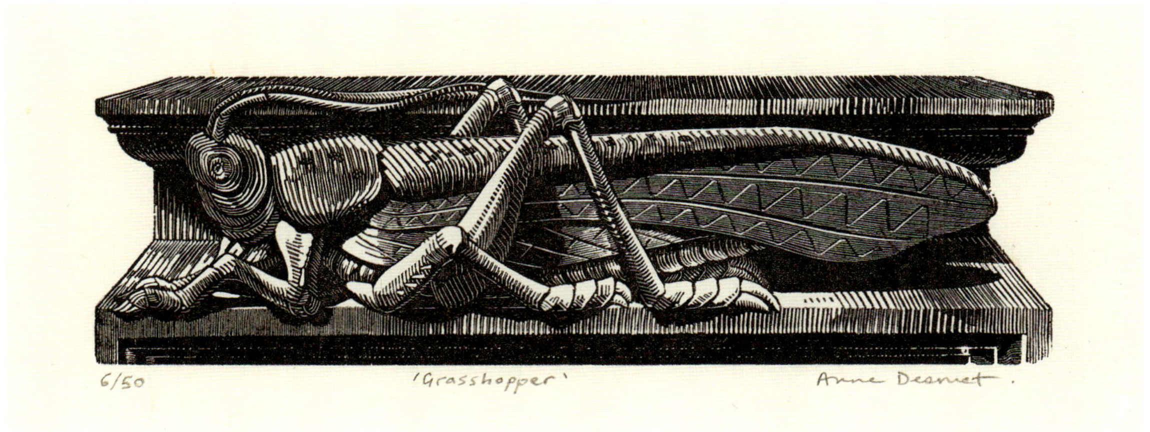

Dr Jennifer Dickson RA
The Fishers of Hadspen Garden
Archival inkjet and watercolour print
51 × 62 cm

Howard Phipps
Dorset Coast, Seacombe
Wood engraving
11 × 15 cm

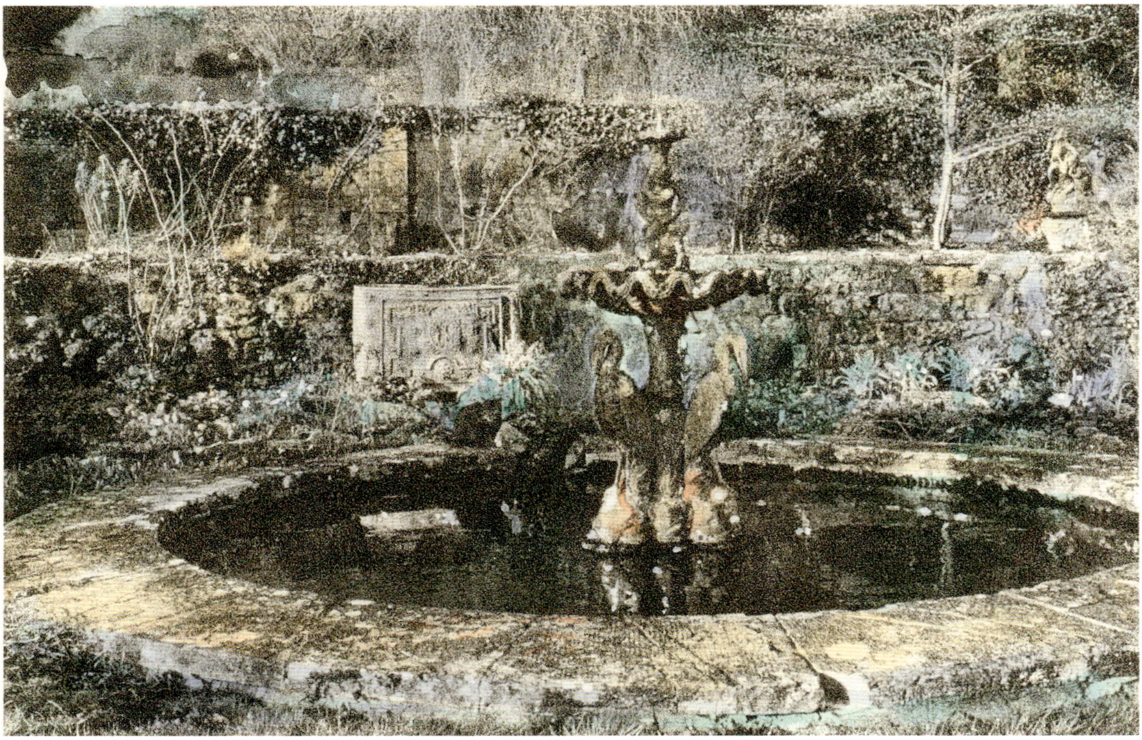

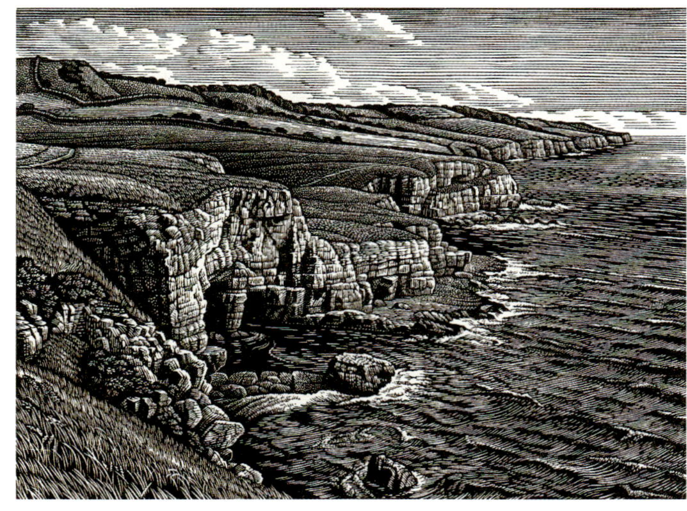

Elliot Melvin
Broad Street, Virginia
Woodcut
21 × 27 cm

Irmgard Parth
Descent to Vent
Woodcut
66 × 49 cm

Rosemary Farrer
Track
Woodblock
15 × 15 cm

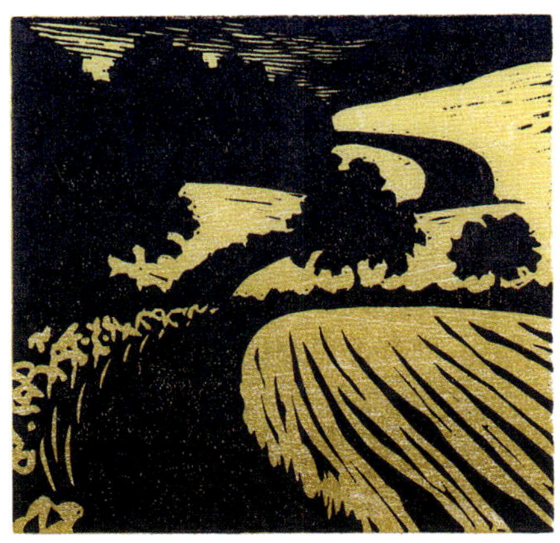

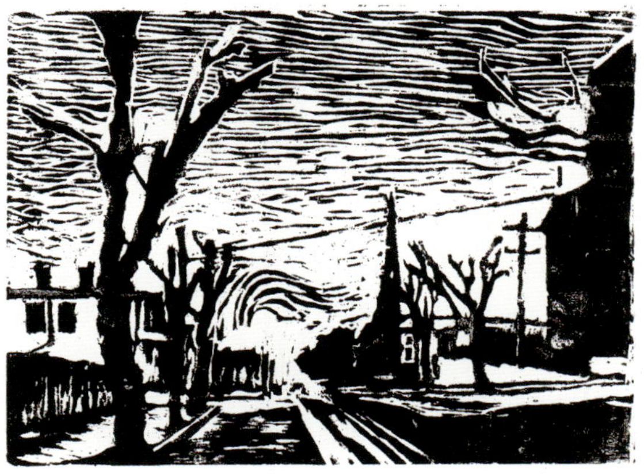

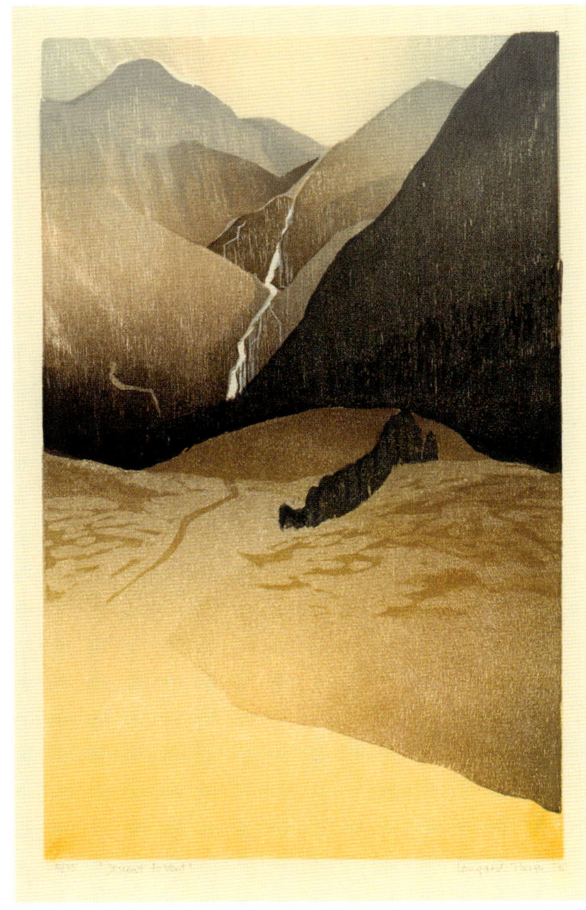

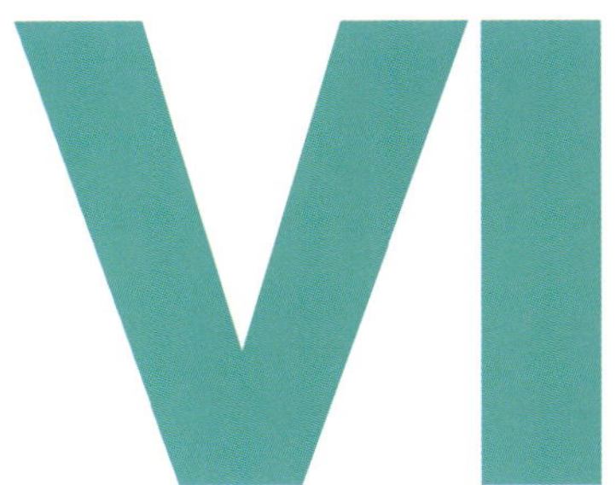

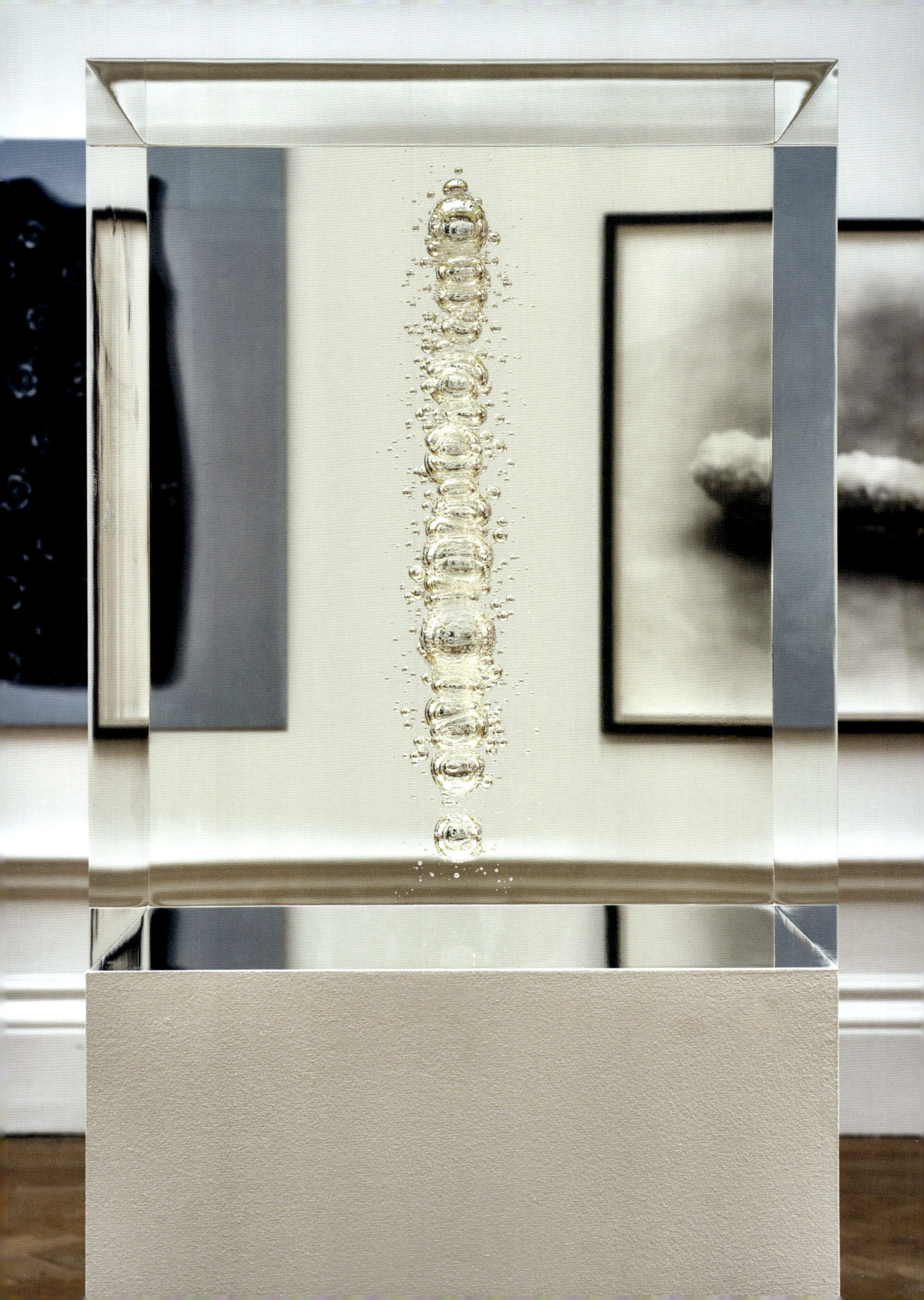

Prof Fiona Rae RA
Figure 1
Oil and acrylic
183 × 129 cm

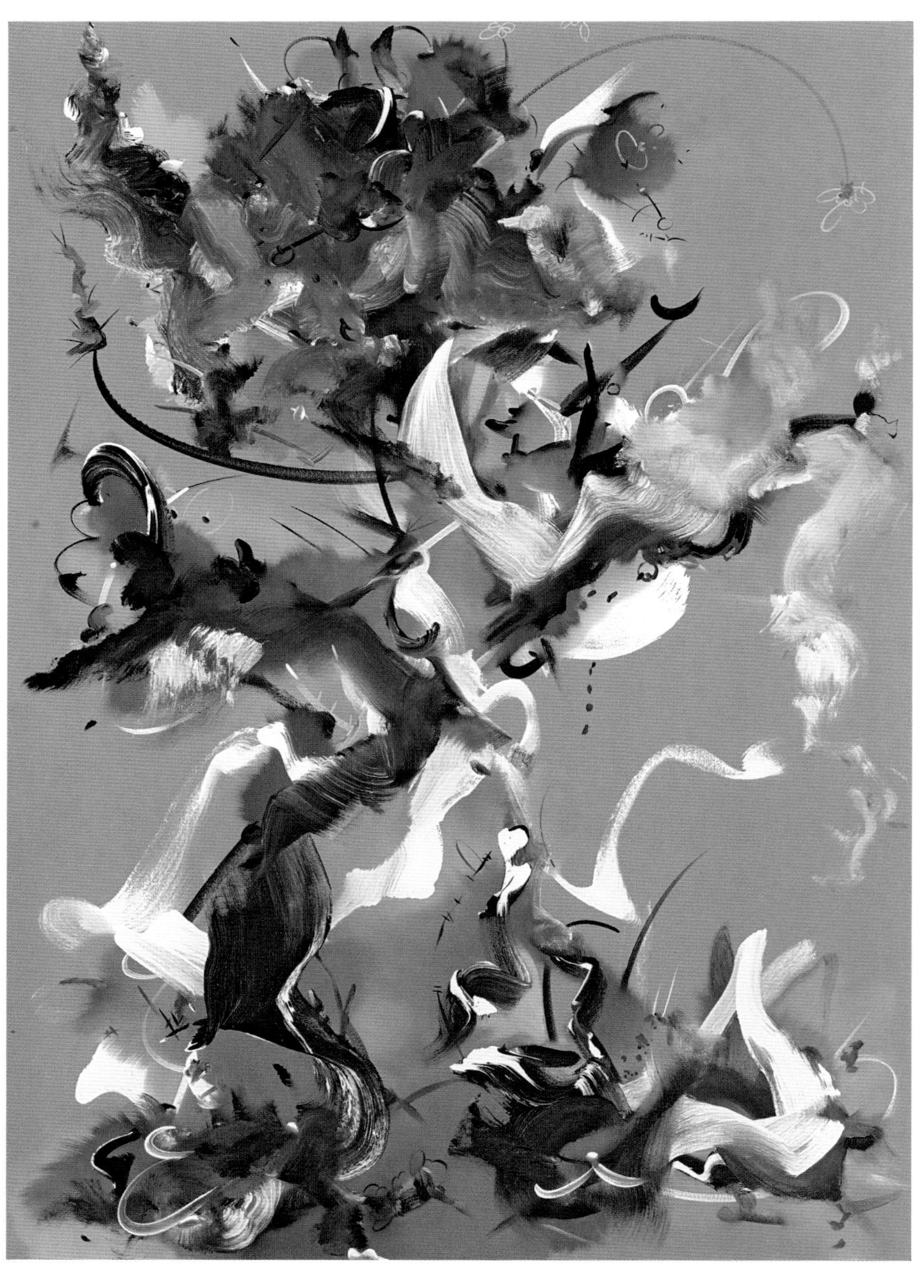

Rose Hilton
Red Studio
Oil
122 × 122 cm

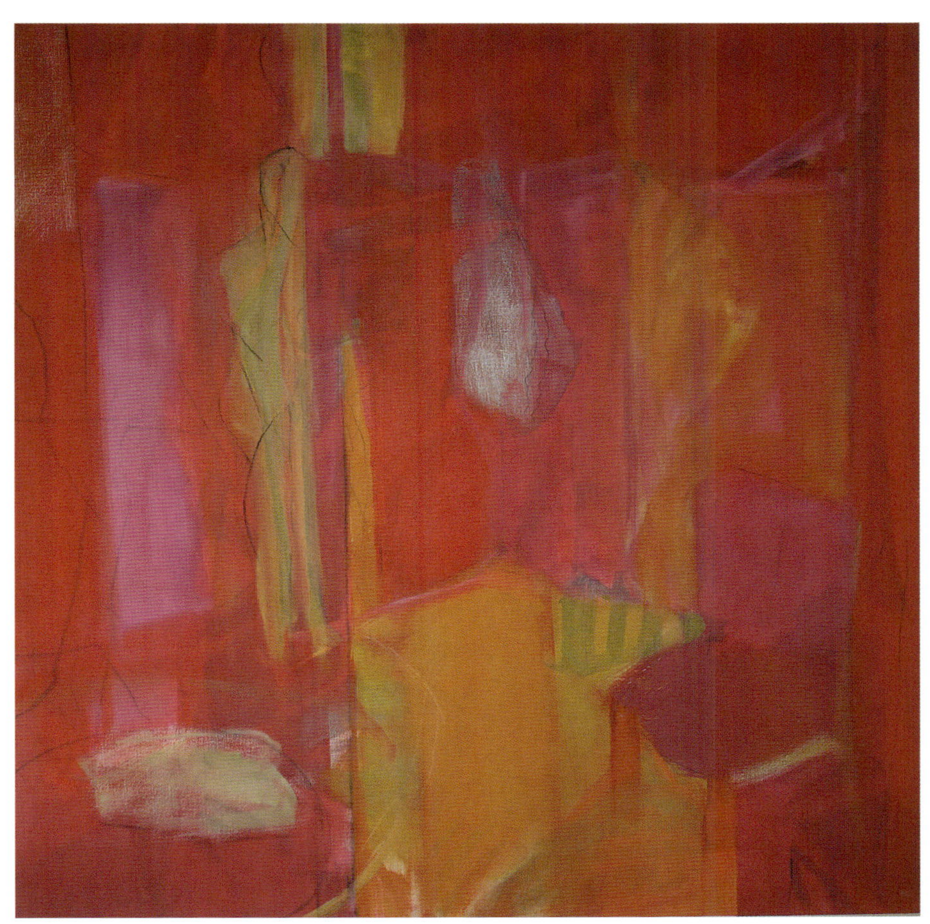

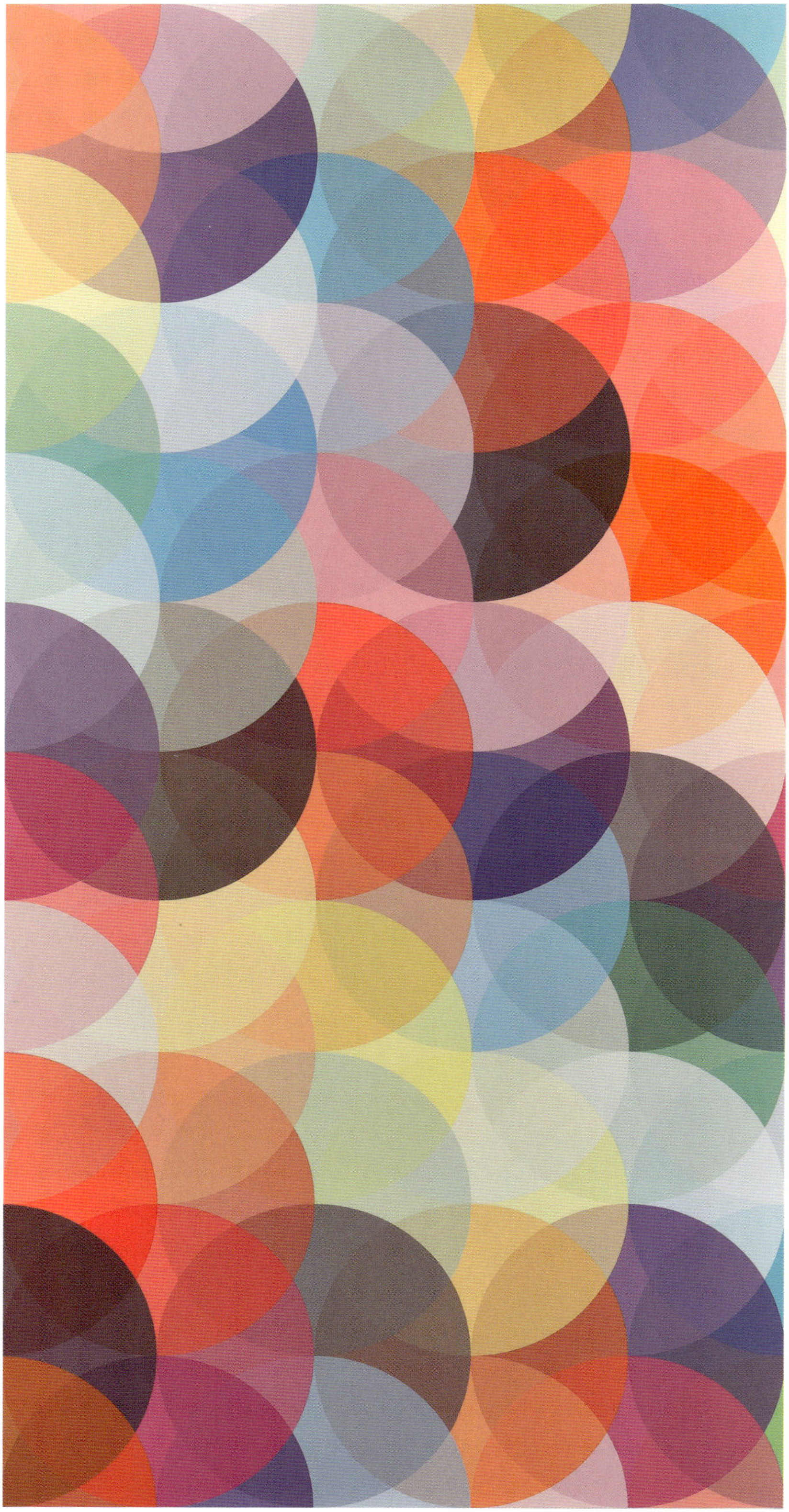

Tim Head
Fictions 3 (Invisible Cities)
UV inkjet print on acrylic
250 × 125 cm

Jon Thompson
Sponge (From the Lyotard Suite)
Oil and acrylic
190 × 155 cm

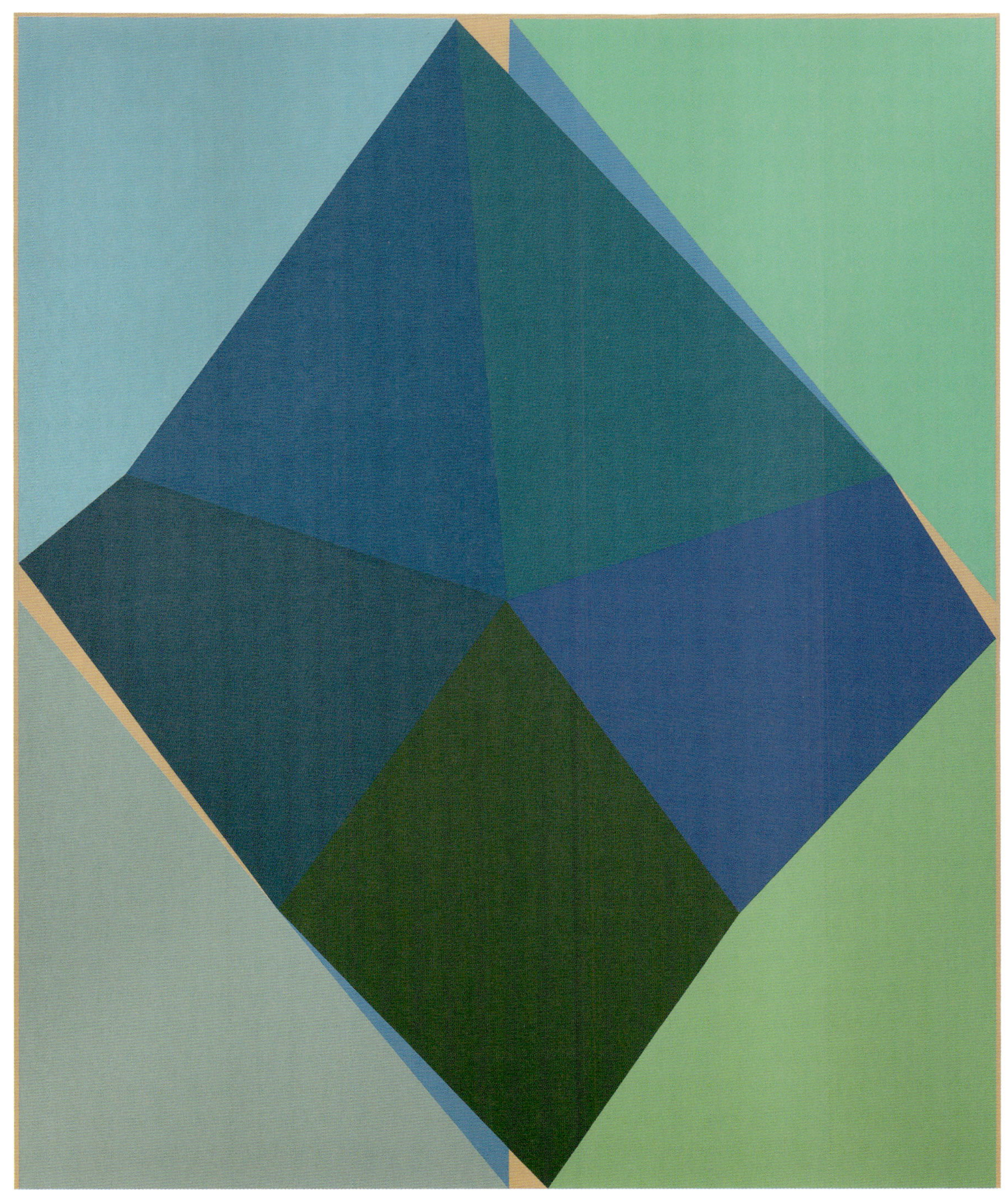

Lisa Milroy RA
Black Dress
Oil
152 × 104 cm

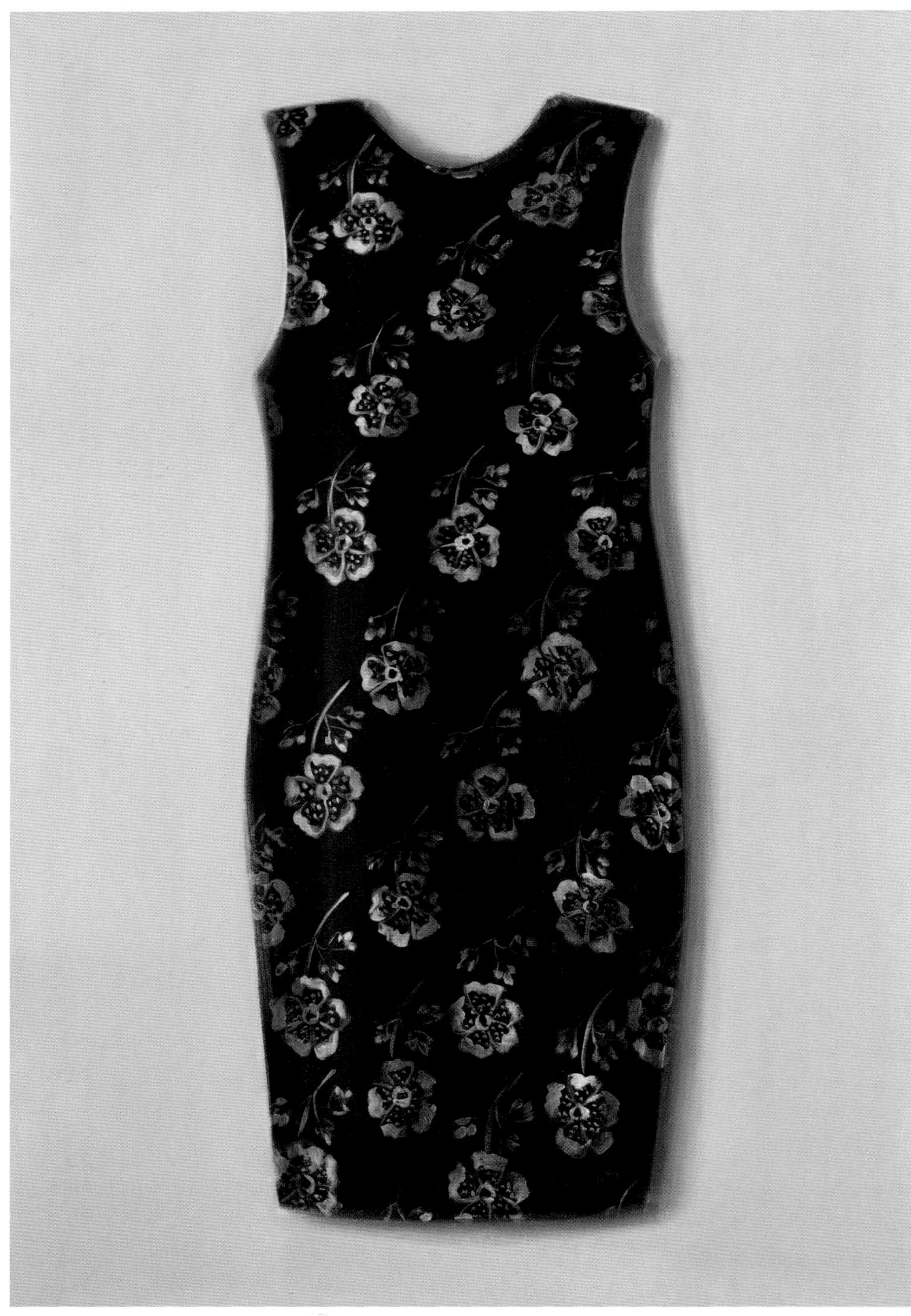

John Hilliard
Height, Distance and Possession
Pigment print
107 × 140 cm

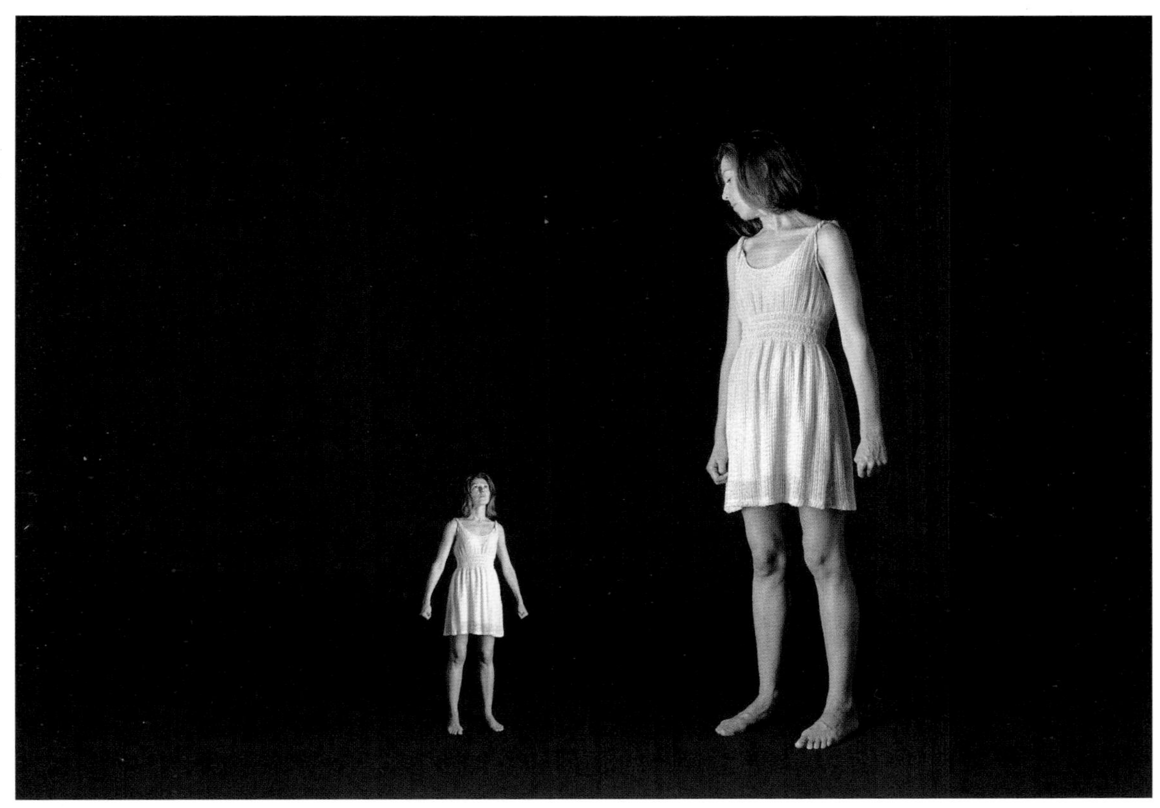

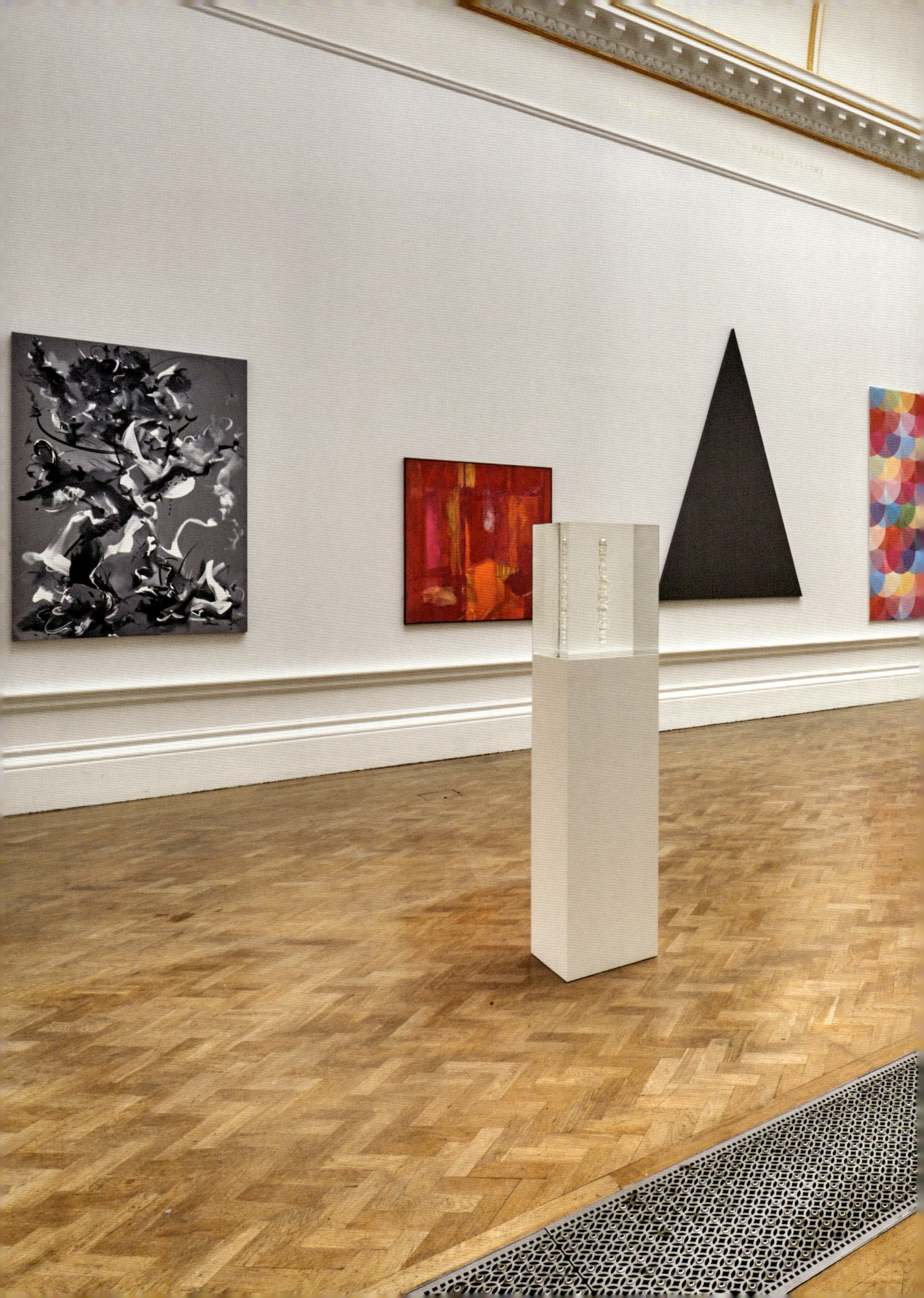

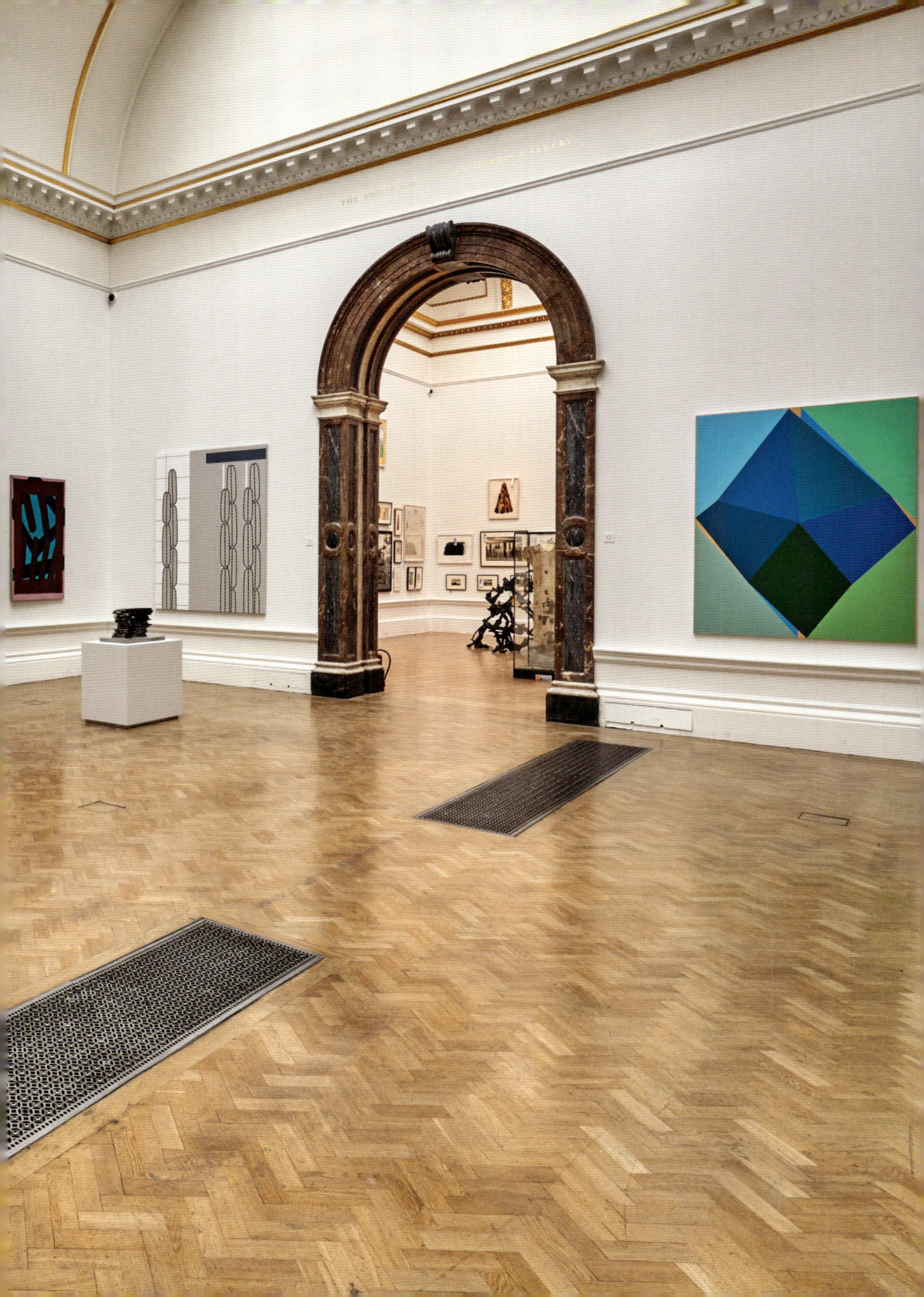

Gary Hume RA
The Blue Ground
Gloss on aluminium
166 × 124 cm

Alan Charlton
Triangle Painting
Acrylic
244 × 180 cm

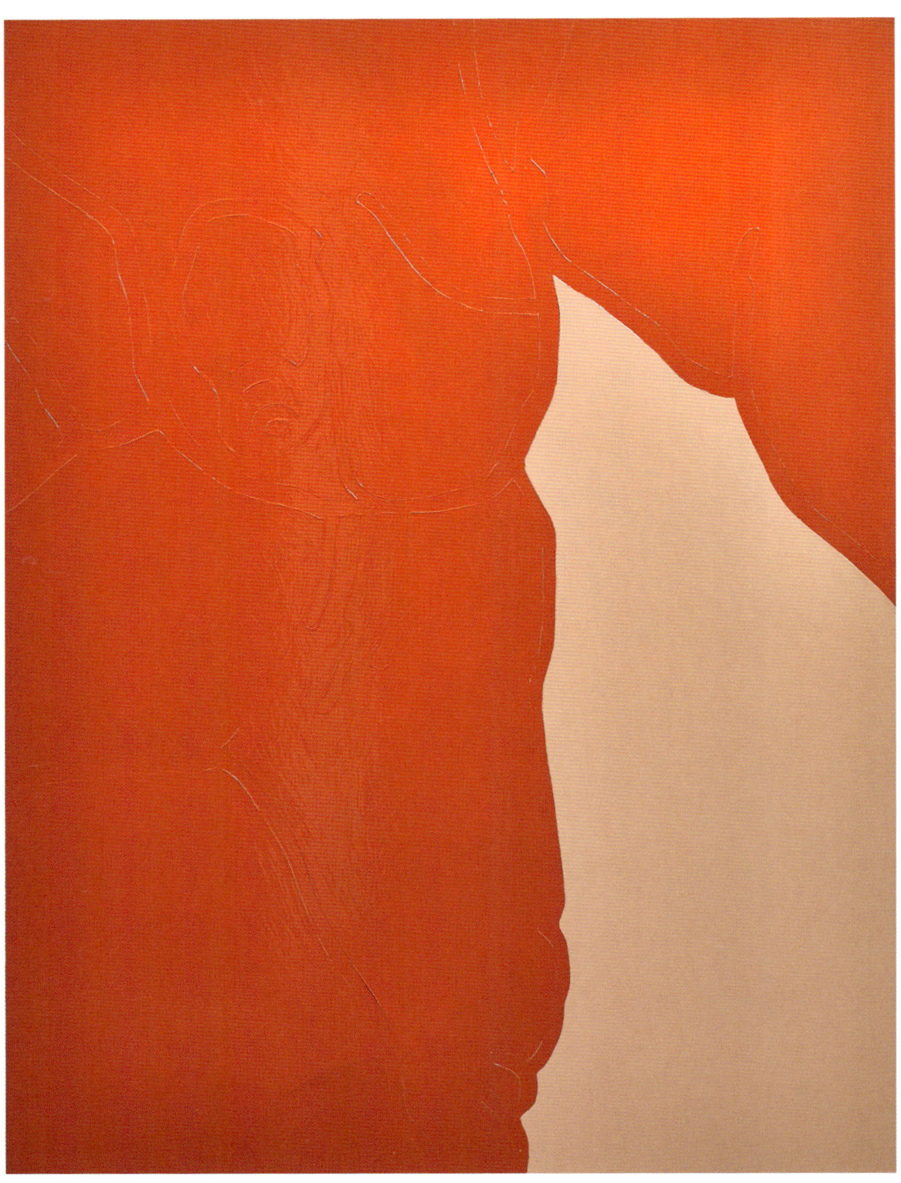

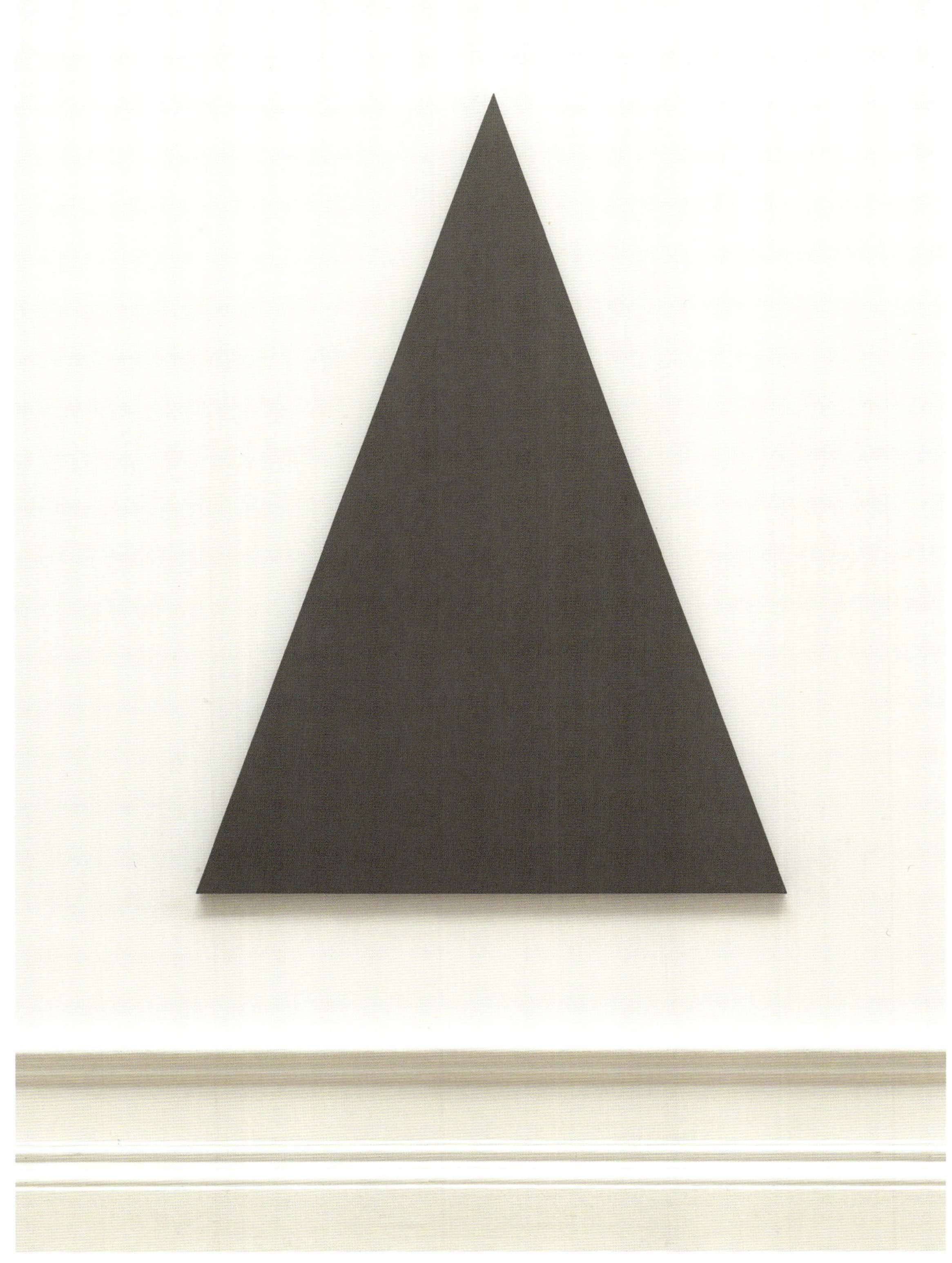

Gerard Hemsworth
Screen
Acrylic
200 × 175 cm

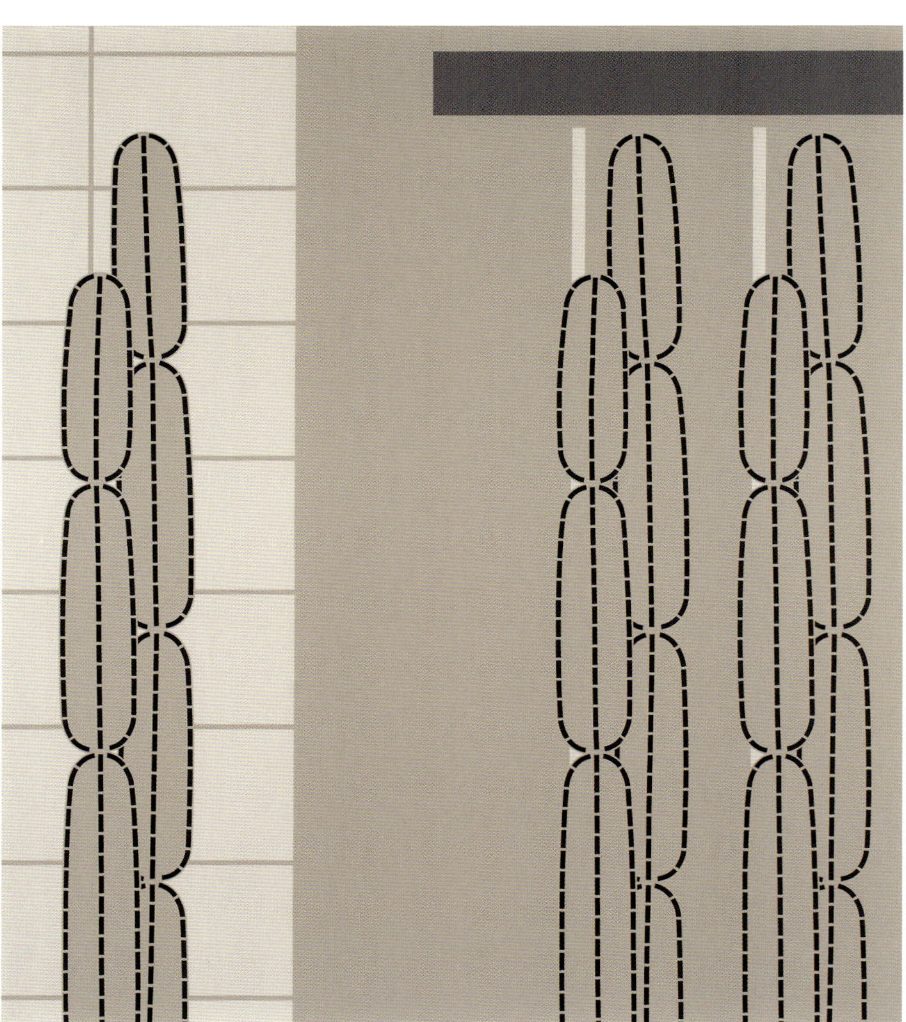

Tacita Dean OBE RA
The Tail End of Film
Photograph
133 × 169 cm

Richard Smith
In House
Acrylic on linen
152 × 115 cm

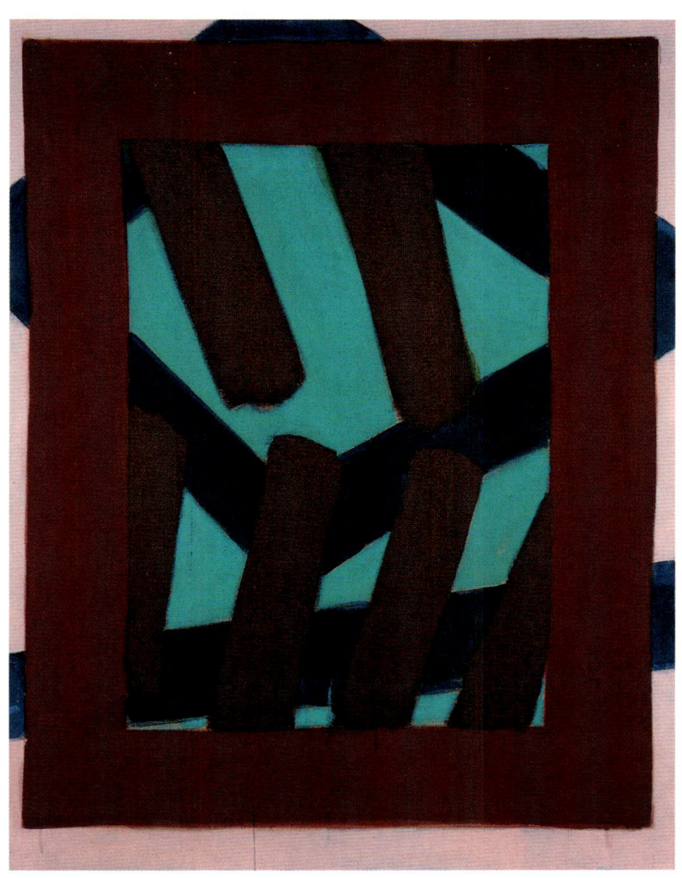

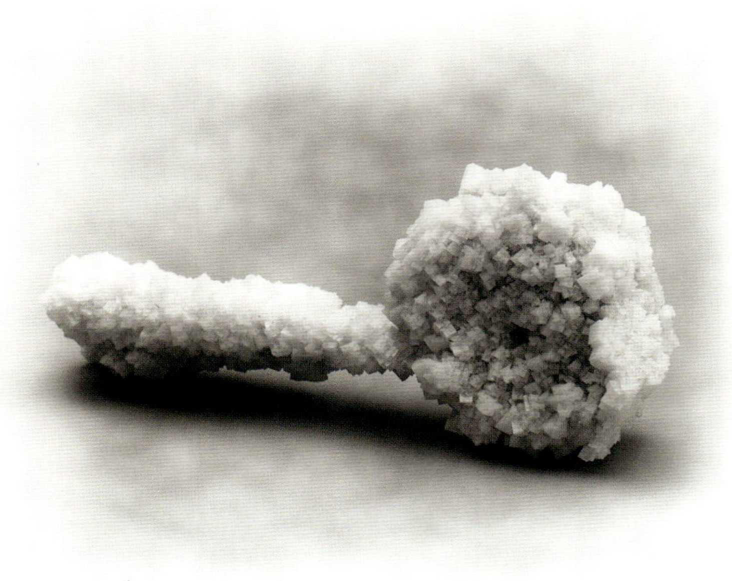

Bernard Cohen
Place Games
Acrylic on linen
137 × 168 cm

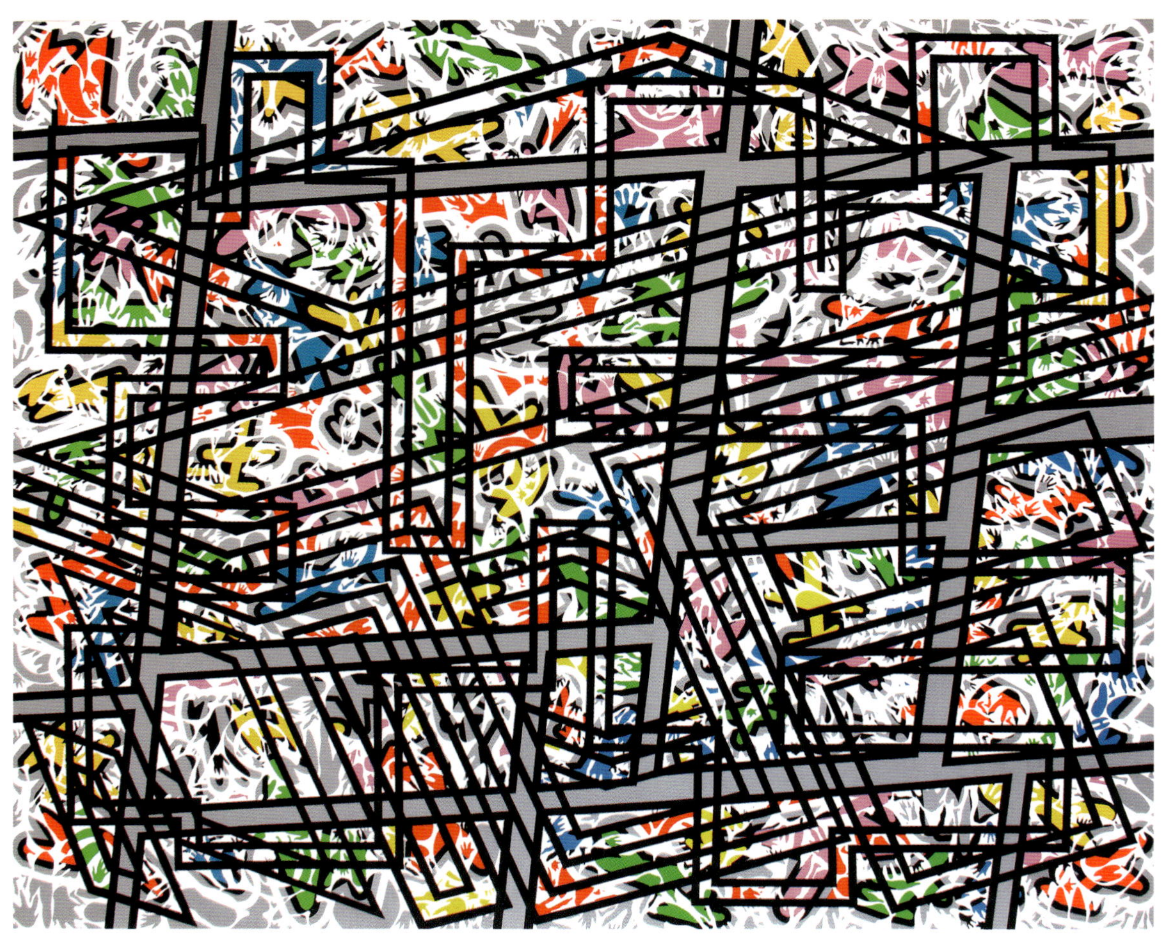

Keith Milow
First and Last
Acrylic
100 × 200 cm

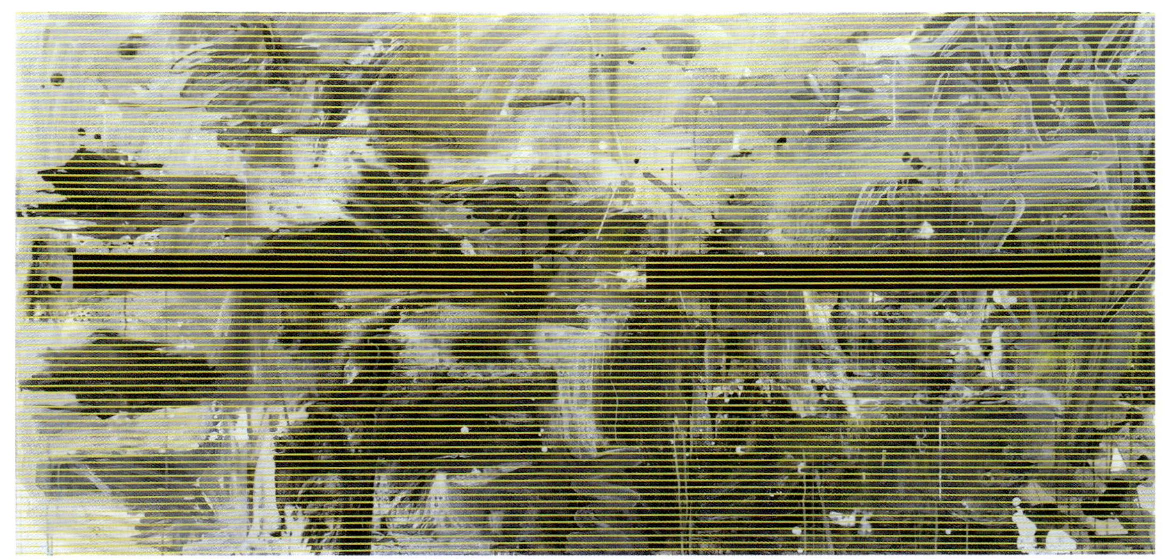

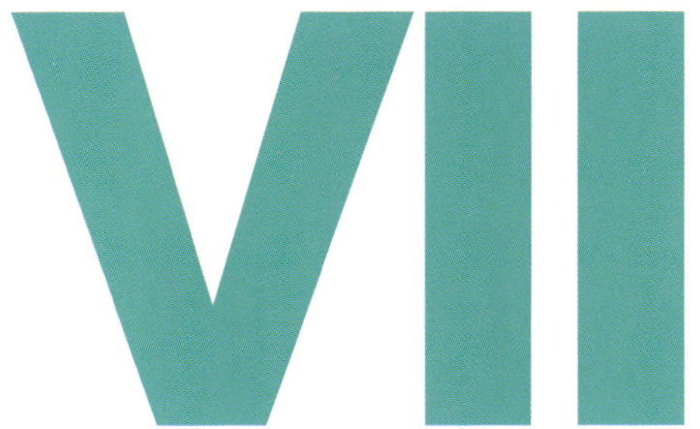

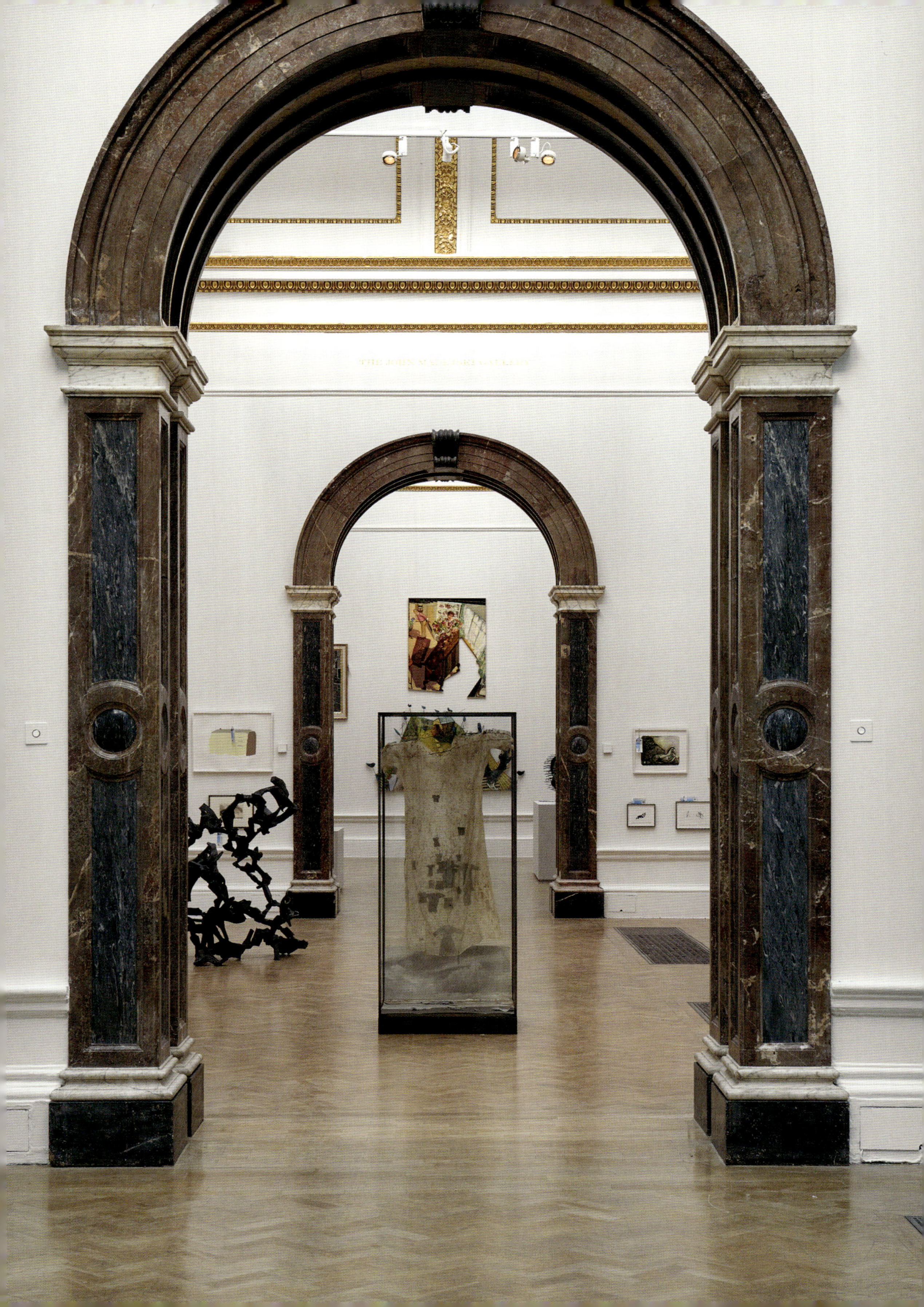

Bob and Roberta Smith RA

David Nott Interviewed by Eddie Mair

Screenprint

80 × 60 cm

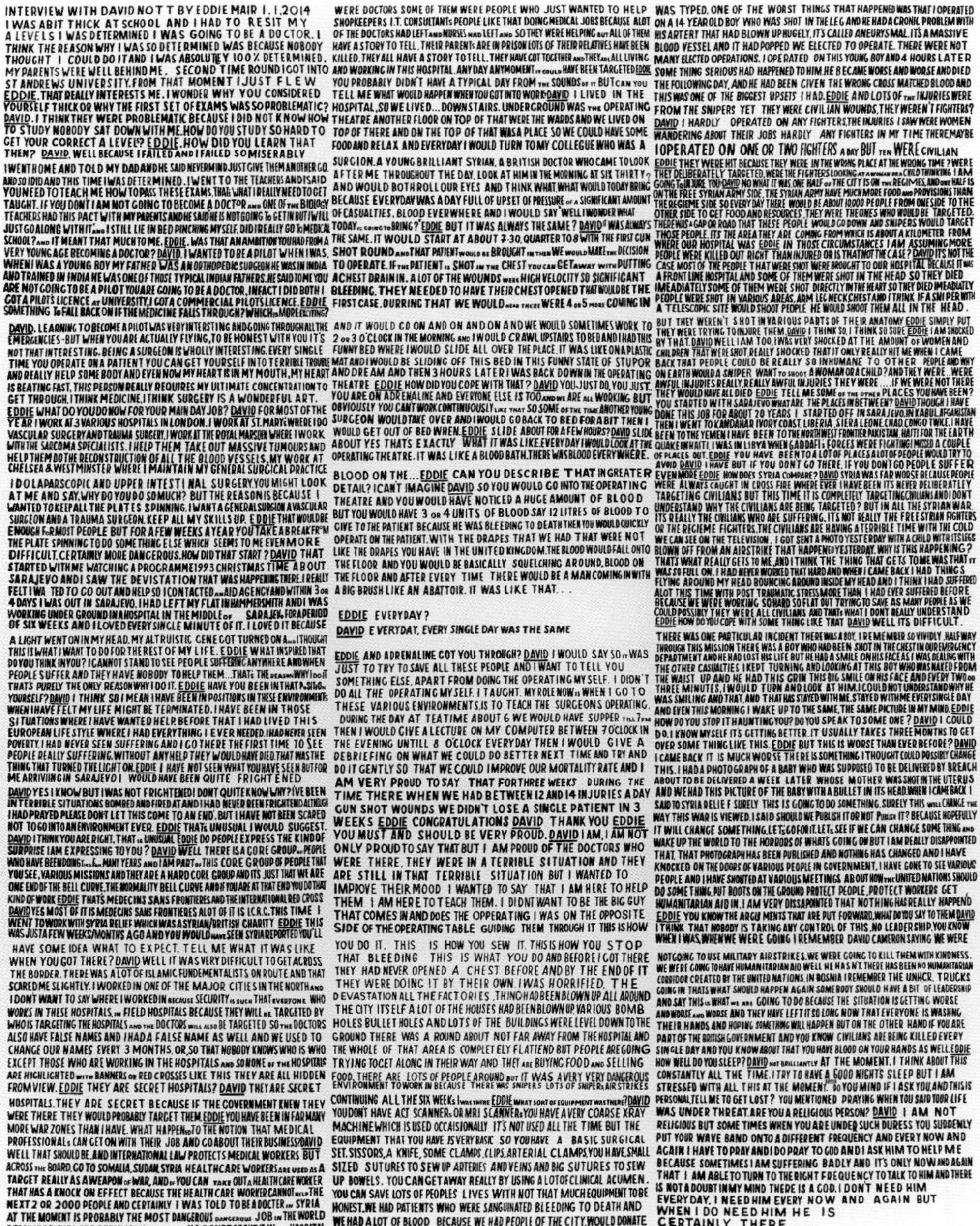

INTERVIEW WITH DAVID NOTT BY EDDIE MAIR 1.1.2014

I WAS A BIT THICK AT SCHOOL AND I HAD TO RESIT MY A LEVELS I WAS DETERMINED I WAS GOING TO BE A DOCTOR. I THINK THE REASON WHY I WAS SO DETERMINED WAS BECAUSE NOBODY THOUGHT I COULD DO IT AND I WAS ABSOLUTLEY 100% DETERMINED. MY PARENTS WERE WELL BEHIND ME. SECOND TIME ROUND I GOT INTO ST ANDREWS UNIVERSITY. FROM THAT MOMENT I JUST FLEW EDDIE. THAT REALLY INTERESTS ME. I WONDER WHY YOU CONSIDERED YOURSELF THICK OR WHY THE FIRST SET OF EXAMS WAS SO PROBLEMATIC? DAVID. I THINK THEY WERE PROBLEMATIC BECAUSE I DID NOT KNOW HOW TO STUDY NOBODY SAT DOWN WITH ME. HOW DO YOU STUDY SO HARD TO GET YOUR CORRECT A LEVEL? EDDIE. HOW DID YOU LEARN THAT THEN? DAVID. WELL BECAUSE I FAILED AND I FAILED SO MISERABLY

I WENT HOME AND TOLD MY DAD AND HE SAID NEVERMIND JUST GIVE THEM ANOTHER GO. AND SO I DID AND THIS TIME I WAS DETERMINED. I WENT TO THE TEACHERS AND I SAID YOU NEED TO TEACH ME HOW TO PASS THESE EXAMS. THAT'S WHAT I REALLY NEED TO GET TAUGHT. IF YOU DONT I AM NOT GOING TO BECOME A DOCTOR AND ONE OF THE BIOLOGY TEACHERS HAD THIS PACT WITH MY PARENTS AND HE SAID HE IS NOT GOING TO GET IN BUT I WILL JUST GO ALONG WITH IT AND I STILL LIE IN BED PINCHING MYSELF, DID I REALLY GO TO MEDICAL SCHOOL? AND IT MEANT THAT MUCH TO ME. EDDIE. WAS THAT AN AMBITION YOU HAD FROM A VERY YOUNG AGE BECOMING A DOCTOR? DAVID. I WANTED TO BE A PILOT WHEN I WAS. WHEN I WAS A YOUNG BOY MY FATHER WAS AN ORTHOPEDIC SURGEON HE WAS IN INDIA AND TRAINED IN INDIA HE WAS ONE OF THOSE TYPICAL INDIAN FATHERS. HE SAID TO ME YOU ARE NOT GOING TO BE A PILOT YOU ARE GOING TO BE A DOCTOR, INFACT I DID BOTH I GOT A PILOTS LICENCE AT UNIVERSITY, I GOT A COMMERCIAL PILOTS LICENCE. EDDIE SOMETHING TO FALL BACK ON IF THE MEDICINE FALLS THROUGH? WHICH IS MORE EXCITING?

DAVID. LEARNING TO BECOME A PILOT WAS VERY INTERSTING AND GOING THROUGH ALL THE EMERGENCIES-BUT WHEN YOU ARE ACTUALLY FLYING, TO BE HONEST WITH YOU IT'S NOT THAT INTERESTING. BEING A SURGEON IS WHOLLY INTERESTING. EVERY SINGLE TIME YOU OPERATE ON A PATIENT YOU CAN GET YOURSELF INTO TERRIBLE TROUBLE AND REALLY HELP SOME BODY AND EVEN NOW MY HEART IS IN MY MOUTH, MY HEART IS BEATING FAST, THIS PERSON REALLY REQUIRES MY ULTIMATE CONCENTRATION TO GET THROUGH. I THINK MEDICINE, I THINK SURGERY IS A WONDERFUL ART. EDDIE WHAT DO YOU DO NOW FOR YOUR MAIN DAY JOB? DAVID FOR MOST OF THE YEAR I WORK AT 3 VARIOUS HOSPITALS IN LONDON. I WORK AT ST. MARY'S WHERE I DO VASCULAR SURGERY AND TRAUMA SURGERY. I WORK AT THE ROYAL MARSDEN WHERE I WORK WITH THE SARCOMA SPECIALISTS. I HELP THEM TAKE OUT MASSIVE TUMOURS AND HELP THEM DO THE RECONSTRUCTION OF ALL THE BLOOD VESSELS, MY WORK AT CHELSEA & WESTMINSTER WHERE I MAINTAIN MY GENERAL SURGICAL PRACTICE

I DO LAPARSCOPIC AND UPPER INTESTINAL SURGERY. YOU MIGHT LOOK AT ME AND SAY, WHY DO YOU DO SO MUCH? BUT THE REASON IS BECAUSE I WANTED TO KEEP ALL THE PLATES SPINNING. I WANT A GENERAL SURGEON A VASCULAR SURGEON AND A TRAUMA SURGEON. KEEP ALL MY SKILLS UP. EDDIE THAT WOULD BE ENOUGH FOR MOST PEOPLE BUT FOR A FEW WEEKS A YEAR YOU TAKE A BREAK FROM THE PLATE SPINNING TO DO SOMETHING ELSE WHICH SEEMS TO ME EVEN MORE DIFFICULT, CERTAINLY MORE DANGEROUS. HOW DID THAT START? DAVID THAT STARTED WITH ME WATCHING A PROGRAMME 1993 CHRISTMAS TIME ABOUT SARAJEVO AND I SAW THE DEVISTATION THAT WAS HAPPENING THERE. I REALLY FELT I WANTED TO GO OUT AND HELP SO I CONTACTED AN AID AGENCY AND WITHIN 3 OR 4 DAYS I WAS OUT IN SARAJEVO. I HAD LEFT MY FLAT IN HAMMERSMITH AND I WAS WORKING UNDER GROUND IN A HOSPITAL IN THE MIDDLE OF SARAJEVO FOR A PERIOD OF SIX WEEKS AND I LOVED EVERY SINGLE MINUTE OF IT. I LOVED IT BECAUSE

A LIGHT WENT ON IN MY HEAD. MY ALTRUISTIC GENE GOT TURNED ON AND I THOUGHT THIS IS WHAT I WANT TO DO FOR THE REST OF MY LIFE. EDDIE WHAT INSPIRED THAT DO YOU THINK IN YOU? I CANNOT STAND TO SEE PEOPLE SUFFERING ANYWHERE AND WHEN PEOPLE SUFFER AND THEY HAVE NOBODY TO HELP THEM... THAT'S THE REASON WHY I DO IT THATS PURELY THE ONLY REASON WHY I DO IT. EDDIE HAVE YOU BEEN IN THAT POSITION YOURSELF? DAVID I THINK SO I MEAN I HAVE BEEN IN POSITIONS IN THESE ENVIRONMENTS WHEN I HAVE FELT MY LIFE MIGHT BE TERMINATED. I HAVE BEEN IN THOSE SITUATIONS WHERE I HAVE WANTED HELP. BEFORE THAT I HAD LIVED THIS EUROPEAN LIFE STYLE WHERE I HAD EVERYTHING I EVER NEEDED. I HAD NEVER SEEN POVERTY. I HAD NEVER SEEN SUFFERING AND I GO THERE THE FIRST TIME TO SEE PEOPLE REALLY SUFFERING. WITHOUT ANY HELP THEY WOULD HAVE DIED THAT WAS THE THING THAT TURNED THE LIGHT ON. EDDIE I HAVE NOT SEEN WHAT YOU HAVE SEEN BUT FOR ME ARRIVING IN SARAJEVO I WOULD HAVE BEEN QUITE FRIGHTENED

DAVID YES I KNOW BUT I WAS NOT FRIGHTENED I DONT QUITE KNOW WHY I'VE BEEN IN TERRIBLE SITUATIONS BOMBED AND FIRED AT AND I HAD NEVER BEEN FRIGHTENED ALTHOUGH I HAD PRAYED PLEASE DONT LET THIS COME TO AN END. BUT I HAVE NOT BEEN SCARED NOT TO GO INTO AN ENVIRONMENT EVER. EDDIE THAT'S UNUSUAL I WOULD SUGGEST. DAVID I THINK YOU ARE RIGHT. THAT IS UNUSUAL EDDIE DO PEOPLE EXPRESS THE KIND OF SURPRISE I AM EXPRESSING TO YOU? DAVID WELL THERE IS A CORE GROUP OF PEOPLE WHO HAVE BEEN DOING IT FOR MANY YEARS AND I AM PART OF THIS CORE GROUP OF PEOPLE THAT YOU SEE, VARIOUS MISSIONS AND THEY ARE A HARD CORE GROUP AND ITS JUST THAT WE ARE ONE END OF THE BELL CURVE. THE NORMALITY BELL CURVE AND IF YOU ARE AT THAT END YOU DO THAT KIND OF WORK EDDIE THATS MEDECINS SANS FRONTIERES AND THE INTERNATIONAL RED CROSS DAVID YES MOST OF IT IS MEDECINS SANS FRONTIERES ALOT OF IT IS I.C.R.C. THIS TIME I WENT TO WORK WITH SYRIA RELIEF WHICH WAS A SYRIAN/BRITISH CHARITY EDDIE THIS WAS JUST A FEW WEEKS/MONTHS AGO AND YOU WOULD HAVE SEEN SYRIA REPORTED YOU'LL

HAVE SOME IDEA WHAT TO EXPECT. TELL ME WHAT IT WAS LIKE WHEN YOU GOT THERE? DAVID WELL IT WAS VERY DIFFICULT TO GET ACROSS THE BORDER. THERE WAS A LOT OF ISLAMIC FUNDEMENTALISTS ON ROUTE AND THAT SCARED ME SLIGHTLY. I WORKED IN ONE OF THE MAJOR CITIES IN THE NORTH AND I DONT WANT TO SAY WHERE I WORKED IN BECAUSE SECURITY IS SUCH THAT EVERYONE WHO WORKS IN THESE HOSPITALS IN FIELD HOSPITALS BECAUSE THEY WILL BE TARGETED BY WHO IS TARGETING THE HOSPITALS AND THE DOCTORS WILL ALSO BE TARGETED SO THE DOCTORS ALSO HAVE FALSE NAMES AND I HAD A FALSE NAME AS WELL AND WE USED TO CHANGE OUR NAMES EVERY 3 MONTHS. OR, SO THAT NOBODY KNOWS WHO IS WHO EXCEPT THOSE WHO ARE WORKING IN THE HOSPITALS AND SO NONE OF THE HOSPITALS ARE HIGHLIGHTED WITH BANNERS OR RED CROSSES LIKE THIS THEY ARE ALL HIDDEN FROM VIEW. EDDIE THEY ARE SECRET HOSPITALS? DAVID THEY ARE SECRET

HOSPITALS. THEY ARE SECRET BECAUSE IF THE GOVERNMENT KNEW THEY WERE THERE THEY WOULD PROBABLY TARGET THEM. EDDIE YOU HAVE BEEN IN FAR MANY MORE WAR ZONES THAN I HAVE. WHAT HAPPENED TO THE NOTION THAT MEDICAL PROFESSIONALS CAN GET ON WITH THEIR JOB AND GO ABOUT THEIR BUSINESS? DAVID WELL THAT SHOULD BE. AND INTERNATIONAL LAW PROTECTS MEDICAL WORKERS BUT ACROSS THE BOARD, GO TO SOMALIA, SUDAN, SYRIA HEALTHCARE WORKERS ARE USED AS A TARGET REALLY AS A WEAPON OF WAR, AND IF YOU CAN TAKE OUT A HEALTHCARE WORKER THAT HAS A KNOCK ON EFFECT BECAUSE THE HEALTHCARE WORKER CANNOT HELP THE NEXT 2 OR 2000 PEOPLE AND CERTAINLY I WAS TOLD TO BE A DOCTER IN SYRIA AT THE MOMENT IS PROBABLY THE MOST DANGEROUS DANGEROUS JOB IN THE WORLD BECAUSE DOCTORS ARE DEFINATLEY TARGETED NO DOUBT ABOUT IT. IN THE HOSPITAL WHERE I WORKED THERE WAS A GROUP OF SAY 60 PEOPLE SOME OF THEM WERE DOCTORS SOME OF THEM WERE PEOPLE WHO JUST WANTED TO HELP SHOPKEEPERS I.T. CONSULTANTS PEOPLE LIKE THAT DOING MEDICAL JOBS BECAUSE ALOT OF THE DOCTORS HAD LEFT AND NURSES HAD LEFT AND SO THEY WERE HELPING BUT ALL OF THEM HAVE A STORY TO TELL. THEIR PARENTS ARE IN PRISON LOTS OF THEIR RELATIVES HAVE BEEN KILLED. THEY ALL HAVE A STORY TO TELL. THEY HAVE GOT TOGETHER AND THEY ARE ALL LIVING AND WORKING IN THIS HOSPITAL. ANY DAY ANY MOMENT IT COULD HAVE BEEN TARGETED EDDIE YOU PROBABLY DIDN'T HAVE A TYPICAL DAY FROM THE SOUNDS OF IT BUT CAN YOU TELL ME WHAT WOULD HAPPEN WHEN YOU GOT INTO WORK? DAVID I LIVED IN THE HOSPITAL, SO WE LIVED... DOWNSTAIRS. UNDERGROUND WAS THE OPERATING THEATRE ANOTHER FLOOR ON TOP OF THAT WERE THE WARDS AND WE LIVED ON TOP OF THERE AND ON THE TOP OF THAT WAS A PLACE SO WE COULD HAVE SOME FOOD AND RELAX AND EVERYDAY I WOULD TURN TO MY COLLEGUE WHO WAS A

SURGION. A YOUNG BRILLIANT SYRIAN, A BRITISH DOCTOR WHO CAME TO LOOK AFTER ME THROUGHOUT THE DAY. LOOK AT HIM IN THE MORNING AT SIX THIRTY? AND WOULD BOTH ROLL OUR EYES AND THINK WHAT, WHAT WOULD TODAY BRING BECAUSE EVERYDAY WAS A DAY FULL OF UPSET OF PRESSURE OF A SIGNIFICANT AMOUNT OF CASUALTIES. BLOOD EVERWHERE AND I WOULD SAY 'WELL I WONDER WHAT TODAY IS GOING TO BRING?' EDDIE BUT IT WAS ALWAYS THE SAME? DAVID IT WAS ALWAYS THE SAME. IT WOULD START AT ABOUT 7-30, QUARTER TO 8 WITH THE FIRST GUN SHOT ROUND AND THAT PATIENT WOULD BE BROUGHT IN THEN WE WOULD MAKE THE DECISION TO OPERATE. IF THE PATIENT IS SHOT IN THE CHEST YOU CAN GET AWAY WITH PUTTING A CHEST DRAIN IN. A LOT OF THE WOUNDS WERE HIGH VELOCITY SO SIGNIFICANT BLEEDING. THEY NEEDED TO HAVE THEIR CHEST OPENED THAT WOULD BE THE FIRST CASE. DURRING THAT WE WOULD HEAR THERE WERE 4 OR 5 MORE COMING IN

AND IT WOULD GO ON AND ON AND ON AND WE WOULD SOMETIMES WORK TO 2 OR 3 O'CLOCK IN THE MORNING AND I WOULD CRAWL UPSTAIRS TO BED AND I HAD THIS FUNNY BED WHERE I WOULD SLIDE ALL OVER THE PLACE. IT WAS LIKE ON A PLASTIC MAT AND I WOULD BE SLIDING OFF THIS BED IN THIS FUNNY STATE OF STUPOR AND DREAM AND THEN 3 HOURS LATER I WAS BACK DOWN IN THE OPERATING THEATRE EDDIE HOW DID YOU COPE WITH THAT? DAVID YOU JUST DO, YOU JUST. YOU ARE ON ADRENALINE AND EVERYONE ELSE IS TOO AND WE ARE ALL WORKING BUT OBVIOUSLY YOU CAN'T WORK CONTINUOUSLY LIKE THAT SO SOME OF THE TIME ANOTHER YOUNG SURGEON WOULD TAKE OVER AND I WOULD GO BACK TO BED FOR A BIT THEN I WOULD GET OUT OF BED WHEN. EDDIE SLIDE ABOUT FOR A FEW HOURS? DAVID SLIDE ABOUT YES THATS EXACTLY WHAT IT WAS LIKE. EVERYDAY I WOULD LOOK AT THE OPERATING THEATRE. IT WAS LIKE A BLOOD BATH. THERE WAS BLOOD EVERYWHERE.

BLOOD ON THE... EDDIE CAN YOU DESCRIBE THAT IN GREATER DETAIL? I CAN'T IMAGINE DAVID SO YOU WOULD GO INTO THE OPERATING THEATRE AND YOU WOULD HAVE NOTICED A HUGE AMOUNT OF BLOOD BUT YOU WOULD HAVE 3 OR 4 UNITS OF BLOOD SAY 12 LITRES OF BLOOD TO GIVE TO THE PATIENT BECAUSE HE WAS BLEEDING TO DEATH THEN YOU WOULD QUICKLY OPERATE ON THE PATIENT. WITH THE DRAPES THAT WE HAD THAT WERE NOT LIKE THE DRAPES YOU HAVE IN THE UNITED KINGDOM. THE BLOOD WOULD FALL ONTO THE FLOOR AND YOU WOULD BE BASICALLY SQUELCHING AROUND, BLOOD ON THE FLOOR AND AFTER EVERY TIME THERE WOULD BE A MAN COMING IN WITH A BIG BRUSH LIKE AN ABATTOIR. IT WAS LIKE THAT...

EDDIE EVERYDAY?

DAVID EVERYDAY, EVERY SINGLE DAY WAS THE SAME

EDDIE AND ADRENALINE GOT YOU THROUGH? DAVID I WOULD SAY SO IT WAS JUST TO TRY TO SAVE ALL THESE PEOPLE AND I WANT TO TELL YOU SOMETHING ELSE. APART FROM DOING THE OPERATING MYSELF. I DIDN'T DO ALL THE OPERATING MYSELF. I TAUGHT. MY ROLE NOW IS WHEN I GO TO THESE VARIOUS ENVIRONMENTS, IS TO TEACH THE SURGEONS OPERATING. DURING THE DAY AT TEATIME ABOUT 6 WE WOULD HAVE SUPPER TILL 7PM THEN I WOULD GIVE A LECTURE ON MY COMPUTER BETWEEN 7 O'CLOCK IN THE EVENING UNTILL 8 O'CLOCK EVERYDAY THEN I WOULD GIVE A DEBRIEFING ON WHAT WE COULD DO BETTER NEXT TIME AND TRY AND DO IT GENTLY SO THAT WE COULD IMPROVE OUR MORTALITY RATE AND I AM VERY PROUD TO SAY THAT FOR THREE WEEKS DURING THE TIME THERE WHEN WE HAD BETWEEN 12 AND 14 INJURIES A DAY GUN SHOT WOUNDS WE DIDN'T LOSE A SINGLE PATIENT IN 3 WEEKS EDDIE CONGRATULATIONS DAVID THANK YOU EDDIE YOU MUST AND SHOULD BE VERY PROUD. DAVID I AM, I AM NOT ONLY PROUD TO SAY THAT BUT I AM PROUD OF THE DOCTORS WHO WERE THERE, THEY WERE IN A TERRIBLE SITUATION AND THEY ARE STILL IN THAT TERRIBLE SITUATION BUT I WANTED TO IMPROVE THEIR MOOD I WANTED TO SAY THAT I AM HERE TO HELP THEM I AM HERE TO TEACH THEM. I DIDNT WANT TO BE THE BIG GUY THAT COMES IN AND DOES THE OPPERATING I WAS ON THE OPPOSITE SIDE OF THE OPERATING TABLE GUIDING THEM THROUGH IT THIS IS HOW

YOU DO IT. THIS IS HOW YOU SEW IT. THIS IS HOW YOU STOP THAT BLEEDING THIS IS WHAT YOU DO AND BEFORE I GOT THERE THEY HAD NEVER OPENED A CHEST BEFORE AND BY THE END OF IT THEY WERE DOING IT BY THEIR OWN. I WAS HORRIFIED. THE DEVASTATION ALL THE FACTORIES. THING HAD BEEN BLOWN UP ALL AROUND THE CITY ITSELF A LOT OF THE HOUSES HAD BEEN BLOWN UP. VARIOUS BOMB HOLES BULLET HOLES AND LOTS OF THE BUILDINGS WERE LEVEL DOWN TO THE GROUND THERE WAS A ROUND ABOUT NOT FAR AWAY FROM THE HOSPITAL AND THE WHOLE OF THAT AREA IS COMPLETELY FLATTEND BUT PEOPLE ARE GOING TRYING TO GET ALONG IN THEIR WAY AND THEY ARE BUYING FOOD AND SELLING FOOD. THERE ARE LOTS OF PEOPLE AROUND BUT IT WAS A VERY VERY DANGEROUS ENVIRONMENT TO WORK IN BECAUSE THERE WAS SNIPERS LOTS OF SNIPERS AIR STRIKES CONTINUING ALL THE SIX WEEKS I WAS THERE EDDIE WHAT SORT OF EQUIPMENT WAS THERE? DAVID YOU DON'T HAVE A CT SCANNERS OR MRI SCANNERS YOU HAVE A VERY COARSE X-RAY MACHINE WHICH IS USED OCCAISIONALLY IT'S NOT USED ALL THE TIME BUT THE EQUIPMENT THAT YOU HAVE IS VERY BASIC SO YOU HAVE A BASIC SURGICAL SET. SISSORS, A KNIFE, SOME CLAMPS, CLIPS, ARTERIAL CLAMPS, YOU HAVE, SMALL SIZED SUTURES TO SEW UP ARTERIES AND VEINS AND BIG SUTURES TO SEW UP BOWELS. YOU CAN GET AWAY REALLY BY USING A LOT OF CLINICAL ACUMEN. YOU CAN SAVE LOTS OF PEOPLES LIVES WITH NOT THAT MUCH EQUIPMENT TO BE HONEST. WE HAD PATIENTS WHO WERE SANGUINATED BLEEDING TO DEATH AND WE HAD A LOT OF BLOOD BECAUSE WE HAD PEOPLE OF THE CITY, WOULD DONATE BLOOD. WE DID HAVE A PROBLEM WITH CROSS MATCHING TO INSURE THE BLOOD WAS TYPED. ONE OF THE WORST THINGS THAT HAPPENED WAS THAT I OPERATED ON A 14 YEAR OLD BOY WHO WAS SHOT IN THE LEG AND HE HAD A CRONIC PROBLEM WITH HIS ARTERY THAT HAD BLOWN UP HUGELY. IT'S CALLED ANEURYSMAL. IT'S A MASSIVE BLOOD VESSEL AND IT HAD POPPED WE ELECTED TO OPERATE. THERE WERE NOT MANY ELECTED OPERATIONS. I OPERATED ON THIS YOUNG BOY AND 4 HOURS LATER SOME THING SERIOUS HAD HAPPENED TO HIM. HE BECAME WORSE AND WORSE AND DIED THE FOLLOWING DAY, AND HE HAD BEEN GIVEN THE WRONG CROSS MATCHED BLOOD AND THIS WAS ONE OF THE BIGGEST UPSETS I HAD. EDDIE AND LOTS OF THE INJURIES WERE FROM THE SNIPERS YET THEY WERE CIVILIAN WOUNDS, THEY WEREN'T FIGHTERS? DAVID I HARDLY OPERATED ON ANY FIGHTERS, THE INJURIES I SAW WERE WOMEN WANDERING ABOUT THEIR JOBS HARDLY ANY FIGHTERS IN MY TIME THERE MAYBE I OPERATED ON ONE OR TWO FIGHTERS A DAY BUT TEN WERE CIVILIAN

EDDIE THEY WERE HIT BECAUSE THEY WERE IN THE WRONG PLACE AT THE WRONG TIME? WERE THEY DELIBERATELY TARGETED, WERE THE FIGHTERS LOOKING AT A WOMAN OR A CHILD THINKING I AM GOING TO INJURE YOU? DAVID NO WHAT IT WAS, ONE HALF OF THE CITY IS ON THE REGIMES, AND ONE HALF IS ON THE FREE SYRIAN ARMY SIDE. THE SYRIAN ARMY HAVE MUCH MORE FOOD AND PROVISIONS THAN THE REGIEME SIDE SO EVERY DAY THERE WOULD BE ABOUT 10,000 PEOPLE FROM ONE SIDE TO THE OTHER SIDE TO GET FOOD AND RESOURCES. THEY WERE THE ONES WHO WOULD BE TARGETED. THERE WAS A GAP OR ROAD THAT THESE PEOPLE WOULD GO DOWN AND SNIPERS WOULD TARGET THOSE PEOPLE. ITS THE AREA THEY ARE COMING FROM WHICH IS ABOUT A KILOMETER FROM WHERE OUR HOSPITAL WAS EDDIE IN THOSE CIRCUMSTANCES I AM ASSUMING MORE PEOPLE WERE KILLED OUT RIGHT THAN INJURED OR IS THAT NOT THE CASE? DAVID IT'S NOT THE CASE MOST OF THE PEOPLE THAT WERE SHOT WERE BROUGHT TO OUR HOSPITAL BECAUSE IT WAS A FRONT LINE HOSPITAL AND SOME OF THEM WERE SHOT IN THE HEAD SO THEY DIED IMEADIATELY SOME OF THEM WERE SHOT DIRECTLY IN THE HEART SO THEY DIED IMEADIATLY PEOPLE WERE SHOT IN VARIOUS AREAS, ARM LEG NECK CHEST AND I THINK IF A SNIPER WITH A TELESCOPIC SITE WOULD SHOOT PEOPLE HE WOULD SHOOT THEM ALL IN THE HEAD.

BUT THEY WEREN'T SHOT IN VARIOUS PARTS OF THEIR ANATOMY EDDIE SIMPLY PUT THEY WERE TRYING TO INJURE THEM. DAVID I THINK SO, I THINK SO SURE EDDIE I AM SHOCKED BY THAT. DAVID WELL I AM TOO, I WAS VERY SHOCKED AT THE AMOUNT OF WOMEN AND CHILDREN THAT WERE SHOT, REALLY SHOCKED THAT IT ONLY REALLY HIT ME WHEN I CAME BACK THAT PEOPLE COULD BE REALLY SO INHUMANE TO OTHER PEOPLE AND WHY ON EARTH WOULD A SNIPER WANT TO SHOOT A WOMAN OR A CHILD? AND THEY WERE.. WERE AWFUL INJURIES REALLY, REALLY AWFUL INJURIES THEY WERE.... IF WE WERE NOT THERE THEY WOULD HAVE ALL DIED EDDIE TELL ME SOME OF THE OTHER PLACES YOU HAVE BEEN? YOU STARTED WITH SARAJEVO WHAT ARE THE PLACES IN BETWEEN? DAVID THOUGH I HAVE DONE THIS JOB FOR ABOUT 20 YEARS I STARTED OFF IN SARAJEVO, IN KABUL AFGANISTAN THEN I WENT TO KANDAHAR IVORY COAST, LIBERIA, SIERA LEONE, CHAD, CONGO TWICE. I HAVE BEEN TO THE YEMEN I HAVE BEEN TO THE NORTHWEST FRONTIER PAKISTAN, HAITI FOR THE EARTH QUAKE IN HAITI. I WAS IN LIBYA WHEN GADDAFI'S FORCES WERE FIGHTING I MISSED A COUPLE OF PLACES OUT. EDDIE YOU HAVE BEEN TO A LOT OF PLACES A LOT OF PEOPLE WOULD TRY TO AVOID. DAVID I HAVE BUT IF YOU DON'T GO THERE, IF YOU DONT GO PEOPLE SUFFER EVEN MORE EDDIE HOW DOES SYRIA COMPARE? DAVID SYRIA WAS FAR WORSE BECAUSE PEOPLE WERE ALWAYS CAUGHT IN CROSS FIRE WHERE EVER I HAVE BEEN ITS NEVER DELIBERATLEY TARGETING CIVILIANS BUT THIS TIME IT IS COMPLETELY TARGETING CIVILIANS AND I DONT UNDERSTAND WHY THE CIVILIANS ARE BEING TARGETED? BUT IN ALL THE SYRIAN WAR, ITS REALLY THE CIVILIANS WHO ARE SUFFERING. ITS NOT REALLY THE FREE SYRIAN FIGHTERS OR THE REGIEME FIGHTERS. THE CIVILIANS ARE HAVING A TERRIBLE TIME WITH THE COLD WE CAN SEE ON THE TELEVISION. I GOT SENT A PHOTO YESTERDAY WITH A CHILD WITH ITS LEGS BLOWN OFF FROM AN AIRSTRIKE THAT HAPPENED YESTERDAY. WHY IS THIS HAPPENING? THATS WHAT REALLY GETS TO ME, AND I THINK THE THING THAT GETS TO ME WAS THAT IT WAS SO FULL ON. I HAD NEVER WORKED THAT HARD AND WHEN I CAME BACK I HAD THINGS FLYING AROUND MY HEAD BOUNCING AROUND INSIDE MY HEAD AND I THINK I HAD SUFFERED ALOT THIS TIME WITH POST TRAUMATIC STRESS MORE THAN I HAD EVER SUFFERED BEFORE BECAUSE WE WERE WORKING SO HARD SO FLAT OUT TRYING TO SAVE AS MANY PEOPLE AS WE COULD POSSIBLY THEY WERE ALL CIVILIANS AND THAT'S WHAT I DONT REALLY UNDERSTAND EDDIE HOW DO YOU COPE WITH SOME THING LIKE THAT DAVID WELL ITS DIFFICULT.

THERE WAS ONE PARTICULAR INCIDENT THERE WAS A BOY, I REMEMBER SO VIVIDLY. HALF WAY THROUGH THIS MISSION THERE WAS A BOY WHO HAD BEEN SHOT IN THE CHEST IN OUR EMERGENCY DEPARTMENT AND HE HAD LOST HIS LIFE BUT HE HAD A SMILE ON HIS FACE AS I WAS DEALING WITH THE OTHER CASUALTIES I KEPT TURNING AND LOOKING AT THIS BOY WHO WAS NAKED FROM THE WAIST UP AND HE HAD THIS GRIN THIS BIG SMILE ON HIS FACE AND EVERY TWO OR THREE MINUTES, I WOULD TURN AND LOOK AT HIM. I COULD NOT UNDERSTAND WHY HE WAS SMILING AND THAT, AND THAT HAS STAYED WITH ME. STAYED WITH ME EVERY SINGLE DAY AND EVEN THIS MORNING I WAKE UP TO THE SAME, THE SAME PICTURE IN MY MIND. EDDIE HOW DO YOU STOP IT HAUNTING YOU? DO YOU SPEAK TO SOME ONE? DAVID I COULD DO. I KNOW MYSELF IT'S GETTING BETTER. IT USUALLY TAKES THREE MONTHS TO GET OVER SOME THING LIKE THIS. EDDIE BUT THIS IS WORSE THAN EVER BEFORE? DAVID I CAME BACK IT IS MUCH WORSE THERE IS SOMETHING I THOUGHT COULD POSSIBLY CHANGE THIS. I HAD A PHOTOGRAPH OF A BABY WHO WAS SUPPOSED TO BE DELIVERED BY BREACH ABOUT TO BE DELIVERED A WEEK LATER WHOSE MOTHER WAS SHOT IN THE UTERUS AND WE HAD THIS PICTURE OF THE BABY WITH A BULLET IN ITS HEAD. WHEN I CAME BACK I SAID TO SYRIA RELIEF SURELY THIS IS GOING TO DO SOMETHING. SURELY THIS WILL CHANGE THE WAY THIS WAR IS VIEWED. I SAID SHOULD WE PUBLISH IT OR NOT PUBLISH IT? BECAUSE HOPEFULLY IT WILL CHANGE SOMETHING. LET'S GO FOR IT. LET'S SEE IF WE CAN CHANGE SOME THING AND WAKE UP THE WORLD TO THE HORRORS OF WHATS GOING ON BUT I AM REALLY DISAPPOINTED THAT. THAT PHOTOGRAPH HAS BEEN PUBLISHED AND NOTHING HAS CHANGED AND I HAVE KNOCKED ON THE DOORS OF VARIOUS PEOPLE IN GOVERNMENT. I HAVE GONE TO SEE VARIOUS PEOPLE AND I HAVE SHOUTED AT VARIOUS MEETINGS ABOUT HOW THE UNITED NATIONS SHOULD DO SOME THING. PUT BOOTS ON THE GROUND PROTECT PEOPLE, PROTECT WORKERS GET HUMANITARIAN AID IN. I AM VERY DISSAPOINTED THAT NOTHING HAS REALLY HAPPEND EDDIE YOU KNOW THE ARGUMENTS THAT ARE PUT FORWARD, WHAT DO YOU SAY TO THEM DAVID I THINK THAT NOBODY IS TAKING ANY CONTROL OF THIS, NO LEADERSHIP, YOU KNOW WHEN I WAS, WHEN WE WERE GOING I REMEMBER DAVID CAMERON SAYING WE WERE

NOT GOING TO USE MILITARY AIR STRIKES. WE WERE GOING TO KILL THEM WITH KINDNESS. WE WERE GOING TO HAVE HUMANITARIAN AID WELL HE HASN'T. THERE HAS BEEN NO HUMANITARIAN CORRIDOR CREATED BY THE UNITED NATIONS. IN BOSNIA I REMEMBER THE UNHCR. TRUCKS GOING IN THATS WHAT SHOULD HAPPEN AGAIN SOME BODY SHOULD HAVE A BIT OF LEADERSHIP AND SAY THIS IS WHAT WE ARE GOING TO DO BECAUSE THE SITUATION IS GETTING WORSE AND WORSE AND WORSE AND THEY HAVE LEFT IT SO LONG NOW THAT EVERYONE IS WASHNG THEIR HANDS AND HOPING SOMETHING WILL HAPPEN BUT ON THE OTHER HAND IF YOU ARE PART OF THE BRITISH GOVERNMENT AND YOU KNOW CIVILIANS ARE BEING KILLED EVERY SINGLE DAY AND YOU KNOW ABOUT THAT YOU HAVE BLOOD ON YOUR HANDS AS WELL. EDDIE HOW WELL DO YOU SLEEP? DAVID NOT BRILLIANTLY AT THE MOMENT. I THINK ABOUT THIS CONSTANTLY ALL THE TIME. I TRY TO HAVE A GOOD NIGHT'S SLEEP BUT I AM STRESSED WITH ALL THIS AT THE MOMENT. EDDIE DO YOU MIND IF I ASK YOU, AND THIS IS PERSONAL, TELL ME TO GET LOST? YOU MENTIONED PRAYING WHEN YOU SAID YOUR LIFE WAS UNDER THREAT. ARE YOU A RELIGIOUS PERSON? DAVID I AM NOT RELIGIOUS BUT SOME TIMES WHEN YOU ARE UNDER SUCH DURESS YOU SUDDENLY PUT YOUR WAVE BAND ONTO A DIFFERENT FREQUENCY AND EVERY NOW AND AGAIN I HAVE TO PRAY AND I DO PRAY TO GOD AND I ASK HIM TO HELP ME BECAUSE SOMETIMES I AM SUFFERING BADLY AND IT'S ONLY NOW AND AGAIN THAT I AM ABLE TO TURN TO THE RIGHT FREQUENCY TO TALK TO HIM AND THERE IS NOT A DOUBT IN MY MIND THERE IS A GOD. I DON'T NEED HIM EVERYDAY. I NEED HIM EVERY NOW AND AGAIN BUT WHEN I DO NEED HIM HE IS CERTAINLY THERE.

1/50 Interview Bob + Roberta Smith 2015

Tammy Mackay
Everlasting
Mixed media
43 × 59 cm

Tracey Emin CBE RA
Hare
Polymer gravure
21 × 18 cm

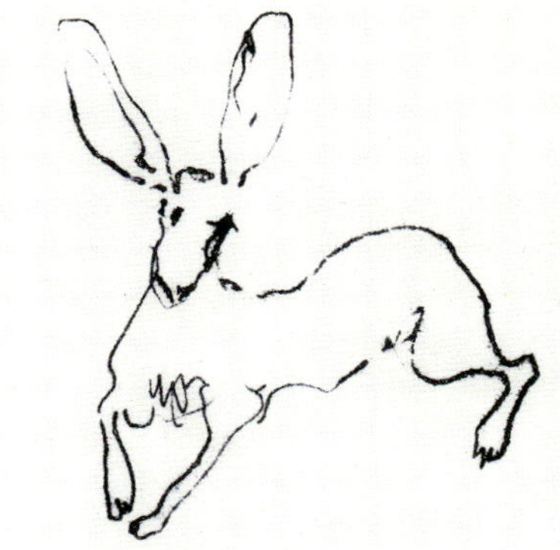

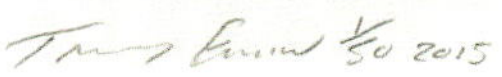

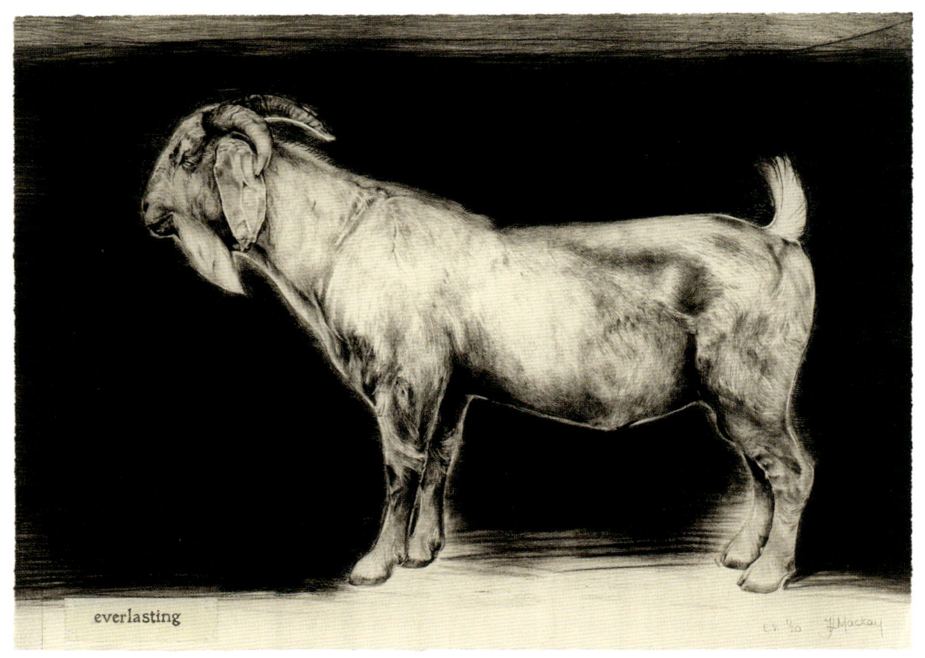

Prof Norman Ackroyd CBE RA
Morning Sunlight Bempton
Etching
74 × 102 cm

Martin Davidson
Stream
Linocut
28 × 18 cm

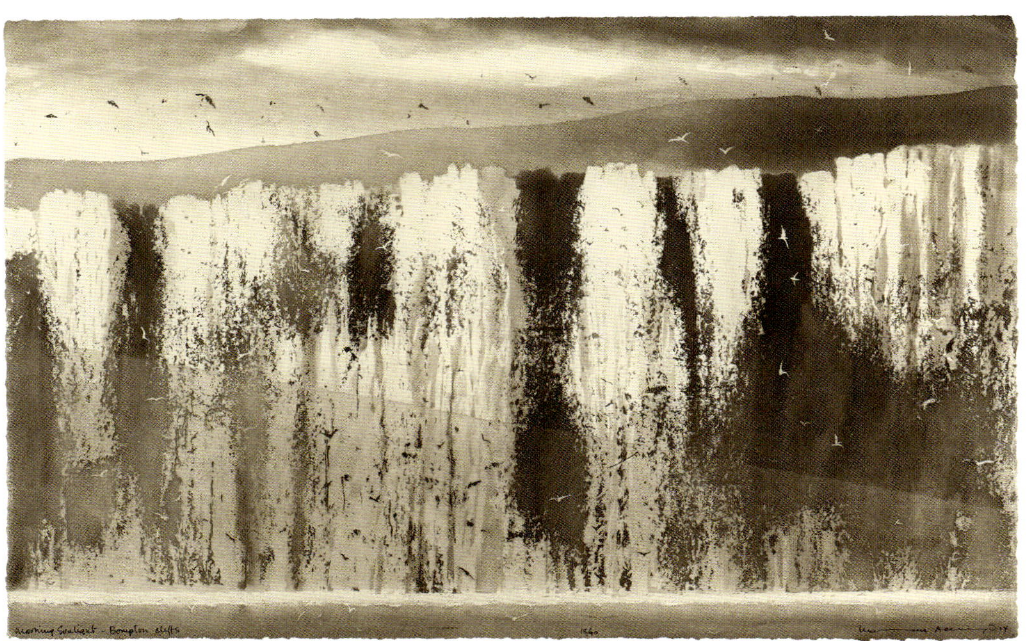

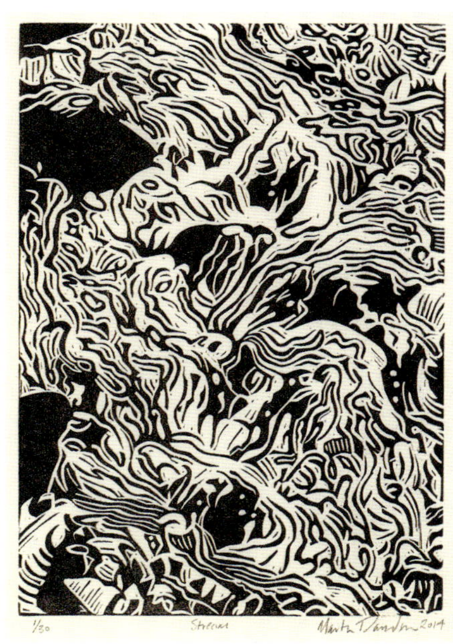

George Shaw
Fuck Me Fuck You Tree
Lithograph
74 × 59 cm

Pamela Silver
Tapestry of Feelings
Sugarlift, spit bite and chine collé
40 × 40 cm

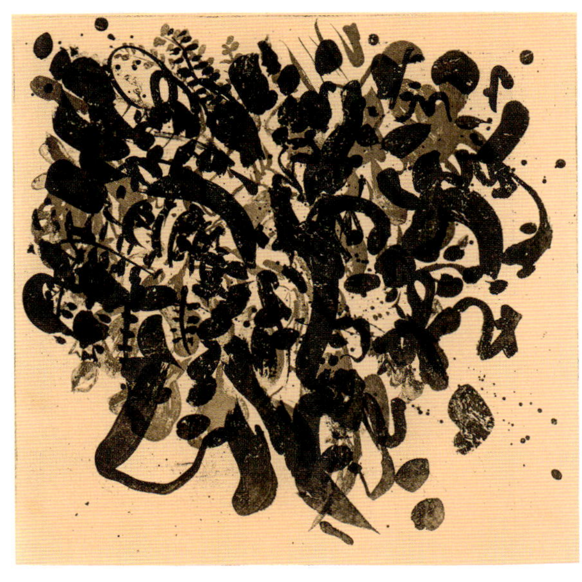

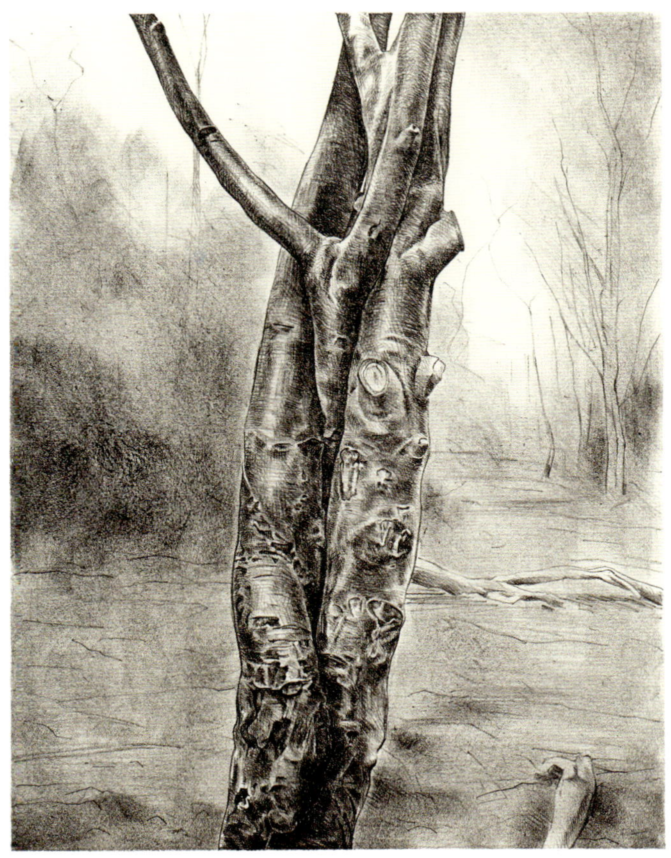

Prof Chris Orr MBE RA
Land of My Father
Engraving and watercolour
68 × 128 cm

Joe Tilson RA
Stones of Venice, L'Arco del Paradiso, Venusia
Screenprint and carborundum
100 × 100 cm

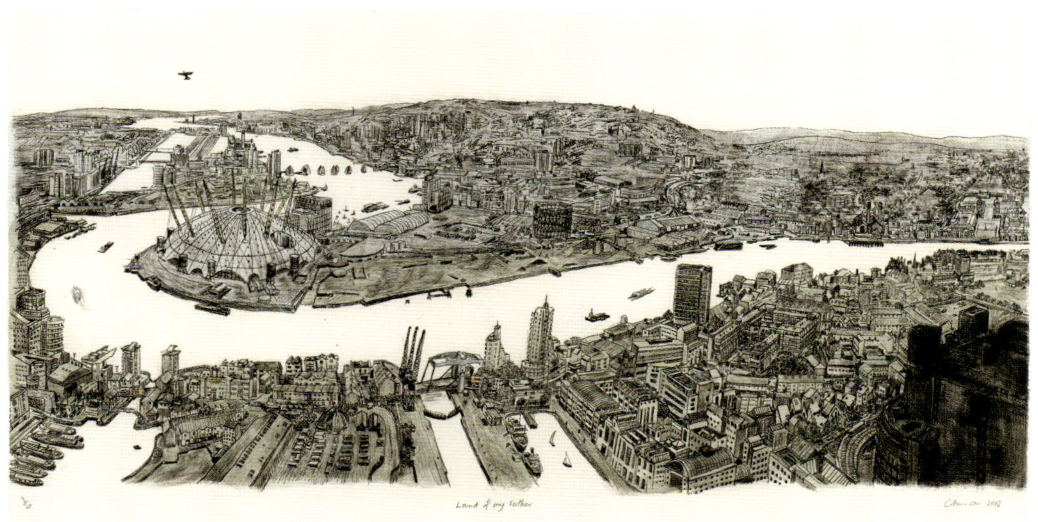

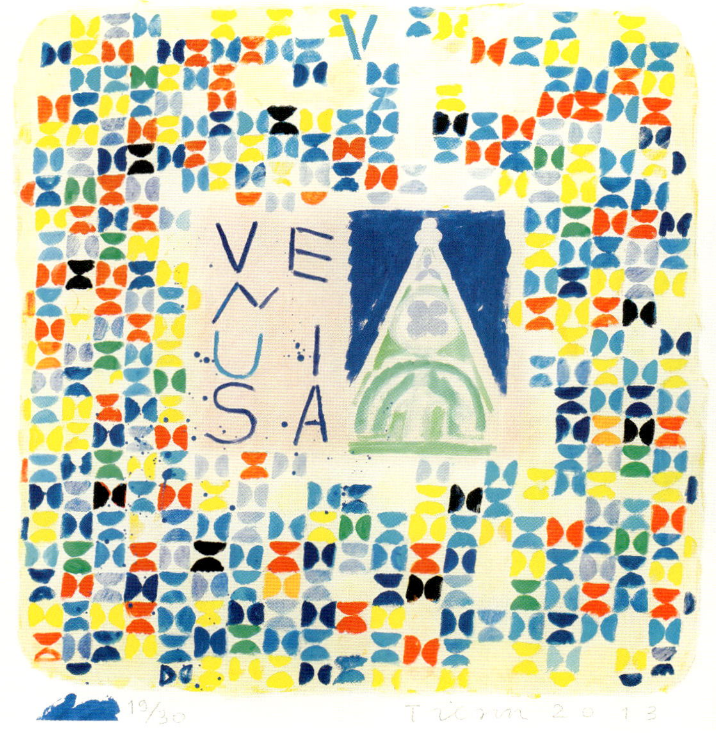

Allen Jones RA
Second Thoughts
Lithograph
62 × 91 cm

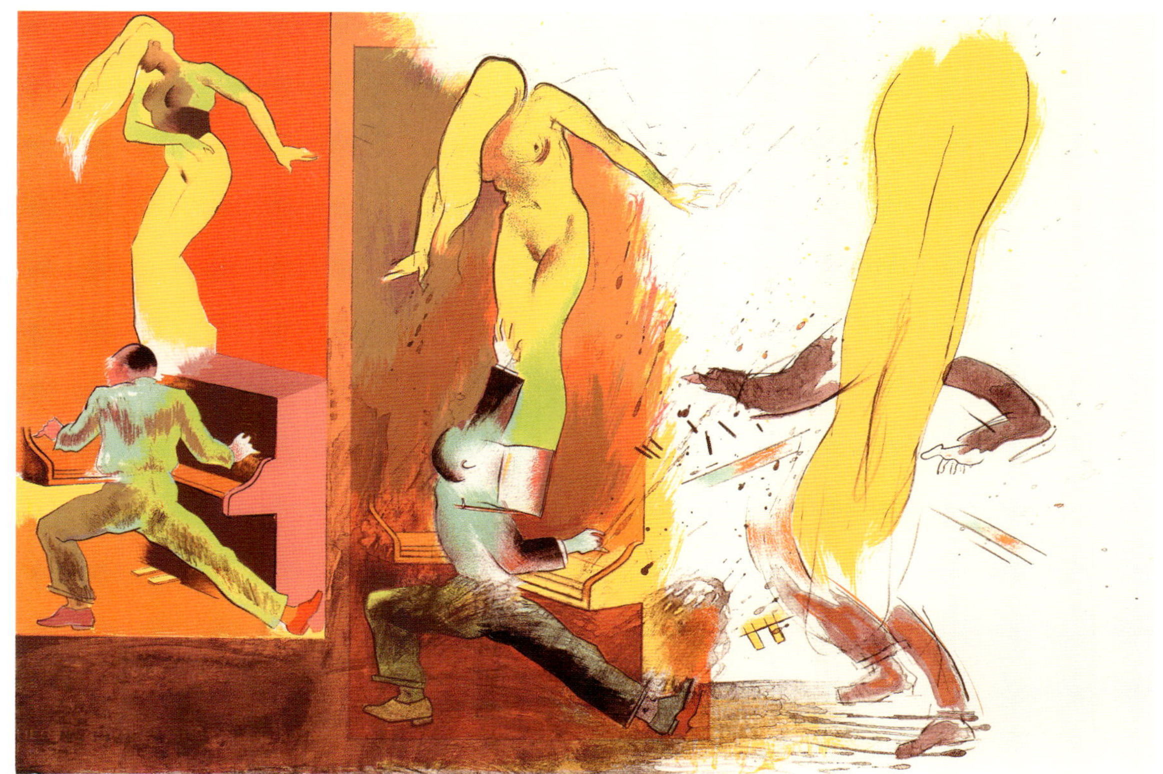

Merlyn Chesterman
Atlantic Roller
Woodcut
40 × 137 cm

Bill Jacklin RA
Stars and Sea at Night III
Monotype
69 × 54 cm

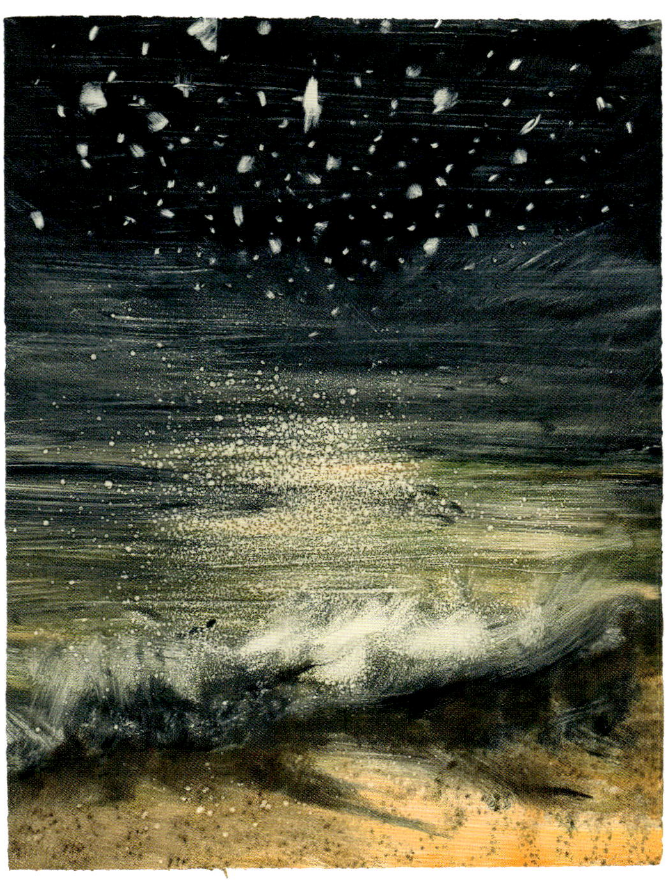

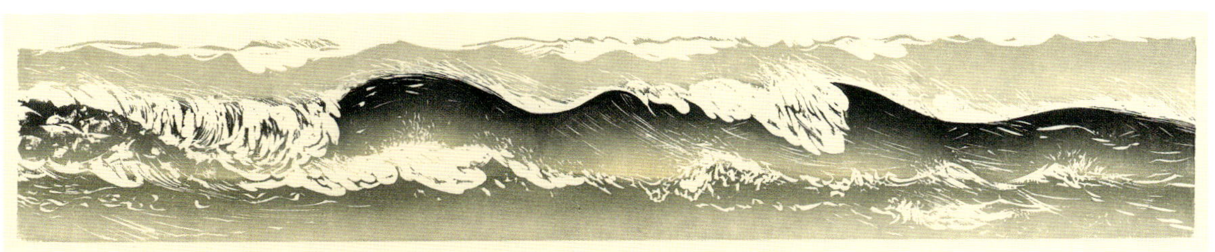

Jonathan Lloyd
Altarpiece in Dazzle Camouflage (Thornham Parva)
Woodcut
40 × 106 cm

Frederick Cuming RA
Night Studio with Self-portrait
Etching
73 × 60 cm

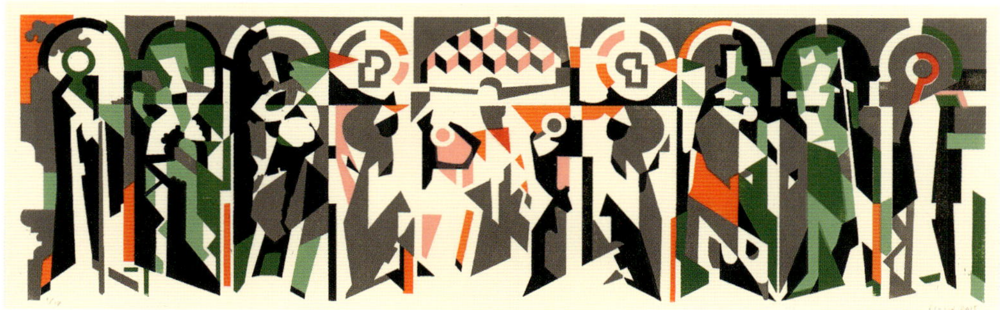

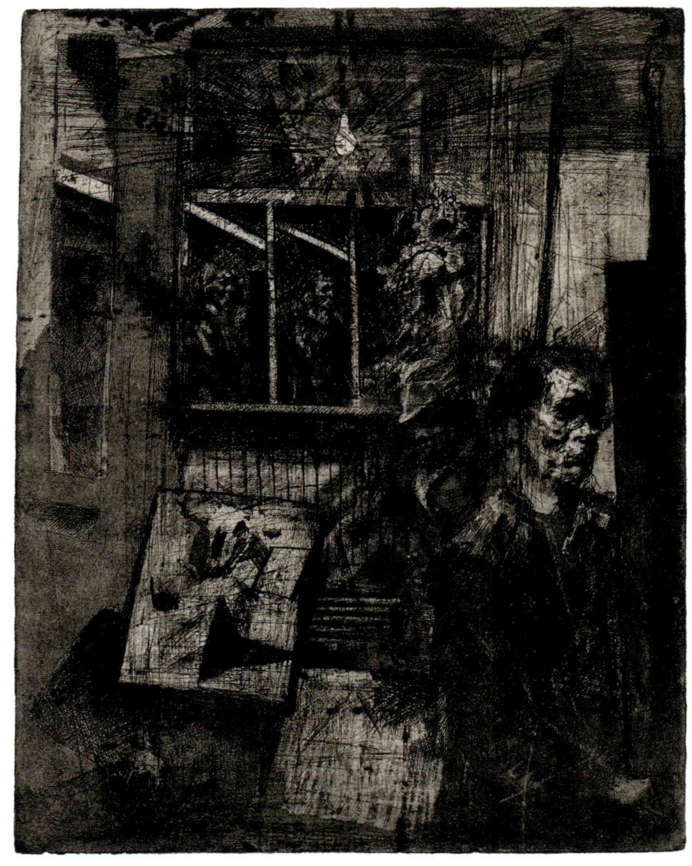

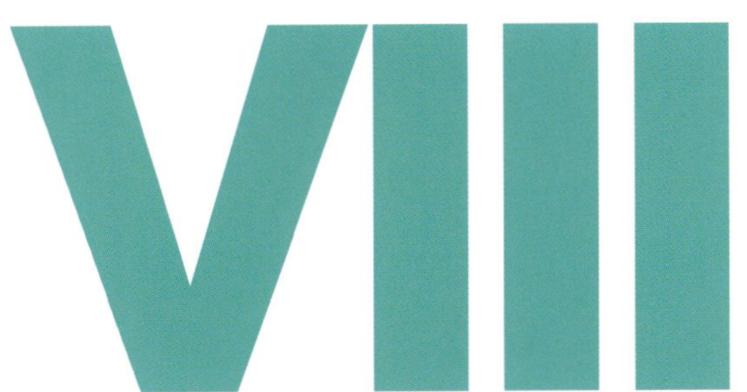

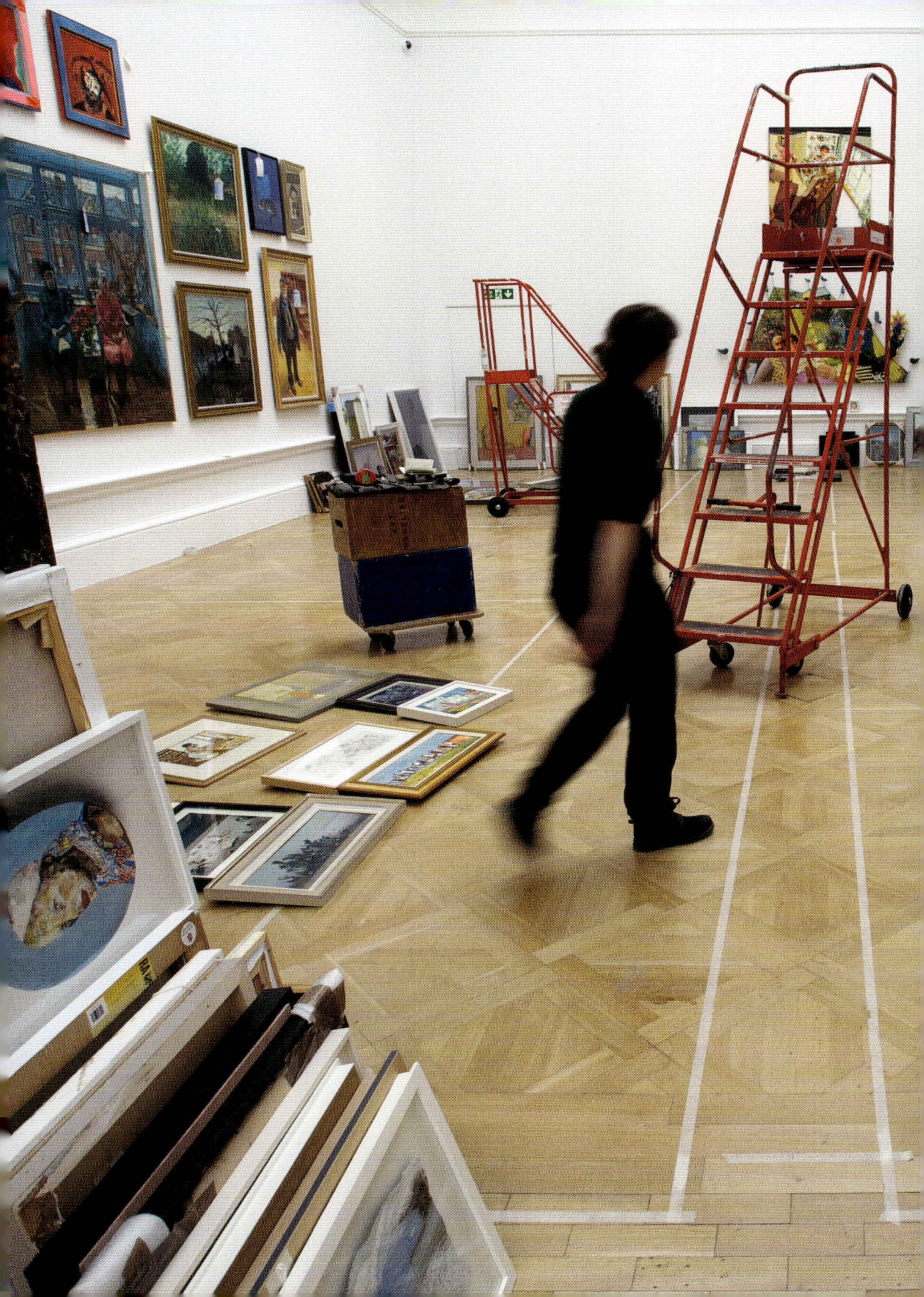

Mick Rooney RA
Just Landed
Oil
165 × 112 cm

James Butler MBE RA
Soldier
Bronze
H 65 cm

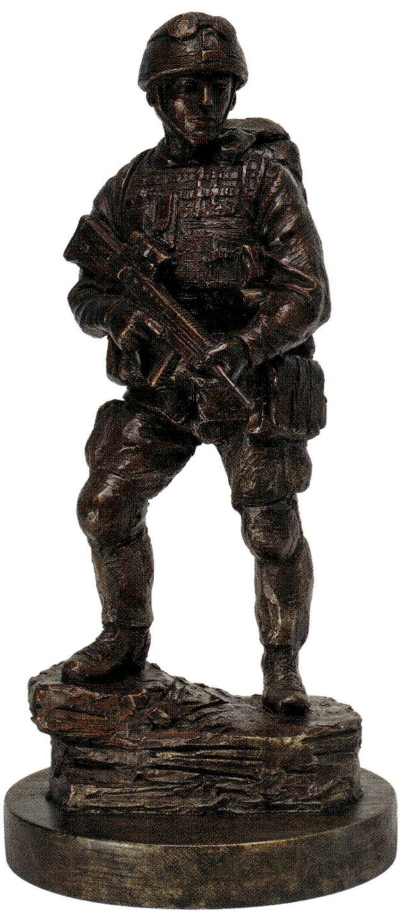

Prof David Mach RA
Sunimi
Coat hangers
H 55 cm

Ken Howard OBE RA
Pescheria Duet (detail)
Oil
65 × 137 cm

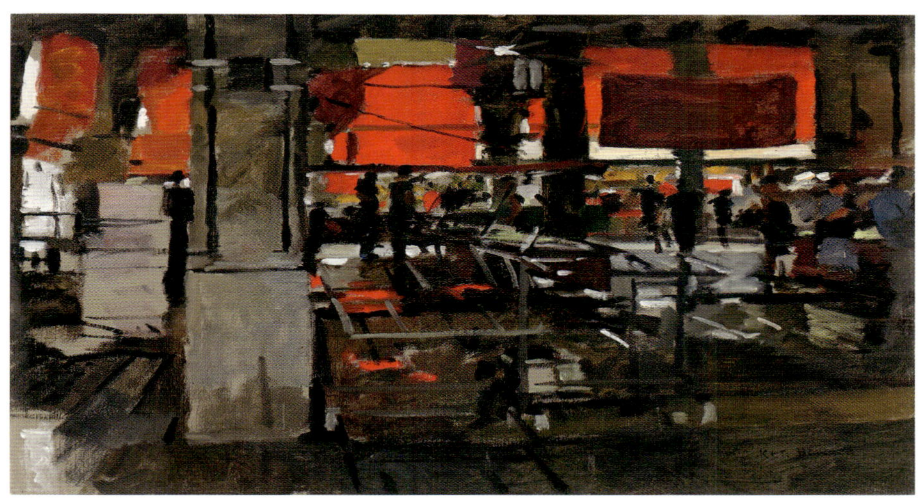

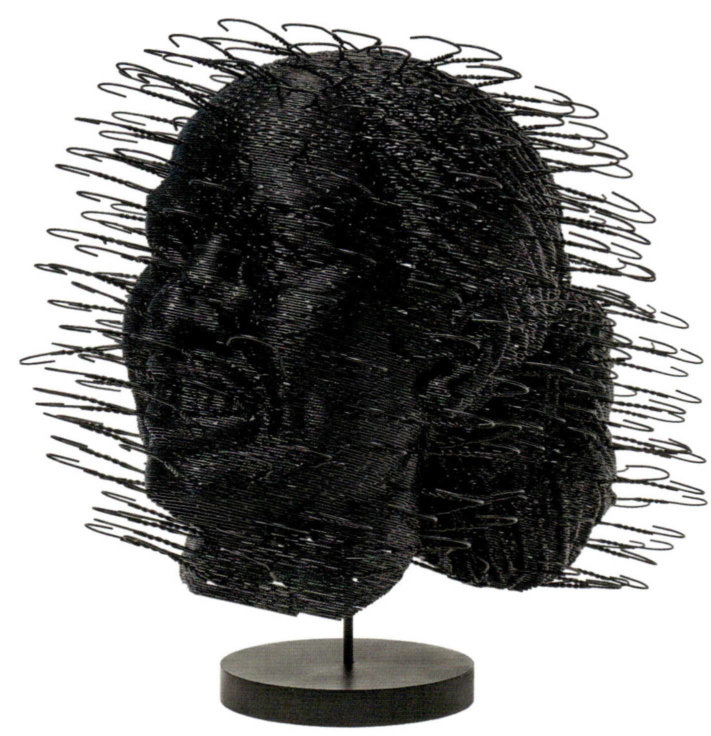

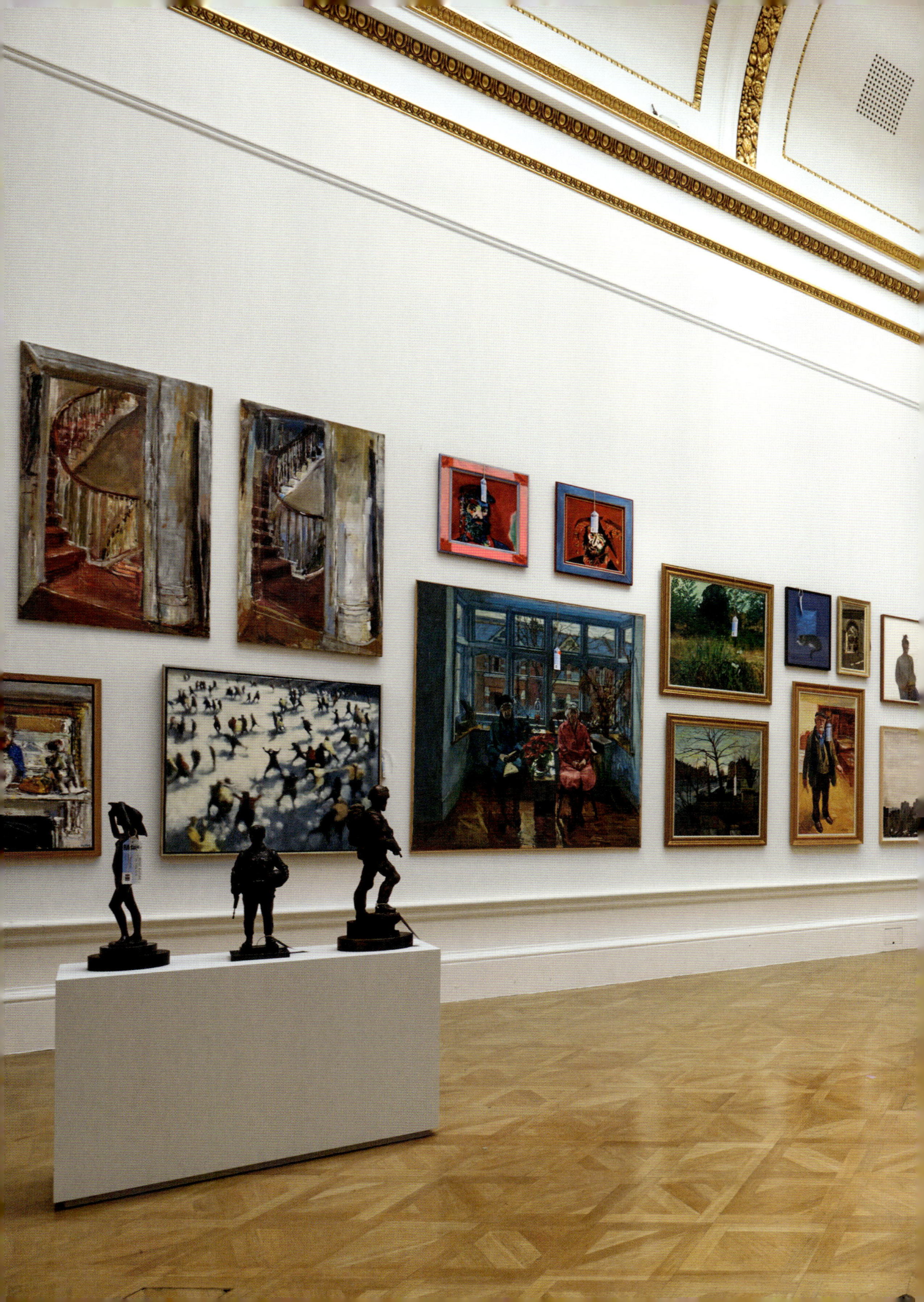

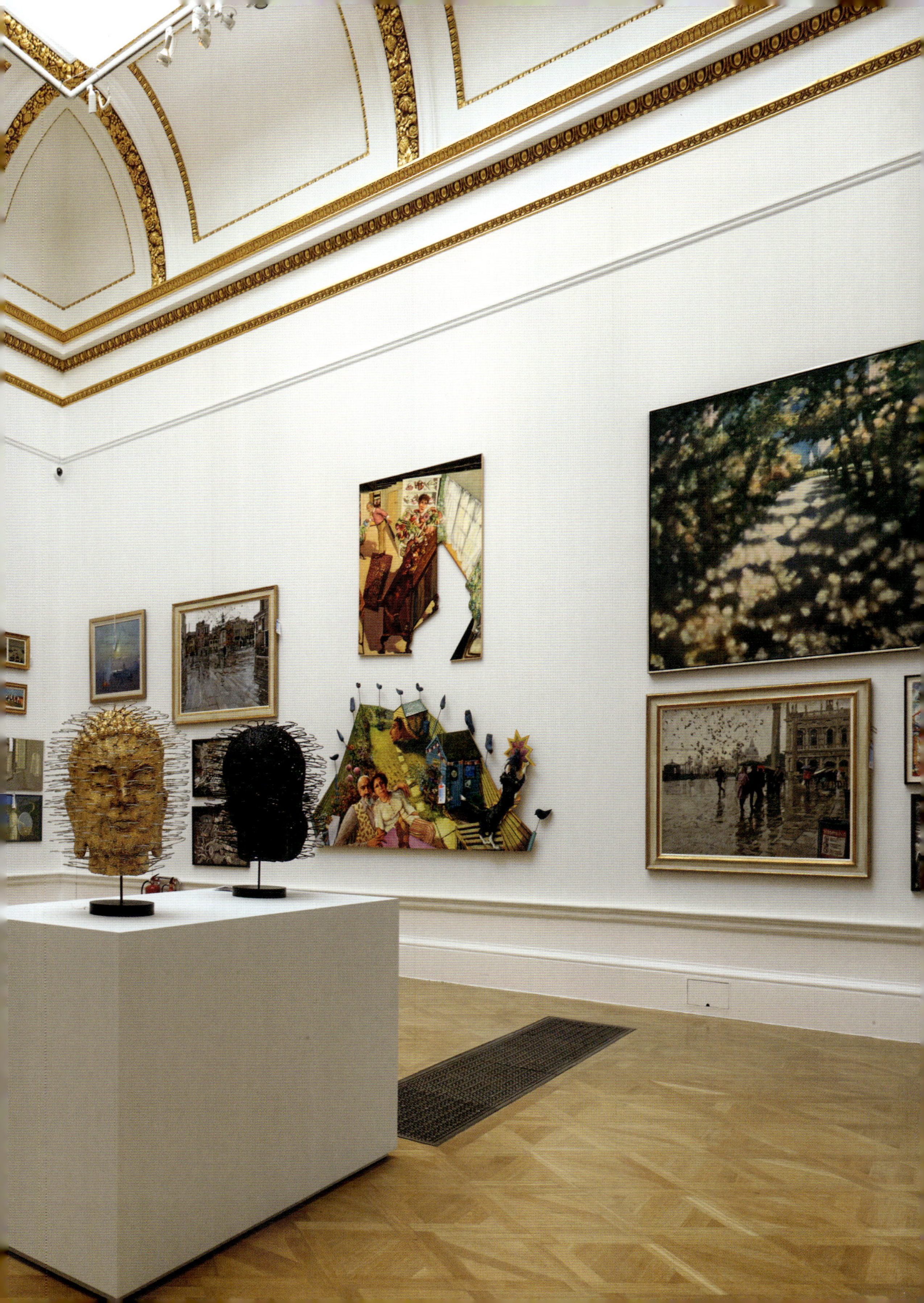

The late William Bowyer RA
The Sisters
Oil
183 × 183 cm

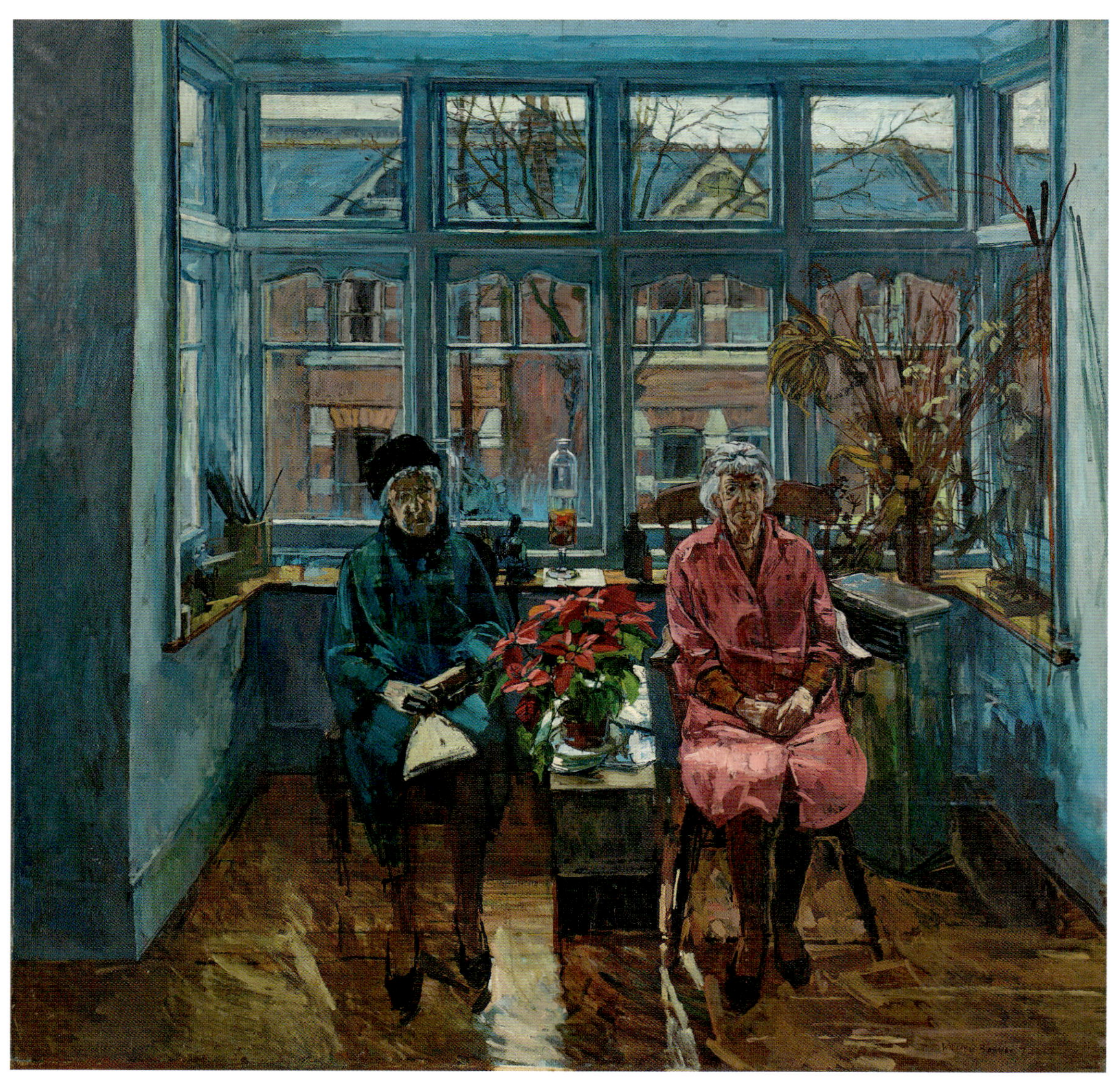

Anthony Green RA
The Birds/A Second Marriage
Oil on MDF
124 × 220 cm

John Wragg RA
The Reader
Acrylic
110 × 110 cm

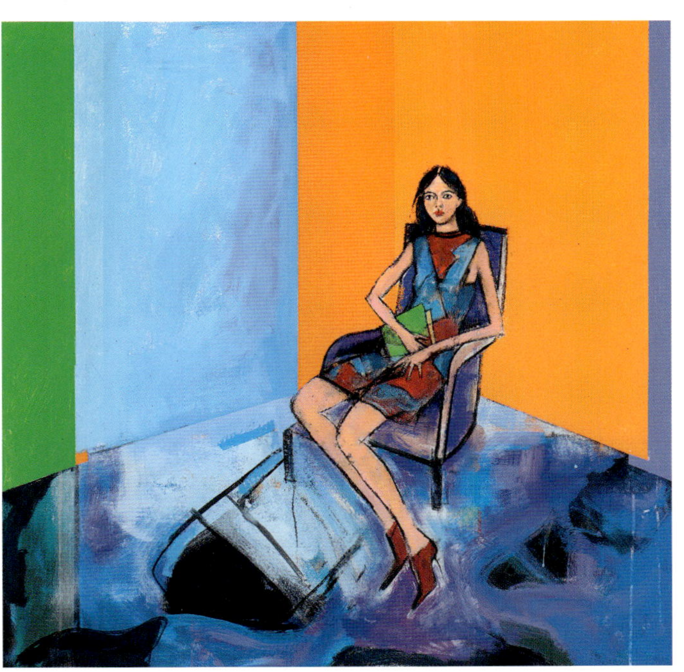

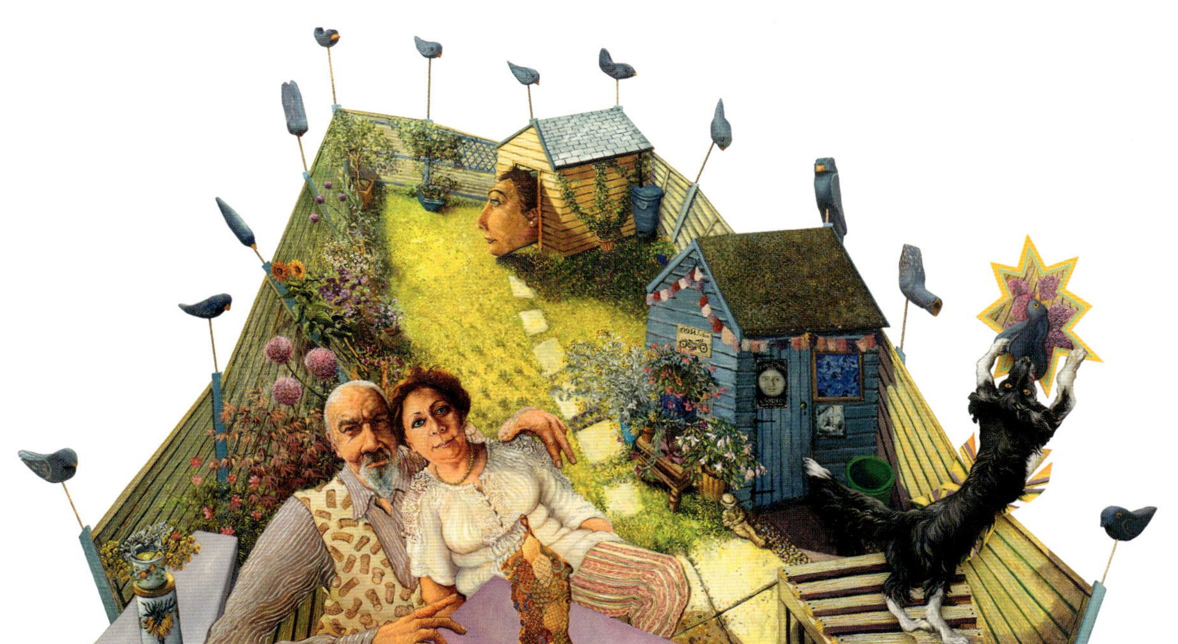

Jeffery Camp RA
Bus in a Storm
Oil
50 × 40 cm

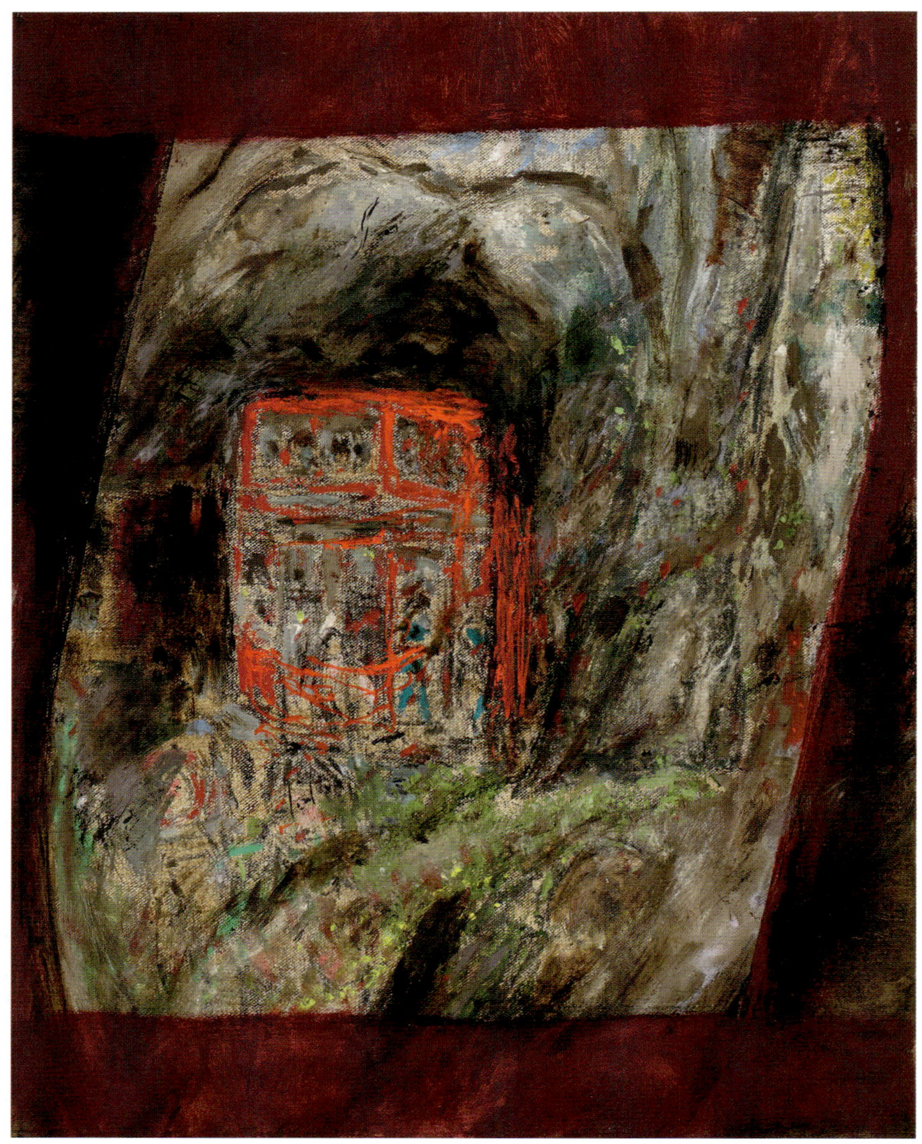

Anthony Eyton RA
Staircase by Night
Oil
147 × 87 cm

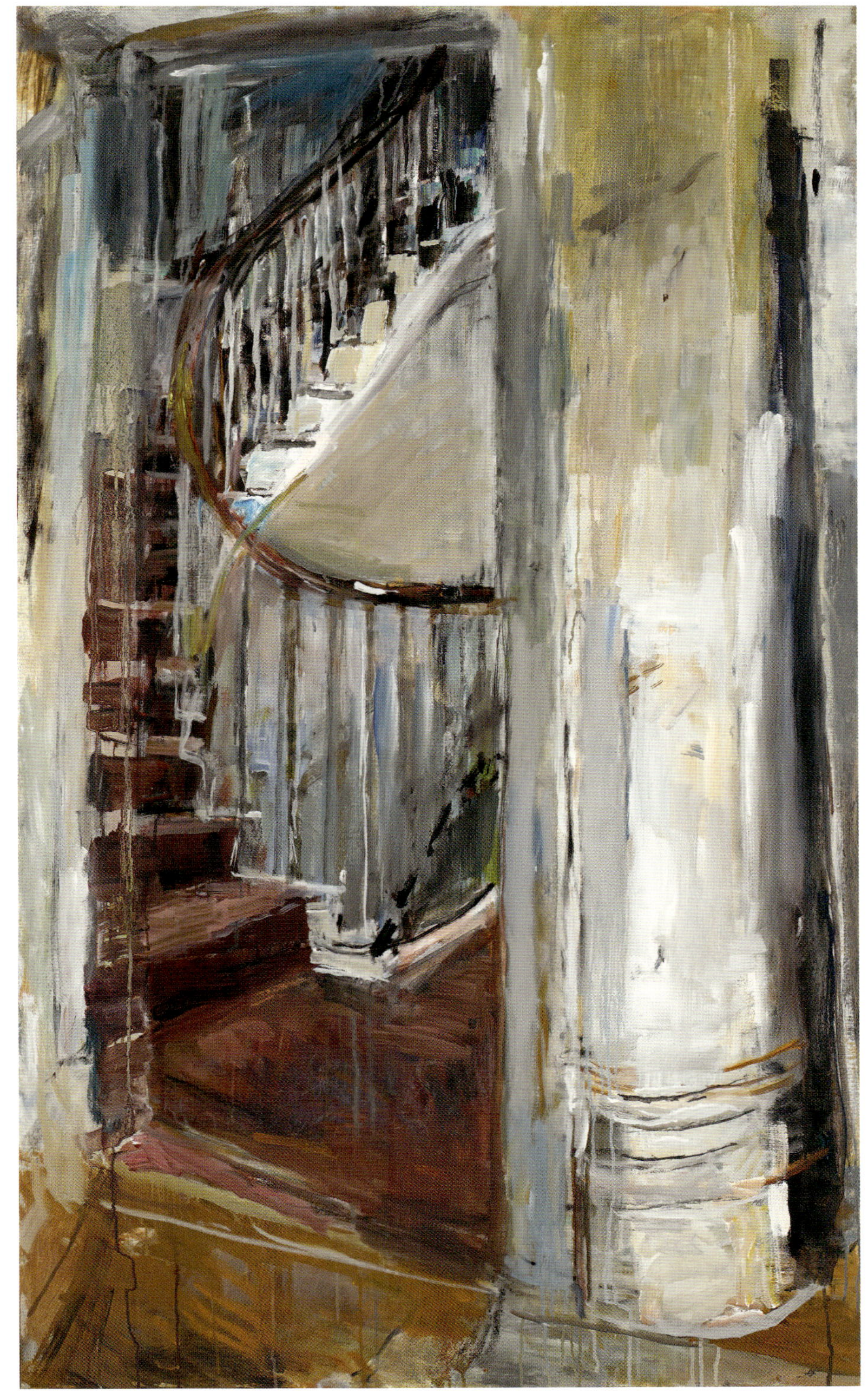

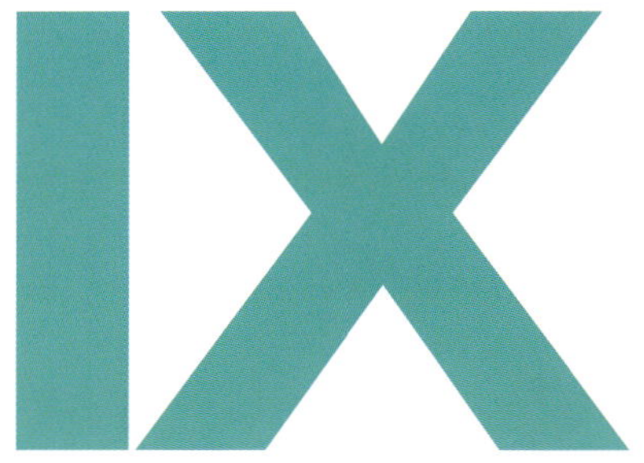

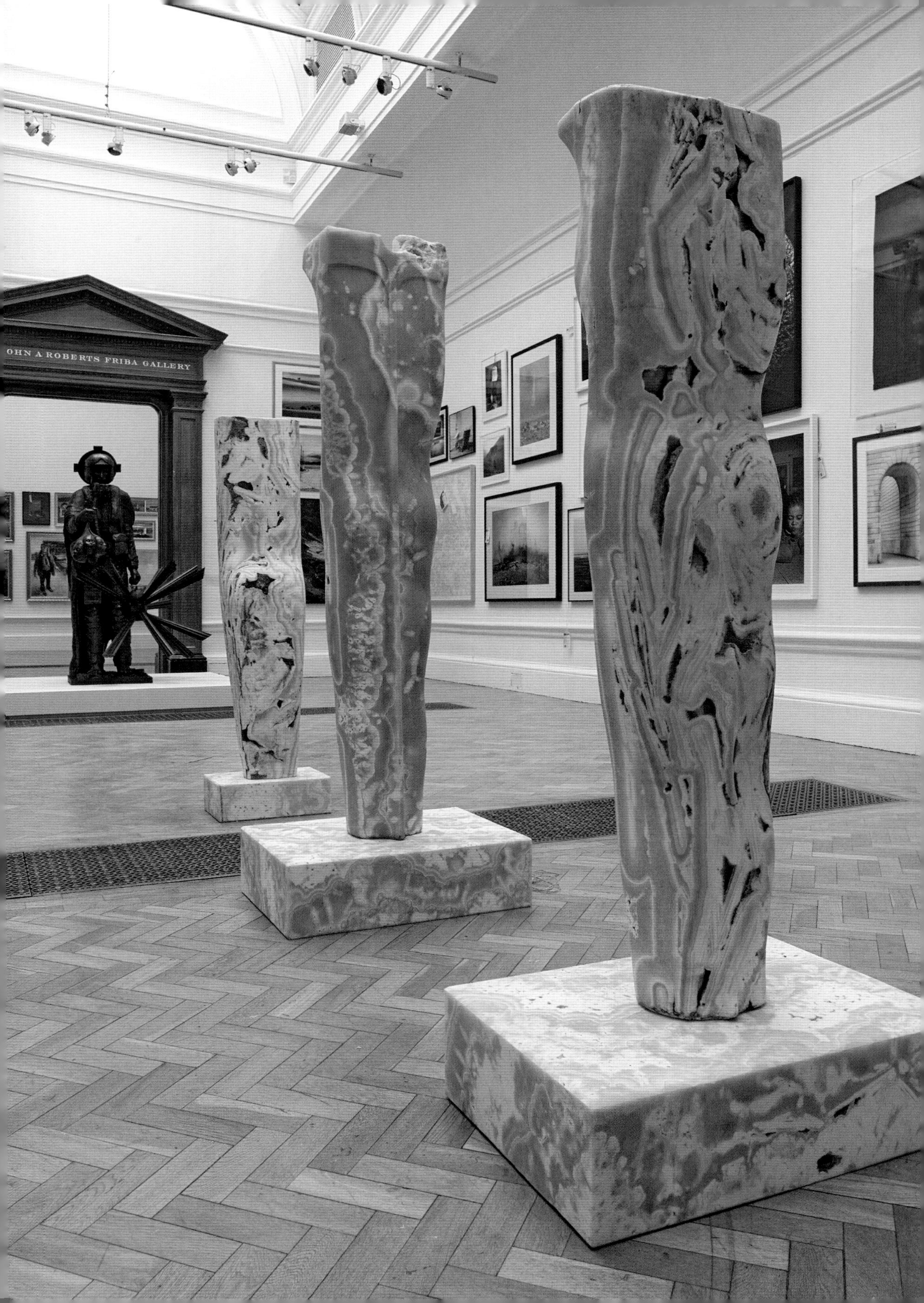
OHN A ROBERTS FRIBA GALLERY

Jean Macalpine
The Island
Inkjet print
113 × 153 cm

Robin Friend
Gaewern Slate Mine (Abandoned in 1970) – From the Series 'Formations'
C-type print
154 × 122 cm

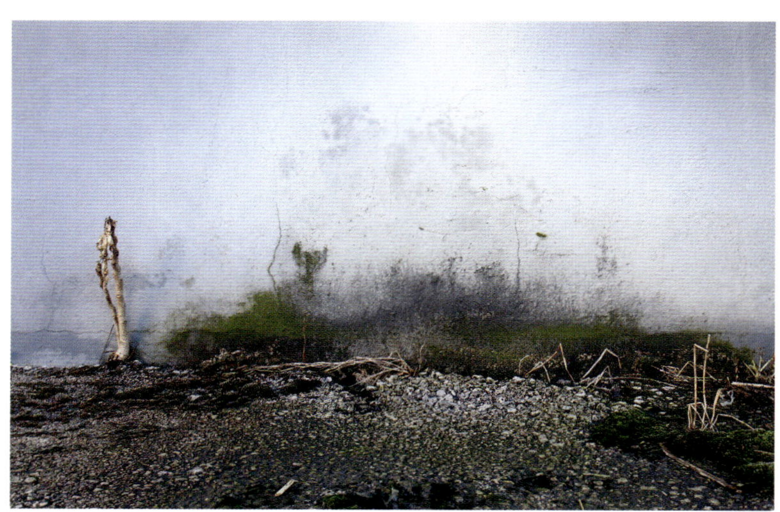

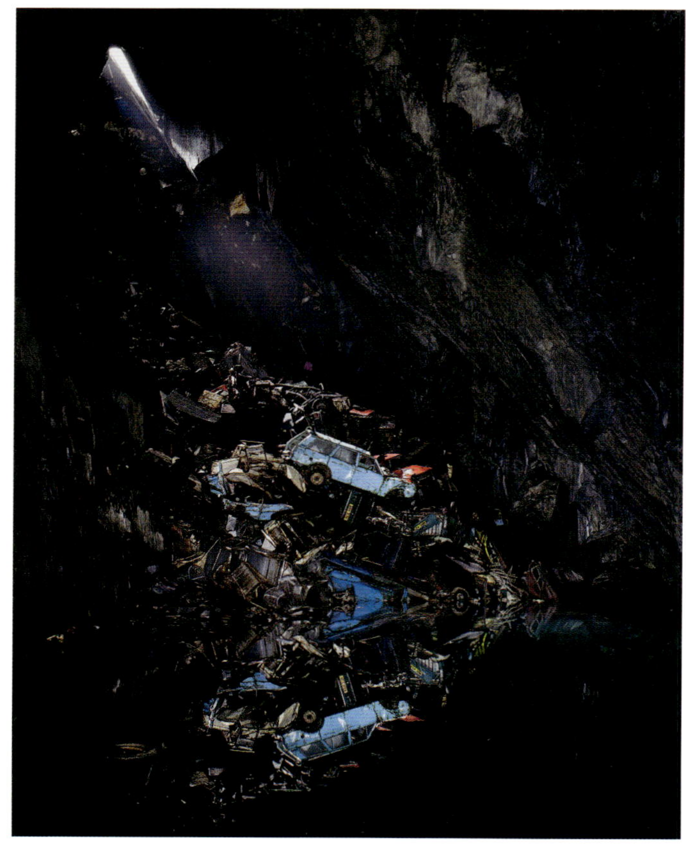

Mark Neville
Somerford Grove Adventure Playground in Tottenham
C-type print
120 × 154 cm

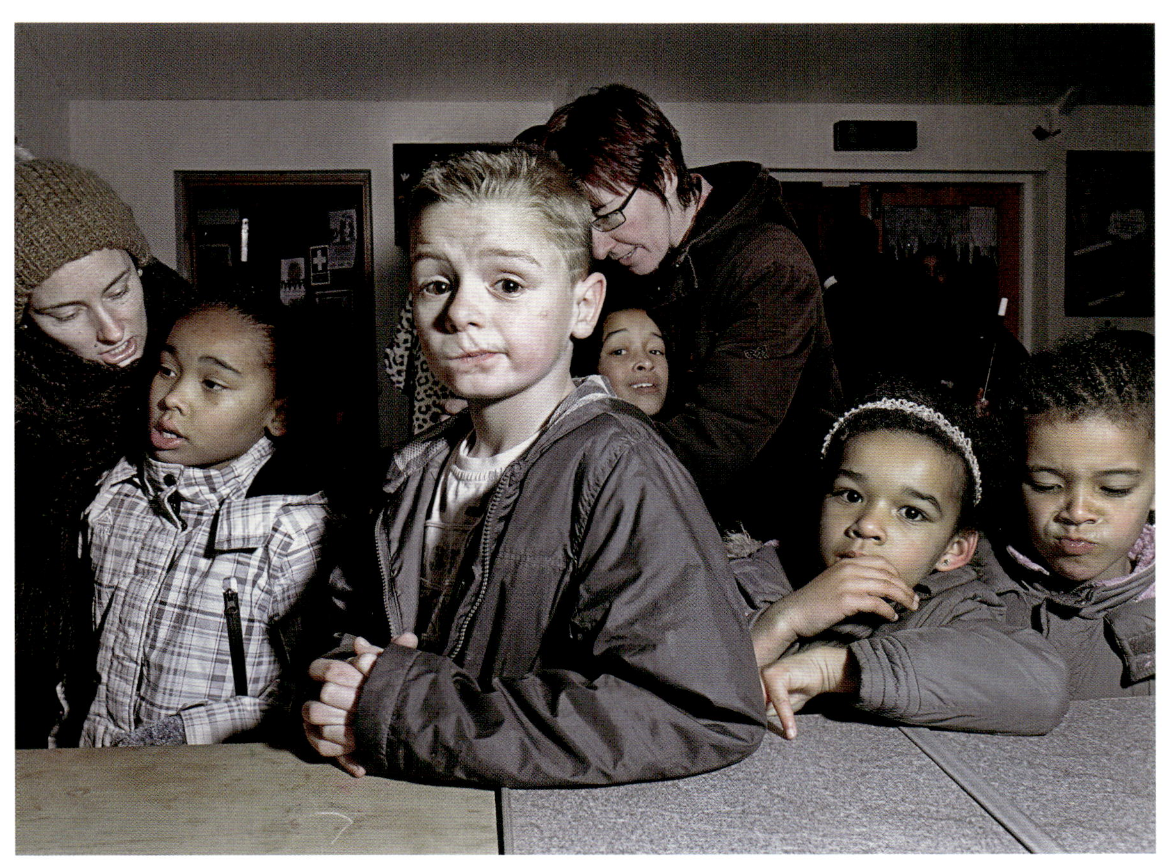

Prof Michael Sandle RA
As Ye Sow So Shall Ye Reap: An Allegory (Acknowledgements to Holman Hunt)
Bronze
H 210 cm

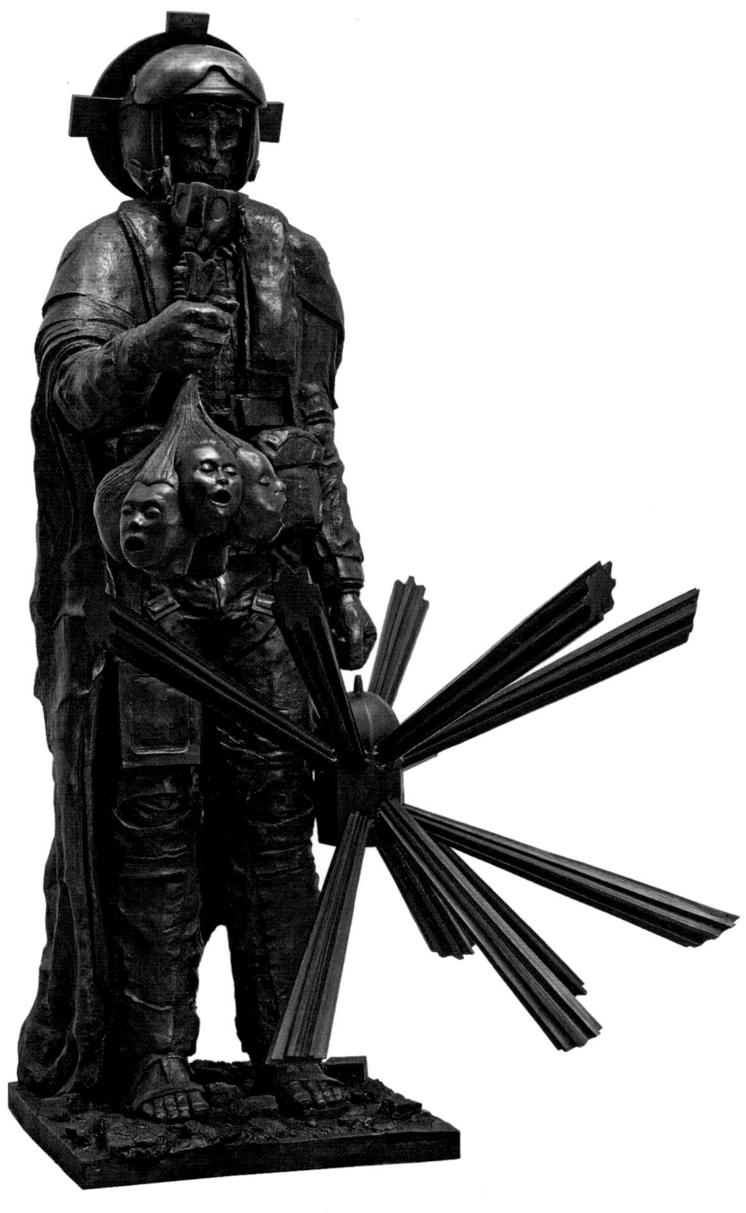

Suzanne Moxhay
Topologies 1
Archival print on paper
62 × 45 cm

Scott Mead
Looking Back
C-type print
153 × 122 cm

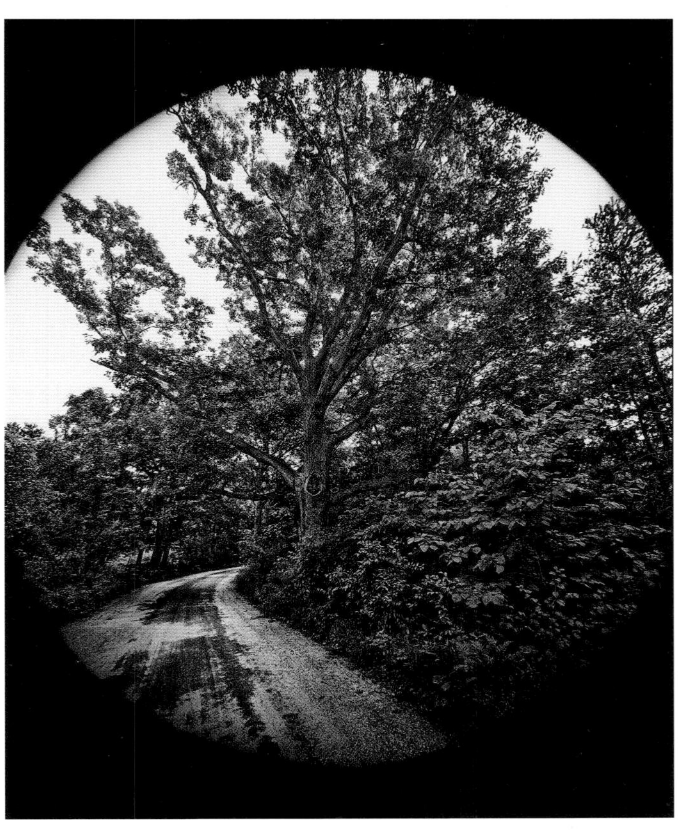

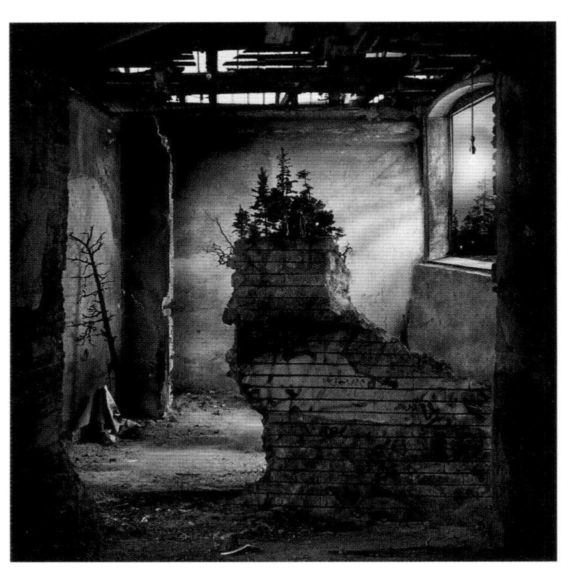

Lecture Room

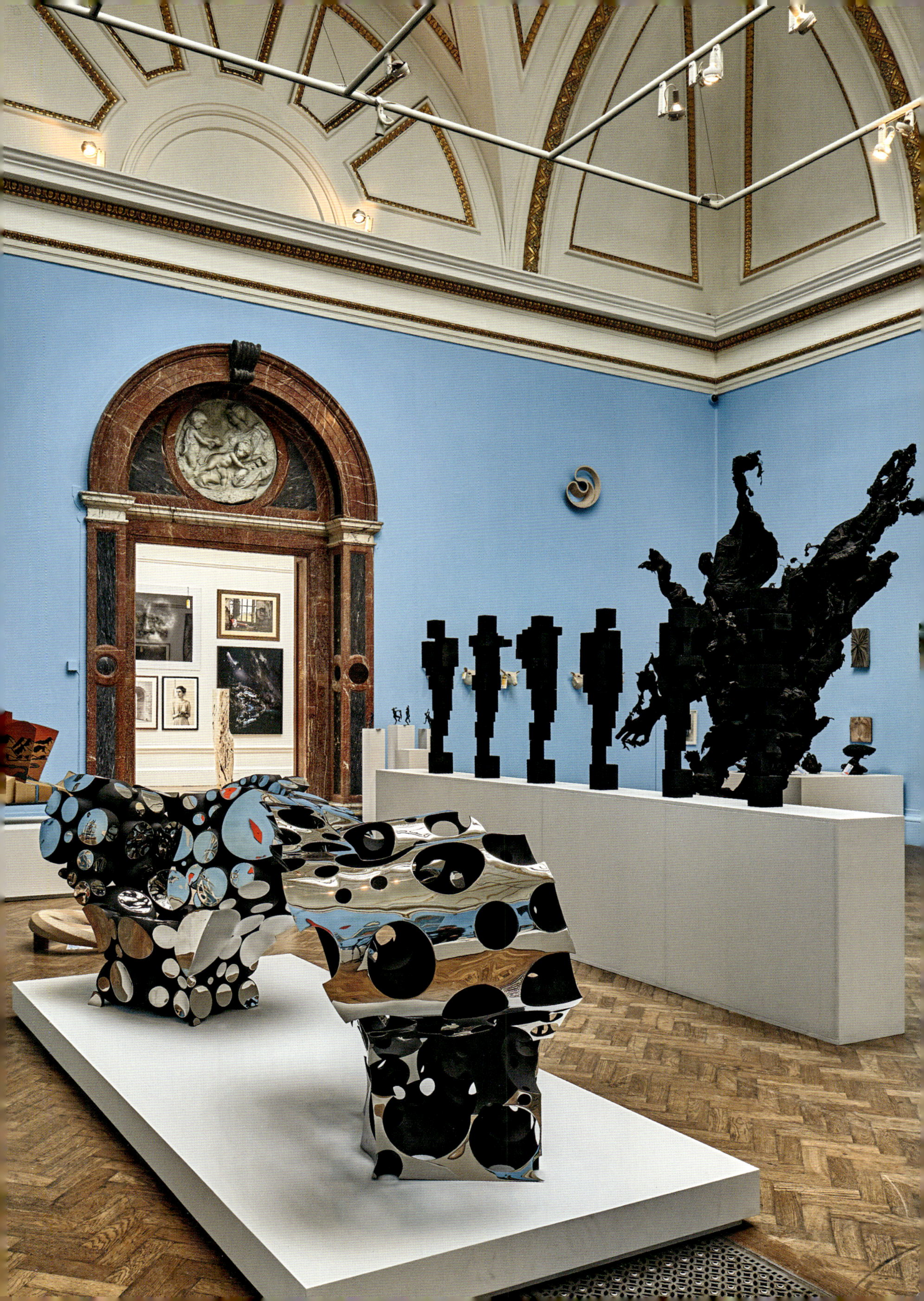

John Carter RA
Pierced Red Shape (From the Maquette of 1985)
Acrylic with marble powder on plywood
145 × 119 cm

Alison Wilding RA
Killjoy
Cast iron and bleached feather
H 12 cm

Ann Christopher RA
From the Edges of Silence
Bronze
H 75 cm

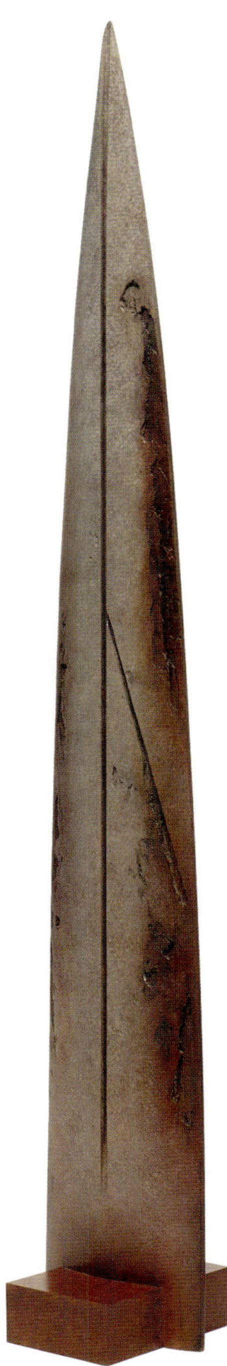

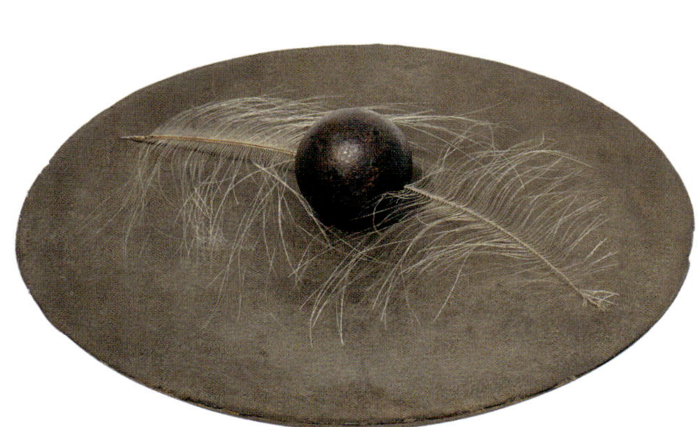

Sir Antony Gormley OBE RA
Left to right:
Small Look, 2014
H 103 cm
Small Slew, 2014
H 97 cm
Small Collect, 2014
H 104 cm
Small Hide, 2014
H 103 cm
Small Reserve, 2014
H 107 cm
Small Spin, 2014
H 108 cm
All works cast iron

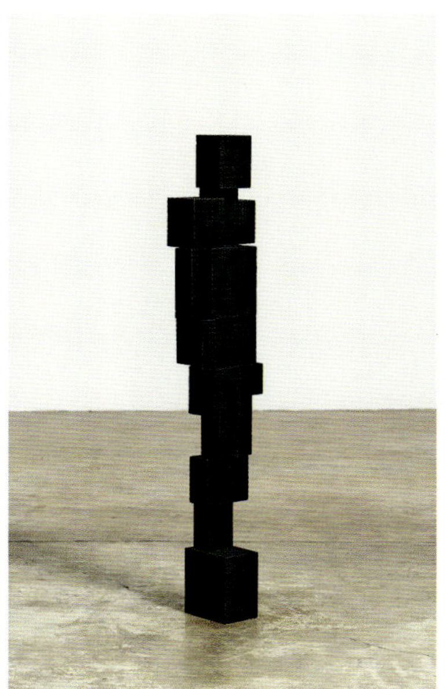

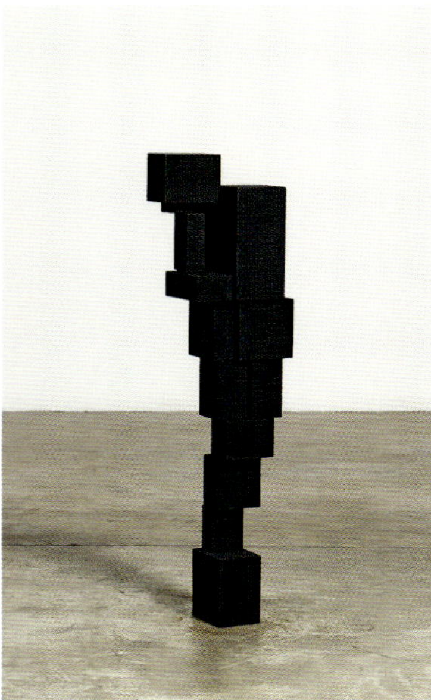

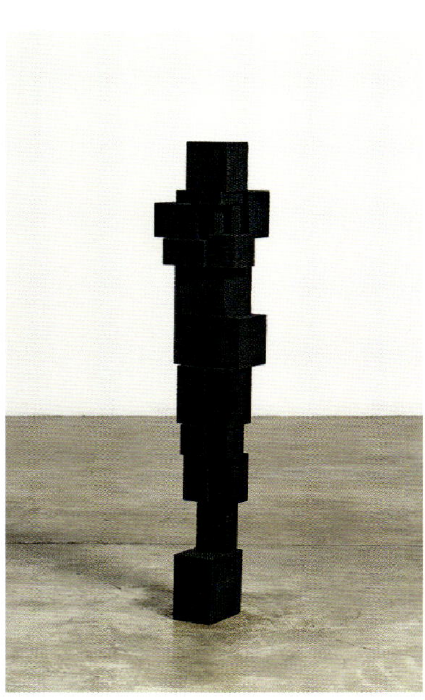

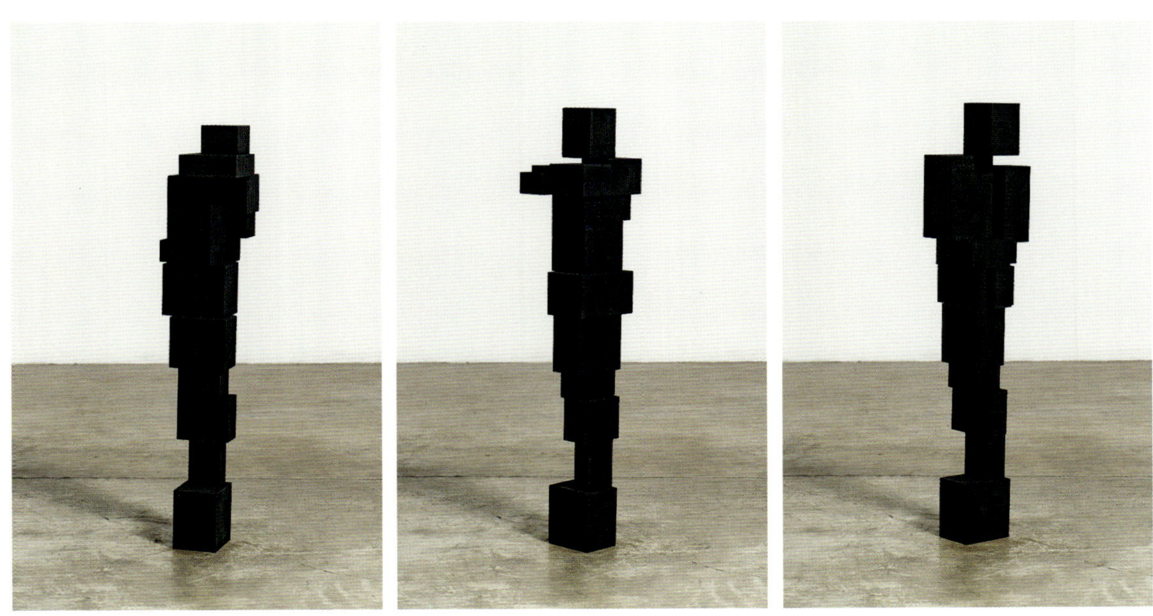

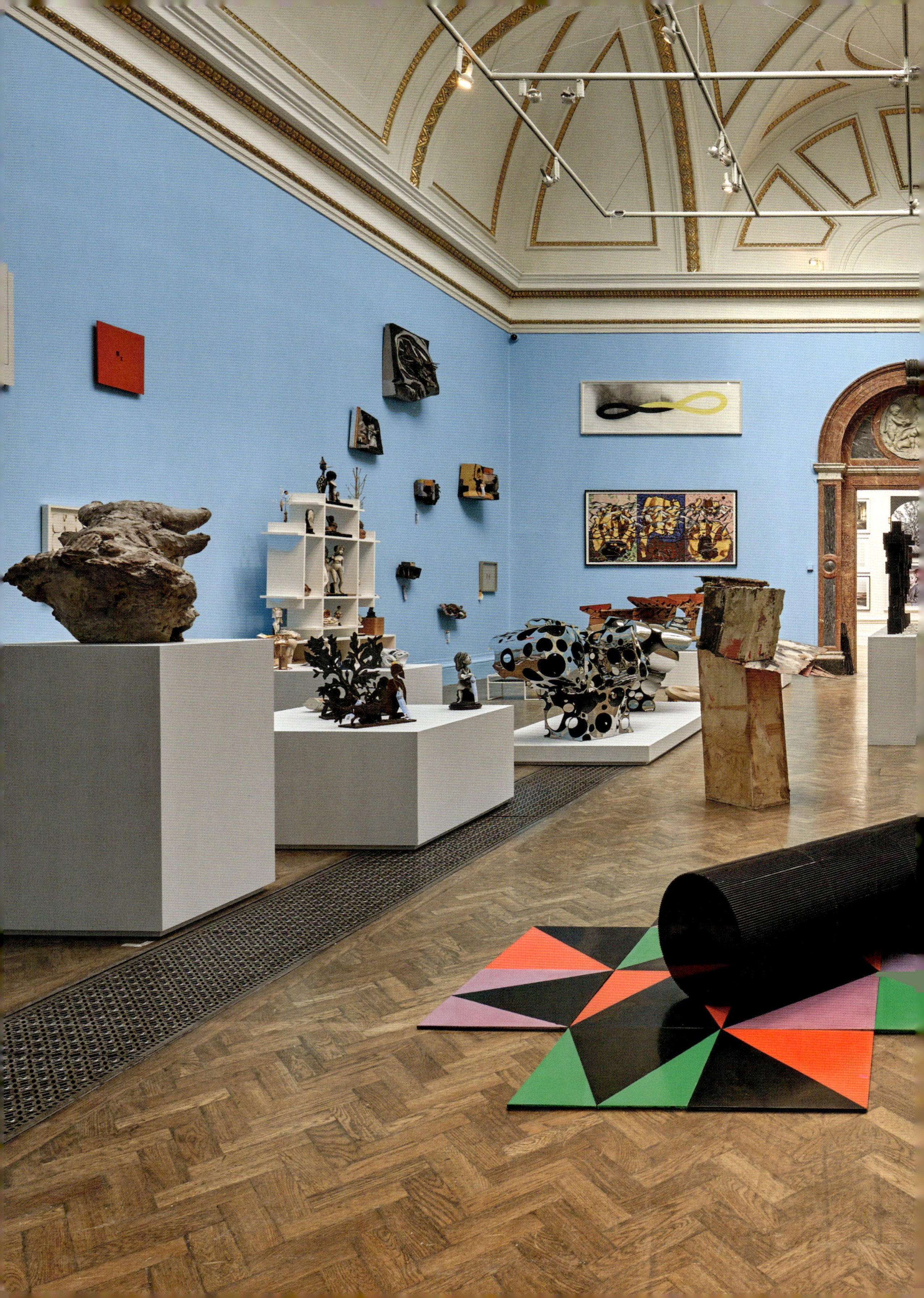

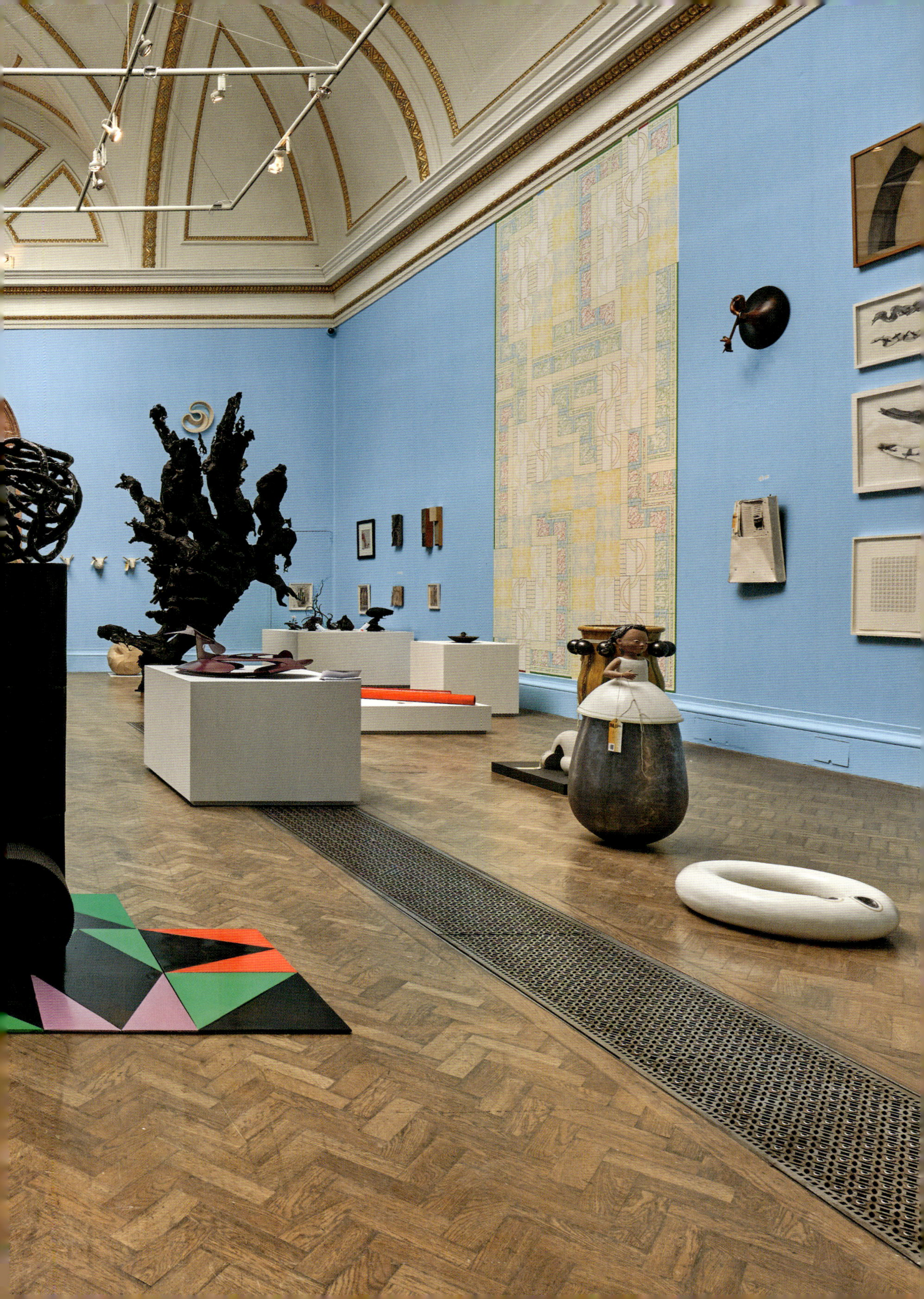

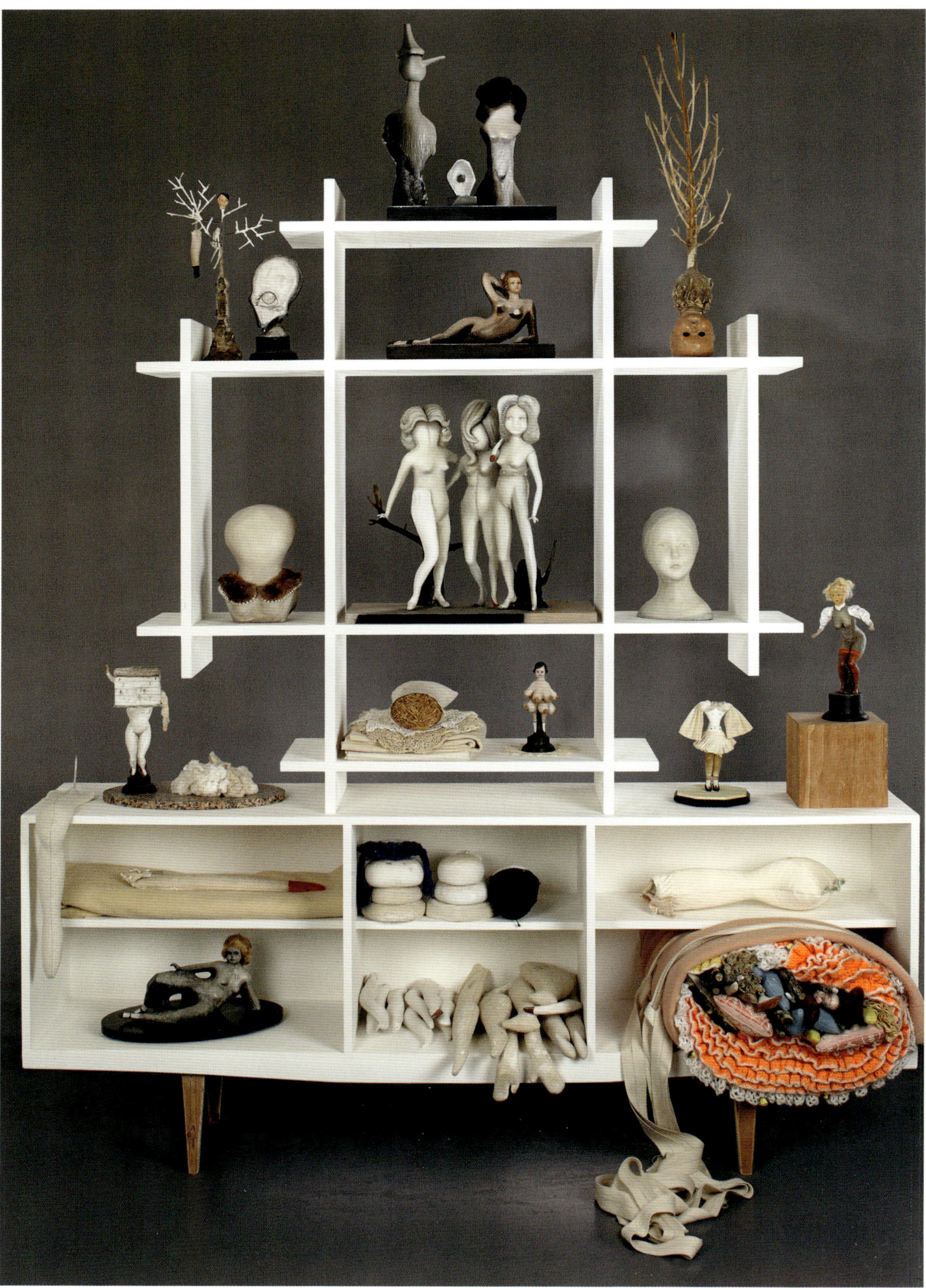

Cathie Pilkington RA
Tall Boy
Mixed media
H 270 cm

The late Geoffrey Clarke RA
Pilgrim
Mixed media
H 221 cm

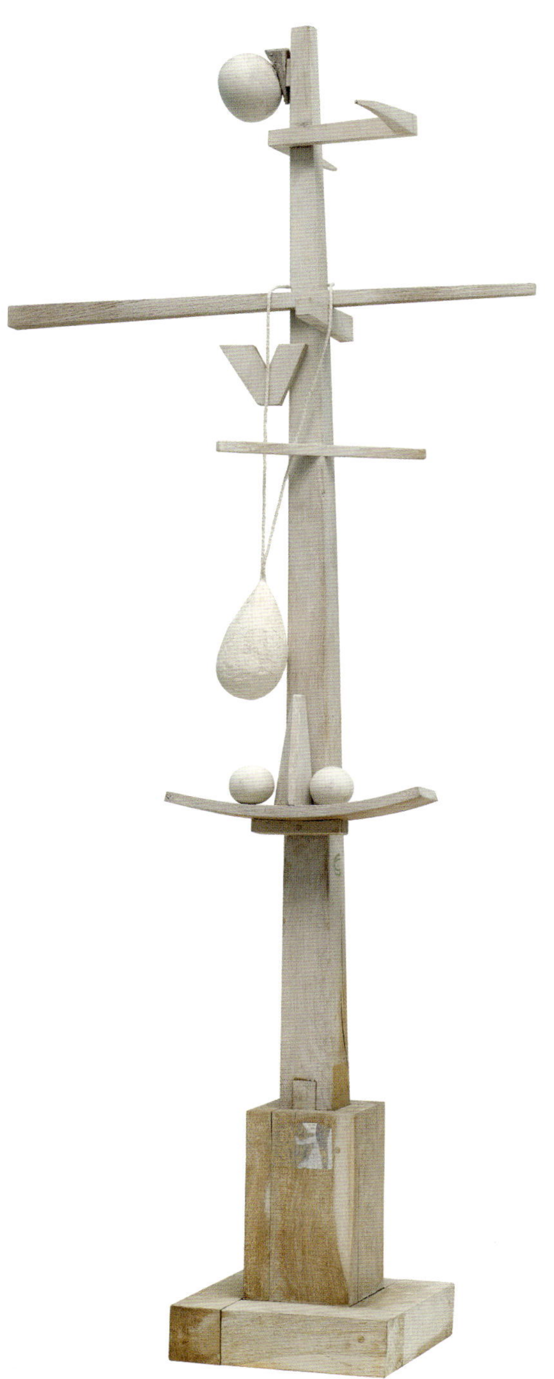

Nigel Hall RA
Winterreisse
Polished wood
D 123 cm

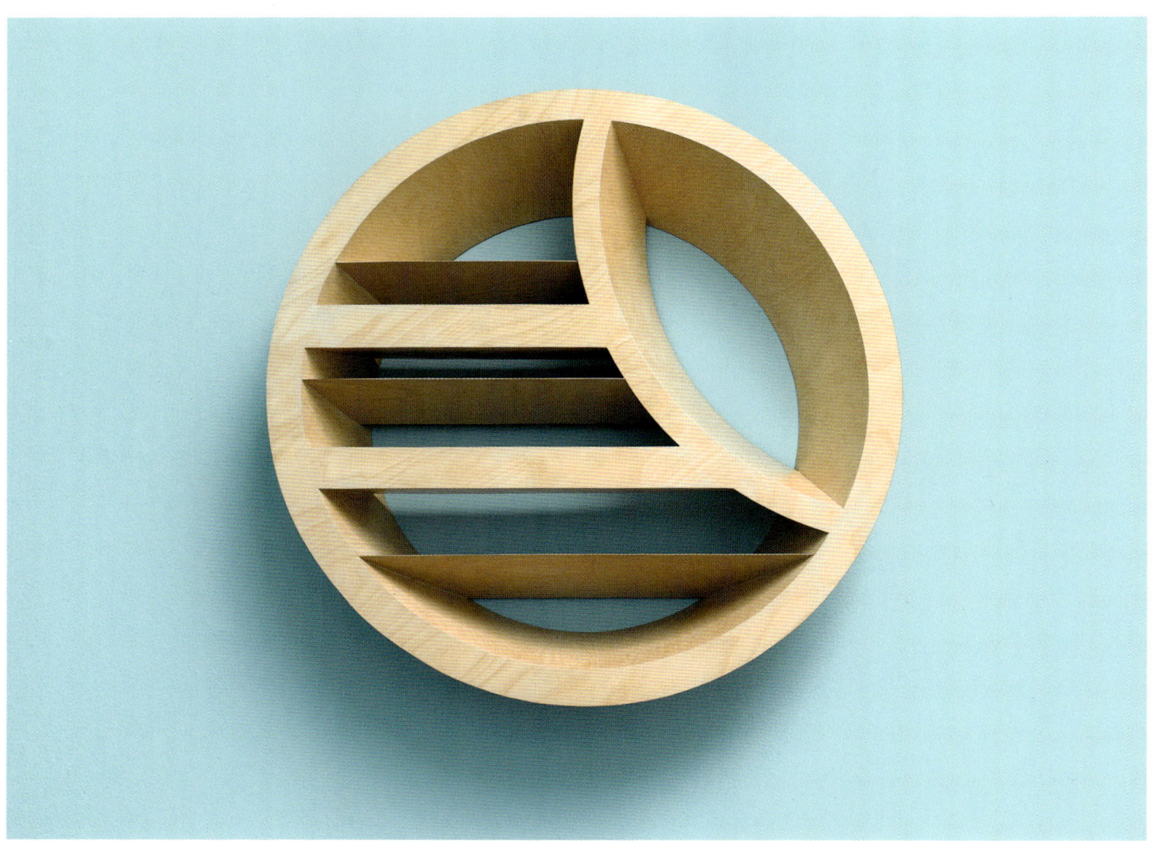

Prof Richard Wilson RA
Slipstream, Draft 2
Mixed media
46 × 63 cm

Prof Bryan Kneale RA
Untitled
Ink and watercolour
72 × 52 cm

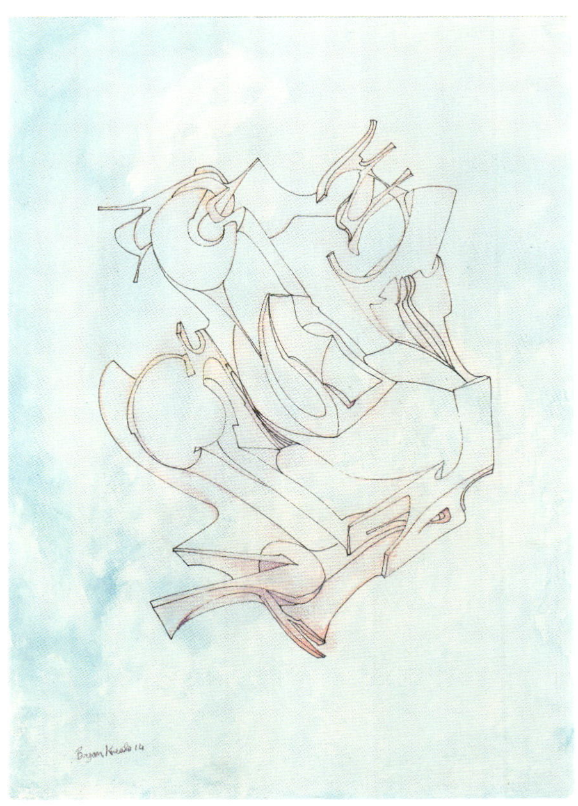

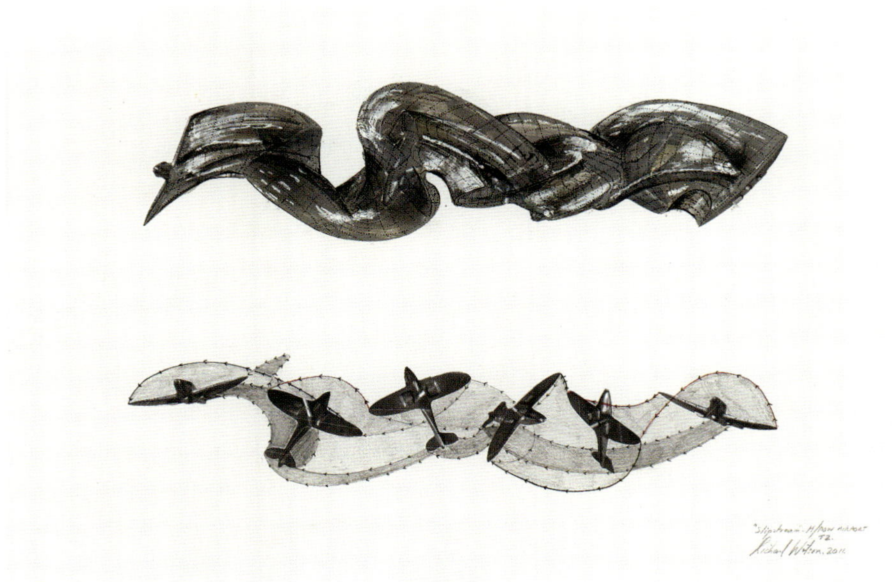

Bill Woodrow RA
Plain Ranger
Wood, cardboard, paint and oilstick
H 83 cm

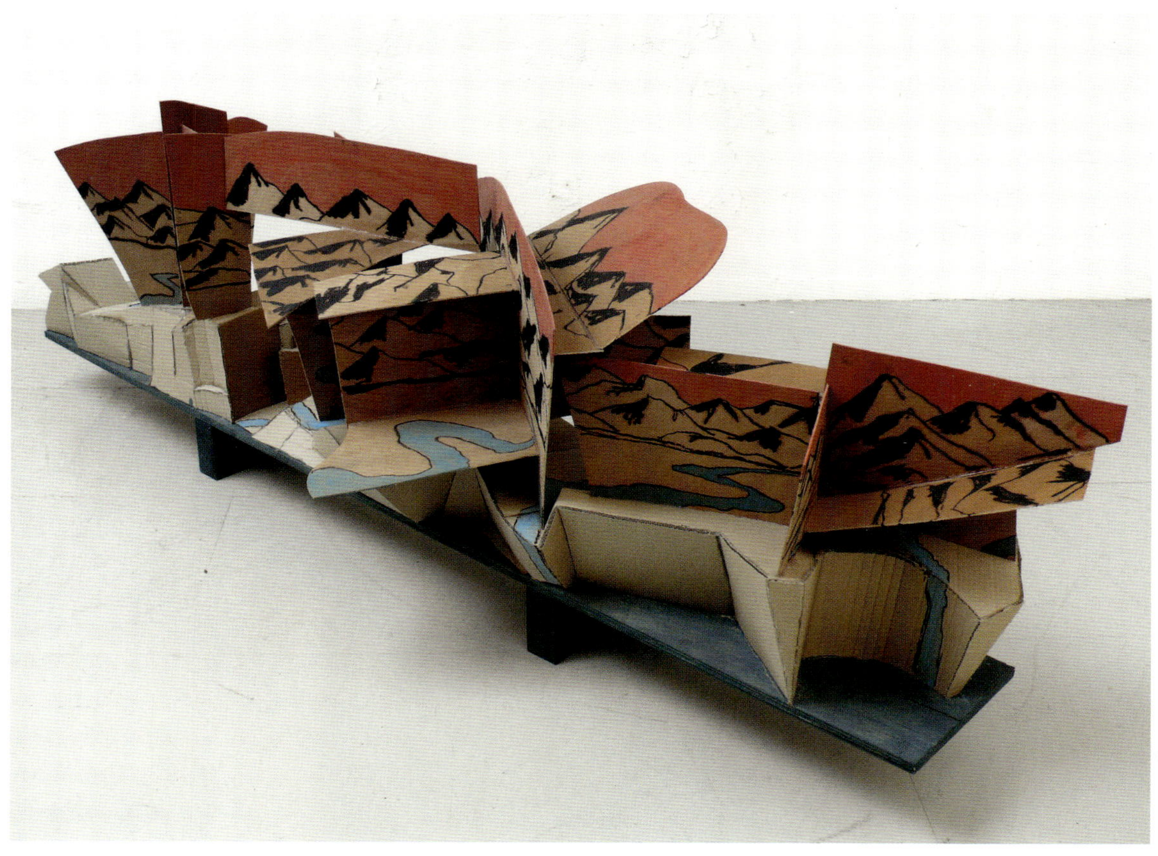

Neil Jeffries RA
Three Holes
Oil on aluminium
H 53 cm

Kenneth Draper RA
Overcast
Mixed media
H 32 cm

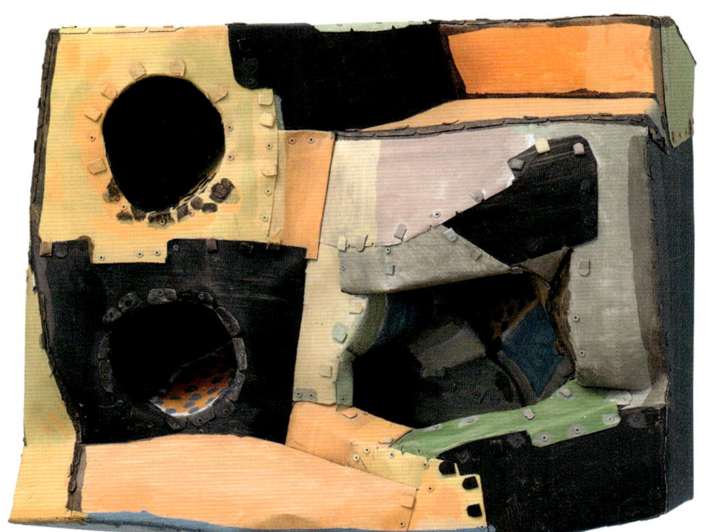

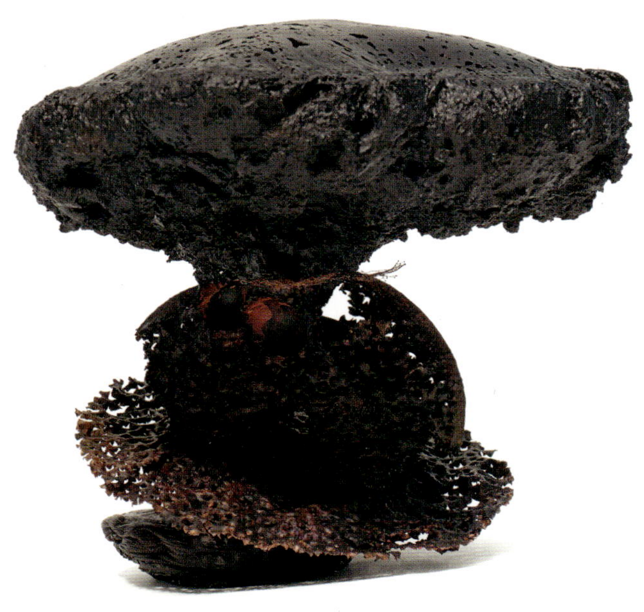

The late Prof Ivor Abrahams RA
Walking the Dog
Acrylic on wood
H 145 cm

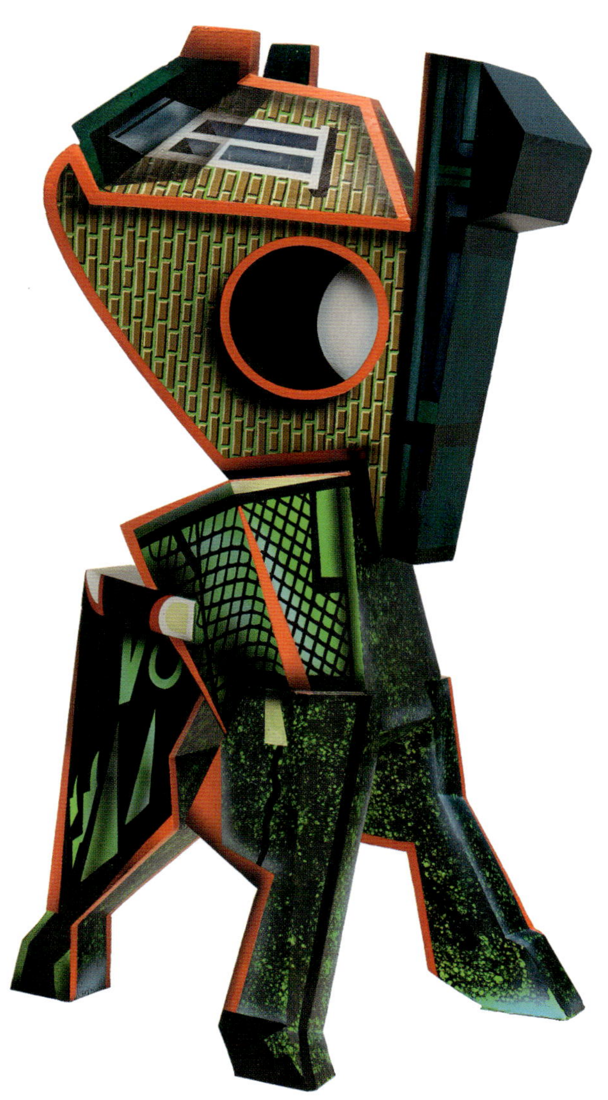

Prof Phillip King CBE PPRA
The Unpainted Gum Tree
Mixed media
230 × 230 cm

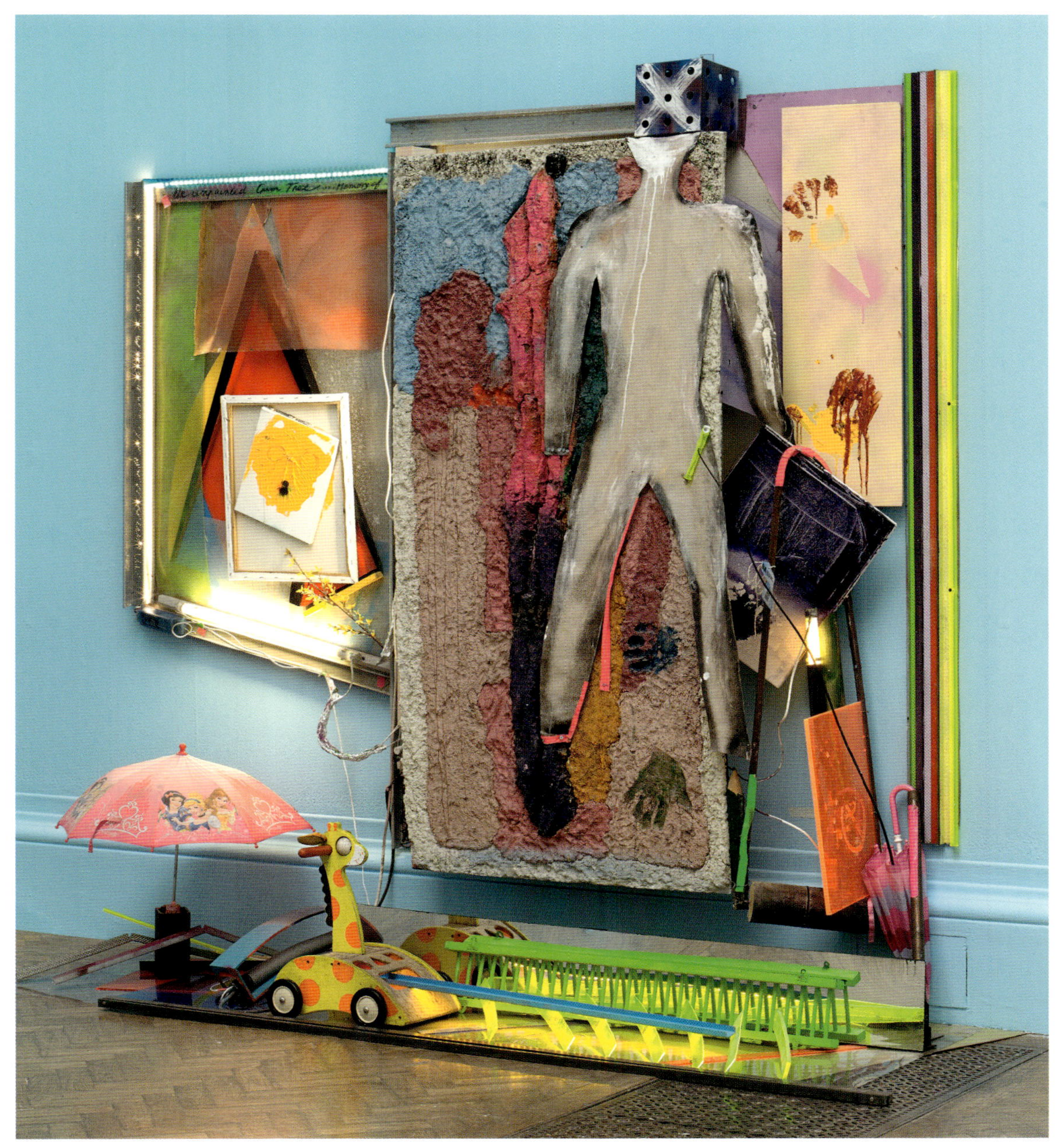

John Maine RA
Segments
Conté
79 × 104 cm

William Tucker RA
The Sculptor 2
Monotype
38 × 28 cm

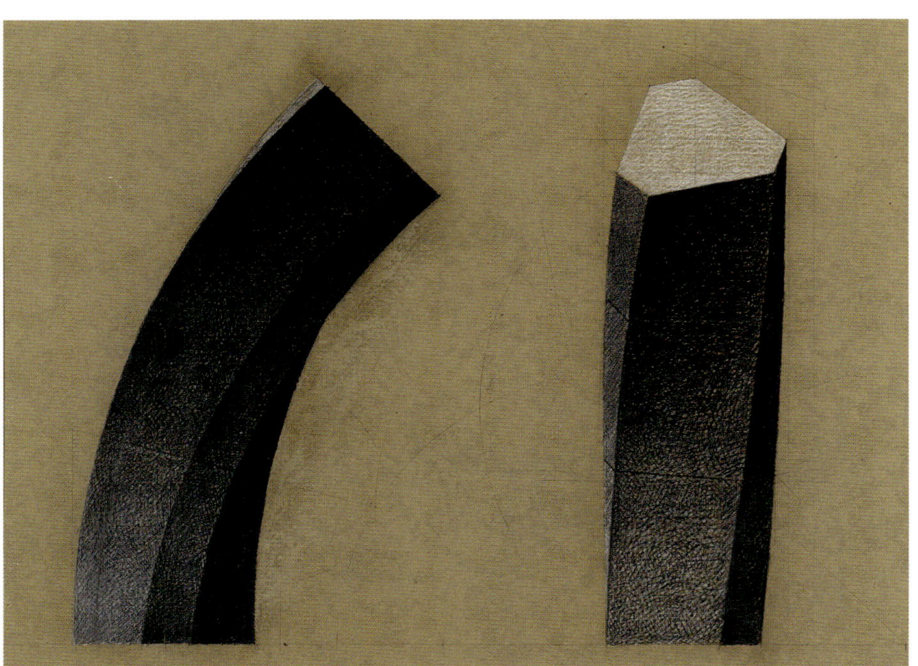

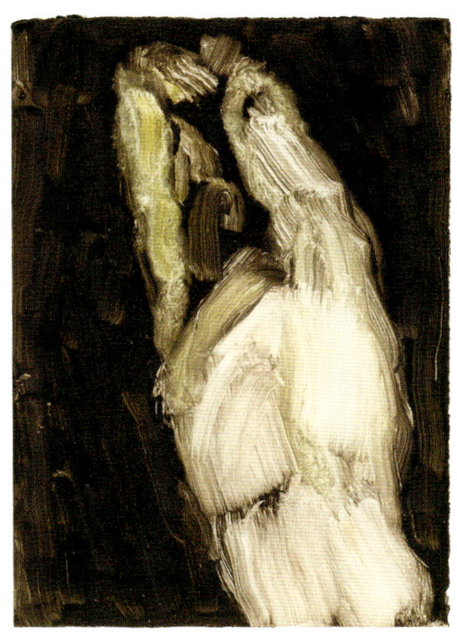

Tim Shaw RA
Erebus (Man of Fire Version II)
Mixed Media
H 350 cm

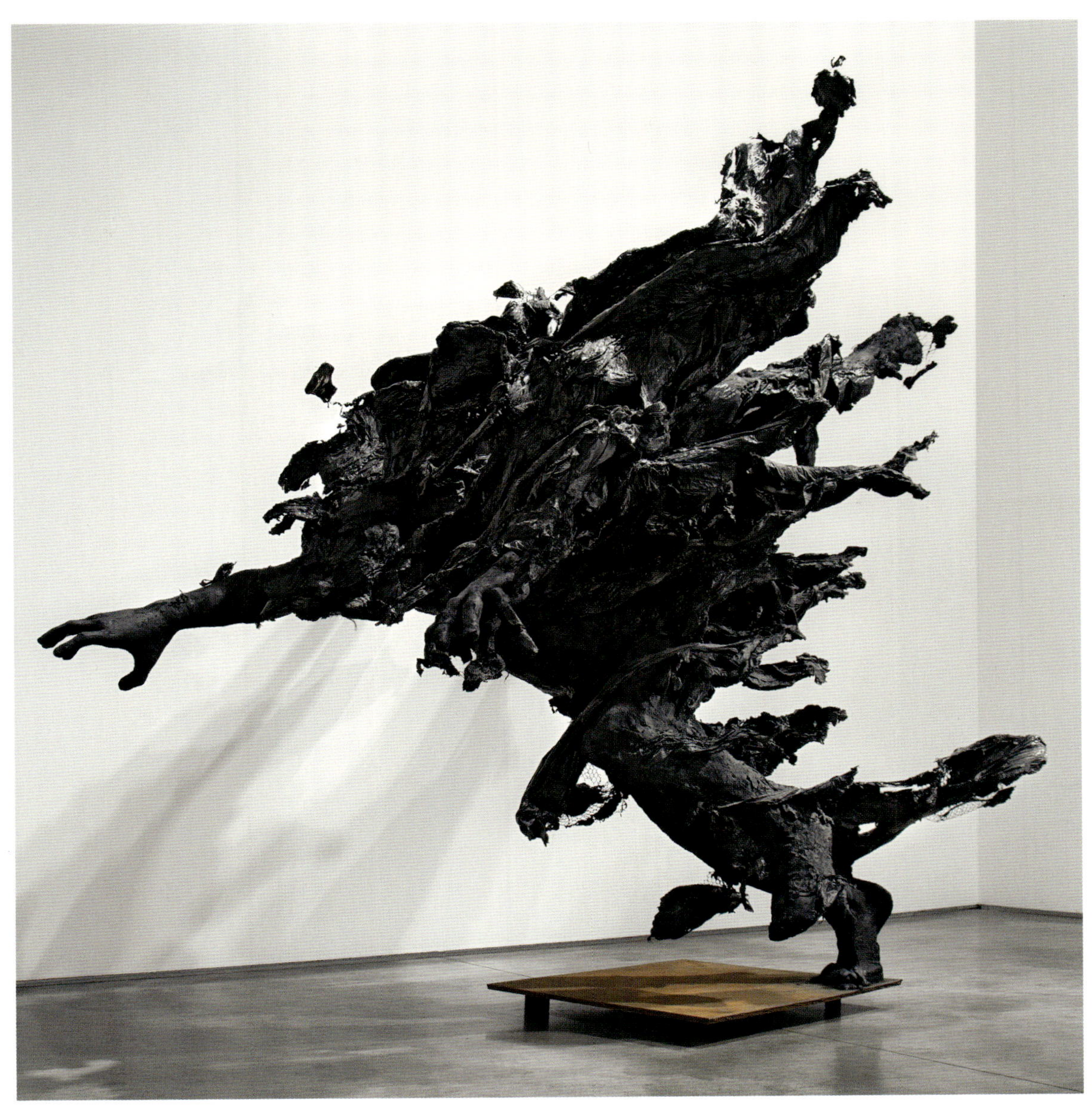

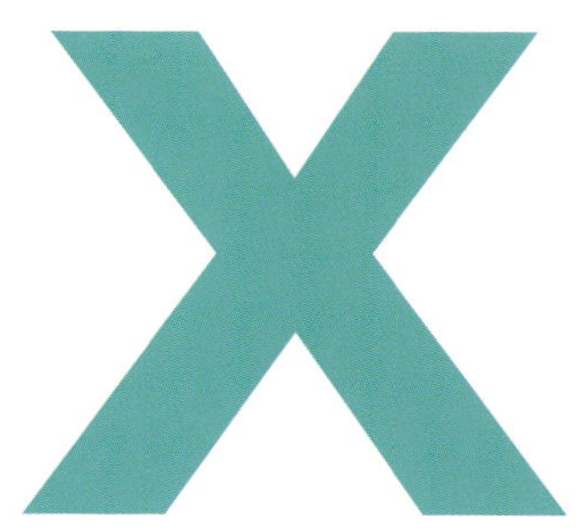

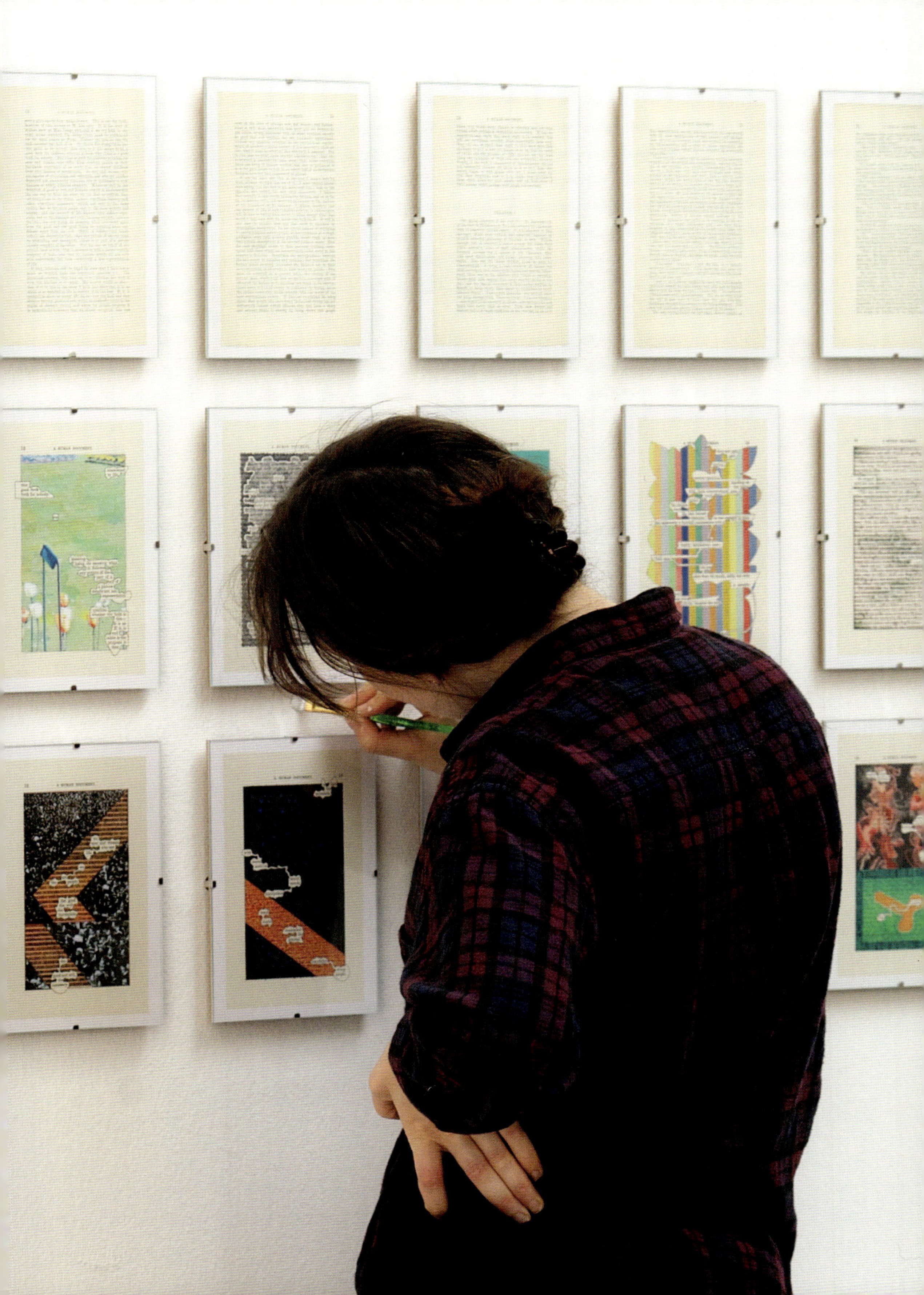

Tom Phillips CBE RA
A Humument, 1966–
Pen, ink, gouache and collage on bookpage
21 × 14.8 cm (each individual picture)

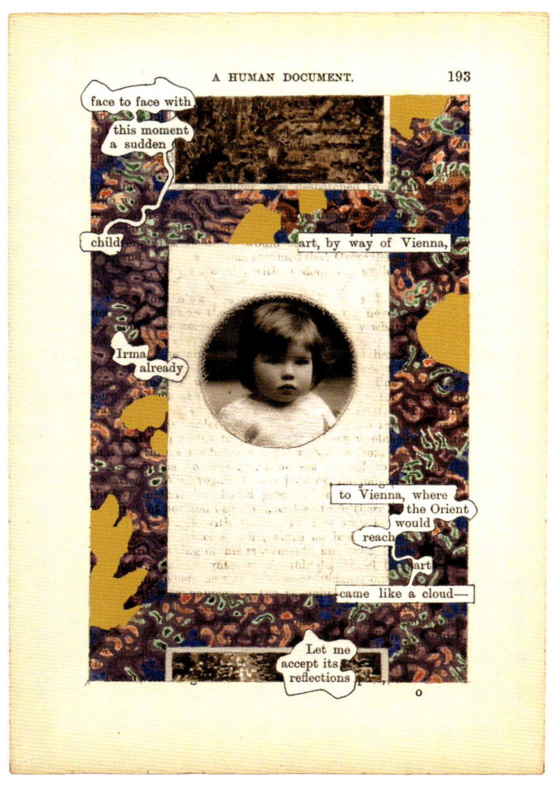

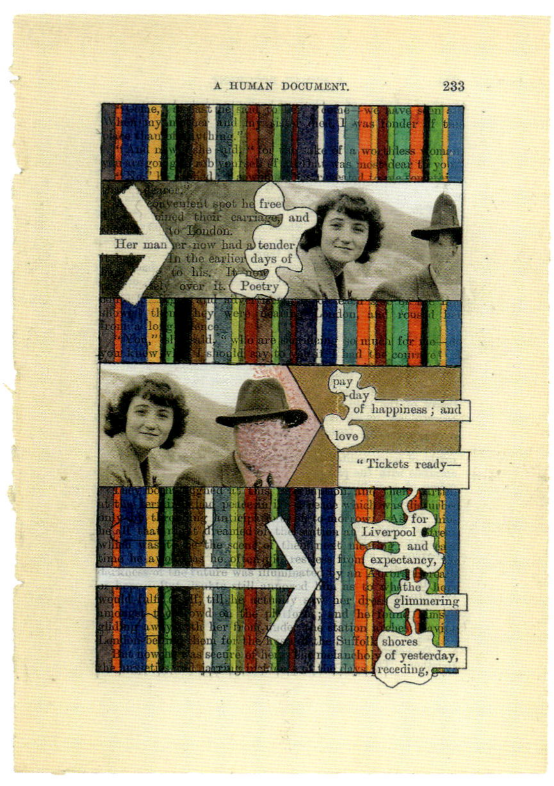

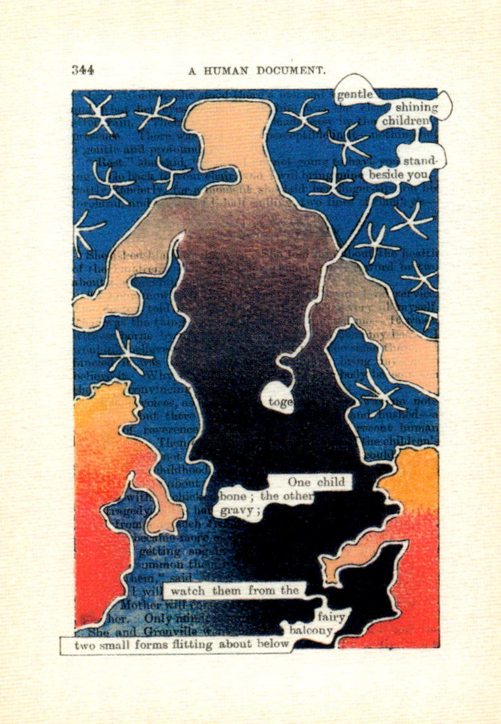
344
A HUMAN DOCUMENT.
gentle
shining
children
stand-
beside you
toge
One child
bone; the other
gravy;
watch them from the
fairy
balcony
two small forms flitting about below

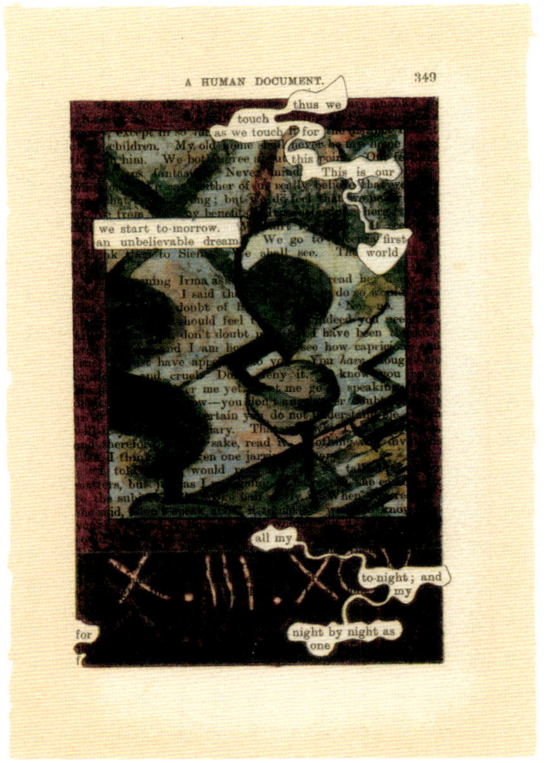
A HUMAN DOCUMENT.
349
thus we
touch
as we touch it for
This is our
we start to-morrow.
an unbelievable dream
first
world
all my
to-night; and
my
night by night as
one

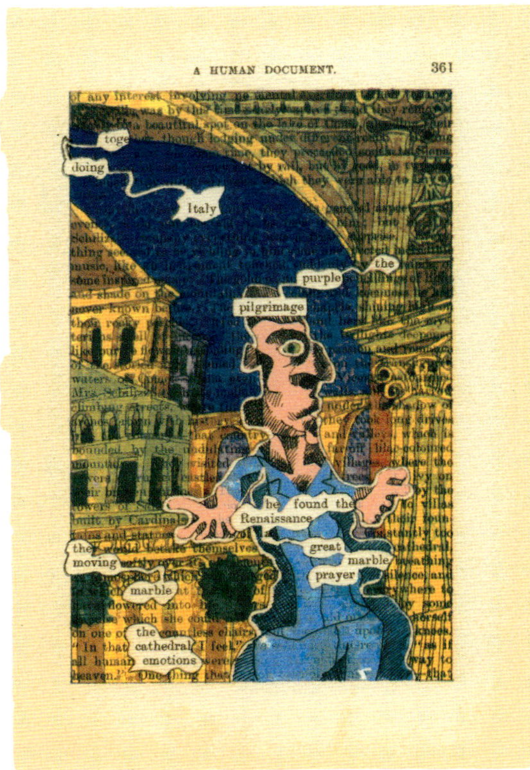
A HUMAN DOCUMENT.
361
toge
doing
Italy
the
purple
pilgrimage
he found the
Renaissance
great
marble
prayer
they
moving
marble
the
cathedral
emotions

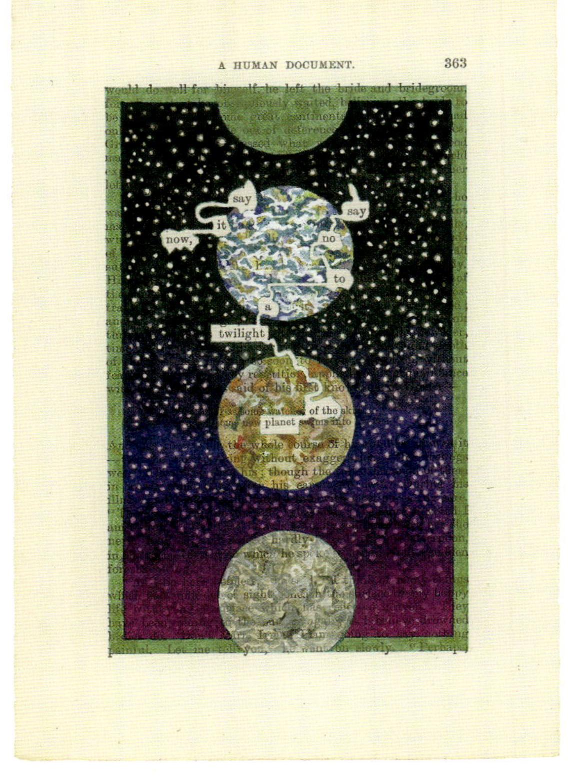
A HUMAN DOCUMENT.
363
say
it
say
now,
no
to
a
twilight
planet

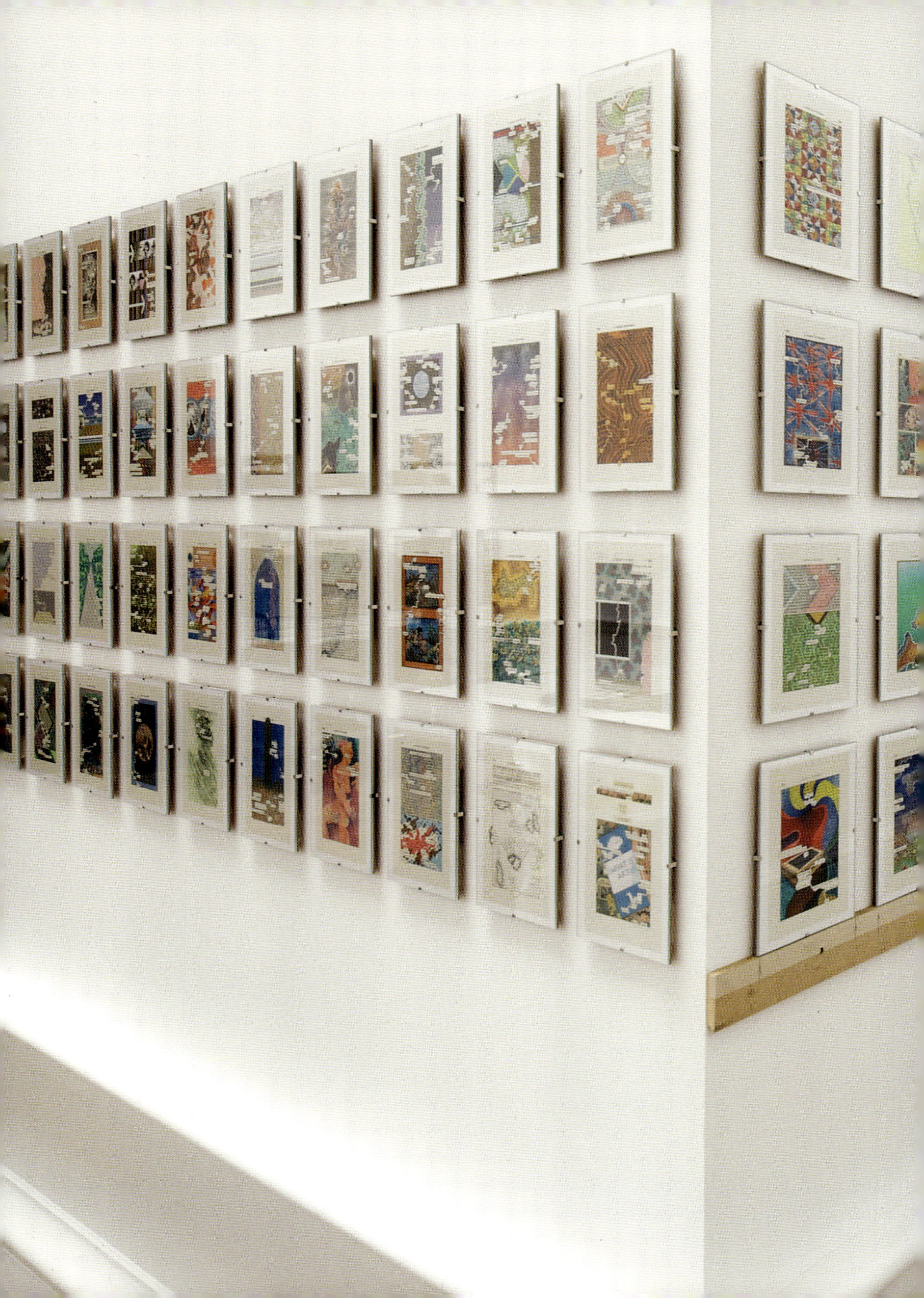

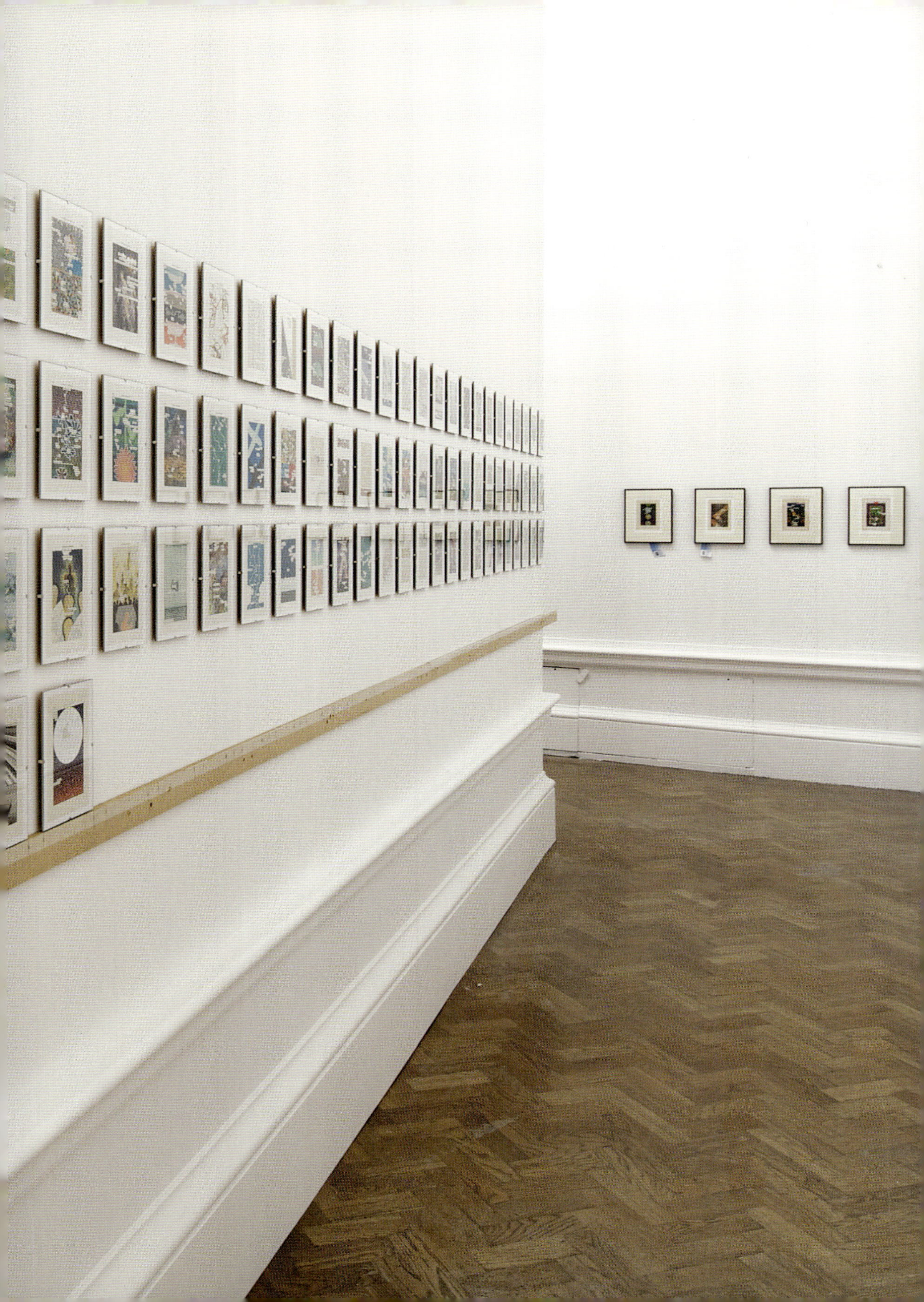

Index

Royal Academy of Arts in London, 2015

Registered charity number 1125383

Officers

President: Christopher Le Brun PRA
Keeper: Eileen Cooper RA
Treasurer: Prof Chris Orr MBE RA
Secretary and Chief Executive:
Dr Charles Saumarez Smith CBE

Past Presidents

Sir Nicholas Grimshaw CBE PPRA Prof Phillip King CBE PPRA

Senior

* Prof Norman Ackroyd CBE
Diana Armfield
Gillian Ayres CBE
Basil Beattie
Dame Elizabeth Blackadder DBE
* Olwyn Bowey
Frank Bowling OBE
James Butler MBE
Jeffery Camp
Prof Sir Peter Cook
Edward Cullinan CBE
Frederick Cuming HON DLITT
Prof Trevor Dannatt
Dr Jennifer Dickson
Bernard Dunstan
Anthony Eyton
Peter Freeth
Lord Foster of Thames Bank OM
Anthony Green
David Hockney OM CH
Sir Michael Hopkins CBE
Ken Howard OBE
Prof Paul Huxley
Tess Jaray
Eva Jiricna CBE
Allen Jones
Prof Phillip King CBE PPRA
Prof Bryan Kneale
Paul Koralek CBE
Sonia Lawson
Dr Leonard McComb
Leonard Manasseh OBE
Michael Manser CBE
Mick Moon
John Partridge CBE
Tom Phillips CBE
Lord Rogers of Riverside CH
Prof Michael Sandle
Terry Setch
Philip Sutton
Joe Tilson
Dr David Tindle
William Tucker
Anthony Whishaw
John Wragg
Rose Wylie

Academicians

Prof William Alsop OBE
Ron Arad
Phyllida Barlow
Prof Gordon Benson OBE
Tony Bevan
John Carter
Stephen Chambers
Sir David Chipperfield CBE
Ann Christopher
Eileen Cooper
Stephen Cox
Prof Tony Cragg CBE
* Michael Craig-Martin CBE
* Gus Cummins
Richard Deacon CBE
Tacita Dean OBE
Spencer de Grey CBE
Anne Desmet
Kenneth Draper
Jennifer Durrant
Tracey Emin CBE
Prof Stephen Farthing
Sir Antony Gormley OBE
Prof Piers Gough CBE
Sir Nicholas Grimshaw CBE PPRA
Dame Zaha Hadid DBE
Nigel Hall
Thomas Heatherwick CBE
Gary Hume
Louisa Hutton
Timothy Hyman
Bill Jacklin
Neil Jeffries
Chantal Joffe
Sir Anish Kapoor CBE
Prof Michael Landy
* Christopher Le Brun PRA
Richard Long CBE
* Jock McFadyen
Prof David Mach
Prof Ian McKeever
John Maine
Lisa Milroy
Prof Dhruva Mistry CBE
Mali Morris
Farshid Moussavi
David Nash OBE
Mike Nelson
Prof Humphrey Ocean
Hughie O'Donoghue
Prof Chris Orr MBE
Cornelia Parker OBE
Eric Parry
Grayson Perry CBE
Cathie Pilkington
Dr Barbara Rae CBE
Prof Fiona Rae
* David Remfry MBE
* Prof Ian Ritchie CBE
* Mick Rooney
Eva Rothschild
Rebecca Salter
Jenny Saville
Sean Scully
Tim Shaw
Conrad Shawcross
Yinka Shonibare MBE
Bob and Roberta Smith
Alan Stanton OBE
Emma Stibbon
Wolfgang Tillmans
Rebecca Warren
Gillian Wearing OBE
* Alison Wilding
Chris Wilkinson OBE
Prof Richard Wilson
* Bill Woodrow

* *Hanging Committee 2015*

Honorary Royal Academicians

Marina Abramovic
Prof El Anatsui
Prof Tadao Ando
Georg Baselitz
Jim Dine
Marlene Dumas
Frank O Gehry
Prof Rebecca Horn
Prof Arata Isozaki
Jasper Johns
Ellsworth Kelly
William Kentridge
Anselm Kiefer
Per Kirkeby
Jeff Koons
Daniel Libeskind
Bruce Nauman
Mimmo Paladino
Ieoh Ming Pei
Senator Renzo Piano
Ed Ruscha
Julian Schnabel
Richard Serra
Cindy Sherman
Frank Stella
Rosemarie Trockel
James Turrell
Ai Weiwei
Peter Zumthor

Royal Academy of Arts

The Royal Academy of Arts has a unique position as an independent institution led by eminent artists and architects whose purpose is to promote the creation, enjoyment and appreciation of the visual arts through exhibitions, education and debate. The Royal Academy receives no annual funding via government, and is entirely reliant on self-generated income and charitable support.

You and/or your company can support the Royal Academy of Arts in a number of different ways:

- Almost £60 million has been raised for capital projects, including the Jill and Arthur M Sackler Wing, the restoration of the Main Galleries, the restoration of the John Madejski Fine Rooms, and the provision of better facilities for the display and enjoyment of the Academy's own collections of important works of art and documents charting the history of British art.
- Donations from individuals, trusts, companies and foundations also help support the Academy's internationally renowned exhibition programme, the conservation of the Collections and education projects for schools, families and people with special needs; as well as providing scholarships and bursaries for postgraduate art students in the Royal Academy Schools.
- As a company, you can invest in the Royal Academy through arts sponsorship, corporate membership and corporate entertaining, with specific opportunities that relate to your budgets and marketing or entertaining objectives.
- If you would like to preserve the Academy for future generations, please consider including a gift to the Academy in your will. Your gift can be a sum of money, a specific item or a share of what is left after you have provided for your family and friends. Any gift, large or small, could help ensure that our work continues in the future.

To find out ways in which individuals can support this work, or a specific aspect of it, please contact Karin Grundy, Head of Patrons, on 020 7300 5671.

To explore ways in which companies, trusts and foundations can become involved in the work of the Academy, please contact the Project Giving Office on 020 7300 5629/5979.

For more information on remembering the Academy in your will, please contact Matthew Watters on 020 7300 5677 or legacies@royalacademy.org.uk

Membership of the Friends

The Friends of the Royal Academy was founded in 1977 to support and promote the work of the Royal Academy. It is now one of the largest such organisations in the world, with around 90,000 members.

As a Friend you enjoy free entry to every RA exhibition and much more...

- Invites to Preview Days before exhibitions open to the public
- Bring one adult family guest and up to four family children under 16 to any exhibition for free
- Use of the Friends Room
- Receive the quarterly *RA Magazine*
- Access to a programme of Friends events
- Keep up to date with the Friends e-news, packed with events, news and offers

Why not join today?

- At the Friends desk in the Front Hall
- Online at www.royalacademy.org.uk/friends
- Ring 020 7300 5664 any day of the week
- E-mail friends.enquiries@royalacademy.org.uk

Head of Summer Exhibition and Curator (Contemporary Projects)
Edith Devaney

Summer Exhibition Organisers
Jemma Johnson-Davey
Katherine Oliver
Paul Sirr
Ria Sloan

Royal Academy Publications
Beatrice Gullström
Alison Hissey
Carola Krueger
Simon Murphy
Peter Sawbridge
Nick Tite

Book design: Adam Brown_01.02
Photography: John Bodkin, DawkinsColour
(unless otherwise stated)
Colour reproduction: DawkinsColour
Printed in Wales by Gomer Press

British Library
Cataloguing-in-publication Data
A catalogue record for this book
is available in the British Library

ISBN 978-1-907533-95-2

Illustrations

Page 2: Michael Craig-Martin CBE RA in front of *Mississippi River Blues* by Richard Long CBE RA in Gallery III
Page 3–4: Conrad Shawcross's *The Dappled Light of the Sun*, 2015 in production
Page 6: Installation of Jim Lambie's *Zobop Colour*
Page 9: Installation view of Wohl Central Hall with Matthew Darbyshire's *CAPTCHA No. 11 – Doryphoros* in the centre and above Liam Gillick's *Applied Projection Rig*
Page 10: Detail of *Untitled* by Sir Anish Kapoor CBE RA
Page 29: Christopher Le Brun PRA *Can't or Won't?* (detail)
Pages 32–33: Installation view of Wohl Central Hall featuring Tess Jaray RA, *Thorns Purple and Yellow*, Prof El Anatsui Hon RA, *Blood of Sweat* and Michael Simpson, *Squint (17), Second Version*
Pages 34–35: Installation view of Wohl Central Hall featuring in the foreground Andrew Lord's *In Electric Light, in the Studio (Gauguin)*, to the left works by Anthony Stokes and above Jim Dine Hon RA
Page 41: Installation view of Gallery III
Pages 62–63: Installation view of Gallery III featuring Richard Long RA, *Mississippi River Blues*
Page 71: Installation of Gallery II in progress
Page 77: Gus Cummins RA and Olwyn Bowey RA during installation of Gallery I
Page 91: Prof Ian Ritchie RA during installation of the Large Weston Room
Pages 100–101: Installation view of the Large Weston Room
Page 111: William Kentridge Hon RA, *If You Have No Eye* (detail)
Pages 112–113: Installation view of the Small Weston Room with works by William Kentridge HON RA
Page 117: David Remfry RA installing Sue A'Court's *Desire & Longing 10* in Gallery IV
Page 120: View from Gallery V through to Gallery IV with Mimmo Paladino HON RA's *Untitled* in the foreground
Pages 122–123: Installation view of Gallery IV
Page 127: Prof Norman Ackroyd CBE RA installing Gallery V
Pages 132–133: Installation view of Gallery V
Page 139: Sir Anish Kapoor CBE RA, *Untitled*
Pages 146–147: Installation view of Gallery VI
Page 155: Installation view towards Gallery VII with Anselm Kiefer Hon RA's, *Lilith am Roten Meer*
Page 165, 168–169: Installation views of Gallery VIII
Page 175: Installation view of Gallery IX with Stephen Cox's works *Bek I, Bek II, Bek III* in the foreground
Page 181: Installation view of the Lecture Room with Ron Arad RA, *Even the Odd Balls?* in the foreground
Pages 186–187: Installation view of the Lecture Room with Phyllida Barlow RA, *Untitled: Slidingupturnedhouse* and in the foreground Eva Rothschild RA, *What the Eye Wants*
Pages 199, 202–203: Installation view of Tom Phillips RA, *A Humument* in Gallery X

Photographic Acknowledgements

Pages 2, 12, 17, 21, 22, 25, 26, 41, 71, 77, 91, 111, 114, 115, 117, 127, 165, 199, 202, 203 Photography: Phil Sayer
Pages 4–5: Photography: Marc Wilmot
Pages 6, 15: Benjamin Norton Photography
Page 15: Top image Courtesy the artist and Victoria Miro Gallery, London
Page 43: Courtesy Michael Craig-Martin and Gagosian Gallery
Page 44: Courtesy of the Artist and UNION Gallery, London
Page 45: © Chantal Joffe. Photography: Robert Glowacki
Page 47: © Jasper Johns/VAGA, New York and DACS, London. Photograph by Jerry Thompson.
Page 53: Courtesy Gillian Ayres and Alan Cristea Gallery
Page 54: Courtesy of the Artist and Maureen Paley © Wolfgang Tillmans
Page 55: © Ed Ruscha. Courtesy the artist and Gagosian Gallery
Page 61: © Derek Boshier, courtesy of Flowers Gallery London and New York
Page 87: Courtesy the artist, Paragon / Contemporary Editions and Victoria Miro, London
Page 98: Photography: Dirk Lindner
Page 99: Photography: Peter Durant
Page 129: © Julian Opie. All rights reserved, DACS 2015 Courtesy Julian Opie and Alan Cristea Gallery
Page 129: © Yinka Shonibare. All rights reserved, DACS 2015. Image courtesy the artist
Page 140: © Fiona Rae. Courtesy Timothy Taylor Gallery, London. Photography: Antony Makinson at Prudence Cuming Associates, London.
Page 142: © Tim Head 2015. Courtesy Parafin, London Photography: Peter Mallet
Page 143: Courtesy Anthony Reynolds Gallery, London
Page 148: © Gary Hume. All rights reserved, DACS 2015. Photo: Steve White
Page 151: © Richard Smith, courtesy of Flowers Gallery London and New York
Page 152: © Bernard Cohen. All rights reserved, DACS 2015. Photo © Bernard Cohen, courtesy of Flowers Gallery London and New York
Page 157: © Tracey Emin. All rights reserved, DACS 2015
Page 184–185: Photograph by Stephen White, London © The Artist
Page 187: Courtesy of the artist and Marlborough Fine Art
Page 200–201: © Tom Phillips. All rights reserved, DACS 2015